Advance praise for *Treaty Justice: The Northwest Tribes, the Boldt Decision, and the Recognition of Fishing Rights*

"This book illuminates more than the law and issues of tribal sovereignty during the Northwest Fishing Wars but how the voices of Native People elevate and inspire justice for all life. Charles Wilkinson, with all his eloquence and empathy, intelligence and passion, brings us into an understanding of why the legal rights and treaties of Indigenous People must be honored, maintained, and fought for in the name of dignity, while protecting cultural knowledge held deep within their enduring relationships within their own home ground. *Treaty Justice* is a final testament to all that this beloved writer of the American West and Indian histories gave his life to: love and justice."

TERRY TEMPEST WILLIAMS | writer-in-residence at the Harvard Divinity School

"Charles Wilkinson has left us with a gift of great knowledge, just as the tribal elders he speaks of gave to us. His dedicated research will help present and future generations understand the cultural, political and legal resilience of the Boldt Decision. This book honors all those who fought for treaty fishing rights, the ancient traditions of the Northwest salmon people and their right to co-manage their fisheries as sovereign government."

LEONARD FORSMAN | Suquamish Tribe chairman and president of the Affiliated Tribes of Northwest Indians

"The Boldt Decision was, to say the least, a watershed moment in the history of the Pacific Northwest and beyond. A half century on, Wilkinson has given us the inside story of this critical case: the labor that went into its manifestation, its implications for all who live in these places, and most importantly the Indigenous land, water, and more-than-human relations that are at its core. A must-read."

COLL THRUSH | author of *Native Seattle: Histories from the Crossing-Over Place*

"Charles Wilkinson was intimately involved in tribal treaty fishing rights by writing about this issue for many years. He was a legal expert and personally involved right up to the time that he sadly passed away."

JOHN ECHOHAWK | executive director of the Native American Rights Fund

"The annual salmon run is one of the wonders of the world and central to the cultures and economies of the Native peoples of the Pacific Northwest. *Treaty Justice* offers an authoritative account of the groundbreaking Boldt Decision that restored fishing rights to 'the Salmon people.' Wilkinson's clear and compelling narrative traces the long, winding road that led to this foundational court case and explores how it continues to sustain Native communities today."

CLAUDIO SAUNT | author of *Unworthy Republic: The Dispossession of Native Americans and the Road to Indian Territory*

Treaty Justice

TREATY JUSTICE

The Northwest Tribes,
the Boldt Decision,
and the Recognition
of Fishing Rights

CHARLES WILKINSON

University of Washington Press   Seattle

Treaty Justice was supported by a generous grant from the Northwest Indian Fisheries Commission, made possible in part thanks to the support of the Jamestown S'Klallam Tribe and Lower Elwha Klallam Tribe.

This book was also supported by the Tulalip Tribes Charitable Fund, which provides the opportunity for a sustainable and healthy community for all.

Additional funding was provided by a grant from the Hugh and Jane Ferguson Foundation.

Treaty Justice was also made possible by generous gifts from Michael Burnap and Irene Tanabe, Vasiliki Dwyer, Ellen Ferguson, Kelby Fletcher and Janet Boguch, Mary Hotchkiss and Mary Whisner, Barbara Johns in memory of David Getches, Sandeep Kaushik and Elizabeth Goodwin, Suzanne Kotz and Stephen Tarnoff, Michael Repass, and Cynthia Sears.

27 26 25 24 23   5 4 3 2 1

UNIVERSITY OF WASHINGTON PRESS   *uwapress.uw.edu*

Cataloging information is available from the Library of Congress

Library of Congress Control Number: 2023948995

ISBN 9780295752723 (hardcover)

ISBN 9780295752730 (ebook)

∞ This paper meets the requirements of ANSI/NISO Z39.48-1992 (Permanence of Paper).

This book is dedicated
to the courageous,
sovereign tribes of the
Pacific Northwest.

Contents

Preface

The late 1960s and early '70s marked the beginnings of the upswelling of jobs in several areas of public interest law. I had gone to law school to practice civil rights law but when I graduated in 1966, there were almost no public interest jobs. When that changed, just a few years later, I was in private practice and began to think about the new civil rights, environmental, and other public law programs.

Several people suggested that I might look at the new firm, the Native American Rights Fund, which was practicing Indian and environmental law. I applied and on October 11, 1971, joined NARF as a staff attorney. Early on, I thanked my lucky stars. I was thrilled that my professional life would now involve working on issues that I cared about personally. Now, more than half a century later, I realize that walking through the front door that long-ago day as a NARF attorney was the moment that law became technicolor for me.

NARF was still in its first year. Youth and idealism spread throughout the offices. All of the dozen attorneys were less than thirty years old. They were an impressive lot; the new public interest work attracted some of the best young lawyers. NARF attorneys had already filed a number of truly major cases (most of them, ambitious though they were, proved to be successful in whole or in part).

One was a lawsuit on behalf of the tribes of Western Washington against the state of Washington charging that the state had long violated tribal fishing rights for salmon under treaties with the United States. This is the litigation that became known as the Boldt Decision, which, along with its broad and lasting impact on law, environment, and society, is the subject of this book. The state argued that tribal fishing rights were minimal and cracked down on Indian fishermen through often violent raids, arrests, and jail time. The tribes believed that they had extensive rights under their treaties with the United States and that, among other things, Indians were entitled to as many Pacific salmon as necessary to meet their needs.

I never worked on the case, but it caught my attention from the beginning. At that point, I had a rudimentary knowledge of Indian law and knew only that this was a difficult legal case, highly controversial in Washington and Oregon, where these state tribal-fishing disputes were commonly referred to as "fish wars." Also, I couldn't help but notice that the case revolved around fish, Pacific salmon no less. I made up my mind to follow it.

After four years at NARF, I spent the rest of my time in law teaching, first at the University of Oregon in Eugene and then at the University of Colorado in Boulder. I have taught Indian law, water law, and federal public land law, all oriented toward the American West. Wanting to get a sense of the region, I did plenty of book research. I also made a priority of getting out on the ground and conducting interviews with, among others, federal and corporate officials, conservation groups, ranchers and farmers, scientists, and Indian leaders and tribal members.

The Indian interviews were especially fruitful. I was basically the first Indian law professor to get out in the field in Oregon and by then the tribes were into the modern Indian sovereignty movement. Many Indian people in Oregon, and Washington as well, invited me out to their reservations.

Delbert Frank of the Warm Springs Tribe of Oregon took me down to his family fishing ground, which is still in use, on the Columbia River 4,000 feet below the rim of the Columbia River Gorge. Over the course of a full day, he explained in precise, loving detail where all of the people worked and slept, and still do, and talked at length about the cultural and religious relationships between his people and salmon. At the end of the day, we went out and pulled up a few salmon with dip nets, but Delbert's bighearted idea was for me to get a sense of what that landscape has always meant culturally and religiously and how it was used for thousands of years.

Other people from Washington, Oregon, northern California, and Idaho showed me around, also taking me to their sites and explaining the historical, cultural, and religious contexts. They also took me out to dip net and long net operations on the ocean and Puget Sound. I went to two or three small dip net operations on small tributaries. The Indian people explained how the tribes have benefited from salmon as food and sometimes sales. Everywhere, including my visit with Delbert, I saw traditional canoes, spears, and apparel as well as more modern items such as contemporary boats, rifles, and fishing gear.

As the years passed by, I focused more and more on Pacific salmon. I increasingly brought them into my writing. I also took on projects involving salmon—mediations and arbitrations between tribes and state and federal agencies, speeches, media interview requests, and giving advice on proposed legislation or settlements. Pacific salmon became my favorite animal.

Then, I found myself wanting to be absolutely clear on the *place*, the *importance*, of the Pacific salmon. Why do people write statements like these?

"The definition of the Pacific Northwest is anywhere that Pacific salmon run."

"Salmon are the soul of the Pacific Northwest."

"Since the ice ages, this Pacific Northwest muscular fish has embodied the health and vitality of this region."

"Salmon are an icon."

Why do Indian people and tribes often describe themselves as "the Salmon People"?

We prize oven-grilled and backyard-barbecued salmon at home and in terrific salmon restaurants in Seattle, Portland, and other places in the Northwest. That is important and relevant but it doesn't justify calling salmon the soul of the Pacific Northwest. The same is true with the joy that sport fishers feel about getting out in the open water and catching these strong, powerful, and beautiful fish. So, too, with the significant economic benefits to the commercial fisheries industry and the considerable economic contributions that sport fishing provides through payment of government license fees, equipment purchases, and travel, lodging, and other expenses paid by visitors.

What is uniquely different and compelling about Pacific salmon is their life story. How, possibly, can they do what they do? There is much public film on Pacific salmon migrations and Americans nationally have a sense of those spectacular long-distance journeys. Much better, if we are able to get out to the rivers at the right time (most return salmon runs are in the fall), do our own research, or get directions from people who know the runs, we can catch sight of parts of these arresting journeys. I have been lucky to have experienced quite a lot of those moments. They are still vivid to me.

Amy Cordalis and her aunt, Sue Masten, are staunch advocates for the Klamath River of northwestern California and its salmon. To them, the river and its salmon are members of their own Yurok families. Amy and Sue took me to the cliff on the north side of the mouth of the Klamath, where the river's outgoing flows hit the Pacific. The chinook salmon were returning from their years in Alaska. It was a noisy, hyperactive scene. The salmon were jumping, diving, and playing in the ocean foam while competing with birds and each other for shrimp and small fish amid the screeching of the gulls and pelicans. We watched for a good hour.

Phillip Martin Sr., a gentle, traditional man with detailed knowledge of his Quinault tribal history, took me to a waterfall high up on his tribe's

Billy Frank Jr. and the author having a discussion on traditional Nisqually land at the southerly reach of Puget Sound, April 2000. Photograph by Mary Randlett. *Courtesy of University of Washington Libraries, Special Collections, MPH2628.*

river. We were there at the right time. The Quinault blueback sockeye salmon run was returning and we could see the power of these fish as they charged up the furious waterfall, leaping, climbing, and swimming to conquer the imposing flow.

Billy Frank Jr., Nisqually, one of the people most responsible for the Boldt Decision, allowed me to join him on a trip to spawning grounds on Muck Creek in the upper Nisqually River watershed. During spawning, all is slower and quieter because the females are releasing their eggs. Soon after, the males and females will both finish their lives. Billy and I were viewing animals that had just completed a round-trip journey of several thousand miles.

Pacific salmon: so exquisite and inspiring, so rare. Based on my reading, talking with people, getting out on the water and the ground, and my own thinking, I was convinced that it is accurate to describe this grand animal by terms such as "the soul of the Pacific Northwest" and a "muscular fish that embodies the health and vitality of this region."

Another subject that I have given special attention to, starting with my time at NARF and continuing throughout my career, is American Indian tribal sovereignty. Tribal sovereignty is one of the most powerful and valuable public ideas that has ever touched my mind. I say that, not just because of tribal sovereignty's legal and intellectual worth, but because it also has proved to be so invincible. The world's most powerful nation tried to terminate tribal sovereignty over the course of many generations, but could not because it meant so much to Indian people, small minority that they were, and they refused to give in.

Sovereignty—the capacity to act as a government—is a technical word but it has numerous real-world ramifications and is a living reality to Indians. To them, the reservations are islands where tribal culture and religion are protected from encroaching dominant society. Sovereignty encompasses the question of whether the law of the tribe or of the white society—in other words, the state—will apply. In America, there are three sources of sovereignty: the United States; the states, including their county and city subdivisions; and the Indian tribes. For more than a century after the treaties of the mid-1850s, the actual practice of tribal sovereignty declined due to aggressive, forced state and federal assimilation policies designed to eliminate the sovereignty and separatism. Modern courts, however, have found that the sovereign treaty rights are still alive.

On the reservations, tribal sovereignty is the lifeblood of the governmental authority that empowers tribes to decide on matters that really count: children, schools, family, health care, natural resources, their lands, and the environment. State fish and game laws such as licensing requirements, bag limits, and seasons do not apply on the reservations. The tribes are free to follow their own time-proven practices.

In some regions, especially the Pacific Northwest and Great Lakes, federal treaty negotiations resulted in treaty provisions allowing fishing, hunting, and gathering rights on off-reservation lands. That means that those tribes have treaty rights beyond the reservation boundaries, allowing tribal members to take Pacific salmon and other marine resources.

In 2013, Billy Frank Jr., chairman of the Northwest Indian Fisheries Commission, asked me if I would be willing to write a comprehensive book on the Boldt Decision, such a monumental event for the Northwest tribes, Indian country generally, and beyond. Billy explained that many tribal members had not even been born when the decision was announced. Other tribal members lacked a context for the decision. Also, the general public in the Northwest and nationally should have a readable and accessible book presenting the Boldt Decision. The Fisheries Commission provided a generous grant for my research assistants, travel, and other expenses related to the book. I would write independently and would receive no honoraria, stipend, or other payments to me personally.

By that time, I had written quite a lot about natural resources and tribes in the American West and nationally; I regularly referred to the Boldt Decision in my work. Like Billy and the Northwest Indian Fisheries Commission, and doubtless many others, I also believed that the Boldt Decision deserved a full treatment. With its fiftieth anniversary coming up, this was a good time to do it. I enthusiastically began work on it.

Treaty Justice is my book about this historic and sweeping judicial ruling. The Boldt Decision, handed down by a federal district court in 1974, announced tribal, state, and federal rights to harvest and environmentally manage salmon and other marine fisheries in the Pacific Northwest. Judge George Boldt's opinion was affirmed nearly completely by the

United States Supreme Court. (When people, including myself, refer to the body of law contained in those two opinions, they often refer to them collectively as "the Boldt Decision," probably because the Supreme Court relied so heavily on Judge Boldt's opinion.)

These court opinions rest in part on constitutional provisions addressing treaties, congressional authority, state police power, tribal sovereignty, and the supreme law of the land. This book presents those in a straightforward nonlegalistic way. Importantly, such constitutional terms often take shape in a context of history, culture, economics, and the actual workings of state and tribal governments. The Boldt Decision, then, did decide constitutional provisions but very much on the judges' minds were salmon, tribal sovereignty and culture, community participation, the economics of salmon harvesting, tribal and nontribal fishing practices, and the performances and effectiveness of state, tribal, and federal fisheries offices.

The Boldt Decision has had an exceptionally broad reach into the future. This book explains the effects of that decision on people, governments, and the environment in Washington, Indian country, other states, the nation, and even other countries as well. We can hope and expect that Judge Boldt's earnest and wise words will continue.

Treaty Justice

THE TWENTY TRIBES OF THE BOLDT CASE AREA

1 Fury on the Puyallup River

The police "were all up on the bridge, with rifles,
and we could see their rifles kicking, and you could feel
the bullets going by; there was nowhere you could go."

Washington's Puyallup River, such a fine breeding ground for Pacific salmon, originates in the glacial waters of Mount Rainier and, gathering cool water from tributaries, runs north and northwest through mountain meadows and forests of cedar, fir, and hemlock before flowing into Puget Sound. The Puyallup riverbank near the Pacific Highway bridge in Tacoma is calm now, but in the summer of 1970, it provided the site for one of the most terrifying police raids during the violent "fish wars" of the 1960s and '70s. Indian fishermen believed they were exercising long-standing rights under treaties with the United States, to fish for salmon in their traditional ways. The state officers believed that the fishermen were violating valuable state conservation laws. Whether measured in dollars, recreational enjoyment, or Indian culture, Pacific salmon were a mainstay of the Pacific Northwest.

In the summer of 1970, with chaotic conflicts regularly erupting on most of northwestern Washington's rivers, events came to a head. Early in August, to support the fishermen down on the river, hundreds of committed Indian people established an encampment on the banks of the Puyallup River. On August 13, tribal leaders announced that state officers were not welcome and that the tribes themselves would police Indian fishing at the Puyallup encampment.

Early September marked the time when the big chinook (also called king) salmon—the most prized of the Pacific salmon—made their summer run up the full-bodied currents of the Puyallup River to spawn. State police scouted the encampment area by boat early in the morning of September 9. Sure enough, the chinook were charging up the river and the Indian fishermen were busily working their nets. Indians at the encampment fired four warning shots near the police boat. Indian people, their supporters, and curious citizens were streaming into the area. Everyone knew this would be the day.

A few hours later, the police—hundreds of them—attacked. Their rifle shots pierced the air and the stench of teargas hung over the encampment. Ramona Bennett, chair of the Puyallup Tribe and the highest tribal official at the encampment, lived the violence that day, recalling that the police "were all up on the bridge, with rifles, and we could see their rifles kicking, and you could feel the bullets going by; there was nowhere you could go. I was so scared that my legs were stiff; it was like that Frankenstein walk you do when you are so absolutely terrified."

The police prevailed. They arrested more than sixty people, including five children. They confiscated the fishermen's catch, nets, and traditional carved cedar canoes. They dragged the fishermen up the rough, rocky riverbanks, making good use of their fists and billy clubs, and jailed them with bail of up to $3,500. Then they bulldozed the tipis, wood shelters, and fire pits of the summer-long encampment. Almost miraculously, no one was killed or suffered long-term physical injuries.

The "fish wars" were a long time in the making. The Indian treaties of the mid-1850s in the Pacific Northwest had supposedly settled the pressing issue of Indian fishing rights. The arriving settlers coveted the salmon for food and economic opportunity. The tribes were Salmon People, and for them the fish were as important as the land. Territorial Governor Isaac Stevens, tough, smart, and bent on acquiring as many acres of Indian land as possible, pushed hard and successfully to locate the tribes on small reservations.

The "fish wars" encompassed many conflicts, but the events on the Puyallup River in August 1970 drew special attention. They were notably violent. They were widely reported nationally and convinced federal officials in Washington, DC, and Seattle to bring litigation to protect tribal rights. The clouds of teargas shown here were photographed by Dolores Varela Phillips on September 9, 1970, PH Coll 1210. *Courtesy of University of Washington Libraries, Special Collections, Dolores Varela Phillips, photographer, UW41875.*

Tribal leaders, however, refused to sign off on the land transfers unless the United States agreed to guarantee tribes the right to fish on the homelands that the tribes transferred to the United States. The government acceded, and each of the five "Stevens Treaties" promised tribes "the right of taking fish" at their traditional fishing grounds "in common with the citizens of the Territory." While the reservations were only small remnants of the tribes' traditional lands, these off-reservation rights covered most rivers and marine waters in Western Washington.

The settlers, believing that Indians should be limited to their reservations, were hostile to these off-reservation rights from the beginning. They forced Native people off their longtime fishing grounds, cut their nets, and stole or damaged their canoes. When tempers flared, local judges were quick to back up the settlers by jailing the Indian fishermen. When Washington became a state in 1889, the legislature passed laws restricting off-reservation Indian fishing.

The stresses heightened into the twentieth century. The salmon runs declined due to logging, dam construction, and steadily increasing commercial and sport fishing by non-Indians drawn to the green Pacific Northwest. By the post–World War II era, lines had hardened. The state expanded and intensified its crackdown on Indian fishing with brutal arrests, confiscations of catch and gear including canoes, and jail time with high bail.

The tribes claimed the sovereign right to regulate Native fishing under the terms of their treaties with the United States. Under the US Constitution, treaties were the "supreme law of the land," meaning that treaty promises overrode inconsistent state laws and actions.

State enforcement officers would have none of it. They and their government superiors claimed that the Indian fishermen were "renegades" and "poachers" who were thumbing their noses at important state wildlife conservation laws.

Every Indian fisherman felt the pressure. Some quit fishing entirely. Many eschewed the daylight hours and limited themselves to "dark time" fishing. One early morning in December 1945, Billy Frank Jr., Nisqually fisherman and perhaps the most luminous figure in the long line of events from treaty time to the present, suffered the first of his many arrests, confiscations, and jailings. He was fourteen years old at the time.

Just as the pace of arrests multiplied, so did the tribes' resistance. By the mid-1960s, the tribes, learning from the tactics of the civil rights movement, were conducting well-publicized fish-ins at the Puyallup, Nisqually, Green, and White Rivers to demonstrate their determination and build public support. By then, the national commitment to civil rights was helping the tribes. The state law enforcement agencies, however, were benefitting from the civil rights conflicts in a very different way.

In 1965, twenty years after his first arrest, Billy Frank Jr. and his brother-

in-law, Al Bridges, were fishing on the Nisqually River in a traditional cedar canoe on a placid autumn afternoon. All of a sudden, out of a slough
on the far side of the river, a massive, high-speed motorboat was charging
at them full-throttle. "[T]his boat was coming at me and Bridges like a
bat out of hell. We turned upstream and tried to run them into another
net but we never made it. Those bastards rammed us at full speed and
knocked us clean over. We had our hip boots on and it was harder'n hell
to swim. I honestly thought I was going to drown. We finally got to shore
and other guys were waiting for us. 'Stop or we'll shoot.'

"At the beginning, these guys had no idea how to run a boat on this
river. . . . But they got real serious about this. And this was the time of
Selma; there was a lot of unrest in the nation. Congress had funded some
big law enforcement programs and they got all kinds of training and
riot gear—shields, helmets, everything. And they got fancy new boats.

"These guys had a budget. This was a war."

On September 8, 1970, Stan Pitkin, the hard-charging young United
States Attorney for Western Washington, walked downstairs in the fed-
eral courthouse in Seattle to the clerk's office and filed the complaint in
United States v. Washington. The chief federal legal officer for Western
Washington, Pitkin had no clear idea of how the case would unfold. A
Republican appointed by President Nixon, he passionately believed in
the rightness of the cause of his clients, twenty Indian tribes in the Puget
Sound–Olympic Peninsula area. He knew about the "fish wars"—everyone did. As the months wore on, Washington looked more and more
like Mississippi and Alabama. In addition to enforcing tribal rights, the
United States Attorney earnestly wanted to use the legal system to help
end the ugliness on the rivers and in the streets.

Pitkin (and the lawyers who intervened in the litigation on behalf of
the tribes) could not project how the case would turn out because the
legal terrain was so uncertain. Federal Indian law was an ancient body

Stan Pitkin walking up the courthouse steps, May 5, 1971. *Courtesy of the Museum of History and Industry, Seattle, Image no. 2000.107.141.36.01.*

of law, protective of Indian treaties, and federal attorneys specializing in Indian law were generally optimistic about this case, but the field had lain mostly dormant for generations.

Besides, the United States and the tribes were seeking extraordinary and unprecedented relief. Pitkin's original complaint called for the court to allocate a "fair share" of the off-reservation salmon runs to the tribes. In time, the Justice Department and tribal lawyers agreed that the tribal allocation should be quantified at 50 percent of the off-reservation fisheries. The accepted principles for interpreting the meaning of words in Indian treaties were that courts should give heavy weight to the intent of the tribes and should construe ambiguous treaty terms in the tribes' favor. The legal team became satisfied that verbal statements made at the treaty negotiations (Isaac Stevens, for example, told the tribal negotiators that "this paper secures your fish"), coupled with court decisions dating back to leading opinions handed down by Chief Justice John Marshall in the 1830s, supported a 50 percent tribal share.

Washington State Fish and Game officials, while acknowledging that the physical conflicts on the rivers caused some political problems, announced that the 50 percent claim was "ridiculous." Tribal fishermen were taking only 2 to 5 percent of the salmon, depending on the tribe. The commercial fishing industry was taking more than 90 percent. Requiring a 50 percent share for the tribes would mean a wholesale reworking of a regional economy that was, after all, commonly described at that time as "timber, salmon, and Boeing." Sport fishers accounted for a small part of the annual harvest, but river and ocean sport fishing was enjoyed by a large and passionate segment of the population. The federal-tribal 50 percent position was counterintuitive to most of the general public.

Was the 50 percent allocation fair? Was it realistic? Could a judge do it? Could the citizenry accept it? Could the political system? Fifty percent of the salmon to 1 percent of the population? After all, the treaties said only that the tribes could take salmon "in common with" the non-Indian citizens.

Still, unlikely as it might have seemed, Judge Boldt's final opinion of over 200 pages found for the tribes on virtually every issue, large and small. His main ruling was that the treaties, in guaranteeing to the tribes the "right to fish in common with the citizens of the territory," meant that the tribes were entitled to harvest 50 percent of the fisheries after accounting for conservation of the runs. Judge Boldt handed down his opinion on February 12, 1974, deliberately choosing Abraham Lincoln's birthday.

Judge George Boldt's ruling, affirmed by the US Supreme Court in 1979, is a landmark in the American civil rights movement. It belongs in the same company as *Brown v. Board of Education* and a select few other court cases in terms of bringing justice to dispossessed peoples. Like those opinions, the Boldt Decision's ramifications are many and still felt today. And, like those cases, the Boldt Decision vividly displays the brilliance and worth of the American system of justice and the moral and tangible benefits it can achieve at its heights.

2 The Salmon People

"Those Fraser River salmon are like blood in your veins.
It's part of you."

When Stan Pitkin filed *United States v. Washington* in 1970, no one could
have known, or even imagined, all that it would accomplish. How did
that come about? What drove Judge Boldt and the Supreme Court justices to find that the tribes reserved in the treaties a full one-half of the
entire fishery in northwestern Washington, a result so bold, so disruptive
of a settled, powerful, economic and social regime? On first read, the
treaties were opaque: the tribes had the right to fish "in common with
the citizens of the Territory."

The ultimate answers to these questions, though, are not found in the
law books. Under long-established American law, judges do not read
treaties in isolation. Words in treaties can be understood only in light
of the entire context. At its heart, this case about law was a case about
history. What brought the United States and the tribes to the treaty
proceedings in the 1850s? What did the United States want to gain and
what did the tribes want to preserve? What did the United States intend?
What did the tribes intend? What were the historical circumstances?

The most critical matter in this exploration of life in the Pacific Northwest in the mid-1800s and before was an understanding of the kind
and level of reliance that those tribal societies placed on salmon. The
United States, the state of Washington, the tribes, and outside scholars,
all steadily prodded by Judge Boldt to do their best work, produced a voluminous amount of information. What emerged was a comprehensive
historical portrait that was informative, rich, and notably different from
the impressions held by most Americans of ancient Indigenous peoples.

The twenty Boldt Case area tribes have always been known as "Salmon People." What does that mean, especially in the aboriginal, precontact times before the treaties were negotiated? How important were the salmon to those people?

All the tribal stories and anthropological and historical research make it clear that these oceangoing fish were pervasive in their lives. Salmon was the staple in their diets. Salmon carried great cultural and spiritual meaning. The tribes established mature and robust economies with salmon as the main driver. Internally, salmon was the principal measure of social status, which depended upon how many material goods, but especially salmon, were distributed to the needy. Beyond the villages, salmon were essential in commercial trade relations that extended up and down the coast and across the Cascades to the east. This elaborate regime required huge amounts of the big fish, and the tribes annually achieved prodigious harvests—several times larger than the takes by all participants in the salmon fishery combined, including the largest commercial vessels, in the twenty-first century.

And there was something simpler, a treasured constant for the people. They loved going out with their nets, spears, and weirs into the bracingly fresh air, onto the open seas and the rivers that flowed through the thick, wet, and misty green forests that so distinguished their homelands. They had the satisfaction of fishing in the same way in the same places as their ancestors had fished for thousands of years.

Some 10,000 years ago, after the glaciers from the Wisconsin Glaciation melted and released their grip on the landscape, ancestors of the twenty tribes in the Boldt Case area began to settle in what is now northwestern Washington and southwestern British Columbia. Eventually this area became one of the most populated by Natives in North America and

Puyallup salmon ceremony, August 30, 1977, from Tacoma's News Tribune.

it is easy to see why it was so attractive. The North Pacific current, like the Gulf Stream in the North Atlantic, brings in moderate temperatures while the Cascade Mountains contain the western warm air and create a barrier against cold air from the plains to the east. Leaving aside the high peaks of the Cascade and Olympic ranges, the land was mostly heavily wooded, usually right down to the water. Given the regular rains and the marine location, water was everywhere—creeks, streams, rivers, bays, and wide-open stretches of the Salish Sea and the Pacific Ocean.

The thick, big-tree forests had disadvantages. They allowed little overland travel. Elk and deer, grazing animals, did not use the deep timbered areas, although both, along with mountain goats and bears, could be found around lightly forested places and those flat prairies that interrupted the woods. But the forests gave much to the Native people. These towering, inspiring mixed stands of Douglas fir, spruce, hemlock, yellow cedar, and, beloved by the people most of all, red cedar, gave great trunk lengths for canoes; lumber for homes; firewood; and bark, branches, and foliage for fishing nets, clothing, healing, and other uses. And the behemoths that together let in little light and rose up out of sight offered another extraordinary gift: the ground-level understory.

With all the moisture, good growing temperatures, shade, still air, and soft soils enriched by fallen giants of millennia past, the forest floors were a spongy wet mass of organic matter—ferns, fungi, skunk cabbage, salal, vine maple, grasses, fallen leaves along with decomposing animals, earthworms, millipedes, and microorganisms. This breeding ground did many things, including providing nutrients for live trees to use. The understory also helped create some of the best salmon habitat in the world by storing water and releasing it slowly and steadily, clean and cool, sometimes on the surface, mostly underground, into rivers and tributaries.

The ocean awaited the young salmon born in the healthy, reliable forest and river habitat. After moving down the rivers and entering the Pacific either directly or via the Salish Sea, some runs headed south to Oregon or California waters and beyond. Other fish traveled as far north as the Gulf of Alaska and feasted on herring, anchovies, shrimp, eels, and other saltwater delicacies. Then the mature runs began the return legs of their miraculous life journeys, often thousands of miles, heading for their native streams and the very spawning beds where they had hatched. The full round-trip took three to five years depending on the species and other factors. At the end, the adult fish spawned, assuring future runs, and died.

The Natives learned the patterns of the runs in their home areas and were ready when the fish returned, harvesting at the most productive locations with nets, traps, and spears. The five species of Pacific salmon—chinook (or king), sockeye, coho (or silver), pink (or humpback), and chum (or dog)—and the steelhead, an oceangoing large trout, were found in abundance in this Northwest landscape, although not all rivers hosted all species.

The waterways contributed to Native societies in another way by allowing for transportation that the forests mostly impeded. Employing river and ocean canoes carved from red cedar, the people used the waters to reach nearby salmon sites and big-game and berry-picking grounds and, depending on the tribe, to reach distant whale, seal, and halibut locations. The sea and ocean also were highways for travel to faraway trading locales and visits to relatives in distant villages for births, weddings, deaths, and social visits. Villages were independent but there was considerable intermarriage so that people commonly had kin in other locations.

These demands of business, family, and subsistence, including the practice of having winter homes and summer hunting, gathering, and fishing camps, combined to make these tribes mobile, and often long-distance, travelers. There was no United States–Canada boundary and the Coast Salish tribes had many relationships with villages in what is now British Columbia. A modern reminder of this is the revival of the Canoe Journey, when, every summer, pullers in hundreds of canoes from both sides of the international line paddle to a host Native Nation and gather together for ceremonies. Thousands of spectators, Native and non-Indian, join in the colorful celebrations.

In referring to the times before contact with white people, Indian people today often say that their people were "rich" or "wealthy." Anthropologists and other scholars regularly agree, describing the tribes of northwestern Washington as having been "prosperous" or "wealthy," or emphasizing the strength of their economies. There is very little understanding of this in the majority society, but it stands to reason. After all, the natural world presented a great opportunity: the climate, rains, forests, and proximity to the ocean made for salmon runs not exceeded anywhere. Because of the elk, deer, and marine species including whales, seals, and sea lions—but especially salmon—the Pacific Northwest pro-

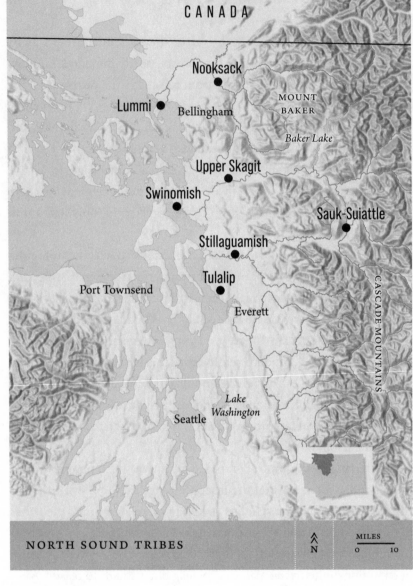

CANADA

Nooksack

Lummi
Bellingham

MOUNT
BAKER

Baker Lake

Upper Skagit

Swinomish

Sauk-Suiattle

Stillaguamish

Tulalip

Port Townsend

Everett

CASCADE MOUNTAINS

Lake
Washington

Seattle

NORTH SOUND TRIBES

N

MILES
0   10

duced more protein per acre than virtually any place in North America. Tribal people, with hundreds of generations of experience, developed effective systems for harvesting, using, and sustaining the runs. They built their societies and economies on those systems.

All treaty tribes in the Boldt Case area shared the same reliance and dependence on salmon and other fish and marine resources. They were all "place oriented" in that they resided along key waterways that provided access to these important marine resources. Having readily available bountiful food resources allowed these tribes to develop cultures rich in religion, art, song, and dance. Their storytelling and ceremonies were focused on the varied, abundant natural resources that surrounded their homeland, much of which centered on salmon and other marine resources. The reliance of all tribes on these natural resources, and a sense of what they all had to gain and what they had to lose at treaty time, can be made clear by examining the particular situations of several tribes.

Lummi Nation

The modern Lummi Nation traces to ancestors in twenty villages where Coast Salish lived in the area of Bellingham Bay and the archipelago now called the San Juan Islands. The Lummi villages, though independent politically, spoke the same Salishan dialect; employed the specialized technology of reef-net fishing, a method of salmon harvesting used in few other places; and had similar societies, institutions, customs, and traditions. These groups had continuing social contacts with each other and were tied together by intermarriage.

Like all of the Northwest tribes, the Lummi faced disruptions—large storms, slow years in the salmon runs, and some violent combat and even wars with other tribes—but their lives were fundamentally stable. They had their bearings. They were Salmon People and they settled their villages right on the water because they also were People of the Sea. Hereditary Chief Bill James tells "Whale Story," which ends with the man swimming toward the light and following a whale underwater. He thought the light was the surface but when he reached it, he found himself on the seafloor. When he looked around, he saw all the different sea creatures, including the whale, who peeled off their skin and revealed that they were actually human beings: "brothers and sisters, all my relations." Another modern Lummi, Jeremiah Julius, speaking for himself and the feeling his Lummi people have always held, said that when he gets on a boat and heads out to sea, he is "returning home."

There was a sturdiness about these villages that had persevered for so long. These large houses were usually in the range of forty to sixty feet wide and hundreds of feet long. Constructed of solid planks fashioned from red cedar, the houses, five to twenty in each village, were not divided into rooms but the brightly painted support posts served as divisions for a house's many families, each with two, three, or four generations. Every family had its own fire pit for cooking, warmth, and conversation. Outside would be various work areas, wood carvings, many canoes, and wide-open views of the sea.

The Lummi, and the other Northwest tribes as well, had a way of life anchored in sharing. A major concern was the acquisition and distribution of food. The society was stratified into three groups, the majority being high class, with a smaller middle class and a still smaller lower class.

The Lummi and the other tribes valued status and wealth, and high respect and prestige were accorded to those who shared food and access to it. The best salmon fishing sites, camas meadows, and clam beds, for example, were held by particular families, but this was not ownership as it is known in the majority society. A family's right to a specific location carried with it obligations. A rights-holding family needed to consider the needs of fishers at other locations, including communities beyond, so that they did not, especially in the case of salmon, overharvest to the disadvantage of others.

Sharing was also done by extensive gifting, and high class status depended upon this generosity. The ceremony of potlatching played a key role. In addition to food, the wealth given out at these elaborate, often extravagant, occasions included blankets, baskets, canoes, and other goods. The generosity established the stature of the family holding the potlatch. Critically, it also accomplished the redistribution of wealth and in some cases, if combined with generosity in the distribution of food, allowed people in the lower classes to move upward.

Salmon was the most important food to the Lummi and the largest takes came from reef-net fishing. This harvesting method was an accommodation to the fact that most of the Lummi villages were located on the shores of the Salish Sea, not on rivers. Harvesting salmon runs could be done efficiently in relatively narrow rivers, where fishers could use weirs, dip nets, and spears. Fishing in open waters, however, had advantages: the fish had all of their fat—and were most nutritious and delicious—before entering freshwater and beginning to lose their fat.

Expansive reef nets could be set and anchored in kelp beds or other reefs, which attracted feed for the returning salmon. Six to twelve fishers in two canoes, two on each side of the net, pulled the net up with their catch. A variation, used in deep water where there were no kelp beds, involved weaving an artificial "kelp bed" with grasses, attaching it to a large net, and suspending it above the ocean floor to simulate a rising reef and attract salmon. Then the men in the parallel canoes would haul up the net and the catch.

Reef netting was a major enterprise. Given a good run, this innovation could produce thousands of fish in a single day.

A high point every year took place when word spread excitedly through the Lummi villages that the late-summer sockeye run was charging through the Strait of Juan de Fuca bound for the Fraser River. Everyone was ready—the men, who would work the reef nets, and the women, who would do the butchering, the hanging of fillets and racks, and the smoking. Fishing for this famous run with the effective reef-net technology out on the open sea allowed for taking the sockeyes when they still had all their fat, making them more delicious and more

Lummi fishermen catching salmon with reef nets ca. 1930–1933. PH Coll 77.37. *Courtesy of University of Washington Libraries, Special Collections, Eugene H. Field, photographer, NA1810.*

susceptible to storage. These runs, coinciding with the ripening of the evergreen huckleberries, would make the village even more prosperous over the next year, when the sockeyes would return again. It was hard work, lasting for three or four days, but satisfying in so many ways. As Lummi tribal member Steve Solomon said, these Fraser River runs are "like the blood in your veins. It's part of you."

Makah Tribe

The dramatic homeland of the Makah Tribe, the northwest corner of the Olympic Peninsula and the northwesternmost point in the Lower 48 states, joins with the Pacific Ocean on the west and, to the north, with the Strait of Juan de Fuca, with British Columbia's long and high Vancouver Island rising in the near distance. Rather than a Salish dialect, the Makah language is related to the Nootkans on the coastal side of Vancouver Island. The Quileute, even more remote, speak a "language isolate," found only within that tribe.

Nor are the Makah "Salmon People" in the sense that the other nineteen tribes are. While the Makah collected many foods, the largest harvests of these marine people consisted of halibut, whales, and seals. The Makah considered halibut a greater delicacy than salmon and, in any event, large quantities of halibut were more available to them. Several streams in the Makah region have runs of salmon, and the Makah took salmon from them, but there are no large rivers with headwaters in the interior mountains, as is the case with the other nineteen tribes, including the Quileute to the south and the Klallam to the east.

The tribal preference for halibut was reflected in a detail of Makah architecture. The large Makah residences—multifamily, multigenerational, thirty feet wide and up to seventy feet long and constructed of red cedar—had much in common with the Lummi and other Coast Salish tribes. Those other tribes' buildings, though, had steep, pitched roofs, whereas the Makah roofs were flat. The reason for the difference is that salmon are smoked in smokehouses, while the Makah eschewed smoking the delicate halibut fillets. Instead, they dried and preserved the halibut in the open air on the accessible flat roofs.

The Makah, with thousands of years of experience, mastered the tricky and dangerous ocean hunt, operating as far as a hundred miles offshore. They took fifty- to hundred-pound halibut in close-in areas with hand lines and U-shaped hooks. Northern fur seals, favored over other seal species for their taste and oil, were taken in expeditions of canoes pulled by three or four men with harpoons. Whaling had a pervasive presence in the five Makah villages. The most powerful chiefs were whalers and would take several thirty- to forty-ton whales annually, mostly grays and humpbacks. Consistent with the spiritual attitude that infused all aspects of whaling, whalers readied themselves for a hunt by purifying

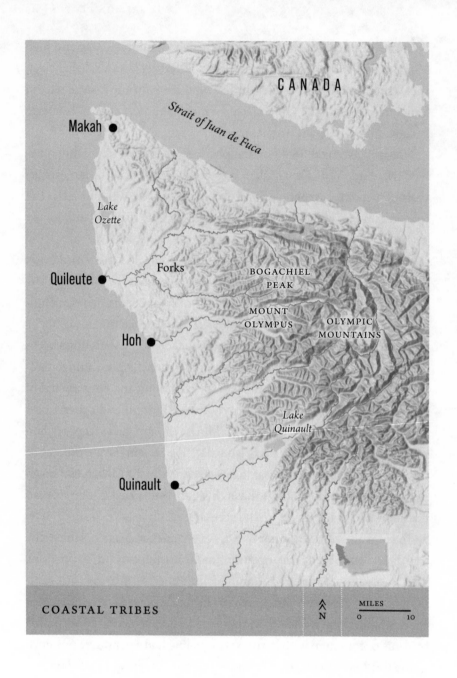

CANADA

Strait of Juan de Fuca

Makah ●

Lake Ozette

Forks

Quileute ●

BOGACHIEL PEAK

MOUNT OLYMPUS

OLYMPIC MOUNTAINS

Hoh ●

Lake Quinault

Quinault ●

COASTAL TRIBES

N

MILES
0   10

themselves through prayer or fasting in private places for weeks. Working from large canoes and singing traditional songs, the Makah used harpoons, not to kill, but to wound and secure sealskin floats that tired the big animals when they made runs after the harpoon strikes. The kill was made by lance. Towing the whale back to shore was slow and draining. The arrival in the village was a grand occasion with thanks, prayers, songs, and celebration over yet another renewal of all that the whales gave to the people.

"The ocean made us rich," explained Janine Ledford, executive director of the Makah Cultural and Research Center. "The ocean made us wealthy for so many years." The whales were used extensively for subsistence and trade. In addition to harvesting the meat, oil was rendered from the blubber and used in the ways that olive oil and butter are today. The skin and bones both had many uses.

Makah commercial trade was extensive. The oil and blubber were high-value exports along with seal and sea otter furs, herring, woven cedar bark clothing, and other goods. In return, the Makah could receive goods—salmon and, especially, red cedar. The cedar stands in Makah territory were relatively modest compared to the big trees on Vancouver Island. The Makah traded with other tribes on the Olympic Peninsula and over Puget Sound. The cultural and family connections with the Nootka tribes on Vancouver Island, however, were deepest and so were the trade relations.

The ocean landscape that lay at the heart of Makah culture, economy, and sovereignty encompassed some 500 miles south to north, reaching from the mouth of the Columbia River up past the Strait of Juan de Fuca all the way to the north end of Vancouver Island. While there were disputes among tribes in this large area, accommodation was the rule. Out of kinship, trade relations, and pragmatism, each of these governments established firm, well-known boundaries. Within those borders, in a fashion not dissimilar from nations in today's world, a governing tribal nation's authority was supreme. The marine highway assured that information traveled quickly by canoe and that intertribal trading ventures and social occasions were commonplace.

A historic conflict at the very front edge of the European incursions highlighted the elaborate Native system that had existed for so long.

In 1788, just four years after the first European arrival commandeered by the Spaniard Juan Pérez, John Meares of Britain sought to enter Makah Territory. Chief Tatoosh was ready for him. Meares had traded with Mowachaht and Clayoquot chiefs, 160 and 100 miles to the north respectively, and the word had quickly spread down to Tatoosh, who intended to block any unauthorized entry by the foreign ship into his domain.

Four hundred Makah warriors in war canoes surrounded Meares's *Felice Adventurer*. When Tatoosh boarded the invading vessels the Englishman, Meares, a veteran of the Royal Navy, described him as "so surly and forbidding a character we had not yet seen." Meares reported that Tatoosh angrily advised him that "the power of [the Clayoquot Chiefs] ended here, and that we were now within the limits of his government, which extended a considerable way to the Southwest." Meares pulled back and made a few other incursions, including attempts to enter the Strait of Juan de Fuca, but Tatoosh and his legions repelled all of them. Meares soon set out for the south, sailing well offshore. He returned a few weeks later, to no better result, and finally retreated to the north.

To Tatoosh, the rules were so obvious and should automatically be obeyed. The Makah had a border and foreign ships could not enter without permission. In a tradition used throughout the Northwest, and Polynesia as well, an outsider wishing to enter or come ashore (on island or mainland) must sing a song asking—imploring—for the right to enter. The host nation may deny entry, singing a loud and strident rejection song, or grant it by singing an upbeat, welcoming song. Such were the prerogatives of the host government. Unauthorized entry was a trespass and cause for violent punishment.

The system was easy to understand and, until the outsiders arrived, extremely effective. The northwestern Washington tribes warred but not to a greater extent than other nations, then and now. Rather, their arrangement among sovereigns created stability among peoples. With the rules set and accepted, trade and social travel could proceed in a steady and mutually beneficial way. It was very civilized.

Quinault Indian Nation

Seventy-five miles south of the Makah, the Quinault River reaches the Pacific. This is a big river, with its headwaters in the snowpacks and thick, wet, and giving forest of the Olympic range and Olympic National Park. At the coast, the long shoreline stretches out north and south. The Quinault River watershed is the homeland of the Quinault Indian Nation.

The people worked the river for the salmon, especially the delicious blueback sockeyes, renowned among the northwestern Washington tribes in the fashion of the Fraser River sockeyes. Out on the shore, the shellfish included the Quinault razor clams, a delicacy for all the generations back and Seattle and Portland restaurants today. A favorite saying among the tribes is "when the tide goes out, the table is set."

Quinault country was endowed with plentiful stands of high-quality western red cedar, which played a large role in the lives of all northwestern Washington Indians. Red cedar is strong, light, rot-resistant, and easy to split. The northwestern Washington tribes used the different parts of red cedar for all manner of purposes. They used the wood to build canoes, houses, carved poles, and steam-bent boxes. They used the bark to construct sweat houses, baskets, mats, and cordage; the soft shredded bark was employed for clothing, diapers, menstrual pads, and napkins. The roots were used for baskets and sewing jobs. The withes (branchlets that hang down from the main branches) were used for nets, lashing and sewing, and baskets. One professor of metallurgical engineering measured the tensile strength and found that "a fairly slender, untwisted withe of red cedar" had a breaking load of 425 pounds.

The strength and lightness of red cedar allowed the construction of the large residences favored by northwestern Washington tribes. The British captain John Meares, in spite of his difficulties with the Makah, took away some favorable impressions. He wrote of the impressiveness of their buildings:

> The trees that supported the roof were of a size which would render the mast of a first-rate man of war diminutive, on a comparison with them; indeed our curiosity as well as our astonishment was on its utmost stretch, when we considered the strength that must be necessary to raise these enormous beams to their present elevation; and how such strength could be found by a people wholly unacquainted with mechanical powers.

The light and durable red cedar trees supported fishing operations of gargantuan size. The Quinault constructed expansive weir systems. As just one example, one of these operations had been inundated by mud and lost to memory. Then, because of recent excavation and because the cedar was so durable, a Quinault V-shaped weir system was discovered. The elaborate operation was over one mile long and some one hundred yards wide at the downriver end, all constructed of thick cedar planks and heavy wood pilings. The site is in Grays Harbor where the Chehalis River pours into the harbor, perfectly located at the exact point where the salmon entered freshwater at the peak of their fat, taste, and nutrition. Carbon dating establishes that the site is approximately 1,000 years old.

Quinault canoes, in the fashion of all the Northwest Coast tribes, allowed for long-distance travel. They frequently journeyed to Vancouver Island for family visits and trade. To the south, they canoed to the mouth of the Columbia River and then worked their vessels upstream. Phillip Martin Sr. remembers such a trip in the 1920s, when he was a boy, and his family made a traditional Quinault journey. One spring they went, not just to the lower Columbia, but paddled upstream to Celilo Falls. This was perhaps the greatest fishing place in North America, where the River of the West narrows and breaks through the Cascade range. For thousands of years, people had come from all over the Columbia watershed and far beyond. This was the best trading locale because the goods were so numerous and diverse. Martin explained what they were looking for: "We don't get a spring chinook run so we would go to Celilo Falls." As usual, the trading was successful: Martin's family obtained plenty of Columbia River chinook jerky—these are the largest and meatiest salmon—and there was high demand for ornate Quinault cedar clothing and renowned Quinault blueback salmon jerky.

Nisqually Indian Tribe

The Nisqually people came north from the Great Basin, across the Cascade Mountains, and erected their first village near what is now called Skate Creek. As for when they first arrived, tribal historian Cecelia Svinth Carpenter has this report: "When asked of the Nisqually elders how long the Nisqually have lived on this Nisqually River, the answer was

Salmon bakes continue to be a staple among Northwest tribal members. Here, Nisqually tribal member Hanford McLeod, center in the traditional cedar hat, does the cooking. *Courtesy of Debbie Preston, Nisqually Tribe Communications and Media Services.*

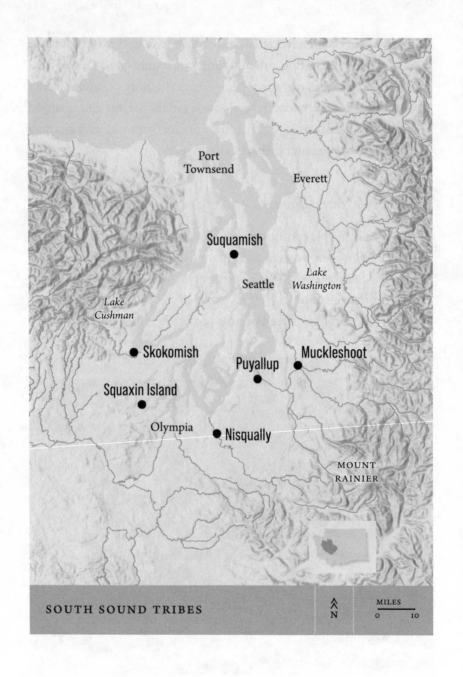

Port
Townsend

Everett

Suquamish
●

Seattle

Lake
Washington

Lake
Cushman

Skokomish
●

Puyallup
●

Muckleshoot
●

Squaxin Island
●

Olympia

Nisqually
●

MOUNT
RAINIER

SOUTH SOUND TRIBES

N

MILES
0   10

'we have always been here. There were no people here when we came. If others had been here before us, they left no signs.'" The Nisqually made their homeland, with its villages of sturdy cedar-plank buildings, in the Nisqually watershed, which reaches from Puget Sound up to the snowfields and glaciers of Mount Rainier. Their largest village was settled at the mouth of the Nisqually River, with an additional twelve villages located up the watershed at points where streams entered the main river. As with all of the northwestern Washington tribes, "Nisqually" basically meant a language and a geological grouping of villages that had much in common, but there was no overarching independent government. Instead, every village was sovereign, independent and self-governing.

The tribe acknowledges on its website both the importance of salmon and the tribe's responsibility to preserve it. "The Nisqually have always been a fishing people. The salmon has not only been the mainstay of their diet, but the foundation of their culture as well. The Nisqually Tribe is the prime steward of the Nisqually River fisheries." As Professor Barbara Lane explains, "Like most of their [tribal] neighbors in western Washington, the Nisqually held the salmon in special esteem and were concerned to ensure that the supply would never fail. To this end, a complex of special rights and observances were performed."

Nisqually people feel a special connection with the towering and beautiful Mount Rainier, rising 14,411 feet above sea level. Rainier, called Ta-co-bet by the Nisqually and meaning "nourishing breasts" and "the place where the waters begin," sends clear and cool water for the salmon runs, family uses, and ceremonies. It affords comfort: "The mountain was always there, never failing, friend, companion, home of the most high of spirit powers even when sequestered behind the clouds."

Ta-co-bet could also be at once a place to have fun and a place to connect with the natural world. Billy Frank Jr. told the story about trips his father and grandfather made up to the peak every fall: "They visited the thermal springs and they actually walked inside the glacier. Big holes. They wanted to know what was in there. Big chunks of ice. Inside the mountain. That's where the river starts, a special place. My dad talked about it; his dad talked about it." As for Billy Frank Jr. himself, whenever he gave a talk in northwestern Washington on a clear day, he would begin by fondly noting that "our mountain is stickin' up there today."

The Nisqually were one of the few coastal tribes to have horses. Some tribal members referred to themselves as "horse Indians." The horses gave them greater mobility out on the open prairies and afforded them access to forest trails. "The thunder of hundreds of horses running on the plains above the Nisqually River once signaled the Nisqually Tribe's prosperity previous to foreign settlement."

Salmon was the single most important food for the Nisqually, and they made much of the shellfish and other marine resources of Puget Sound. At the same time, their name for themselves—the Squalli-absch, meaning "People of the Rivers and Prairies"—made clear the high station of those open, sweeping, and productive prairie landscapes. Joseph Clark, an early American visitor in the 1840s, was moved by the beauty of the Nisqually prairies:

> Everywhere, in this part of the country, the prairies open wide, covered with a low grass of a most nutritious kind, which remains good throughout the year. In September there are slight rains, at which time the grass commences a luxuriant growth, and in October and November, there is an abundance of green grass, which remains until the ensuing summer, about June, it is ripe, and drying without being wet, is like our hay in New England; in this state, it remains until the Autumn rains begin to revive it.

What Joseph Clark did not know was that the fire regime of the Nisqually helped create the vibrant scene, including the "low grass of a most nutritious kind" that Clark witnessed. The people prized the sweet, color-rich camas bulbs, which they harvested in the late spring and then cooked in fire pits, ate fresh, and stored for year-round use as a staple in much the same way modern people use sweet potatoes and oatmeal. The prairies also produced onion bulbs and roots including those of sunflowers, tiger lilies, and carrots. They also picked many kinds of berries including huckleberries, strawberries, blackberries, and salal berries, eating them fresh or drying them on special racks built over a low-burning fire. The camas, other bulbs and roots, and berries all needed open and sunny prairies free of encroaching trees and brush.

The Nisqually and the other northwestern Washington tribes responded with active land management practices. They made extensive use of fire to encourage growth of the prairies' bulbs and roots. So, too, with forestlands. The tribes burned thick timber stands in order to create sunny forest openings so that native grasses could move in and create good grazing habitat for deer and elk, a reminder that these tribes were hunters and gatherers, as well as fishers.

Lower Elwha Klallam Tribe

The Olympic Peninsula is bordered to the west by the Pacific Ocean and the high Olympic Mountains. The east side of the peninsula meets Puget Sound and a number of low mountains and alpine ridges. In the wild interior of the peninsula, the Elwha River runs north and flows into the Strait of Juan de Fuca near what is now the town of Port Angeles. Today, the mouth of the river is within the reservation of the Lower Elwha Klallam Tribe. Two other Klallam tribes made their homelands along the Strait of Juan de Fuca and today the Jamestown S'Klallam Tribe and Port Gamble S'Klallam Tribe have reservations on the Olympic Peninsula.

Historically, the Lower Elwha Klallam people had about thirty-three villages, mostly within the Elwha watershed, but a few villages were located on lower Vancouver Island across the Strait of Juan de Fuca in what is today British Columbia, Canada. The largest village and burial ground, where downtown Port Angeles now lies, was named Tse-whit-zen. In the villages, family dwellings, about twenty by thirty feet, were built in a single row with the doors facing the water. Each village had a potlatch house, about fifty by two hundred feet in size. All of the village structures were made of thick wooden cedar planks and, except for the

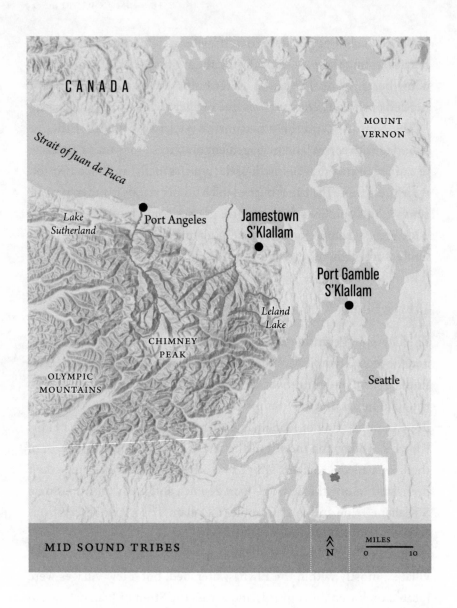

CANADA

MOUNT
VERNON

Strait of Juan de Fuca

*Lake
Sutherland*

Port Angeles

**Jamestown
S'Klallam**

**Port Gamble
S'Klallam**

*Leland
Lake*

CHIMNEY
PEAK

OLYMPIC
MOUNTAINS

Seattle

MILES

MID SOUND TRIBES

N

0   10

potlatch house, had gabled roofs. The sidewalls of the homes were about twelve feet high and were covered with rush mats, which also served as beds. A few planks in the roofs were always left loose so they could be moved to leave smoke holes.

The Lower Elwha Klallam were intimately connected to the Elwha River and its watershed. Veteran environmental journalist Lynda V. Mapes observed that "the river wound through every aspect of tribal members' lives: what they ate, what they wore, what they built, their art, worship, and healing arts." The Lower Elwha Klallam ate a variety of seafood including humpback, silver, and two varieties of dog salmon, steelhead, halibut, lingcod, flounder, herring, smelts, and candlefish. The Klallam would occasionally hunt whales if they were close to the shore of the village, but did not hunt them to the extent that the Makah Tribe did. In addition to the many villages on the lower part of the watershed, near the Strait of Juan de Fuca, some members chose to live upriver because of the better hunting and vegetation gathering. Adeline Smith, Klallam tribal leader from an upriver family, described the thriving society: "People who lived up the river hunted, then came down the river and exchanged. That way everyone tasted everything. My mother gathered the fruit and went down to the small village at Ediz Hook and treated them with apples and pears. We would get flounder."

Still and all, salmon had a pervasive importance to the Lower Elwha. Salmon were the most important food source for the Klallam. They were valuable trade items. The salmon also informed the tribe's culture: "[l]ike the salmon, the Klallams showed their wealth by gifting and did not waste or hoard the largesse of the river, sea, mountains, and meadows that sustained their lives."

Historically, the Elwha watershed was as good as salmon habitat gets. This interior region of the peninsula, its heartland, was bracingly wild: free-running creeks, streams, and rivers heading in pristine snowfields and lush rain forests and meadows. In its natural state, including thousands of years as home to Lower Elwha people, the Elwha River watershed produced a spectacular array of salmon runs of all five Pacific salmon species and steelhead, including some fish in excess of one hundred pounds. As the National Park Service put it, before treaty times and the construction of dams and clear-cutting, "[s]ome of the richest runs of salmon outside of Alaska crowded upstream to their spawning grounds in the wild Elwha River."

Tribal members sometimes fished the highly productive close-by Strait of Juan de Fuca, where so many runs returned from the ocean to spawning grounds on Puget Sound rivers. Nonetheless, the great majority of Lower Elwha Klallam fishing took place at home, on the salmon-rich Elwha River.

Before the treaties, then, the whole watershed was the Lower Elwha Klallam Tribe's homeland. Their villages, potlatch facilities, fishing spots, stories, and culture were located there. They had their pristine water and landscape all to themselves.

The same was true for all of the Pacific Northwest tribes. Everything depended on the gathering of food, which pulsed through their whole existence—the meals, the potlatches, the trade—but everywhere, it was long and arduous work, and year-round. Salmon harvesting was often done in driving rains or other bad weather and wrestling the big fish out of the water into the canoes or up onto the banks was grueling. As for whaling, the Makah did the most but the Quinault, Quileute, Hoh, and Klallam also did some. Pursuing whales and other marine species far offshore required seemingly insurmountable effort and danger, but they did it. Harvesting the shellfish meant cold, wet conditions and all the bending and transporting the catches in baskets was hard on the joints. All of that was mostly spring and summer work.

In the summer and autumn, the tribes established temporary camps for hunting deer and elk, and in some places mountain goats, ducks, and geese. Huckleberry gathering in the fall was a favorite activity, as was the gathering of camas and wild carrots, potatoes, and onions from the open meadows.

Winter, with its storms, was a quieter time but there was still much to do. Nets had to be repaired or new ones created from red cedar, vine maple shoots, or spruce roots. Baskets and waterproof cooking pots were woven. Women and men made hammers, mauls, adzes, chisels, scrapers, and cutting tools from rocks, bones, and shells. Often there would be need for canoes, which required locating a promising cedar tree and hauling it back to the village. Workers hacked and stripped off the bark and limbs, then hollowed out the inside. Separately carved bow and stern pieces added height and length to the canoe. Once the sides and bottom were thinned, the canoe was soaked and steamed so that the finishing touches, sometimes including painting, could be made. The job of creating a canoe usually took two or three years.

The shorter days, difficult weather, and slower pace of winter also set the stage for one of the Salmon People's main institutions. Story-telling, done on winter evenings amid the fragrance and warmth of cedar fires in the cedar-plank buildings, bound together past, present, and future generations. Conscientious elders, male and female, passed on to enthralled young people vivid, precisely worded accounts—variously exciting, scary, and hilarious—all carrying heartland aspects of a people's creation, history, culture, and values. Memorable characters included Raven, Salmon, Crow, Coyote, Transformer, and Thunderbird. Raven, the mischievous trickster, often brought ill to people and other creatures. But Raven's deviousness could also do much good, as when he gave the sun to the world:

"Before Raven came, the earth was dark and cold. When he saw people living without shadows, he began a search for light. He finds it at the house of Sky Chief, who does not want to share it. Raven changes himself into a pine needle and floats down into the water that Sky Chief's daughter is drinking. In her stomach, he turns into a baby, to Sky Chief's delight. When the baby asks for and receives the shiny ball in the box, he turns back into Raven and flies into the sky, placing the ball where all may enjoy it. That is why Native Americans of the Pacific Northwest feed the raven."

Thunderbird, like Raven, had many sides to his personality and was the subject of many stories. The most powerful of all creatures, he wrought thunder, volcanoes, hurricanes, and tsunamis. Thunderbird's benevolence, however, also greatly benefited the people. A long time ago, the giant Mimlos-whale was eating nearly all of the killer whales—the orcas. This was hard on the Hoh and Quileute people, who needed the orcas' meat and oil. Thunderbird attacked the Mimlos-whale and a great battle ensued. Thunderbird, with his powerful claws and enormous wings, lifted the whale up in the air, flew it many miles to dry land, and dropped it. The great whale was injured but alive. Thunderbird lifted it far up into the air and dropped it again, this time killing it. To this day, there are still orcas in the Salish Sea, and Pacific Northwest Native people continue to give thanks to Thunderbird.

But change was to come to these culturally distinct, stable, independent, family-oriented, and economically productive Indigenous communities who harvested prodigious amounts of salmon without affecting the sustainability of the runs.

3 Natives and Europeans Collide

"In this bottle I hold the smallpox safely corked up;
I have but to draw the cork and let loose the pestilence
to sweep man, woman, and child from the face
of the earth."

The thousands of years when Native Americans were the exclusive occupants of the Pacific Northwest came to an end in the late eighteenth
century. The Spanish came first. Starting in 1769, the Spaniards began
what quickly became an elaborate network of presidios, missions, and
towns in what is now coastal California. Spanish leaders had long claimed
California as a Spanish colony but worried about Russian and British initiatives to the north, and sent out ships to determine what their imperial
rivals had accomplished in the Pacific Northwest. The three nations had
much at stake: rich agricultural land, trade with the Indians, and control
of the Northwest Passage, if that mythic route to the Pacific existed.

The first explorer to make landfall in the Pacific Northwest may have
been a pilot named Juan de Fuca, a Greek citizen sailing under the flag
of Spain. He claimed to have reached in 1592 what is now known as the
Strait of Juan de Fuca, the large channel between Vancouver Island and
the Olympic Peninsula that connects the Pacific to the inland Salish Sea,
where he traded with Natives. To this day, the claim of de Fuca's discovery is unverified, but in the late 1700s the possibility of this answer to the
Northwest Passage animated Spanish adventurers in the New World.

In 1774, Juan José Pérez Hernández commanded a voyage which,
while Pérez failed to spot the Strait of Juan de Fuca (its mouth is often

Word gradually went out among outsiders that the Pacific Northwest had arresting beauty and potential for family settlement and resource development. This view was taken from shore across a waterway with Mount Baker in the background. *Courtesy of the Bancroft Library at the University of California, Berkeley, Admiralty Inlet from Port Townsend, Washington, Robert B. Honeyman Jr. Collection of Early Californian and Western American Pictorial Material, BANC PIC 1963.002:0827-C.*

wrapped in fog), was the first, save for de Fuca's possible landing, to make landfall in the Pacific Northwest, at Nootka Harbor on Vancouver Island. Pérez and his men traded with the Nootka Indians and had peaceful relations with them. The Spanish government in Madrid then decreed that another expedition would sail in 1775, led by Bruno de Hezeta. His two ships, the *Sonora* and the *Santiago*, which missed the entrance to the Strait of Juan de Fuca, anchored at Point Grenville, just south of the mouth of the Quinault River. Combat with Natives broke out—the cause is not known—and seven Spanish sailors were killed.

Then the British came forward. In June 1788, as reported earlier, John Meares, a Royal Navy veteran, captained the *Felice Adventurer* and traded with tribes on Vancouver Island before he was repulsed by

Makah Chief Tatoosh for entering Makah Territory without tribal permission. The same year, Captain James Cook made landfall on Nootka Sound on Vancouver Island on the third and last of his whirlwind tours of the South Sea, which had earlier taken him to Australia, New Zealand, Hawaii, and other points. The ship stayed for a month and Cook's men traded for some 1,500 sea otter pelts. The very dense fur proved to be much sought after in China and Europe as well—sea otter pelts became known as "soft gold"—and the sailors did very well when they later sold the furs. The episode jump-started the rush of British and American fur traders that made up a significant part of the Northwest economy for decades thereafter. The trade made the British ever more determined to control the region. Spain and Britain came close to war,

Foreign ships, including war vessels, became commonplace. Here, two vessels were anchored in Bellingham harbor, ca. 1859: an American two-masted steamship and a larger British three-masted steamship. *Courtesy of the Bancroft Library at the University of California, Berkeley, Military vessels in Bellingham Bay, Washington, Robert B. Honeyman Jr. Collection of Early Californian and Western American Pictorial Material, BANC PIC 1963.002:1293-B.*

but Britain's military strength led to the Nootka Convention of 1790, which effectively cemented British trade rights in the Northwest over those of Spain. Ignacio de Arteaga captained the last Spanish voyage, in 1779, making several stops on Vancouver Island and Alaska. In time, of course, the Americans would establish sovereignty in the Pacific Northwest, as against Spain, Russia, and France.

This early exploring and jousting among European nations, which provided the setting for the first contact between tribes and newcomers in the Pacific Northwest, did not result in any significant permanent occupants, buildings, or towns. Numerically, very few citizens from outside nations came to the Northwest during these years. There were no wars, just a few skirmishes and the loss of a few people on both sides, but only a few. There were no changes on the land from mining, logging, or even road building. Still, the impacts were immense—and grotesque. The Europeans unwittingly brought killing diseases from which Native people had no protection. The epidemics wrought ravages exceeding all that happened afterward, and certainly before.

There is no certainty over when, and from where, the first epidemics hit in the mid- to late 1770s. Early Russian explorers did bring viruses but their landings were in Alaska and the northern end of Vancouver Island; those contagions probably did not reach as far south as what is now Washington. Captain Cook's people, in 1788, were the healthiest and kept the most complete records, which made no reference to smallpox. That left the Spaniards.

The two most authoritative sources acknowledged that there is no firm answer, with Elizabeth Fenn concluding that the Arteaga Expedition in 1779 probably lit the first fuse and Robert Boyd leaning toward the 1775 Hezeta voyage. The ships made just a few brief landings, but smallpox is a speedy long-distance traveler and it moved from village to village and person to person. Native people were mystified by this invisible force that was killing and maiming their family members and villagers. "Old timers said that the sickness came from the south—it just came by itself."

The impacts of the epidemics are hard to comprehend. Epidemiologists and demographers emphasize the immensity of the impacts of European diseases on Indigenous peoples in the Americas since 1492. Prominent geologist William Denevan described it as "possibly the greatest demographic disaster in the history of the world." In the United States, the commonly accepted range of Native Americans before contact was 5 to 7 million. By 1900, the Native population hit its all-time low of 250,000, a drop of approximately 95 percent. Wars and violence account for only a small amount.

The Pacific Northwest Natives suffered the same cataclysmic population loss as Indian people nationally, almost all of it due to the epidemics. The effects on individuals, families, and tribal societies were immeasurable. Many plagues, including smallpox, measles, influenza, cholera, typhus, and venereal diseases, ravaged Indian civilizations remote from Europe who had not built up immunities. The most destructive of all was *Variola major*, smallpox:

> *Variola*'s relationship to humankind is both parasitic and paradoxical. To thrive and multiply, the virus has to have a host. But for the host species—unlucky *Homo sapiens*—*Variola* is the most unruly of guests. It inflicts unspeakable suffering upon its victims. It blinds, scars, and maims. In the end, it also confers either immunity or death. For the parasite, this presents a problem. *Variola* consumes its human hosts as a fire consumes its fuel, leaving spent bodies, dead or immune, behind. To survive, the virus has to find a constant supply of new victims. In a large urban population, such individuals might become available through immigration or childbirth. But elsewhere, if *Variola* is to succeed, it has to travel. It has to find more hosts and then, inexorably, still more.

Early British explorers witnessed the impacts. In 1792, Captain George Vancouver, after meeting with members of the Twana (now Skokomish) Tribe at Hood Canal, wrote in his journal:

[A]t the extremity of the inlet ... about sixty [people]. ... : one or two had visited us on the preceding Thursday morning [at Port Discovery]; particularly one man who had suffered very much from the small pox. This deplorable disease is not only common, but it is greatly to be apprehended is very fatal among them, as its indelible marks were seen on many; and several had lost the sight of one eye ... owing most likely to the virulent effects of this baneful disorder.

On the same expedition, Peter Puget summarized his meetings with Natives of Puget Sound and the Strait of Georgia:

the Small pox most have had, and most terribly pitted they are; indeed many have lost their Eyes, & no Doubt it has raged with uncommon Inactercy [sic] among them

Smallpox exploded over the land and by 1800 had invaded the entire Native population. Villages, even entire tribes, were decimated. Meriwether Lewis of the Lewis and Clark Expedition observed this when he met with Lower Columbia River Chinook Indians in 1806:

The smallpox has distroyed a great number of the natives in this quarter. It prevailed about 4 years since among the Clatsops and distroy several hundred of them, four of their chief fell victyms to it's ravages. Those Clatsops are deposited in their canoes on the bay a few miles below us. I think the later ravages of the small pox may well account for the number of remains of vilages which we find deserted on the river and Sea coast in this quarter.

The contagions continued their onslaught for most of the nineteenth century, with major epidemics in the Pacific Northwest in 1801–2, 1824–25, 1836–37, 1852–53, and 1862. In the late 1890s, ethnologist Charles Hill-Tout interviewed Mulks, "the old historian of the tribe," the Squamish of the Lower Fraser River. He was "about 100 years old" and related this:

One salmon season the fish were found to be covered with running sores and blotches, which rendered them unfit for food. But as the people depended very largely upon these salmon for their winter's food supply, they were obliged to catch and cure them as best they could, and store them away for food. They put off eating them till no other food was available, and then began a terrible time of sickness and distress. A dreadful skin disease, loathsome to look upon, broke out upon all alike. None were spared. Men, women, and children sickened, took the disease and died in agony by hundreds, so that when the spring arrived and fresh food was procurable, there was scarcely a person left of all their numbers to get it. Camp after camp, village after village, was left desolate. The remains of which, said the old man, in answer by my queries on this, are found today in the old camp sites or midden-heaps over which the forest has been growing for so many generations.

The European diseases wrought more than death and disfiguration. Blindness was common among survivors, as were famine and malnutrition. Most infected pregnant women and the children they carried died upon birth or shortly thereafter. Tribal customs were stunted: survivors, suffering from fatigue, hunger, and pain, were often unable to give the good nursing care, including food, that the tribal communities traditionally provided.

One tribal healing practice—the afflicted person would go to the sweat lodge and then dive into a nearby lake or river—was not suited for *Variola*. The steam heat of the lodge increased the smallpox fever and the trip to a river was even worse. As one fur trader observed, "the unfortunate Indians, when in the heat of the fever, would plunge into the river, which generally caused instant death."

The diseases, which battered the Salmon People for a full century, impacted the future, not just the time of specific epidemics and outbreaks. Reminders were all around: The disfigurations of surviving fellow tribal members. The empty age-old villages, graves, and scattered human remains. The memories of lost parents, brothers and sisters, relatives, and friends. The growing presence of the newcomers, who, the tribal people came to realize, brought the germs.

Some rogue Europeans put an exclamation point on the threat of smallpox. The most dramatic incident was delivered by Duncan Mc-Dougall, a prominent Scottish fur trader. Bitter over a conflict in June 1811 with Indians at Clayoquot Sound on Vancouver Island that resulted in the loss of his ship, the *Tonquin*, and his crew, McDougall wrongly believed that the Lower Columbia River Indians were involved. Incensed, he called Clatsop and Chinook leaders to Port Astoria, at the mouth of the Columbia, to strike fear in their hearts:

> He assembled several of the chieftains who[m] he believed to be in
> the conspiracy. When they were all seated around, he informed them
> that he had heard of the treachery of some of their northern brethren
> towards the Tonquin, and was determined on vengeance. "The white men
> among you," said he, "are few in number, it is true, but they are mighty
> in medicine. See here," continued he, drawing forth a small bottle and
> holding it before their eyes, "in this bottle I hold the small-pox safely
> corked up; I have but to draw the cork, and let loose the pestilence, to
> sweep man, woman, and child from the face of the earth."

This "smallpox in a bottle" threat terrified the Chinook and Clatsop leaders, whose peoples had been ravaged by *Variola*. The word, carried by the ease of canoe travel and the elaborate trail systems linking the tribes, spread throughout the Northwest. The Indians already knew of the white men's might. This was much worse.

The Northwest tribes, for so long strong, wealthy, and stable peoples, now felt loss, confusion, and fear. Professor Richard White described it as "fatalism." Facing these new arrivals, they had much less leverage than when they were at full strength. They had lost many leaders. Their military capability was diminished. They were weakened, off balance, pulled into a new world with fewer assets. While they did not realize it in the early part of the 1800s, they would be called upon in the 1850s to negotiate treaties that would define their rights to land, salmon, and self-determination—their futures. Would they be ready at treaty time?

At the turn of the nineteenth century, trade was on every country's mind and there were four main international players in the Pacific Northwest: Russia, Spain, Great Britain, and America. The area was still distant but the nations all coveted the right to vie for the land ownership and trade opportunities in the territory's spectacular waters and abundant forests. The Northwest offered direct access to the ocean and the trade routes that came with it. The Russian and Spanish claims would all be extinguished by 1825, leaving only the British and Americans. The powerful Hudson's Bay Company had become the only British entrant when it absorbed the North West Company, a Canadian enterprise, in 1821.

With the international expansion of trade and the fight for control of the area, one must remember the key figures in the narrative that kept the trade and forts afloat. The Native tribes were the very heartbeat of the trade enterprise in the Northwest and instrumental to the survival of the fur traders who moved there. Though more non-Natives were gradually advancing into the region, Natives still held the majority, as would be the case for many years to come. Interest in the area slowly increased, trade grew, the Northwest was gradually opened, and interactions with the Natives expanded.

From 1820 through the mid-1840s the British and American traders were moving into the region. They took drastically different approaches when interacting with the Indigenous peoples of Puget Sound. Where the British were more accommodating and fairer in their dealings with the tribes in order to coexist, the Americans were looking toward the future of the region and how it would benefit them. According to Vine Deloria Jr., "The Americans tended to be mostly whites, contemptuous of the Indians of the area and interested only in a quick profit. The British sought a well-regulated trade and eventually settled at the trading posts." The Natives were not fond of the Americans either: "The first experience of the Indians with the Americans, whom they came to call 'Bostons' because every ship seemed to be from Boston, left a distinct dislike among them." The Natives preferred the "King George Men," as they called the British, over the Bostons. The King George Men acknowledged the importance of conducting themselves with a sense of diplomacy when dealing with the Natives. As Deloria explains, this is not to say that the Englishmen were completely benevolent toward the tribes, but they realized that, strategically, without them they would not endure:

> For a twenty-year period, from 1820 to 1840, the Indians and the "King George" men lived in comparative peace and harmony in the Puget Sound–British Columbia region. The British always went out of their way to ensure justice to the Indians and treated them with fairness even in legal matters. If an Indian harmed a white man he was promptly called to account, but if a white man harmed an Indian he was called before the same officer and given the same sentence for the offense that the Indian would have gotten. Such evenhanded justice endeared the British to the Indians, and they developed a great loyalty to the British.

This loyalty was also strengthened by the fact that British traders tended to take Native wives. For traders it was beneficial to have a Native American wife from a local tribe. Taking a wife from a local tribe meant that these women would be able to speak the different languages of the villages they came from. It was even more beneficial if she was the daughter of a leader because that almost guaranteed commerce with that tribe. Also, Native women were used to working more laborious jobs (tanning leather, carving canoes, and gathering firewood and food) than their white counterparts, which would come in handy when married to traders.

The relative harmony between the British and the tribes is seen in the creation of its forts in the Northwest. The British were the first to make a lasting and consistent trading enterprise in the Puget Sound area. The Hudson's Bay Company selected locations convenient to several tribes and emphasized that each fort would be a reliable, fair, and consistent trading partner and employer. An example is Fort Nisqually, founded in 1833 and located between present-day Tacoma and Olympia. It was the first permanent non-Indian settlement on Puget Sound. Over the course of two decades, the top figure for Hudson's Bay was Dr. William Fraser Tolmie, who took an interest in the culture and customs of the tribes and learned the Nisqually language. Professor Richard White wrote that Dr. Tolmie was one of the few white men to "approach the Indians with a modicum of humanity, humor, and commonsense." While Hudson's Bay had Dr. Tolmie, at Fort Nisqually and other forts there was a pragmatic working agreement between Hudson's Bay and the tribes that each side would attempt to understand the other and make reasonable adjustments. There were ups and downs, but for roughly a generation the British and the tribes had relationships that led to good economic results and social stability. Here is how Nisqually historian Cecelia Svinth Carpenter summarized it:

> Fort Nisqually became a place where many Nisqually people found employment and where several young Nisqually maidens found husbands. The peacefulness of the scene fast disappeared when American families started arriving and building fences around choice Nisqually land.

The election in 1844 of James Knox Polk as United States president triggered events that moved Indian treaties in the Northwest to the forefront. Aggressively expansionist, Polk had campaigned on the idea of the United States acquiring all lands west of the Louisiana Purchase out to the far Pacific Ocean. He successfully achieved that extravagant program, which expanded the country's borders by more than one-third, through treaties with Mexico, the Republic of Texas, and England.

As for England, he campaigned on the battle cry "54–40 or fight." At the time, the "Oregon Country," basically today's Pacific Northwest, was governed by the Joint Occupancy Agreement of 1818 between the United

States and Great Britain. The two nations mutually consented to jointly occupy—basically covering settlement and fishing—the landscapes in the Oregon Country.

Wanting full, not just joint, United States land title and jurisdiction in the Pacific Northwest, Polk pressed for a new treaty from the beginning of his term. Although he argued for "54–40," he finally put the fifty-fourth parallel aside and settled for a northern boundary of the forty-ninth parallel. The land above the forty-ninth parallel had been settled mostly by Great Britain and his main objective was to secure complete federal authority to the Pacific Northwest. The resulting 1846 treaty put the future states of Oregon, Washington, and Idaho, along with parts of Montana and Wyoming, exclusively and permanently in federal hands.

Relationships changed in the Pacific Northwest. Tensions between American settlers and Native people increased. With the Oregon Trail now established as a reliable route to the Northwest, the Polk administration encouraged American settlement in Oregon, especially the Willamette Valley. The days of harmony between the British and the Natives were steadily coming to an end. Skirmishes increased in the Northwest, the most notable being the 1847 Whitman Massacre near present-day Walla Walla, Washington. The Cayuse Tribe came to resent the settlers, especially when an outbreak of measles took out half of their tribe in 1847. Marcus Whitman, an American physician, tried to help out but could do little to combat the disease. The Cayuse killed Whitman and fourteen others in their belief, shared with other tribes, that men of medicine and healing should be held accountable for the deaths of patients they could not save. Word of the Whitman Massacre spread quickly and tensions flared up in both white and Indian communities in the Northwest.

Expansion-oriented politicians in Washington, DC, and settlers out in the field wanted to move to territorial status so there would be a formal governmental apparatus. It would be short of statehood, and Congress would make final decisions, but territorial status would establish some home rule. And it would be yet another marker to Britain and other foreign nations that the Northwest was solidly American. In 1848, Congress officially established the Territory of Oregon, encompassing the future states of Oregon and Washington along with Idaho, and western parts of Montana and Wyoming.

The population of the Oregon Territory was still very small. The 1850 Census reported just 13,000 people, mostly in the Willamette Valley. North of the Columbia River there were sparse settlements and, farther north still, the first Americans to settle did not arrive on Puget Sound until 1845, when the Simmons Party arrived with four families and two single men.

Still, populous or not, the Oregon American citizens had support for expansion—determined leaders in Congress, led by Senator Thomas Hart Benton of Missouri and Senator Stephen Douglas of Illinois. Territorial status helped. Oregon now had a member, although nonvoting, in Congress, Samuel Thurston, who was enthusiastic and effective in pushing for a land program allowing land grants for settlers and opening Indian land for homesteading: Thurston "was an indefatigable promoter of a Donation Land Act for his Oregon constituents. In the East he interviewed editors, Congressmen, and executive officers, always urging a land grant."

The matter of tribal land possession was no minor or theoretical matter. Under controlling federal law, announced first by Chief Justice John Marshall in the 1823 decision *Johnson v. McIntosh*, before the treaties, tribes were "rightful occupants of the soil, with a legal, as well as just, claim to retain possession of it, and to use it to their own discretion." The United States, in other words, had obtained land title to all of the West as against foreign nations but the tribes retained their right of occupancy. Under American law, the United States could obtain tribal land by war or treaty, with the strong preference for proceeding with treaties. Settlers could not move onto tribal land without formal federal approval in a treaty.

This principle was well known in Washington, DC, and by land office officials in the West. Individual settlers were told by local federal officials that homesteads could not be made on Indian land but settlers often would have none of it and went ahead, with conflicts becoming ever more numerous. The issue was not going to go away. Settlers kept coming and tribal land extended to virtually every acre in the Territory.

Congress adopted a two-part strategy: move the Oregon tribes out of the Willamette Valley and then enact comprehensive legislation for settlement of Oregon by Americans. In 1850, Congress passed the Oregon Indian Treaty Act for "the extinguishment of their claims to lands lying west of the Cascade Mountains; and, if found convenient and practicable, for their removal east of said mountains." Oregon Indians universally hated the Oregon Indian Treaty Act. To these tribes, the Willamette Valley, other valleys in western Oregon, and lands north of the Columbia and west of the Cascades were their homelands and always had been. To them, moving "east of the mountains," as the Act contemplated, was ridiculous, totally unacceptable. In a complicated series of events beyond the scope of this book, Willamette Valley tribes were in time removed—not to the east of the mountains—but outside of the Willamette Valley, mostly to the Oregon Coast, which was not desirable to settlers at that time.

A few months after the Oregon Indian Treaty Act, Congress adopted the 1850 Donation Land Act to promote settlement in the Oregon Territory. It was the most ambitious homestead act yet enacted and served as a model for the Homestead Act of 1862. Single males could obtain grants of 320 acres and married couples could claim 640 acres (a full square mile). The inrush of settlers mushroomed. One scholar, Jerry O'Callaghan, exulted that it "came very close to meeting the classic homestead ideal—award the best farmland to the actual settlers."

The Donation Land Act, which was so excellent if only the benefits to settlers and their communities are considered, brought in many more people, with Indian-white conflicts inevitably rising, especially over land. The stampede that was the Gold Rush of 1849 also affected Oregon. Most prospective miners headed for California and stayed there, but a steady number fanned out to Nevada and Oregon. They, too, wanted land but most of it was subject to the Indian right of occupancy, leading to disputes.

The tribes of what is now northwestern Washington, however, then went through a separate round of treaties that are at the heart of this book. American ambitions to obtain tribal rights in the Northwest were galvanized by Washington becoming a separate territory.

It did not take long for Americans east and west to appreciate the immensity of Polk's acquisition of the lands from the Rockies to the Pacific Coast. California gold and silver literally brought the United States into the world economy. California's population jumped from 14,000 in 1848 to 100,000 by the end of 1849, and 223,000 by 1852. California skipped over territorial status and went straight to statehood in 1850, becoming the first state in the West without first being a territory. The 1850 Donation Land Act was less dramatic, but it was highly respected bringing, as it did, thousands of American farm families to the West.

These events inspired Oregonians to accelerate their dreams of statehood. It was realistic. Congress required territories to have a population of at least 60,000 to be eligible for statehood. With the rapidly growing Willamette Valley, Oregon would soon meet that. One political problem came up: the current Oregon Territory was too big, in terms of acreage, for a new state. Citizens in both Oregon and Washington complained that the current size was unmanageable. Citizens north of the Columbia and west of the Cascades would much prefer to travel to a capital in Olympia rather than Salem. A consensus quickly developed: reduce the Oregon Territory to the size of the current state of Oregon by breaking off a new Territory, consisting of the larger, much less populated regions.

In 1853, Congress agreed and reduced the Oregon Territory, which would become a state in 1859. The 1853 bill also created the Territory of Washington.

On one level, this new territory was just a backwater. The town of

Seattle had been founded in 1851 but the total American citizenry in the territory amounted to just 4,000. The Puget Sound country was still little known and lightly populated.

Yet a certain kind of ambitious young man could see it as a bright opportunity. A territorial governor would have to be named and he would be head of a government with a legislature, courts, and administrative officials. The economic value of Washington's marine and forest resources would likely climb. It would be logical that the governor would also be named Commissioner of Indian Affairs since the most important matter for the expansive new territory would be to negotiate treaties with the tribes. This effort was at the very forefront of manifest destiny, erasing the Indian right of Indian occupancy and fully opening the Pacific Northwest for settlement by Americans, from the Pacific Ocean across broad Washington to the mountains of Idaho and Montana. Yes, the territorial governorship of the Washington Territory might well be an important and exciting office indeed.

4 Young Man in a Hurry

"It is almost impossible to do anything without extinguishing [Indian] title and placing them on reservations where they can be cared for and attended to."

Isaac Ingalls Stevens, one of the most consequential figures in the history of the Pacific Northwest, was born on a farm outside of Andover, Massachusetts, in 1818. He was ambitious, aggressive, and erratic in his early days and throughout his life. His legs were unnaturally short and he had an outsize head, yet he was smart, handsome, and articulate and drew people in. Stevens was also driven, and Kent Richards gave his excellent biography of Stevens the title *Young Man in a Hurry*.

He won an appointment to West Point and finished first in his class in 1839. After graduation, Stevens secured a plum position with the Army Corps of Engineers as superintendent of a major construction project at Fort Adams in Rhode Island. He performed so well there that he was appointed to head up, concurrently, construction projects at five separate sites in New England.

For all of Stevens's success, his promotions in the peacetime army came slowly. He requested and received an assignment in 1846 to the Mexican War. A year later, he achieved a transfer to a war zone and served as adjutant to General Winfield Scott, the highest-ranking officer in the US Army. Stevens received high praise for his wartime advice and courage, which included reconnaissance behind enemy lines.

After the war, he returned to the Army Corps of Engineers. Over the years, he befriended a number of high military and political figures,

Isaac Ingalls Stevens, ca. 1860. *Library of Congress, Prints and Photographs Division, Civil War Photographs, 2018666865.*

including General Scott, Senator Stephen Douglas, and Franklin Pierce, United States senator and later brigadier general in the Mexican–American War. When Pierce drew criticism for his leadership in the war, Stevens drew upon his firsthand knowledge and sent letters to several newspapers praising Pierce's leadership. Pierce greatly appreciated his support.

In 1852, General Winfield Scott, a Whig, and Pierce, a Democrat, opposed each other in the 1852 presidential election, with Pierce prevailing.

Stevens knew he would be in line for an appointment. Just before Pierce took office, Congress passed the statute creating the Washington Territory. Stevens jumped on the opportunity, urging Pierce to nominate him as the territorial governor. The new president did put Stevens forward and the Congress approved him.

Stevens didn't stop there and soon requested Pierce to award him two other high positions. The young man wanted to be superintendent of Indian Affairs for the territory, since the biggest issue out in the territory would be eliminating vast amounts of Indian land title in order to open for homesteading as much fertile farm country as possible. It was customary for territorial governors to head up Indian Affairs as well.

Pierce acceded to that request and a third one: commander of the survey of the northern route for the transcontinental railroad, from Minnesota to Fort Vancouver. Ever organized, Stevens, who reported to the Secretary of War for the survey, assembled a company of 120 men. He conducted his fieldwork on the survey by traveling from Washington, DC, to the West Coast with his staff, seeking to identify the best route for the transcontinental rail line. When he reached Washington Territory, he assumed his duties as governor and top official for Indian Affairs.

Stevens arrived in Olympia, the territorial capital, on November 25, 1853. Founded seven years earlier, the town had grown steadily albeit slowly and became one of the largest settlements in the territory, with two sawmills, a gristmill for grain, and a population of 150. He received a warm and enthusiastic welcome from the civic leaders. Stevens and the political leaders who greeted him heartily agreed on one thing: the great majority of Indian lands must be opened for settlement, and soon. The citizenry out across the territory believed that also. Part of it was the Americans' simple desire to own their own family homes, resting on productive farmlands in this glorious landscape, but there was more. From the beginning, American settlement of the open West carried with it powerful philosophical, religious, and moral imperatives.

President Thomas Jefferson had put the finishing touches on the Lou-

This cityscape of downtown Olympia in 1856 was created by artist Robert Chamberlain, and Lynn Erickson was author and researcher for the project. *Courtesy of the Olympia Historical Society.*

isiana Purchase from France in 1803, thus acquiring the vast western domain out to the Rockies. For Americans, settlement of this place, which doubled the size of the nation, would be the embodiment of the Jeffersonian Ideal, holding that the highest form of governance, democracy, would be a nation primarily based on agrarian communities of small, self-sufficient family farms—rather than on manufacturing. Farming, Jefferson believed, promoted hard work, a direct connection to the land, freedom, sustainability, and honesty. Manufacturing, on the other hand, meant greed, dependence, and corruption. For Jefferson, "Those who labor in the earth are the chosen people of God." The West would be "an empire of liberty."

When Stevens made his maiden trip to the Washington Territory in 1853, the Jeffersonian Ideal continued to inspire western homesteaders. But the American mind-set about western lands had added to it a sharper edge. The second titanic acquisition of western lands—President James Polk's additions from 1846 through 1848 of Texas, the northern Mexican lands, and the Pacific Northwest, from the Rockies all the way to the Pacific—amounted to even more real estate than the Louisiana Purchase.

The lure of western land, with homesteading now coupled with gold fever, spiked to a new level. President Polk, picking up on a paper written by John O'Sullivan, a New York columnist and expansionist, adopted a new term, "manifest destiny," to join with the Jeffersonian Ideal:

> Our claim to Oregon would still be best and strongest. And that claim is by the right of our manifest destiny to overspread and to possess the whole of the continent which Providence has given us for the development of the great experiment of liberty and federated self-government entrusted to us.

As O'Sullivan asserted, the American claim of manifest destiny, with its overt nationalist and religious imperatives, struck the right note with American leaders and citizens alike. The United States had a superior right to western lands that superseded any claims by Britain, Texas, or Spain. Nor did there seem to be any significant room for Indian tribes. Chief Justice John Marshall's recognition of tribal legal rights to their lands was officially acknowledged by the federal government, but his formulation seemed to have evolved from a legal, constitutional, and moral obligation to a bureaucratic procedural matter.

The loudest official recognition of the diminished federal respect for tribal land rights was sounded in the pivotal Donation Land Act of 1850 in which Congress, during the Polk years, threw open the "land" in the Oregon Territory (which still included Washington) to wide-open homesteading by Americans. Every previous land act had expressly excluded Indian land, recognizing the shared ownership between the United States and tribes: homesteading on Indian land could not be allowed unless the tribes had ceded lands to the United States by treaty. The Oregon Indian Treaty Act, companion legislation to the Donation Land Act, directed commissioners to negotiate treaties with the tribes for the "extinguishment of their claims" west of the Cascades, and, if practicable, "for their removal east of the Cascades." This put severe stress on the tribes, which continued until the Washington treaties were completed five years later. Settlers out in the West made it clear that they wanted homesteads on land, even if occupied by Natives. Federal officials in Washington, DC, and out West felt pressure to complete the treaties quickly.

As Americans saw it then, it may be that the tribes had a right to their ancestral land, but that could be changed by war or, more likely, by treaty, and the treaties should promptly and fully honor the United States' manifest destiny as designed by Providence. That view was especially held out in the West, where settlers were waiting for their land.

Stevens had gotten off to a high-octane start on his first visit to Olympia. He arrived on November 25, 1853, a day early, drenched by heavy rains. No matter. The local whites had been enthusiastically looking forward to his visit and responded in kind. They saw that the governor had put on dry clothes and retreated to an impromptu fine dinner at the Washington Hotel, with civic leaders offering warm speeches and toasts. They knew Stevens's agenda and he knew theirs, and they matched perfectly. They applauded his obvious energy and drive: "I have come here, not as an official for mere station, but as a citizen as well as your chief magistrate to do my part towards the development of the resources of this Territory, and combining the elements of national organization and strength on the western coast. A great field opens to our view, and we can labor with the conviction that from our hands as the pioneers on the Northern Pacific, an imperial domain will descend to our children, and an accession of power result to our country, all too in the cause of freedom and humanity." The booster newspaper, the *Washington Pioneer Democrat*, reported that the celebratory group proclaimed, "We confidently assume that Washington Territory has the best corps of federal officers on the Pacific coast, and a *model* Governor—one who will be a Governor of the whole people."

Stevens had found plenty of time on his long overland journey from Washington, DC, to put together his thoughts on a program. He knew he had to please both his superiors back East and his constituents in the territory. He had long been exposed to the policies of high federal officials. As for the settlers, he had met only a few on his trip out, but the priorities and attitudes of Americans on the frontier were well known back East. For the most part the two matched up well, and with his own beliefs also.

Starting with the dinner at the Washington Hotel, the governor put forth a three-part program on development of the territory's resources and regularly presented it with precision and color. It began with the adage that the most important thing to be done for a new country is the "laying-out and construction of roads." Stevens had rock-solid credentials: everyone was enthusiastic about the Northwest rail line from Minnesota, which Stevens headed up, and the business it could bring west. The governor also learned all of the area's roads—many just trails—that needed construction. His second priority, necessary but less immediate, was to complete work on matters left over from the 1846 treaty with Britain that solidified American title to the Northwest. The northern boundary of the nation and territory remained in dispute, as did compensation to the Hudson's Bay Company for the value of their lands now under United States ownership.

Third, and perhaps most important, treaties needed to be made so that Indian title could be extinguished. Development depended on it. Existing settlers could not begin making the land profitable until they had title. Future homesteaders wanted certainty before journeying west. He made up his mind early. A few weeks after arriving in Olympia, he wrote Indian Commissioner George Manypenny that "it is almost impossible to do anything without extinguishing their title and placing them on reservations where they can be cared for and attended to."

Understandably, Stevens's wife, Meg, and their young children could not accompany him on the rigorous survey trip west, and he was able to throw himself completely into his governmental duties. Anxious for support and information about this new government and complex landscape, he met relentlessly for the next four months with influential locals individually and in small groups. He developed an inner circle of about thirty. While the governor and his constituents discussed unending details, agreement on the three overarching goals remained solid and the common commitment to accomplish them deepened.

In addition to the stuff of politics, Stevens had much on his mind. Most of the fieldwork for the Northern Pacific Railroad Survey was completed but the elaborate, highly praised final report—thanks to the vision and insistence of Stevens, the project's highest official—would not be finalized for seven more years. Secretary of State William Marcy directed Stevens to address the two still unresolved issues from the Treaty of 1846—the boundary dispute and the Hudson's Bay Company's claims for compensation. All of this required, during Stevens's quite short visit to the territory, negotiations with different sets of British officials around Puget Sound and on Vancouver Island. He also needed to get out to several roads in order to understand their conditions.

This left little time for dealing with the tribes in the northwestern part of the territory in the Puget Sound and Olympic Peninsula areas. While almost all federal officials agreed that those treaties should come first, Stevens seemed to place a higher priority on the tribes in the far eastern part of the territory, the Blackfeet, Crow, Yakama, and others, which were larger and militarily more powerful than the western tribes. With little time to spare out in Olympia, the governor took a "hurried" midwinter trip, visiting Steilacoom, Seattle, Bellingham Bay, and Victoria on Vancouver Island. He had business with American and British officials in all of those places but did meet with some Indian people from nearby locations. This approach, so minimal compared with his relations with virtually every other significant interest group in the region, certainly wasn't due to a lack of energy—he had plenty of that—but it did display a lack of interest and respect.

He also lacked knowledge of Indian people. In his youth, he saw surviving Natives in Maine but had no contact with tribes during his years at West Point or in the military. The railway survey expedition had scattered exchanges with Indians, but he delegated those relationships to staff, and his direct meetings with tribes were superficial. Stevens clearly saw whites as superior to Indians and believed that Americans were destined to control the Pacific Northwest fully and finally with little respect to the tribes. Without any understanding of tribal cultures, societies, or philosophies, he offhandedly opined that the tribes had no need for vast lands since they would become farmers on small plots.

These opinions were starkly contrary to the tribes' views. Stevens looked down on Indians, but did not believe in military action against them: the sweeping changes he advocated should be made through voluntary treaty negotiations. It might be anathema to Indian people to sign away almost all of their lands, but Stevens, totally committed intellectually to manifest destiny and the overriding value of farming communities, was certain that the extinction of Indian land title he would force upon tribes at treaty time was both inevitable and (as he claimed) a benefit to them.

Regardless, Stevens made an excellent choice for his advisor on tribal cultural matters. George Gibbs grew up in an intellectual household near

Astoria, Long Island, graduated from Harvard, and became a lawyer. When word of the California Gold Rush created high excitement on the East Coast, Gibbs, just thirty-three, took notice. To him, the allure was not the heralded chance to get rich, but the mountains, forests, and Indian tribes of the West Coast. In 1849, he headed not to California but to Oregon. He threw himself into Indian culture, interviewing Indians on the trip west and in Oregon, California, Washington, and Idaho, finally settling on a farm in Steilacoom, Washington Territory. Intelligent, organized, and committed, he became a self-made anthropologist before the field became a recognized science.

In the summer of 1853, Gibbs signed up with Stevens's railway survey as an ethnologist and geologist to study possible routes across the Cascade range in the territory. Among other things, he wrote a number of papers on Indian culture that Stevens relied on in his final report. By then, Gibbs was widely recognized as the most knowledgeable American on the Indians of the Pacific Northwest.

The two worked closely on the treaties. Gibbs had no impact on Stevens's determination to extinguish huge amounts of Indian title or on the governor's race to early treaty negotiations. Gibbs did, however, bring forth important treaty provisions that responded to tribal interests.

The governor's choice as a second aide on tribal matters was much less auspicious. Michael Simmons, a leader of the first settlement on Puget Sound, had accomplished little economic success, may have been illiterate or nearly so, and held Indians in low regard. At the same time, the rugged Kentuckian was popular among the whites and would bring an extinguishment-now perspective shared by most of the settlers.

After giving his formal address to the territory's first legislative assembly on February 28, 1854, which was resoundingly well received, Stevens began making plans to make a trip back to the nation's capital. He had need for congressional appropriations to support the railway survey report, roads, and treaty negotiations but mail was slow and unreliable in those prerailroad days. In addition, he knew from his experience that successful dealings with Congress and the executive agencies required face-to-face meetings. In making arrangements during his absence, he appointed Charles Mason as acting governor. Stevens had already made Mason, a lawyer from Providence, his territorial secretary, second in command; Mason had done well and the government was in good hands when the governor was out of the territory.

Stevens then initiated a heavy-handed strategy that had lasting consequences. Federal policy had always been to negotiate with political leaders—"chiefs." The Native political structure of much of the Northwest was based on local villages, each an independent sovereign. But, numerically, that would require too many "tribes" to make treaties with. So, before Stevens left, he instructed Simmons to determine the identity of tribes, even if it meant grouping villages together to create one "tribe." Simmons should also identify the chiefs, who could speak for these often-fictitious units. Simmons soon hired his business partner, Frank Shaw, as an interpreter and collaborator. As the authors of one article in the *Oregon Historical Quarterly* put it, "Simmons and Shaw wielded enormous power over the lives and futures of the Puget Sound Indians. With Stevens absent from the Territory, they were positioned to make most of the decisions about which groups were invited to the Treaty Councils and which individuals were designated as tribal leaders."

With things in order in the territory, Stevens began the long steamboat journey to the East Coast by way of San Francisco and the Panama overland route on March 26, 1854. He arrived in New York two months later, having been away from his wife and children for a full year.

Stevens spent a hectic summer in the nation's capital. He had many balls in the air—time-consuming dealings with Congress, the War Department, and the Office of Indian Affairs in the Interior Department.

By the summer it had become clear that the project closest to Stevens's heart was the railroad survey and report. One author observed that "there is no doubt that during the time that Stevens was Governor . . .

that his first and foremost endeavors at all times were in the interest of the railroad project. Everything else was of lesser importance." It is important to mark down the magnitude of this effort. By the early 1850s, interest was building at all levels of government to create efficient, affordable transcontinental railroads to link the eastern part of the country to the Pacific Coast. This ambitious venture was widely seen as being critical to the national interest but the distances, selection of routes, engineering challenges, construction difficulties, scientific uncertainties, and huge cost made it daunting to the young nation. In 1853, Congress moved forward, directing the Topographic Branch of the Army to conduct, in short order, six intensive surveys identifying the best east-to-west railway routes. As noted earlier in this chapter, Stevens had been named to the prestigious office of commander of the Northern Pacific Railroad Survey.

The bulk of his time that summer was spent on the railroads. The railroad surveys were all the talk in Washington, and most of his top staff were reunited in the capital. Stevens's work had two broad parts: the survey to gather data, and the report, which would present all the findings and recommendations. He substantially completed the survey in 1853 at the end of his onerous trip to Washington Territory with his large and able staff.

The final report took much longer. He was determined to make the full report an elaborate document that went far beyond identifying the proper Northern Pacific routes and justifying them with scientific data, challenging as that work was. He also wanted to present a wide and interesting variety of scientific background research about geology, botany, topography, zoology, and anthropology. Going even further, he aimed for a humanistic package that included maps and many works of art. Although it took until 1859, he succeeded. His report is acknowledged to be the best of the six reports that were prepared for other routes and presented to the Army. There is no doubt about his preeminent role in conceiving and preparing it. One study concluded that his report was "probably the most important single contemporary source of knowledge on Western geography and history and their value was greatly enhanced by the inclusion of many beautiful plates in color of scenery, inhabitants, fauna and flora of the Western country."

Isaac Stevens's work and report led to Congress's passage in 1862 of the Central Pacific and Union Pacific grant to fund a railroad line to San Francisco. (This is the project that produced the ceremonial "golden spike" driven by Leland Stanford at Promontory Summit in Utah Territory to commemorate the joining of Central Pacific Railroad from the west and the Union Pacific Railroad from the east to create the first transcontinental railroad across the United States.) In 1864, two years after Isaac Stevens's death, President Lincoln signed the largest grant, for the Northern Pacific line reaching to Tacoma, which was not fully completed until 1883 when President Ulysses Grant drove the traditional "golden spike" at Gold Creek, Montana.

By the end of his whirlwind Washington, DC, visit, Stevens, and the Franklin Pierce administration as well, wanted to discuss the upcoming Washington Territory treaty negotiations, which they planned to begin by the end of the year. When George Manypenny became Indian Commissioner in 1853, as a sign of the times, he brought in a tougher approach toward treaty making. Later, he prided himself on acquiring a large expanse of Indian title, boasting in an 1856 report to Congress that under his administration the United States had acquired by treaty 174 million acres and that "in no former equal period of our history have so many treaties been made, or such vast accessions of land been obtained."

Manypenny, who wanted to exert some control over the upcoming faraway negotiations, gave Stevens instructions through an acting commissioner. Among other things, he emphasized that he did not want large reservations but, rather, was determined to consolidate all tribes on a single reservation or on "a limited number of reservations . . . in a limited number of districts . . . apart from the settlement of the whites."

For Stevens's part, he had already discussed possible sizes of reservations with several people and he himself leaned toward a single consolidated large reservation. But he knew that George Gibbs, who had the best understanding of anybody, favored a different approach, based on small individual reservations on each tribe's homeland coupled with the right of tribal members to fish, hunt, and gather on lands the tribes would transfer to the United States in the treaties. Before the governor left the capital, he sent an inconclusive report to Manypenny suggesting a large central reservation but not committing himself to it. That would give him the chance to talk with Gibbs and others out in the territory. But time was short and it would turn out that these and other momentous decisions would be made in a hurried, often scattered, manner.

In late September 1854, Stevens, with his wife and children, left Washington, DC, on the steamship rides and the Panama overland leg to the territory. He had spent four months in Washington, DC, and, as well, four months getting there and back (two months each way).

5 Treaty Time

"This paper secures your fish."

Isaac and Meg Stevens, with their children in tow, arrived in Olympia on December 3, 1854. It had been a hard trip. There were sicknesses on the jam-packed steamer to San Francisco. After traveling up to Vancouver, Washington, by sail, they spent a long, wet day in a cramped canoe with Indian pullers and then endured a rainy, muddy three-day wagon trip to Olympia.

The next three weeks leading up to the first treaty council demonstrated the ragtag preparation and heavy-handed "negotiations" that resulted in the transfer of hundreds of thousands of acres of tribal land and set the stage for an additional four treaty councils in the Puget Sound–Pacific Ocean area.

Stevens arrived on the opening day at the second annual session of the Washington Legislative Assembly of the new territory. His address as governor was scheduled for the day after. He spent little time on Indian issues, briefly mentioning in the early part of his address that, while back in Washington, DC, he had obtained funding for the treaty negotiations. However, he dedicated the very last paragraph of his speech to the tribes, issuing a ringing promise that left no doubt what was to come:

> In closing this communication, I will indulge the hope that the same spirit of concord and exalted patriotism which has thus far marked our political existence, will continue unto the end.
>
> Particularly do I invoke the spirit in reference to our Indian relations. I believe the time has now come for their final settlement. In view of the important duties which have been assigned to me, I throw myself

unreservedly upon the people of the territory, not doubting that they will extend to me a hearty and generous support in my efforts to arrange, on a permanent basis, the future of the Indians of this territory.

By now, the die was cast. The United States of America would be deciding the "final," "permanent" future of the tribes. In doing so, Isaac Stevens would be representing the "people of the territory," not the "Indians of the territory."

The governor called an organizational meeting, to be held in Olympia on December 7, for the members of a Treaty Commission, charged with representing the United States at the treaty councils with the tribes. The designated members were himself; Michael Simmons and Frank Shaw; George Gibbs; the locals who had been doing work with the tribes for Stevens during the governor's absence; Hugh Goldsborough, a lawyer from back East who had no knowledge of Indian relations; and young James Doty, who served as secretary. George Gibbs was the only one, including Stevens, with any experience in treaty negotiations; because of his knowledge of Native languages, he played a major role in drafting and negotiating treaties in the Oregon Territory and northern California.

Treaty of Medicine Creek

The first order of business was to discuss the Blackfeet and other tribes in the eastern part of the territory, which was Stevens's top priority. Then the discussion turned to the Puget Sound tribes. Stevens had already made the decision to hold the initial negotiations by the end of December, just a few weeks away, but still had not decided which tribes would be included. At the first commission meeting, they agreed that those would be the Nisqually Indian, Puyallup, and Squaxin Island Tribes. The group also asked Gibbs to draft a treaty quickly, and he agreed to do so.

Three days later, December 10, Gibbs did submit a draft to the group and they agreed to it with minor changes. All understood that the amount of tribal reservation land should be minimal, which, to both Indian Commissioner George Manypenny and Stevens, was automatic. The group felt, however, consistent with Gibbs's views, that reservations should be on traditional homeland areas. The commissioners did not set the boundaries of any reservations, central though that issue was.

The group also continued the existing understanding that the negotiations would be in English and Chinook Jargon, a rudimentary device for trade negotiations, a patchwork of English, French, and various Indigenous languages. The Indigenous languages, however, would not be directly used at the negotiations. The translator would be Frank Shaw, a settler. These were weighty decisions. The Chinook Jargon, with some 500 words, could not possibly speak to sovereignty, land ownership, fishing rights, assimilation, freedom, or the futures of societies. Shaw, as interpreter, had only a moderate grasp of the Chinook Jargon and knew no Indigenous languages. Further, scholars of the Chinook Jargon emphasize the importance of the quality of the translations: "To a great extent, effective communication depends on the ingenuity and imagination of the speaker." Thus, "The way a word is spoken has a tremendous influence on meaning."

In approving George Gibbs's draft treaty, the Treaty Commission gave little attention to Article 3. True, the draft treaty was going to call for small reservations. The Americans intended to obtain almost all Indian land title in the territory and beyond in the upcoming treaty negotiations and the many that would follow; yet these off-reservation provisions in Article 3 would cover vast amounts of American land, for the tribes fished, hunted, and gathered on many millions of acres. Ultimately, it was the few but sweeping words in Article 3 of the Stevens treaties that would consume so much time and energy in the Pacific Northwest a century and a quarter later:

> Article 3. The right of taking fish, at all usual and accustomed grounds and
> stations, is further secured to said Indians in common with all citizens of

Article 3 of the official Medicine Creek Treaty sets out the fishing rights of the tribes. *Official Medicine Creek Treaty, 1854.*

the Territory, and of erecting temporary houses for the purpose of curing, together with the privilege of hunting, gathering roots and berries, and pasturing their horses on open and unclaimed lands.

The written record does not explicitly tell us why the group did not feel a need to address this provision at any length, but the known circumstances explain it.

Stevens respected Gibbs, the drafter of Article 3, whom he had worked with on the railroad survey, and relied upon him. In particular, he had no doubts about Gibbs's knowledge of Northwest Indians. He had seen several of Gibbs's memos and reports on Indians in the survey process. This included Gibbs's remarkable report of March 1855, two hundred manuscript pages in all, *Indian Tribes of Washington Territory*, which became known as the most complete and authoritative treatment of the Northwest tribes ever published up to that time. Gibbs's report burnished Stevens's reputation, since it was a prominent part of the overarching report on the Northern Pacific Railroad, headed up by the governor.

In his lengthy *Indian Tribes* report, Gibbs explained how Indian fishing should be treated in the upcoming treaties. Gibbs believed that reservations did not need to be large. The tribes did, however, need to have access to traditional lands that would be transferred to the United States because "they require the liberty of motion for the purpose of seeking . . . roots, berries, and the fish . . . and of grazing their horses and cattle at large . . . but they do not need the exclusive use of any considerable districts." Thus, the treaties specified "the use of their customary fisheries, and free pasturage for their stock on unenclosed lands should be secured."

At the commission meeting, the governor accepted Gibbs's recommendation, but not because it was fair to the Indians. Every indication is that Stevens wanted only two things: as many acres of Indian land as possible and a short and sweet treaty process. He could trust Gibbs's judgment because Gibbs himself believed that the force of westward expansion made it inevitable that most land would go to settlers and that Indian reservations must be small. As for tribal rights on land transferred by tribes to the United States, to Stevens the key point was that the tribes would not sign the treaties without the off-reservation fishing rights. Gibbs believed that to be true and politely expressed it in his major report, saying that "the subject of the right of fishery . . . is believed to be one concerning which difficulties may arise." And it was true: the tribes consistently made it clear that traditional fishing rights must be guaranteed.

Other beliefs caused American participants not to be concerned about Article 3 fishing rights. Gibbs, reflecting the belief of the time, wrote that off-reservation Indian fishing would likely never conflict with settlers: "A large portion of their territory will, in all human probability, never be occupied by white men." While that turned out to be factually inaccurate, it did allow the treaty process to go more smoothly. Another reason the opinion leaders did not much worry about the off-reservation rights was, as author Alexandra Harmon puts it, that the Americans thought of treaties as a "temporary expedient" with a "short lifespan." Under this version of the Vanishing Indian, the tribes would soon assimilate or die out. That also did not come about.

But whatever perceptions and motives were at work, the Treaty Commission did not see the fishing rights in Article 3 as a problem for the Americans.

At the end of their meeting, the commissioners agreed to get the word out to the tribes, especially through Simmons and Shaw, that the Nisqually Indian, Puyallup, and Squaxin Island Tribes would be expected to come to a "potlatch" and treaty negotiations on December 24 at Medicine Creek, Nisqually traditional land at the southern end of Puget Sound.

Simmons and Shaw advised the Indians that the United Stated wanted peace with the tribes, provided that the tribes would consent to trading their lands for "reservations for their exclusive use" and "such other privileges as could be agreed upon at the council." American settlement of the territory was inevitable and the tribes would have to cooperate. It was, as Simmons and Shaw made clear, necessary that the Indians be at the potlatch and treaty signing. For Stevens, the necessary thing was to complete the treaty and open up the Indian lands so that homesteaders could stake their claims. Consequently, he assured the tribes at the negotiations that their members could continue to take salmon at their traditional sites so he could move on to the signing ceremony.

The members of the federal team had decided upon most of the treaty provisions but they had not addressed all, including the number, size, and location of the tribal reservations. Time was short: they would not meet again until the eve of the first formal treaty council, just two weeks hence.

Simmons and Shaw headed out to the tribal villages to notify the tribes that there would be a "potlatch" on December 24 and a treaty council starting on December 25, Christmas Day. They explained that the United States, in the treaty, would purchase most of their land except for the reservations. They emphasized that Indian people could continue to fish, hunt, and gather food on the purchased land.

It is impossible to know the exact reactions of the tribes at this point.

They knew the Americans were aggressive and were determined to get Indian land, very different from the British. They knew that, while the tribes had significant military capabilities, the United States was more powerful. The tribes themselves had the tradition of large and formal negotiating gatherings to resolve important disputes, but they had no real idea of what a "treaty" was. Overall, they must have hoped that something good would come of this, but mostly Indian people were fearful. And they knew that they had no choice but to go to Medicine Creek on the appointed day.

Simmons and Shaw also arbitrarily designated leaders—chiefs—to speak for tribes, clearly choosing ones who would be unlikely to rock the boat. Perhaps their main targets were Leschi and Quiemuth, Nisqually brothers who lived upriver at Muck Creek, a tributary of the Nisqually River. While they were not known as leaders, they were highly respected by the Nisqually and other tribes as well. Over the years, Americans had many contacts with them and found them levelheaded, honest, and collegial. While never suggesting that Nisqually land should be substantially reduced, the brothers knew that having some settlers was inevitable and recommended, based on their lifelong knowledge of the tribal landscape, the transfer of land to two or three newly arrived families, parcels that would make good farming ground. Those Americans greatly appreciated the information.

The brothers listened carefully to Simmons and Shaw and raised no objections. Of course, they did not know the nature of the reservations that Stevens and his men had in mind because that had not been decided yet.

The treaty council site on Medicine Creek (She-nah-nam in Salish) was an open knoll looking out over broad Puget Sound with low cedar and fir groves to the west and a large Nisqually village nearby. Medicine Creek is short, about four miles long. It runs parallel to the much larger Nisqually River, half a mile to the east, with headwaters from the Nisqually Glacier high on Mount Rainier. Both water courses flow into Puget Sound. Medicine Creek is not a significant salmon stream, but it is spring-fed and rich in shellfish. Of course, the village was well located for salmon, a short walk to the Nisqually or an easy one-mile paddle in a cedar canoe to Puget Sound.

On December 23 a group of settlers went out to prepare the site for the Treaty Council. They cleared more than an acre of brush and logs, situated logs as seats for tribal and federal leaders, and pitched tents for the federal party. They also contributed lavish amounts of food—"carcasses of beef, mutton, deer, elk, and salmon, with a cloud of wild geese, ducks, and smaller game," along with sacks of potatoes, flour, sugar, and salt—to be consumed starting on December 24 when the tribal members, federal representatives, and numerous local settlers would arrive and socialize during the afternoon and evening and continuing through the completion of the negotiations.

This event would be a large gathering. Early in the morning of the twenty-fourth, Native people began to arrive. Some walked from nearby villages. Others came by cedar canoes. Many Nisqually lived on the lower river but several of their villages were upriver on prairies, where they quartered their horses. Some of those tribal members came in dramatically, in a long line of Nisqually riding horseback. Governor Stevens and his party, including his twelve-year-old son, Hazard, arrived later in the day by steamboat. George Gibbs paddled in from Olympia with a colleague. For all three days, the weather was gloomy and chilly. It rained the entire time. Gibbs wrote this:

> Thin temporary huts of mats with the smoke of their numerous camp fires, the prows of canoes hauled upon the bank & protruding from among the huts, the horses grazing on the marsh, the gloom of the firs & cedars with their long depending moss & the scattered & moving groups of Indians in all kinds of odd & fantastic dresses present a curious picture.

Stevens arranged for every Native leader to receive a "certificate of authority," a card designating the holder as a chief, subchief, or other position.

After the socializing on the twenty-fourth, Governor Stevens called the official Medicine Creek Treaty Council to order on Christmas Day. Tribal people, in their best finery, brought all manner of color and pride to the high occasion. One historian believed Stevens should have upgraded his attire, dressed as he was with "his flannel shirt open at the throat, twill pants bloused and tucked into his boots forty-niner style, the ensemble topped by a black felt hat with a pipe rather than a feather in its band. Practical garb to be sure, acceptable to Jacksonian democracy, but to the Indians, with their sense of occasion and concern for dignity, an affront."

We do not know what was said at these negotiations over so much land, for no minutes exist, not even any informal notes jotted down by participants. James Doty, secretary of the Treaty Commission, apparently had the duty to prepare minutes but all that remains is a brief, superficial, extremely general three-page summary that quotes Stevens twice but contains not a single word spoken by the tribal leaders. Formal minutes—notes taken during a meeting to report the key issues discussed, actions taken, important statements, and proposals made, so as to provide an accurate record of what transpired during the meeting—were prepared for virtually every federal-tribal treaty to date, but not at Medicine Creek. This is the entry for the first day:

DECEMBER 25TH The Programme of the Treaty was fully explained to the Indians present. At the evening Session of the Commission the draft of the Proposed Treaty was read, and after a full discussion of its provisions by the gentlemen present, viz Messrs. Simmons, Gibbs, and Doty, it was ordered to be engrossed and is as follows. [The original treaty was sent to Washington, DC, for approval by the Senate and no copy was included with the "minutes."]

The "full" explanation and the reading of the treaty must have been a blur to the assembled Indians. The 500 words of the Chinook Jargon could not possibly have carried the terms of the complex 2,625-word document. Owen Bush, one of the early pioneers, put it this way: "I could talk the Indian languages, but Stevens did not seem to want anyone to interpret in their own tongue, and had that done in Chinook. Of course, it was utterly impossible to explain the treaties to them in Chinook."

At the same time, some treaty matters could be explained in ways other than legalese. A main example was land, especially the reservations. The tribal leaders knew the landscape cold. So they asked the commissioners to identify the reservations' locations. The answer was beyond astounding: all of the three tribes, more than 1,500 people, would move to a single reservation on Squaxin Island, comprised of two sections (roughly 1,280 acres).

The proposal had been Isaac Stevens's idea, for his personal preference was to have one general reservation, as small as possible. George Manypenny and others back in DC liked that approach as well. Stevens knew that Gibbs strongly disagreed. The proposal seems to have been made late on Christmas Eve without a commission meeting, a product of the federal team's hurried, often slapdash way of doing business.

Leschi fumed at the idea. Unlike tribal members down by Puget Sound, he was a "horse Indian" who rode for hunting elk and deer. He quartered up to fifty head of horses and needed open prairie land and its native bulbs, roots, and grasses for his family and the horses. He, his brother Quiemuth, and others had farmhouses and outbuildings. Squaxin Island, with its marine characteristics and trees, allowed none of that. Besides, all of those Indian communities could not live on an island that size! Thinking of the Nisqually, and the other tribes as well, this proposal was completely unfair and insulting. There was no question about it.

Leschi finally spoke up during the afternoon. John Hiton, Nisqually, remembered this:

[H]e stood up before the Governor and said that if he could not get his home, he would fight, and that the Governor then told him it was fight, for the treaty paper would not be changed. . . .

Leschi then took the paper out of his pocket that the Governor had given him to be sub-chief, and tore it up before the Governor's eyes, stamped on the pieces, and left the treaty ground, and never came back to it again.

Quiemuth and about fifty other Nisqually followed Leschi and left the Medicine Creek Treaty Council. At least that is what probably happened. Tribal participants agreed with Hiton. Most, though not all, Americans did not. Signatures of both Leschi and Quiemuth appear on the treaty, signed the next day; they may have been forged but that cannot be proved.

After the first day of the Medicine Creek Treaty Council ended, conversations broke out among commission members, tribal leaders, and

Chief Leschi, who was hanged in 1858, is portrayed in this 1894 watercolor by Raphael Coombs. *Courtesy of the Washington State Historical Society, Tacoma, Washington.*

locals, resulting in a lot of confusion and bad feelings. The governor's tent was a busy place that evening, with Indian leaders exchanging views and asking questions of federal officials and influential settlers. Later on, Stevens and commission members finally relented, deciding to scrap the one-small-reservation approach. Instead, the Squaxin Island Tribe would have its reservation. The Nisqually Indian Tribe would have a reservation of two sections at the mouth of Medicine Creek. The Puyallup reservation of two sections would be located on a rocky hillside on Commencement Bay.

The action did provide additional land to the tribes—four sections totaling 2,560 acres—but not much. The United States was, after all, determined to acquire Indian title from the crest of Mount Rainier to the far side of Puget Sound, a total of 4,000 square miles.

The negotiations continued on December 26. Governor Stevens led off with a speech about "the Great Father" and his "children," the Indian people. "The Great Father wishes you . . . to have homes, pastures for your horses, and fishing places. . . . [H]e now wants me to bargain with you, in which you will sell your lands and in return be provided with all these things."

Secretary James Doty reported in his minimalistic way that "the treaty was then read section by section and explained to the Indians by the Interpreter and every opportunity was given them to discuss it. . . . The Indians has [sic] some discussion and then Gov. Stevens put the question, 'are you ready? If so I will sign it.' There were no objections and the treaty was signed" on December 26 by federal officials, tribal leaders, seventeen local residents, and the governor's son Hazard.

But, in the eyes of the Americans, the treaty was not complete. Two days after the Medicine Creek Treaty Council concluded, George Gibbs and Frank Shaw braved a driving rainstorm to examine the Nisqually reservation that Stevens had presented at Medicine Creek. Shaw was concerned that it might overlap the property on which Shaw's home was built—and it did. So they drew up a new reservation on an adjacent ridge, also two sections in size.

The two men then went to the Puyallup reservation near Commencement Bay and concluded that it, too, conflicted with existing or possible claims, so they replaced it with a nearby two-section parcel. They drew up new maps and submitted them along with the treaty to the Senate for approval. The Americans made these changes unilaterally, after the formal treaty signing, without discussing them with the tribes.

The whole reservation matter was a mess. Stevens's one-small-reservation idea was preposterous, an outrage. The subsequent approaches were hardly any improvement at all. The amount of land was still far, far below the amount of land that would make acceptable residential homelands for these Indian peoples. Not only were the lands far too small, they were not usable. Some Natives did live on Squaxin Island, but most traditionally lived on the adjacent mainland. As for the Nisqually and Puyallup reservations, they were thickly forested, rocky and steep, far from any prairie lands. No Indians, before or after the treaty, ever lived on those "reservations."

All the tribes were resentful, confused, and angry. Leschi felt that way and it seems to have been one of the few times in his life that he experienced raw anger. A levelheaded, gentle person, he had invested a lot of his time working with the settlers and finding ways to live peacefully with them. While he well knew that Stevens and the other Americans wanted a great amount of Indian land, his outburst at Medicine Creek and his reaction to the minimal changes that followed probably reflected an unexpected level of betrayal: "What? This can't be! How did we get hit by a thing like this?!"

After the Medicine Creek Treaty Council, Leschi tried to find ways to convey his distress to federal officials, but to no avail. On December 30, 1854, Stevens shipped the treaty back to Manypenny in Washington, DC, less than a week after the treaty signing; the US Senate ratified it on March 3, 1855; and President Franklin Pierce proclaimed it on April 10, 1855.

Why did the tribes stand back as they did? Why did they allow themselves to be steamrolled? To be sure, Isaac Stevens was a good part of this with his fast-paced, my-way-or-the-highway approach. But Stevens was just one aspect of the unwritten code of faraway, rough-and-ready Washington Territory, awash in patriotic manifest destiny, that sent out warning signs no Indian could ignore. Fifty years after the treaty, the earnest historian Ezra Meeker, who lived his life in northwestern Washington, dug into this. One of Meeker's interviews was with Tyee (Salish for "leader" or "chief") Dick:

"Dick signed the treaty and then [later felt] like a fool for signing," he said.

"Then why did you sign, Dick?" I asked.

"Oh, John Hiton made a speech. This was the second day. Hiton he said we sign treaty, and then we take farms all the same as white man: and then all the whites and the Governor took off their hats and cheered and then the Olympia Indians began to sign, and the Squaxons they signed and I held back, but Simmons come and patted me on the back and told me 'that's a good fellow, Dick, you go and sign, and I will see you are treated right and well taken care of, and I knew Simmons and thought him good man and signed."

"Did you understand what the treaty was?"

"No, I don't think any of the Indians did understand. Why would they agree to give up all the good land, and that was what we found afterwards the treaty read."

"Hiton said, 'The reservation was no good; all stones; all big timber; up on bluff; nobody live there; nobody live there now.'"

"Then why did you sign it?" I asked.

"Why, what's the use for Indians to fight whites? Whites get big guns; lots ammunition; kill off all soldiers, more come; better sign and get something some other way."

By the summer of 1855, tension was in the air. As happened all too frequently in relations between the two disparate cultures, misunderstanding piled upon misunderstanding.

Leschi's dissatisfaction with the treaty was well known. Michael Simmons, James McAllister (a prominent settler), and other locals made clear their belief that Leschi, perhaps in league with the Yakama, was likely to ignite hostilities. With Stevens engaged in treaty negotiations with the Blackfeet, they took their concerns to Charles Mason, the acting governor. In October, Mason responded by writing General John Wool in San Francisco and requesting sufficient ammunition to meet the threat of "2,000 armed Indians." Wool denied the request, believing it exaggerated. The acting governor then met with Leschi but both men held firm.

Mason then took action, directing Captain Charles Eaton, commander of the Volunteer Mounted Rangers, to remove all Indians near the base of the Cascades over to Puget Sound. He gave Eaton chillingly broad authority: "Should you meet any unusual or suspicious assemblage of Indians, you will disarm them, and should they resist, disperse them and put any who resist or use violence to death, or send them to Fort Steilacoom in irons, or bound them as you may deem best." Now all territorial citizens, Indian and white, had reason to worry.

Eaton rounded up nineteen volunteers to bring in Leschi and Quiemuth. The word spread among the Indians, who went on an even higher alert. Feeling threatened, a Nisqually Indian shot and killed one of the volunteers. The same day, Nisqually Indians approached the volunteers' camp, wanting to talk. The volunteers had orders not to shoot, but one of them did, killing one of the Indians.

The resulting Puget Sound War, or Leschi War, as it is variously called, injected the people of Washington Territory with day-to-day anxiety. In military terms, it was not a major war. Fighting was intermittent and what combat there was lasted just five months. There are no records, but fatalities seem to have amounted to three or four dozen on each side.

Leschi and Quiemuth went underground after the hostilities ended. They knew that Stevens wanted to prosecute both of them as murderers.

With the war over, events led to one gratifying accomplishment. On August 4, 1856, Stevens convened a conference, held at Fox Island in southern Puget Sound, to discuss the Nisqually and Puyallup reservations. He had reasons to look back at Medicine Creek. Indian people continued to resent the treaty reservations; those strong and lasting emotions might have led to still more warfare. Perhaps he had second thoughts about the fairness of the treaty. But, beyond that, he faced a widespread backlash over the treaty and the war that followed it. In addition to the revulsion among the tribes, he came under considerable fire among Americans in both the territory and Washington, DC, over the Medicine Creek Treaty and the war. George Gibbs expressed the prevailing criticism in writing that "the Governor's treaties had a great deal to do in fomenting this war there is no doubt. Those on the Sound were much too hurried, and the reservations allowed them were insufficient."

Whatever the motivations, at Fox Island Stevens promised to eliminate the two unusable reservations and replace them with two suitable reservations, not monumental but much larger and well located. He also assured tribes of a substantial reservation on the Green River for the Muckleshoot. He described the reservations and identified them on maps. The tribal people stood and applauded at the end of the day.

It took several years to survey the land and resolve title and conflicts but this was one Stevens promise that was kept. The Nisqually received 4,717 acres (about 7.5 square miles) of heartland in the Nisqually watershed, straddling the river and offering salmon, pasturing ground for horses, and prairie land for wild potatoes, carrots, and other roots and bulbs. The Puyallup reservation was larger, 36 square miles, and it also included ample salmon runs, habitat, and open inland meadowland for pasturing and vegetation. Stevens's promise also included a third reservation, 3,500 acres, of traditional homeland for Muckleshoot Indians in the upper White and Green Rivers country. Leschi and Quiemuth were not at Fox Island, but the actions taken there brought a welcome measure of justice to tribes and vindicated the brothers and their insistence that the treaty was overreaching and wrong. Nonetheless, the pressure among the whites to convict Leschi and Quiemuth did not let up.

Isaac Stevens, who has been described as "obsessed" with Leschi, put a bounty of $500 on Leschi's head. Finally in November 1886, he was arrested. They charged him with the murder of A. Benton Moses, a volunteer soldier during the war. With Stevens wanting a quick result, they tried him immediately, three days after the arrest. A jury of Americans deadlocked and could not agree on a verdict. A second trial, which lasted one day, resulted in a conviction and the judge sentenced him to death. Leschi, who did have a lawyer, appealed to the Territorial Supreme Court.

A few weeks later, Quiemuth came in voluntarily. Almost immediately after he went into custody, he was stabbed to death by the son-in-law of James McAllister. The relative claimed that Quiemuth shot and killed McAllister, although the assertion was never proved. During the appeal, Leschi spoke to the Indian people: "Whatever the future holds, do not forget who you are. Teach your children, teach your children's children, and then teach their children also. Teach them the pride of a great people. ... A time will come again when they will celebrate together with joy. When that happens my spirit will be there with you."

At his appeal to the Territorial Supreme Court, Leschi said through an interpreter, "I do not know anything about your laws. I have supposed that the killing of armed men in wartime was not murder; if it was, the soldiers who killed Indians were guilty of murder too. . . ." Leschi was correct on the law. When a combatant in a war kills a combatant on the other side, there is no crime under civil law.

So Leschi was hung at a gallows near Fort Steilacoom on February 19, 1858, with a gathering of 300 people, including some Nisqually. The hangman, Charles Grainger, saw and felt this:

Leschi was a square-built man, and I should judge would weigh about one hundred and seventy pounds. He was about five feet six inches tall. He had a very strong, square jaw and very piercing, dark brown eyes. He would look almost through you, a firm but not a savage look. His lower jaw and eyes denoted firmness of character. He had an aquiline nose, and different kind of features than these Flathead Indians—more like the Klickitats. His head was not flattened much, if any at all. He had a very high forehead for an Indian.

I saw Leschi in 1853 at McAllister's on the Nisqually. McAllister told me he was a good, faithful Indian. George McAllister and Joe Bunton both told me that Leschi met them on the way and helped them.

He did not seem to be the least bit excited at all, and no trembling on him at all—nothing of the kind, and that is more than I could say for myself. In fact, Leschi seemed to be the coolest of any of the scaffold. He was in good flesh and had a firm step and mounted the scaffold without assistance, and as well as I did myself. I felt then I was hanging an innocent man, and believe it yet.

Over time, Leschi became a respected figure in Washington. Several public places in Seattle bear his name. Indian people kept his vision alive over the years. In 2004, the Washington State Legislature, finding that "Chief Leschi [was] a courageous leader whose sacrifice for his people is worthy of honor and respect," created a Washington Historical Court of Inquiry and Justice to determine whether Leschi's conviction was just. The seven-person court of state and federal judges, including one tribal judge, and with Washington Chief Justice Gerry Alexander as presiding justice, found that justice had not been done because both Leschi and A. Benton Moses were "lawful combatants." The opinion could have no legal effect, but the act of setting the record straight, late though it was, was uplifting to Indian country and many other people in northwestern Washington.

Treaty of Point Elliott

Mukilteo is a shoreline area on Possession Sound looking directly across to Whidbey Island and, in the distance to the west, the high Olympic Mountains. For the Swinomish, Suquamish, Duwamish, and several other tribes, the beach made a perfect landing spot for their cedar canoes. An open meadow lay adjacent to the shore with a forest backdrop of red cedar and Douglas fir, as well as smaller but distinctive red-bark madrone. Mukilteo, meaning "good camping ground" in Salish, served as ceremonial and council grounds for Native people. Today, the town of Mukilteo and the coastal spot of Mukilteo, now called Point Elliott, lie twenty-five miles north of Seattle.

Governor Stevens chose the area for his second treaty, referred to as the Treaty of Point Elliott. He was moving quickly and would complete four treaties in less than five weeks. There would be ten "Stevens Treaties" in all, five with the tribes in the western part of the territory, who would later become the Boldt Case area tribes, and five with the tribes in the expansive eastern part of the territory. In all ten treaties, the governor followed his Medicine Creek regime to the letter, including his insistence that no changes could be made to the treaty he proposed at the councils. As a result, all ten treaties would be almost completely identical, except for the names of the tribes and the descriptions of land conveyed to the United States.

The Point Elliott Treaty Council, which encompassed some twenty-two tribes, drew a large Native attendance. Estimates ranged between 2,300 and 2,500 Indian people.

Once again, Stevens identified a good location from the Native point of view—well liked and convenient by canoe. With the treaty council scheduled for January 22, 1855, Lummi, Duwamish, and other peoples arrived as early as five days in advance. The description in the *Pioneer and Democrat* gave evidence of the importance of the event to the tribes:

The canoes, filled with the natives, as they approached the treat[y] ground, was said to be imposing, and their inimitable and frail crafts, as having been manned with an order and precision that would have been creditable to a military evolution. They advanced along the quiet waters of the Sound in regular platoons, with the most perfect "dress" and order, and weeled into line, fronting the treaty ground, in admirable style.

At the Point Elliott Treaty Council, the tribes transferred their Indian title to the most valuable part of northwest Washington, then and now:

> All land west of the crest of the Cascade Range, from Olympia to the Canadian line, north-south a distance of about 200 miles.

The total amount of land was about six hundred thousand acres. The transaction was "negotiated" at a treaty council that lasted just one day.

Isaac Stevens opened the proceeding with his emotional "Great Father" speech, but he added even more punch at the beginning:

> My Children! You are not my children because you are the fruit of my loins but because you are children for whom I have the same feeling as if you were the fruit of my loins. You are my children for whom I will strenuously labor all the days of my life until I shall be taken hence. What will a man do for his own children? He will see that they are well cared for, that they have clothes to protect them against the cold and rain, that they have food to guard them against hunger, and as for thirst you have your own glorious streams in which to quench it. I want you as my children to be fed and clothed, and made comfortable and happy. . . . We want to place you in houses where you can cultivate the soil, raising potatoes and other articles of food, and where you may be able to pass in canoes over the waters of the sound and catch fish, and back to the mountains to get roots and berries. . . .
>
> The lands are yours, and we mean to pay you for them. Thank you that you have been so kind to all the white children of the Great Father, who come to build mills, till land, build and sail ships. We will put our hearts down on paper. . . . If the Great Father says the paper is good it will stand forever.

With such a large number of tribes, Stevens decided to designate four head chiefs, who would represent their own tribes and others, who were not named, as well. The four head chiefs were Chief Seattle for the Suquamish and Duwamish and nearby tribes; Chief Patkanim, for the Snohomish and neighboring tribes; Chief Goliah, for the Skagit and nearby tribes; and Chief Chow-its-hoot, for the Lummi and other tribes in the Canadian border area. At the end of the day, to be sure, the treaty included all tribes and communities in the sprawling area; eighty-three Native American men, the head chiefs and other tribal members, most identified as subchiefs, would sign the treaty. Stevens offered the head chiefs, but not the others, a chance to deliver remarks. The treaty he put forward that day called for a "general reservation" with modest reserves. There were four: at Tulalip, amounting to thirty-six sections, or 23,040 acres; two reservations of two sections each, one for the Suquamish and Duwamish and one for the Swinomish and tribes in the area; and the island of Chah-choo-sen in the Lummi River area for the Lummi and other tribes in the border area.

Stevens called on Chief Seattle first and the chief made a short statement:

I look upon you as my father. I and the rest regard you as such. All of the Indians have the same good feeling towards you and will send it on paper to the Great Father. All of them, men, old men, women & children rejoice that he has sent you to take care of them. My mind is like yours. I don't want to say more. My heart is very good towards Dr. Maynard [a physician who was present]. I want always to get medicine from him.

After all of the signing was done later in the day, Seattle again addressed the gathering. On behalf of himself and the other chiefs, he presented a white flag to Stevens and said this:

Now by this we make friends and put away all bad feelings if we ever had any. We are friends of the Americans. . . . We look upon you as our Father. We will never change our minds but since you have been to see us will never be the same.

The other three head chiefs made brief conciliatory statements as well. Chief Patkanim said, "Today I understand your heart as soon as you spoke. I understand your talk plainly. . . . We want everything you

This image, the only known photograph of Chief Seattle, was taken
in 1865, just two years before he passed away at the approximate age of
86. Photograph by E. M. Sammis, PH Coll 24.23. *Courtesy of University
of Washington Libraries, Special Collections, E. M. Sammis, photographer,
NA1511.*

said." Chief Chow-its-hoot responded, "I don't want to say much, my heart is good. . . . I have some houses at home. But I will stop building if you wish and I will move to Chah-choo-sen. . . ." Chief Goliah was of the same mind. "I am happy at heart. My heart is good and that of all my friends. I give it to the Governor."

It needs to be said that the written record at Point Elliott has the same deficiencies as the one at Medicine Creek. The "minutes" are hardly that. As at the first treaty council, the official minutes presented long statements by Stevens but very few words by Indian people. George Gibbs, rather than the young and inexperienced James Doty, did the minutes at Point Elliott and more could be expected from Gibbs. Probably Stevens gave him directions. At the same time, there is no reason to doubt that the four chiefs did make the statements reported in the minutes and did intend to be conciliatory.

Why did the tribal leaders react this way, given that they were about to surrender such an expansive block of beloved traditional land that had been homeland since deep antiquity? There is no single answer for there were numerous factors—pressure points—and Native people had different views. In spite of the fact that tribes possessed significant military strength and the Indian population in the territory was much larger than that of the whites, bucking the Americans was problematic. Isaac Stevens was a fearsome figure. Settlers had issued the "smallpox in a bottle" threat decades before but the words still hung in the air; a major epidemic had hit the territory just two years before the Point Elliott Treaty. There was a generalized fear that the whites had no regard for Indian lives and were quick to act violently when, in their view, Native people got out of line.

There is a more intangible reason why the four men spoke as they did. They all had made, over many years, formal presentations in trying to resolve disputes with other tribes. There were protocols, a decorum. While the chiefs did not know exactly what to expect at this treaty council, they probably did think it would call for the kind of diplomacy that was used in their intertribal negotiations. The federal officials understood this.

They themselves spoke and acted in an effusive, flowery way, believing that the tribes expected it on such an occasion.

Still, if the reasons for the language and demeanor might be accepted, how could the leaders have agreed to such a one-sided treaty that cost them so much land? Perhaps they saw some things that made their conduct, given all the circumstances, understandable and necessary, even wise.

The chiefs believed Stevens when he said that the treaty he handed them was nonnegotiable. There was something of a saving grace to that. The Medicine Creek Treaty Council was only a short time past, but Stevens showed that he already realized that he had erred in imposing such a crabbed group of reservations. The four reservations he brought to Point Elliott, while still stingy, met some bare minimum of acceptability in the way that the Fox Island reservations a year later did. The Point Elliott lands, like those at Fox Island, were livable homeland parcels in the way that the Medicine Creek reservations for the Nisqually and Puyallup were not. Most basically, these reservations were Stevens's final offer and the hard-nosed governor would make their lives miserable if they did not accept it.

Besides, the treaty had positive aspects. In addition to land ownership, the treaty dealt with other matters, promising an agricultural and industrial school, a blacksmith, a carpenter, and farmers to "instruct" them in those operations, and of great note, a physician. Native people believed, and were encouraged to by whites, that the services provided to them would allow them to be more like white people. And the treaty was believed to be the foundation for reduced hostilities, peace. The chiefs' warm, congenial presentations, and their white flag, were designed to promote that peace.

The treaty provisions and oral promises that drew the most attention and optimism, however, were in Article 5, announcing their rights to fish, hunt, and gather in the lands they would cede to the United States. Everyone on the federal side, starting with George Gibbs and including Isaac Stevens, knew that the tribes had insisted on this from the beginning and would not sign without it. The tribes had their own nonnegotiable provision. Stevens agreed with it and used it as a main argument for the tribes accepting the treaty. He referred to it multiple times at every treaty council. Tribal people well understood the value of the article and repeatedly and successfully pressured Stevens to reaffirm it. General Gaines, Lummi, reported this in 1895:

> I was at Muckleteoh when Gov. Stevens made the treaty with our people in 1855. Gov. Stevens told the Indians that they could go anywhere on the salt water where they were accustomed to go to catch salmon, or dig clams or hunt deer or ducks; that the treaty would not confine us to the reservation when we wanted to hunt or fish and that we could fish where we used to; our headmen told Gov. Stevens that Chiltenum was their best fishing grounds and they wanted to know whether if they signed the paper they could to go Chiltenum (Point Roberts) just as they always had done.

A nephew of Chief Patkanim also reported how Stevens had firmly assured his uncle:

> In the Treaty my uncle Pat Kanim reserved the salmon, he reserved the deer, he reserved the elk, he reserved the bear, he reserved the beaver, he reserved the clams, he reserved the dry tree, and he reserved the cedar. That is what he claimed and said would be his and that Governor Stevens agreed to let him have all he asked. Governor Stevens said what you will be given today your children will be all right and your son will have land, and your grandchildren will have land and all those will be all right.

There are many other examples of the governor emphasizing Article 5 in arguing that tribal leaders should sign the treaties.

These Article 5 rights were very concrete to the Natives. They did not think in terms of ownership of land but the tribes seem to have believed that Article 5 rights contained almost all of the prerogatives that they needed from land. These off-reservation locations were not where they lived, but they were places where, during all seasons of the year, they obtained essential objects at the center of their lives: salmon, deer and elk meat, sweet berries, and many other natural objects they looked to for food, clothing, tools, and medicine. They gathered them and developed ceremonies, prayers, gear, and practices for obtaining them and ways of thanking the natural world for them. And these rights applied all across the immense landscape to which the tribes conveyed land title. Yes, these rights were *tangible*.

The Point Elliott Treaty reserved them and the people made up their minds to make sure that their treaty rights would continue in all of the years that lay ahead. Every single tribe in the ten Stevens treaties did the same and all these treaties contained Article 5 language. In a sense, all the tribes took Tyee Dick's stand: "Better sign and get something some other way." George Boldt would not even be born for half a century, but the tribes' patience would in time be validated.

Treaty of Point No Point

Isaac Stevens held his next treaty council two days after Point Elliott. The Point No Point Treaty, with the S'Klallam, Skokomish, and Chimakum Tribes of the eastern Olympic Peninsula, was signed at yet another fine site. The formation, low, long, and thin, is called Hahdskus in Salish, meaning "long nose." Spiritually meaningful to the S'Klallam tribes, it was and is an important fishing area for the S'Klallam because the current brings salmon from many different streams to the area.

The vista is breathtaking. The first two treaty sites faced west, looking out to the Olympic range in the distance. Point No Point is located on the northern tip of Kitsap Peninsula, facing east over Admiralty Inlet. The high Cascades stretch out across the horizon. Mount Baker, close to the Canadian border, rises up to the north and, far to the south, eighty miles from Seattle, towers Mount Rainier. Almost all of the splendor had been Indian title until the events of the past three weeks.

Now Isaac Stevens trained his energies on the Olympic Peninsula. At Point No Point, he would obtain for the United States more than half of the peninsula, over a million acres.

The encompassing vista was not available to the eyes of participants when the Point No Point Treaty Council began amid a firestorm on January 24, 1855. The accounts don't address how the crowd of 1,200 Indians and a dozen federal representatives reacted to the storm. Stevens gave his normal "Great Father" speech. The treaty was then "read and interpreted" to the Natives. Stevens then "asked [the Indians] if they had anything to say."

The answers were very different from the few Indian remarks mentioned in the minutes of the first two treaty councils.

Che-lan-teh-tat, Skokomish, spoke first:

> I wish to speak my mind as to the selling of the land. Great Chief! What shall we eat if we do so? Our only food is berries, deer and salmon. Where then shall we find these? I don't want to sign away all my land; take half of it, and let us keep the rest. I am afraid that I shall become destitute and perish for want of food. I don't like the place you have chosen for us to live on. I am not ready to sign the paper.

L'Hau-at-scha-uk, Skokomish, said:

> I do not want to leave the mouth of the River. I do not want to leave my old home, and my burying ground. I am afraid I shall die if I do.

Two others spoke strongly against the treaty. Toward the end of the first day, four tribal leaders supported the transaction, using the kind of conciliatory "you are our father" language that their predecessors employed at Medicine Creek and Point Elliott. As the first day ended, doubts were as real as the rain and wind.

The Point No Point Treaty presented a different mix of difficulties for the tribes. This time, Stevens succeeded in obtaining a basic land arrangement he had favored from the beginning: a single general reservation with a number of tribes on it. The treaty provided for a reservation of six sections, 3,840 acres, which, while nowhere near generous, passed the straight-face test for land size. It was excellent land at the mouth of the Skokomish River at Hood Canal.

But it was not homeland for many of the Native people. Several of the thirty-three Skokomish villages were within it, but the large majority were not. Two of the anguished voices at Point No Point were Skokomish chiefs.

The arrangements with the S'Klallam and Chimakum Tribes' villages were especially hard. Their villages, twenty-six for S'Klallam, many fewer for Chimakum, were up on the Strait of Juan de Fuca, seventy miles or more to the north. The two environments have differences. The Strait of Juan de Fuca has an oceanic climate, with bracing westerly winds, oceanic waves, and a hundred inches of rainfall annually. Hood Canal is inland, more sheltered, not much affected by the ocean, and receives roughly seventy-five inches of rain yearly. Oysters and clams were outstanding at Hood Canal and the salmon were bountiful. The salmon runs at the S'Klallam and Chimakum villages, with the returning big fish, strong and healthy, only hours from the ocean, were even more robust.

The overriding point, though, is that Hood Canal was not remotely S'Klallam or Chimakum homeland. Isaac Stevens's order for them to move out of their territory, home for thousands of years, to an unknown place was brutal.

Resistant though many Indian speakers were, in the end, as with the two earlier treaty councils, the three Point No Point tribes came around, probably for the same reasons as the earlier tribes.

In striving to bring the tribes along, the governor and his people emphasized the importance to the tribes of the Article 5 fishing, hunting, and gathering rights. The minutes show three instances on the first day when, at various points, Frank Shaw, Michael Simmons, and the governor interjected arguments, true to the text of the treaty, that, regardless of the acceptability of the reservations, the tribes would still have access to their traditional lands for salmon and other foods:

Mr. F. Shaw, the Interpreter explained to them that they were not called upon to give up their old modes of living and places of seeking food, but only to confine their houses to the spot.

Mr. Simmons, the Agent explained that if they kept half their country, they would have to live on it and would not be allowed to go anywhere else they pleased. *That when a small tract alone was left the privilege was given of going where-ever else they pleased to fish and work for the Whites.* [emphasis in italics added]

We do not know, but it is likely that Stevens and his men had discussions with tribal leaders that evening, as suggested by the governor's remark at the beginning of the second day that "the Treaty was read to you last night. You have talked it over. Now we will consider it."

The second and last day—Stevens announced that the weather was now "pleasant"—began when "the Indians came up bearing White Flags." The three designated leaders, the Duke of York (S'Klallam), General Pierce (Chimakum), and Nah-whil-luk (Skokomish), gave their support to the treaty. Then Isaac Stevens offered brief remarks in which he put forth a promise that would be important to federal court judges in the late twentieth century: "*This paper secures your fish.* Does not a father give food to his children? Besides fish, you can hunt, gather roots and berries" [emphasis added]. Then to consummate the agreement, "Governor Stevens once more asked [the assembled Indians] if they were satisfied to sign the treaty. They all declared themselves so. It was accordingly signed. And a salute fired from the Steamer at a signal."

By the time the US Senate ratified the treaty four years later, many of the Skokomish who lived outside the small reservation on Hood Canal had relocated at the reservation and most of the others would follow. As for the S'Klallam, it was clear from the beginning that they would not live there. Their homes and their treaty rights to fish at their "usual and accustomed places" were located far to the north. They returned to their homelands near the Strait of Juan de Fuca. Few though their resources were, they refused to give in, first living off public domain land and then, over the years, acquiring lands by purchasing private lands and obtaining public domain parcels through Indian homestead provisions. By the 1950s, they had established reservations at the lower Elwha River, Jamestown, and Port Gamble. A few Chimakum tribal members went to live among the S'Klallam but the tribe had few members and over the course of about two generations disappeared as a distinct tribal entity.

Treaty of Neah Bay

The frenetic pace of treaty making continued. Three days after Point No Point, Governor Stevens and his aides dropped anchor at Neah Bay on a windy January 29, 1855. This was Makah Tribe territory, the far tip of the Olympic Peninsula, the northwesternmost point in the contiguous states. The Makah had received no formal notice of a treaty council although they had learned of it from other tribes. Consistent with his views on reservations, Stevens wanted to include the Quileute, the coastal tribe south of the Makah. But contact had not been made. A quick inquiry made it clear that the Quileute would not go to Neah Bay on such short notice. The Makah might have objected to the inclusion of the Quileute in the Makah Reservation in any event. The Makah had refused to participate in the Point No Point Treaty, saying it wanted its own treaty with the United States.

Two years before, the Makahs had suffered one of the deadliest small-pox epidemics, costing them an estimated 40 percent of their people. Stevens seemed to have thought that "this was the moment."

At the same time, the oceangoing tribe had leverage. Stevens declared them "the most formidable navigators of any in the American territories on the Pacific." He asserted that "the superior courage of the Makahs, as well as their treachery, will make them more difficult of management than most other tribes of this region." Also, as Stevens knew well, the Makah Tribe was a major economic player. The tribe traded salmon and halibut and also oil. Historian Joshua Reid explains:

> Since the maritime fur trade, Makahs had participated in making co-
> lonialism possible in the Northwest Coast. A product harvested and
> processed into a vital commodity for both indigenous peoples and
> newcomers, whale oil was a key ingredient non-Natives used to expand
> colonial spaces in the region. Makah oil heated and lit homes and busi-
> nesses in nearby towns such as Victoria and Port Townsend. Victorian
> era colonialists prided themselves in bringing light—a central compo-
> nent to imperial projects across the world—to the Pacific Northwest.
> Many Victorians believed that wherever the British flag flew, they had a
> "responsibility to import the light of civilization (identified as especially
> English), thus illuminating the supposedly dark places in the world." Lit-
> tle did these Victorians expect, though, that indigenous oil would fuel
> English lamps. Large quantities of Makah oil also greased the skids of
> local logging operations.

Settlers, in other words, resolutely wanted the treaty to be made so that the Makah oil would continue to flow.

On January 30, Stevens and Gibbs spent the day walking the ground to determine where the reservation should be located. They decided on a grudgingly small reservation.

That evening Stevens invited Makah leaders to join him on the schooner *R. B. Potter* to discuss the treaty. He had it explained to them through the blur of the Chinook Jargon and then asked for their comments. It was immediately apparent that the Makah would not be operating from despondence over the loss of so many from the epidemic. If anything, the horror made them all the more determined to protect their traditional prerogatives and ways. Out on the schooner, the Makah forcefully presented a vision of the treaty as fundamentally protecting not just land, but, as well, the traditional Makah vision of ocean and whales. Hence the title of Professor Joshua Reid's book, *The Sea Is My Country*.

Every speaker emphasized marine rights. Kuhl-Choot spoke first: "I ought to have the right to fish and take whales and get food when I like. I am afraid that if I cannot take halibut where I want, I will become poor." Kee-chook said, "I do not want to leave the salt water." Several chiefs spoke to the tribe's elaborate system of marine law, giving descriptions of individual property rights to saltwater tracts and salvage rights over beach tracts. Perhaps the most attention-getting remarks came from Tse-Kauwtl, a high chief at Ozette Village, whom Stevens himself appointed as head chief because the village chiefs all said that they all were equal. He put it succinctly. "I want the sea. That is my country."

The formal Neah Bay Treaty Council, once again just a single day, took place on January 31. Six hundred Makah tribal members attended. There were two departures from the governor's standard script. First, his introduction included a pointed reference to the Makah view of this treaty:

> He knows what whalers you are, how you go far to sea, to take whales.
> He will send you barrels in which to put your oil, kettles to try it out,
> lines and implements to fish with.

The text of the treaty also included an addition to the language in all of the Stevens treaties: "This right of taking fish *and of whaling or sealing* at usual grounds and stations is further secured to said Indians. . . ." [emphasis added]. Those words are the only tribally specific reference in all of the Stevens treaties, save for boundary descriptions, that Stevens was willing to accept.

The Makah Treaty Council came to an end with the usual fanfare and document signings.

The Makah leaders could take considerable pride. They had stood up to Isaac Stevens and had brought new ideas and facts to the treaty negotiations. They succeeded in achieving the express right to hunt whales and seals. The reservation in the official version of the treaty, though, was far less than what they believed Stevens had agreed to.

Six years later, James Swan, a respected schoolteacher, historian, and author who had taught at the Makah villages, became convinced from conversations with many people that the reservation described in the treaty did not reflect the tribe's understanding. Swan wrote up his findings and took them public. This led to an Interior Department order amending the borders in accordance with the Makah's expectations.

Over the years, tribal officials pressed for affirmation from higher authorities than the department. Under legislation and presidential orders, the reservation was expanded to a point very close to what the tribe expected, including a return of two islands. These accomplishments, important in their own right, were also emblematic: starting with the lands granted to tribes at Fox Island, tribes achieved adjustments and reservations in every Boldt Decision treaty in order to modify Isaac Stevens's stingy reservations.

Treaty of Olympia

With the Makah treaty under his belt, Governor Stevens wanted to treat with the Quinault Indian Nation and other tribes south of the Makah and thereby extinguish virtually all Indian title to the entire coast of Washington. He got off to a bad start. For the first time, in the gathering often referred to as the Chehalis Council, his carefully designed system for ramrodding treaty agreements through in one or two days came up empty.

When the treaty council with the Upper and Lower Chehalis, Lower Columbia River Chinook, Cowlitz, and Quinault tribes convened at the Chehalis River February 27, 1855, Isaac Stevens delivered his usual speech to an estimated 370 Indians and had the proposed treaty read and translated. Right from the beginning, leaders from each of the tribes objected. The reservation was unacceptable for two reasons. The reservation would be located on traditional Quinault tribal lands and all the tribes would move to that reservation. Further, the location and size of the reservation were wildly unspecific: the proposed treaty said only that it would be "a tract of land on the Coast of the Pacific between Makah and Grays Harbor and Cape Flattery [a distance of more than

100 miles], sufficient for their wants, to be selected by the President of the United States." The tribes offered many alternative proposals, mostly modest-sized reservations for individual tribes on their own traditional lands, but Stevens would not budge. On March 2, after one week of impasse, he angrily threatened this:

> We have now been here a week. I have heard you all. Only one band the [Quinault] have hearts like mine, but the paper is nothing without all sign. The [Quinault] alone leave it to the Great Father. There can therefore be no Treaty and I shall not call upon you again to treat, but next summer I shall send Col. Simmons through that country to examine it and when a good place is found I shall say to the Great Father put these people upon it. There will then be no treaty, no promises but you will be in the hands of the Great Father to do as we please.

On the next day, George Gibbs reported the end of the Chehalis Treaty Council: "It having been found impracticable to bring the Indians voluntarily upon one reservation, Governor Stevens dismissed them and this morning started on his return."

After the failure on the Chehalis River, Stevens—busy by then with the tribes to the east—sent his Indian agent, Michael Simmons, to act on his behalf and negotiate with the Quinault, Quileute, Hoh, and Queets Tribes to clean up the Chehalis mess. The tribes generally liked Simmons, who dealt with them in a more low-key way than Stevens did.

Simmons's Treaty Council, held at the mouth of the Quinault River for one day on July 1, 1855, was brief and placid. The tribes all signed a document that was almost identical to the one presented at Chehalis. While there was no conflict at the council, there was misunderstanding. The critical reservation issue was dealt with by words similar to those at the Chehalis Treaty Council: "There shall . . . be reserved . . . for the tribes and bands . . . a tract of land sufficient for their wants within the Territory of Washington, to be selected by the President of the United States. . . ." Where would the reservations be? How many? What size?

Regardless, the treaty moved ahead. The governor's signature was still needed. Six months later, a formal signing ceremony took place on January 25, 1856, at the territorial capital in Olympia—the name that was given to the treaty that had been negotiated at the Quinault River. The reservation location (or locations) were still up in the air but one thing was determined for sure: the tribes had conveyed an estimated 200,000 acres of Indian title—one-third of the Olympic Peninsula—to the United States.

In time, as with so many of Stevens's crabbed reservations, tribal inequities were ameliorated if not fully corrected. In 1872, Washington Superintendent of Indian Affairs R. H. Milroy recommended that the Quinault Reservation be substantially enlarged and a year later President Ulysses S. Grant expanded it to nearly 200,000 acres on November 4, 1873. Then executive orders created reservations, with small but excellent traditional land bases, of 837 acres for the Quileute in 1889 and 443 acres for the Hoh. Most Queets people, always closely related to the Quinault, resided on that reservation and today are considered Quinault tribal citizens.

In one year and a month, Isaac Stevens shaped society in a way that few people ever have. With his fierce, focused campaign, he achieved his objective: to obtain Indian title to tens of millions of acres of land in Washington, Idaho, and Montana in the name of the United States and open up vast amounts of western lands for family settlers and resource developers.

In many ways, he ran roughshod over Indian people with utter indifference. He probably fancied himself, and understandably so, as part of "the Vanishing Indian" phenomenon, a dogma of the time that was shorthand for the idea that the end of tribalism would allow Indian people to participate fully in the American dream.

What that thinking didn't account for was the staying power of Native people. In a sense, Indians themselves might not have overtly identified

that staying power. They just *did it*. The elders who participated or observed the treaties did know two things. Their tribes had the status of
governments recognized by the United States of America. They took
pride in that. They knew, also, about the treaty right to hunt, fish, and
gather on tens of millions of acres of land, river, and ocean that was for-
merly Indian title. The old people knew and treasured those things and
wanted them to be passed on, in detail, for generations to come, right
up to the mid-twentieth century and beyond. Then, in a very different
setting than Isaac Stevens's heyday, the staying power would evolve
from stories and dreams into hard results that revived and honored the
age-old cultures and ways.

6 The Long Suppression

"All the Indian there is in the race should be dead.
Kill the Indian and save the man."

After the United States Senate confirmed all of the Pacific Northwest treaties, a calm settled in. The tribes, and non-Indians as well, assumed that the substantial issues had been resolved. But the calm did not last long. The forces behind manifest destiny were alive and well. Settlers still wanted land. Immigrants began to stream in. By the late 1860s, settlers in many places in the Pacific Northwest were complaining that Indians were impeding settlement. Similar complaints were made across the West and became a national concern.

The tribal role in decision-making, limited though it was, diminished after treaty making. The tribes, distant from the nation's capital, primarily spoke their own languages and mostly kept to the reservations. Still non-citizens, they lacked the right to vote and possessed little understanding of how the government worked. They had almost no influence on federal decision-making. Some initiatives, such as individual treaties, are carried out at the local level but national Indian law and policy, developed in Congress and federal agencies in Washington, DC, has always had major impacts on all individual tribes.

Starting in the early 1870s and continuing throughout the next several generations, Congress, and the Bureau of Indian Affairs (BIA), were especially active in Indian matters. The dominant voices wanted to develop western land and had little knowledge about, or concern for, Native American sovereignty, land, or culture. Advocates argued that Indian people would benefit by leaving the reservation and moving into the mainstream society under state jurisdiction. "Assimilation," "civilizing,"

"Americanization," and "detribalization" became code words for federal policy.

The result was a century that was a wasteland, save for a few years in the early Franklin Delano Roosevelt administration, for Indian people all across the country. The tribes lost 90 million acres of reservation land nationally. Tribal traditions, religions, languages, education views, and health practices were suppressed. The epidemics continued. Private citizens were free to insult them on the street and some restaurants and other businesses put "No Indians" signs on their doors. States extended their jurisdiction into Indian country. And leave no doubt about it: Native fishing rights, so central to tribal existence, in the Northwest were denied or scraped to the bone.

By the 1870s, assimilation had become the driving force in Indian policy. The westward expansion was still roaring in the 1880s and homesteaders saw the treaty lands in the West as impediments to settlement. Mining companies, logging firms, and water development interests also were frustrated by having the reservations off-limits. As Professor Francis Paul Prucha wrote in his book *The Great Father*, there now was an "Indian problem":

> No panacea for the Indian problem was more persistently proposed than allotment of land to the Indians in severalty. It was an article of faith with the reformers that civilization was impossible without the incentive to work that came only from individual ownership of a piece of property. The upsurge of humanitarian concern for Indian reform in the post–Civil War era gave a new impetus to the severalty principle, which was almost universally accepted and aggressively promoted until Congress finally passed a general allotment law.

In response, Congress passed the General Allotment Act of 1887, one of the most significant statutes in the history of Indian law. This assimilation statute was sold as a way of providing land to tribal members so they could become farmers and gain the benefits of the majority society. The land, though, would not come from available federal public lands but rather from tribal lands. So Congress authorized the BIA to transfer land from reservations, owned by the tribes, to individual tribal members. These individual parcels, called allotments, amounted to 160 acres for family heads and 80 acres to each single person over eighteen years of age. The statute provided that the allotments would be held in federal trust for twenty-five years, meaning that the allotments could not be transferred or subject to state tax and zoning laws for that period.

Outsiders found ways to get at allotment land by changing the time limit provisions in the laws or waiting out the twenty-five-year period. A prodigious amount of Indian land loss followed, with total Indian land holdings plummeting from 138 million acres in 1887 to 48 million acres in 1934, a total loss of 90 million acres. Some of this was done through arms-length transactions and even more was taken by fraud, sharp dealing, mortgage foreclosures, and tax sales. Noted scholar of Indian history Professor Angie Debo explained the flows of Indian allotments to non-Indian opportunists this way:

> It was immediately apparent that even these advanced Indians, who had supported themselves thriftily and governed themselves well, had no concept of the written instruments—deeds, mortgages, leases, powers of attorney—that regulated the white man's land transactions. Theoretically, as United States citizens they had access to the courts, but the entire legal system of eastern Oklahoma was warped to strip them of their property. The term grafter was universally applied to dealers in Indian land and was frankly accepted by them.

Even so, the largest body of land loss to Indians under the General Allotment Act came from the "surplus land" provisions of the 1887 act. An astounding 60 million acres went straight to settlers because they were "surplus" to the needs of these hunting and fishing tribes who would not need so much land since the tribal members would become

INDIAN LAND FOR SALE

GET A HOME		PERFECT TITLE
OF		❈
YOUR OWN		POSSESSION
❈		WITHIN
EASY PAYMENTS		THIRTY DAYS

FINE LANDS IN THE WEST

IRRIGATED IRRIGABLE	GRAZING	AGRICULTURAL DRY FARMING

IN 1910 THE DEPARTMENT OF THE INTERIOR SOLD UNDER SEALED BIDS ALLOTTED INDIAN LAND AS FOLLOWS:

Location.	Acres.	Average Price per Acre.	Location.	Acres.	Average Price per Acre.
Colorado	5,211.21	$7.27	Oklahoma	34,664.00	$19.14
Idaho	17,013.00	24.85	Oregon	1,020.00	15.43
Kansas	1,684.50	33.45	South Dakota	120,445.00	16.53
Montana	11,034.00	9.86	Washington	4,879.00	41.37
Nebraska	5,641.00	36.65	Wisconsin	1,069.00	17.00
North Dakota	22,610.70	9.93	Wyoming	865.00	20.64

FOR THE YEAR 1911 IT IS ESTIMATED THAT 350,000 ACRES WILL BE OFFERED FOR SALE

For information as to the character of the land write for booklet, "INDIAN LANDS FOR SALE," to the Superintendent U. S. Indian School at any one of the following places:

CALIFORNIA:	MINNESOTA:	NORTH DAKOTA:	OKLAHOMA—Con.	SOUTH DAKOTA:	WASHINGTON:
Hoopa.	Onigum.	Fort Totten.	Sac and Fox Agency.	Cheyenne Agency.	Fort Simcoe.
COLORADO:		Fort Yates.	Shawnee.	Crow Creek.	Fort Spokane.
Ignacio.	MONTANA:	OKLAHOMA:	Wyandotte.	Greenwood.	Tekoa.
IDAHO:	Crow Agency.	Anadarko.	OREGON:	Lower Brule.	Tulalip.
Lapwai.	NEBRASKA:	Cantonment.	Klamath Agency.	Pine Ridge.	WISCONSIN:
KANSAS:	Macy.	Colony.	Pendleton.	Rosebud.	Oneida.
Horton.	Santee.	Darlington.	Roseburg.	Sisseton.	
Nadeau.	Winnebago.	Muskogee.	Siletz.		
		Pawnee.			

WALTER L. FISHER,
Secretary of the Interior.

ROBERT G. VALENTINE,
Commissioner of Indian Affairs.

The "Indian Land for Sale" poster epitomized the federal Indian policy during the century after the treaties. There were many justifications for "assimilation" but almost all led to the acquisition of Indian land and resource rights. The poster shows how the federal government was more than willing to make Indian treaty lands available to potential settlers. *Library of Congress, Rare Book and Special Collections Division, 2015657622.*

farmers. So much for the cynical promise that the General Allotment Act would bring assimilation and lasting benefits to Indian people. Most tribes—three-fourths of all tribes in the country, and nearly all of the tribes in Washington—would have their reservations broken up, first by transferring some tribal lands to tribal individuals and numerous non-Indian purchasers of tribal members' land, and then by having big chunks of their reservations designated as "surplus lands" for non-Indians. President Theodore Roosevelt called the 1887 act "a mighty pulverizing engine to break up the tribal mass. It acts directly upon the family and the individual."

The tribes lost so much. David Treuer captured this exact moment in time for all American Indians in his 2019 book, *The Heartbeat of Wounded Knee*, when he described the meaning of the Wounded Knee Massacre of 1890: "Both sides joined in seeing the massacre as the end not just of the Indians who had died, but of 'the Indian' period. There had been an Indian past, and, overnight, there lay ahead only an American future."

During this long assimilationist period, the Bureau of Indian Affairs, working in concert with the churches, hammered home to tribal members the message that traditional culture was a thing of the past and that assimilation into the larger society was both inevitable and good. Native languages, religions, clothing, and ceremonies were un-American and bad. By the turn of the twentieth century, the BIA had become a suffocating presence on the reservations as the agents bypassed tribal leaders and handed out benefits to cooperating Indians or took disciplinary action on tribal members who refused to accept American ways. These federal officials worked hand-in-glove with the churches. Alvin Josephy explains:

> Agents of the Bureau of Indian Affairs looked away from, or even
> encouraged, missionaries who continued to break up Indian ceremonies

or interfere with and punish individual Indians and their families when they tried to revive languages, arts, and other aspects of their traditional cultures.

Education was a main vehicle for assimilation. Early on, the Friends of the Indian, a politically influential group of self-appointed East Coast Christian advocates for Indians, declared education the foundation for assimilation policy: "The Indian must have a Christian language to enable him to perform the duties of family, the State, and the Church." The BIA churches built up separate systems of on-reservation day schools and boarding schools. When Thomas Morgan became BIA commissioner in 1889, he was an all-out supporter of an intensive Indian education system, announcing that "the Indian youth should be instructed in their rights, privileges, and duties as American citizens; should be taught to love the American flag; should be imbued with genuine patriotism; and made to feel that the United States, and not some paltry reservation, is their home." Captain Richard Henry Pratt, who founded the federal Carlisle Indian School in Pennsylvania, was even blunter in putting forth the basic notion that guided the federal and state schools and epitomized the era: "[A]ll the Indian there is in the race should be dead. Kill the Indian and save the man."

Administrators and teachers faithfully carried out these hard-nosed ideas in the real world of Indian schools for half a century. The pressures on the students and parents were relentless. Allen Slickapoo, Nez Perce, described his experiences at Chemawa Boarding School near Salem, Oregon:

> The boarding schools were highly regimented. Many of these schools used military discipline and force was the word of the day. Many of our students came from homes speaking the Nez Perce language and had to learn English in the boarding schools.
>
> This was very difficult since the general feeling was that English had to be beat into the students. Harsh disciplinary measures were taken to enforce the learning of English. Many of us recall the punishments given

for failure to learn an English word or words. The students, both boys and girls, were required to wear military-style uniforms. The boys were taught to drill. This style of education was practiced up into the 1940s.

By the 1920s, Indian policy began to soften. In 1924, Congress granted citizenship to all Indians. The 1928 Meriam Report, written by the Brookings Institution, called for reform, including increased health

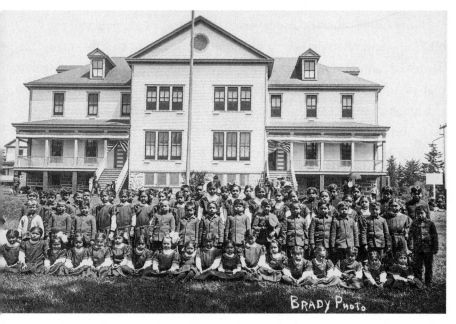

Children stand in front of the girls' dormitory at the federal boarding school, the Tulalip Indian School, near Marysville, Washington, and Tulalip Bay. The students had been removed from their homes and sent to the school, where they were subjected to the rigors of the assimilation program, designed to Americanize and Christianize Indian people, especially the youth. The students were required to attend many church activities and prohibited from using their tribal languages, wearing Indian clothing, and generally doing anything that reflected their Indianness. Photograph by Ferdinand Brady, ca. 1912. *Courtesy of the Museum of History and Industry, Seattle, Image no. 1988.11.13.*

and education support, an end to allotment, and recognition of tribal self-governance.

When Franklin Roosevelt became president in 1933, he named as BIA commissioner John Collier, a dynamic and reform-minded social worker who was praised by Southwestern tribes. Collier, with the active support of Roosevelt and Interior Secretary Harold Ickes, led the charge for the Indian Reorganization Act of 1934, the first omnibus legislation since the General Allotment Act. The IRA prohibited further allotments; allowed tribes to regain surplus lands not homesteaded; increased funding for health, education, and social programs; and invited tribes to adopt constitutions to enhance tribal self-government, which had steadily been weakened for generations.

Under Collier, the BIA also reversed the decades-long policy of prohibiting—and often punishing in administrations and courts—many dances, ceremonies, and other cultural practices with Collier ordering that "no interference with Indian religious life or ceremonial expression will hereinafter be tolerated." In 1942, the FDR administration also produced Felix Cohen's *Handbook of Federal Indian Law*, one of the greatest treatises in American law. Cohen brought back Chief Justice John Marshall's rulings that placed tribal sovereignty and the trust relationship at the center of Indian law. The Cohen treatise was influential then and remains so today.

Collier began to wear thin. While sincerely supportive of tribal interests, his programs suffered from a top-down approach. More and more tribal leaders sensed that Collier thought he knew what was best for Indians and that he often pressured them. Whatever opposition he had from Indian country, his problems with congressional leaders ran much deeper, resulting in accusations that the Indian Reorganization Act, tribal sovereignty, and treaty fishing and hunting rights programs were "communistic." By 1943, there was strong sentiment among members of

the Senate and House Indian Affairs Committees against tribal governments and reservations and in favor of ending federal responsibilities to
Indians. It would not be long before federal Indian policy swung a full
180 degrees, dashing the hope that was high in Indian country under the
FDR programs and contriving the most destructive of all Indian policies.

On August 1, 1953, in a House Concurrent Resolution, Congress
announced the new Indian policy: termination. The title was not chosen lightly. The national legislature, led by the zealous, single-minded
Arthur V. Watkins of Utah, called for a hard-edged elimination of the
far-flung Indian policy system: sell off the reservations, pay off the
Indians, abrogate all the treaties and laws relating to tribes and tribal
members, and make state laws universally applicable.

The Concurrent Resolution set official government policy and would
be carried out through termination statutes for individual tribes. But
the fervor to terminate ran strong and the first sentence in the 1953 resolution proclaimed Congress's determination to terminate tribes and
reservations "as rapidly as possible."

Senator Watkins had strong ideas but virtually no knowledge of Indian
country. Still, he and his allies pushed through six major termination
statutes within a year, hitting the timber-rich Klamath and Menominee
Reservations and the numerous small tribes in Oregon and California.

Congress did not terminate any Washington tribes, although BIA officials brought termination proposals to twenty-one Puget Sound tribes
and other Western Washington tribes throughout the 1950s. Senator
Henry Jackson pressed for termination of the large Colville Reservation
in the eastern part of the state until the late 1960s yet could not achieve
passage.

In all, approximately 109 tribes and bands nationally were terminated.
A minimum of 1,362,155 acres and 11,466 individuals were affected. Statistics on Indian population were notoriously inaccurate, but no more
than 3 percent of all federally recognized Indians were involved. The
total amount of Indian trust land was diminished by about 3.2 percent.

Congress finally repudiated termination in 1973. For the 1950s and most of the 1960s, however, fear of termination burned hot on reservations in Washington and across Indian country nationally.

Unlikely though it might have seemed, the 1950s proved to be the seedbed for the highly spirited and organized activism that led to the Boldt Decision and the accomplishments that followed it. True, during the postwar years, Northwest Indian people had every reason to give in to confusion and depression. The poverty was relentless. Washington claimed that its right to regulate treaty fishing for "conservation" purposes allowed it to regulate all aspects of tribal fishing. State fisheries officers hammered tribal fishermen, arresting them and often jailing them. Tribes could afford only limited legal support. Termination was terrifying: if its proponents prevailed, there would no longer be tribes, treaties, or reservations; all that being an Indian meant would be crippled or destroyed altogether.

Nonetheless, a new kind of thinking was emerging in Indian country. Twenty-three thousand tribal veterans returned from service in World War II and the Korean War. They had gained wide support in the military. They had succeeded in the outside world. These veterans had expectations, were impatient and assertive, and inspired their fellow Indians. Helen Peterson, later executive director of the National Congress of American Indians, declared that "World War Two revived the Indians' capacity to act on their own behalf."

The NCAI, founded in 1944 and today the largest and most influential intertribal organization, had a two-person staff and almost no budget in the 1950s, but tribal leaders Helen Peterson (Cheyenne-Lakota) and Joe Garry (Coeur d'Alene) were forces of nature. From the beginning they saw termination for what it was, and fought it as hard as they could. In Garry's Buick, they went out into Indian country and explained how serious termination was. Garry urged tribal members to fight back, for themselves and all tribes: "Hang on to your lands. Kick and scratch if you have to, but hang on to your lands. Don't sit back and let things happen to you."

Garry and Peterson encouraged tribal members to attend congressional termination hearings on individual tribes. They had little luck in the beginning. Senator Watkins had created a steamroller that led to the several early acts. The coast-to-coast Indian opposition, however, gathered steam, and members of Congress began to take notice. Some bills were blocked and others delayed. The termination policy had become a bad name in many quarters. The termination acts of the early and mid-'50s caused great damage to the affected tribes, but, while hearings continued into the late 1960s, only one termination act was passed after 1959.

As for tribal fishing rights, in the years after the treaties the Northwest tribes endured the suppression, assimilation, and assaults on sovereignty faced by Native people nationally, but the particulars differed.

For two decades after the treaties, the tribes and the settlers had few disputes over fishing rights. The homesteaders were mostly farmers, not fishers, so there was little competition out on the rivers. In fact, the newcomers looked to the Indians for salmon, bartering collaboratively with Natives for fish.

The competition for salmon changed dramatically with the arrival of canneries. Canning was invented in France in 1809. Until then, the preserving of meat, fruit, and vegetables was limited to drying, smoking, pickling, and natural refrigeration. Canning, first in glass bottles, later in tin, was a significant advance. The first canning of salmon took place in Scotland in the 1820s, but it didn't spread to the United States until 1864, when the Hume brothers opened a small operation on the Sacramento River in California. Realizing the greater potential in the Northwest, the Hume brothers promptly moved up to the Columbia River in 1867.

This revolutionized the commercial production of salmon. No longer would entrepreneurs be limited to a small trade of salted salmon

A PUGET SOUND SALMON CATCH

By the 1890s, commercial fishing interests were taking salmon with no regulations in place. The companies created large canneries that allowed them to can great amounts of fish and ship to a worldwide market. This photograph, ca. 1900, shows workers unloading salmon from barges at a Seattle cannery on Puget Sound south of downtown Seattle. *Courtesy of the Museum of History and Industry, Seattle, Image no. SHS10593.*

packed in unwieldy barrels. Immediately, businesspeople could ship great numbers of cases, each containing fifty-eight one-pound cans of Pacific salmon, to literally anywhere in the nation and world. Salmon harvesting exploded.

The first cannery opened in Mukilteo in 1877 with the Mukilteo cannery producing 5,000 cases in its first season. The non-Indian commercial fishery quickly developed into a major industry. By the turn of the twentieth century, some forty-five Puget Sound canneries were producing nearly 1,400,000 cases of salmon annually.

The commercial fishermen, mostly newcomers, built impressive harvesting operations. They took fish with long nets and hook-and-line operations out on the ocean to harvest returning salmon before the runs reached the fishing grounds on bays and rivers. But highly efficient devices on the bays and rivers were even more effective. Fishers built large traps, mostly weirs—V-shaped structures of wood or stone—that guided fish into enclosures for easy capture. They put long gill nets in open water or stretched them across rivers. When fish swam into the gill net, they passed only partway through the mesh; when they struggled and tried to back up, the twine slipped behind their gills and they could not escape.

Fish wheels, creaky new devices, powered by the river current and kept in constant motion, resembled Ferris wheels. The many baskets on each wheel scooped returning salmon out of the water. These fish wheels, some fixed on rock formations, others floating and mobile, were deadly efficient when well located.

These new circumstances—the inventions of canneries and mammoth unregulated harvesting operations—began the decline of the Northwest salmon runs that continues today. In his incisive analysis, *The Fisherman's Problem*, Arthur McEvoy made this observation:

> Here was the fisherman's problem in laboratory form. Access to salmon
> was free to anyone who could put a gill net into the water or who had
> capital to build a cannery. The industry's gauntlet simply permitted too
> few fish to escape upstream to spawn new ones for future runs. Any fisher
> or any canner who might have left a salmon in the water so as to conserve
> the resource would simply have given that fish to competitors.

In 1908, President Theodore Roosevelt lamented the ineffectiveness of state regulation over this common-pool resource:

> The salmon fisheries of the Columbia River are now but a fraction of
> what they were twenty-five years ago. . . . During these twenty-five years
> the fishermen of [Oregon and Washington] have naturally tried to take
> all they could get, and the two legislatures have never been able to agree
> on joint action of any kind adequate in degree for the protection of the
> fisheries.

Non-Indian commercial fishermen affected virtually all salmon waters in the state of Washington. The harvesting boom wreaked havoc on Indian fishing. Tons of returning salmon bound for grounds where tribes had traditionally fished were intercepted and packed in tin cans. The commercial take expanded dramatically while the tribal catches dropped precipitously. Herman Olsen, a Lummi fisherman, explained how the productive tribal reef-net fishery was affected:

> After the canneries started going good, the white man came and put traps right there off Lummi Island to catch salmon for the canneries. Asked no permission or anything, they just put their traps in. Right where the reef nets were. Well, then they just kept moving the Indians out, moving them, moving them until they got all of them crowded clear out. There was no more room left for them. They had to give up. Move away.

The economics and politics of Northwest salmon fishing began to change. Northwesterners had long enjoyed the outstanding sport fishing for salmon and the leaping, tail-walking steelhead. Sport fishers began organizing and urging state legislative action to protect sport fishing. They had some early successes, including state laws prohibiting net fishing on some rivers and tributaries. This impacted the tribes, for most tribal fishing occurred on inland watercourses rather than on bays and open waters. State officials paid little attention to tribal complaints. Ever since statehood in Washington, the state made much of its purported police power, certainly including Indian fishing, treaties or no. The Washington State Supreme Court handed down several such opinions, including the *Towessnute* case of 1916, which made it clear that tribes and their treaties, in the eyes of the state, had little if anything to do with fishing rights on Washington waters:

> The Indian was a child, and a dangerous child, of nature, to be both protected and restrained. In his nomadic life he was to be left so long as civilization did not demand his region. . . . [W]hen off the reservation, [Indians] have ever been subject to the criminal laws of the states. . . .

[T]he police power is indispensable to any commonwealth, and . . . the right of regulating fish and game is a proper exertion of such a right.

The sport fishers, savoring their new influence, succeeded in getting passed a state initiative in 1932, establishing the Department of Game to protect "game fish" (especially steelhead) and representing sport fishers. It joined the Department of Fisheries, which protected "food fish" and represented commercial fishing interests. There was no recognition of the third user group, with its own interests: the treaty tribes.

In 1934, Washington voters approved Initiative 77, a heralded measure that addressed the salmon crisis. By then it was clear that there were two politically powerful user groups, the commercial fishers and the sport fishers. The two, with the common interest of improving the runs, joined together to put the initiative on the ballot and campaign for it. The measure, which prohibited all fixed gear—traps, fish wheels, and set nets—passed by a two-thirds majority.

While the salmon catch did decline, Initiative 77 never lived up to its high objectives. Commercial fishers found ways around it, with purse seining expanding because those nets were dropped down in open water and were not "set nets" under the initiative.

As for the tribes, they were exempted from the gear restrictions in Initiative 77: "The provisions of the Act do not apply to fishing by Indians under federal regulation." This provision was not due to any desire of the initiative's sport fishing drafters to acknowledge any tribal treaty rights; it was probably required by the Washington State Attorney General, who wanted to avoid any part of the initiative being struck down as conflicting with federal laws.

After the passage of Initiative 77, sport clubs went to the Game Department and—despite the exemption of Indian fishing in the Initiative—demanded action against off-reservation tribal net fishing. In 1936, the Game Department, ignoring the exemption, enthusiastically announced its intent to come down hard on Indian net fishing, threatening to arrest all "young bucks," and declared that "the current controversy hinges on the point that Indians are infringing on state rights. The state is not infringing on the privileges of Indians." The state agencies' policy of delivering to commercial and sport interests, while cracking down on treaty fishing, continued into the mid-twentieth century.

Eminent historian of the Pacific Northwest Alexandra Harmon explained how the future Boldt Case area tribes processed and reacted to these emerging societal changes in the 1960s:

> After the 1950s one provision of the century-old treaties negotiated by Isaac Stevens became the predominant emblem of Indian identity in western Washington—the provision for off-reservation fishing. To say this is not to assert that fishing and treaties were previously unimportant to descendants of indigenous people. But the twentieth century was more than half over before they focused almost single-mindedly on the treaty-reserved right to fish as the best expression of their relations to non-Indians and thus a cardinal symbol of their Indianness.
>
> Following World War II and particularly by the late 1950s, Indians could see themselves reflected in non-Indians' eyes as poor, backward, and isolated. They responded in typically varied ways. Many sought spiritual and cultural validation of their worth in new or revived religious ceremonies, festivals, and pan-Indian organizations. Many instead or also took pride in the treaties, identifying themselves with the earliest recipients of solemn U.S. promises. Increasingly, the promise they cited was one that Governor Stevens had included in every treaty: "The right of taking fish at usual and accustomed grounds and stations is further secured to said Indians in common with all citizens of the Territory. . . ." Converging pressures spurred diverse people to proclaim this right the definitive element of their Indian heritage.

7 The Tribes Come Forward

"We better win this one or there won't be another one."

For a full century after the treaties, the Washington tribes—isolated, poor, and unfamiliar with American politics—had done little to respond to the state's determined and expanding efforts to minimize Indian harvesting of salmon. The tribes and their fishermen made no progress with state leaders and agencies. They failed to invoke the support of the federal government. They did not take their story to the public through the media or otherwise. Lacking funds, they rarely hired lawyers to protect tribal rights in the courts. This changed quite abruptly, within just a few years in the early 1960s.

The law on Indian treaty rights, never well settled, became even more unsettled by the late 1950s. In the 1942 *Tulee* case, the United States Supreme Court recognized the validity of off-reservation treaty rights and also general state power to regulate tribal fisheries for "conservation" but did not define the term. Similarly, in 1957 the Washington Supreme Court issued a split decision in *State v. Satiacum*. Four justices, echoing the state's argument that the treaties carried little weight, found broad, nearly unlimited state "conservation" authority over tribal fishing. Four other justices, however, saw little room for state regulation, finding that traditional fishing practices historically exercised by tribal people and embedded in the treaties continued "unimpaired," unless curtailed by Congress.

State officers continued to make raids and arrests, often accompanied by beatings and other rough treatment of Indian fishermen. Some lower court judges fined Indian fishermen or sent them to jail; other local courts dismissed prosecutions as violating the right of tribes to determine their tribal members' fishing seasons, take limits, and use of nets. Just as bad, numbers of private citizens interfered with tribal fishers, blocking access to fishing grounds, cutting their nets, sometimes stealing their canoes and gear, and issuing loud insults when Indian people came into town. Ted Plaster, Lummi tribal member, related, "I was fishing with my son and a white man's boat came right toward my net line and ran over it and cut it all up. They do that all the time to Indians. . . . They think they own all the fish." Indian people received little protection from the police.

It had always been difficult for Indian people to accept how the non-Indian citizenry supported the state's hard-line, discriminatory position on Indian fishing. To be sure, the call for "conservation" of the salmon runs was universally and rightly held high in the state, in and out of government. Yet it was impossible to pin the troubles of the salmon on the tribes. Indian people knew that they had always insisted on conserving the health of the runs. By the early 1960s, tribal fishers were taking only 6 percent of the total Puget Sound harvest while sport fishers took 8.5 percent and commercial fishers took 85.5 percent. The total of all Indian fishers was approximately 800, compared to 6,600 non-Indian commercial fishermen and 283,000 non-Indian sport fishers. True, the runs were declining but that was due in large part to overfishing by non-Indians under the state's loose, generous regulations. Further, it was becoming increasingly obvious that, in addition to the direct harvesting, significant damage was due to wide-scale impacts on salmon habitat because of the postwar influx of new Washington residents, dams, high-yield logging, and the loss of good salmon habitat to new housing, commercial buildings, shopping centers, and roads and highways.

Some opposition to Indian fishing came from a general feeling among many in the white community that it violated American norms of equality for tribal fishermen to use nets prohibited by state law and to fish outside of state seasons. Such concerns were understandable: there was little public information available about the century-old Indian treaties and the reasons for them. The tribes were not bringing much information of that sort to the public.

Opposition to these treaty rights also traced to attitudes unrelated to fishing per se. Racism played a role. More abstractly, the larger public in the late 1950s just did not know much about Indian people, their cultures and traditions, and their relationships to the lands, rivers, and salmon. In that era, as for generations before, most Indian people stayed on the reservations and did not much participate in the majority society.

Public views against tribal fishing and Indian people in general spurred state government action. Ever since the Department of Game's founding in the 1930s, the agency and its vocal sport fishing constituency had become ever more committed to denying Indian treaty rights. The issue had become key because the state was seriously considering going to Congress for major revision or outright abrogation of the treaties. Washington public opinion would play a role on Capitol Hill, led by longtime Washington Attorney General John O'Connell in 1962, who warned that "it is probable that the ultimate solution will have to lie with Congress."

Indian fighters Walt Neubrech, the veteran chief of enforcement for the Department of Game, as well as game department officers and other state officials, went to great lengths to build political opposition to the tribes. Alvin Josephy explained:

Simplistic arguments . . . continued to be used [by fish and game authorities] to rouse public sentiment and prejudice against the Indian fishers. Some of the campaign was deliberately furthered by irritated state game wardens who spied on the Indian fishermen and made secret movies of them catching steelhead in nets out of season to show at meetings of sport fishermen's clubs. Such provocations had their intended effect.

Anger continued to build, editorial writers and politicians seethed, and in 1961, the atmosphere was right for state officials to move once more against the Indians.

And move the state of Washington did. In 1961, it became the first state to resolve to eliminate Indian treaty rights. Washington decided to carry out a major campaign in the courts, with appeals to Congress, and escalated even more aggressive programs of raids and arrests. This time, though, the state would be faced with very different tribal opposition than in the past.

The most viable part of the escalation was the raids, ramped up in both numbers and intensity. On January 6, 1962, during the winter chum salmon run on the Nisqually River, three dozen officers with walkie-talkies and a reconnaissance spotter plane overhead closed in on six Nisqually fishermen, arresting them and confiscating their carved cedar canoes, gear, and catches. The men were charged with fishing with gill nets. Billy Frank Jr. described the pressure that would be exerted for several years to come during any significant salmon runs:

> It was nearly a daily event to get hassled by those guys. It was a good day if you didn't get arrested. After a while, I didn't even bother to tell [my family] because they already knew: 'If we don't come back home, call C. J. Johnson.' He was the bail bondsman.

Now, in light of the all-out campaign against their treaty rights, the tribes talked among themselves and realized that they had to do much more. The civil rights movement gave them hope. They saw the need to take the initiative and strategize, work together, influence public opinion, and

Al Ziontz, 1979.
Courtesy of Ron Ziontz.

be much more active in the courts, the then-current presidential administration, and Congress. Over on the coast, the Quinault Indian Nation protested state policies by closing scenic Lake Quinault, within the reservation but previously open to the public, to all boating, swimming, and fishing by whites. Leaders of the Muckleshoot, Puyallup, and Nisqually Indian Tribes began laying plans, which would soon produce results, to combat state raids on the Nisqually, Puyallup, and Green Rivers. Several tribes began bringing in attorneys. In 1963, the Makah held their initial meeting with Al Ziontz, who opened up a welcomed new approach by telling the tribal council, "If I were representing the Makah Tribe, the principle of tribal sovereignty would be the way I would go about defending your rights." Ziontz did become Makah general counsel and a decade hence would be a major force in the Boldt Decision litigation.

Still, a growing understanding of the state's attacks, coupled with dedicated tribal members and determined traditional fishers out on the rivers were not enough. The tribes lacked effective political and legal strategies if their treaties were to survive.

Enter Hank Adams.

Assiniboine and Sioux, Hank Adams was born on the Fort Peck Reservation in Montana, but his parents and he moved to Washington when he was eighteen months old. They settled at the Quinault Reservation and Hank grew up there. Razor-sharp brilliant and driven—he had a photographic memory and read obsessively—Adams immersed himself in Quinault history and the tribe's many current issues of old-growth timber, salmon, and various forced assimilation policies. He read broadly in American Indian law, history, and policy. After high school, where he was student body president and editor of the school newspaper, he attended the University of Washington, but only briefly.

In early 1963 Adams joined the National Indian Youth Council. NIYC, founded just two years earlier, was the only Indian-led activist organization in the country and was committed to civil disobedience. He was dazzled by it. He met inspiring young Indian leaders such as Clyde Warrior (Ponca), Karen Rickard (Tuscarora), Mel Thom (Walker River Paiute), and Herb Blackford (Navajo). The activist-founded NIYC grew out of a groundbreaking anthropological experiment, the brainchild of Professor Sol Tax of the University of Chicago, who believed that low academic performances of Indian college students were due to mainstream education's failure to address Native American history and culture. In 1956, Tax held the first of a series of Workshops on American Indian Affairs, six-week immersion courses, which brought sixty Indian students every year to Chicago for each workshop.

The workshops were successful from the beginning. The program became even better when Tax turned primary authority of the workshops over to D'Arcy McNickle, a Flathead tribal member from Montana whose eminence and bravery made him a superstar with the college students in the workshops. The brightly taught workshops recognized the value of Native beliefs and experiences and addressed racism, colonialism, cultural preservation, treaty rights, self-determination, and tribal sovereignty. Civil disobedience was taught as one mechanism to protect and further the rights and needs of Native Americans.

The workshops made an impression on the founders of NIYC, as well as on many other Indian college students, and were a significant factor in the activism that rose up in Indian country in the 1960s. It certainly took hold in the Pacific Northwest.

Hank Adams, liking the NIYC crew and their aggressive national approach, threw himself into it. Along with Bruce Wilkie (Makah), he made sure that the Northwest fishing wars were a major NIYC priority. Adams finally arrived at Frank's Landing in February 1963 with his belongings and a pile of ideas. He was nineteen years old.

As the treaty fishing rights cause continued to gather steam, it would be a wide-open process and many voices would be heard. On matters of strategy, though, the daring and creative Hank Adams—always on top of the history, law, culture, and politics—had the most impact.

By the summer, the fishers, the people at Frank's Landing, dozens of tribal leaders and members from the southern Puget Sound tribes, and the omnipresent Adams all recognized that the state had expanded its enforcement actions, openly talking about "extinguishing" Indian fishing rights, and that it was now necessary, especially with termination in the air, for the Indians to take the initiative at the state and national levels. There was much discussion over exactly what actions to take.

The opportunity came in December 1963 when the Washington Supreme Court, which for so long had ruled against tribal fishing rights, handed down *State v. McCoy*. The state had closed the Skagit River and brought charges against a Swinomish tribal member under the Treaty of Point Elliott. In a brief opinion, the court relied on the little-used *Ward v. Race Horse*, an 1896 US Supreme Court opinion requiring that, upon admission to the Union, new states have all of the powers of the original states. Thus the *McCoy* Court ruled that, at statehood, Washington had "acquired all of the sovereign powers of the original states, including the power to preserve its natural resources."

McCoy was a bombshell. No matter that *Ward v. Race Horse* was known as a highly questionable reading of the US Constitution and was largely ignored until the United States Supreme Court formally overruled it in 2019. No matter that, just a few months before *McCoy*, the Ninth Circuit Court of Appeals issued a unanimous, sweeping opinion in *Maison v. Confederated Tribes of Umatilla Indian Reservation* upholding near-complete jurisdiction of tribal treaty rights. *Maison*, which *McCoy* did not even mention, was one of the first cases to honor treaty rights in the way that courts at all levels would view Indian fishing rights and other Indian treaty rights, beginning at the end of the 1960s and through to the present. But no matter. What mattered is that *McCoy*—at the formative and emotional moment it was handed down—purported to give the state carte blanche to regulate or extinguish tribal fishing in virtually any manner it wished.

The tribes saw *McCoy* for the threat it was. The game and fisheries departments would enforce it out on the ground and the state agencies and fishing interests would run with it to the state courts.

The residents at the Frank's Landing settlement on the Nisqually River—Billy Frank Sr., Billy Frank Jr., Al and Maiselle Bridges, Don and Janet McCloud, and others—immediately called an emergency meeting. Fifty Indians from several tribes attended and reached agreement to take action. They decided to start by going to the governor first, in hopes that he might direct the fisheries and game departments. The *McCoy* decision had come down on December 19, 1963. By December 23, the tribes were on the road to Olympia. Governor Albert Rosellini, while never a supporter of Indian rights, did grant them a short meeting, but dismissed them with a curt "Nice to hear your problems. Come back again."

On January 2, 1964, the state fisheries and game departments intensified enforcement even more by going to Frank's Landing and ordering Nisqually fishers to pull up their nets during winter runs of steelhead and chum salmon. The fishers refused. The officials immediately obtained an injunction from a Pierce County judge, closing the lower Nisqually River to net fishing. Wardens then moved in and arrested the fishers. The state, using its seemingly unlimited power under the *McCoy* decision, then closed the Puyallup River and other tribal fishing areas, making a wave of arrests.

The families at Frank's Landing promptly formed an organization, the Survival of the American Indian Association (SAIA). The co-founders, Janet McCloud (Tulalip) and Ramona Bennett (Puyallup), were both fishers who had been active in Northwest fishing rights for years and would be advocates for tribal sovereignty the rest of their lives. Ramona Bennett grew up on the Puyallup Reservation and learned from her

Hank Adams and Ramona Bennett comparing notes on Indian fishing rights. Photograph by Cary Tolman. *Courtesy of the Museum of History and Industry, Seattle, Image no. 2000.107.020.10.03; Cary Tolman, photographer, Seattle Post-Intelligencer.*

Janet McCloud speaking at a press conference in Olympia, July 3, 1968. After her extensive and effective advocacy during the Boldt years, McCloud founded the Sapa Dawn Center located on sacred ground and dedicated to Native culture and spirituality. In addition, over the thirty years after Boldt, she gave many speeches nationally and internationally on Indigenous peoples' rights, culture, and history. She has been described as the "Rosa Parks of the American Indian movement." Photograph by Howard Staples. *Courtesy of the Museum of History and Industry, Seattle, Image no. 2000.107.121.9.01; Howard Staples, photographer; Seattle Post-Intelligencer Olympia, July 3, 1968.*

mother, who was born there in 1903. Ramona declared that the post-treaty "land grabs" and federal and state forced assimilation programs were "racist" and even "genocide." This applied to the loss felt in Indian country over Indian treaty fishing rights. This is how she put it:

> The treaties provided for a means of support, for hunting and gathering and harvesting salmon, and shellfish. If you can support your family you can live with dignity. If you have no means of taking care of your family, if you're on your bloody knees in some welfare line, then you don't have dignity. And our people suffered a deprivation of fishing for ninety years, ninety years. That's twice the length of our median life span.

Janet McCloud explained why this was the time and place to act: "The Nisqually River was targeted because it was so close to Olympia [the state capital]. We were so close to all that police power. That's when we had to organize."

SAIA saw itself as a "fighting" organization, dedicated to civil disobedience. They dismissed the negotiation-and-compromise approach with the state, which the Bureau of Indian Affairs urged upon tribal leaders, as an obvious failure. The SAIA people, as well, looking in part to the actions of Black leaders in the South, believed that tribes had to do more. They hit the ground running, finding an old mimeograph machine at Goodwill and launching a spicy paper called *Survival News* with articles on tribal fishing rights and political strategies. McCloud (her Indian name was Yet-Si-Blue, meaning "Woman Who Speaks Her Mind") served as editor and knew how to tell a story. In 1961, Washington state game wardens descended upon McCloud's home in Yelm, Washington, in search of illegally hunted deer meat. McCloud asked the wardens if they had a search warrant. "They did: It said 'John Doe.' It made me so mad, but that's the way they treated us back then."

Copies of *Survival News* were sent to the mainstream media.

This was also the moment when Billy Frank Jr. became part of the political strategizing and action. He had long been one of the most visible tribal members, suffering his first arrest as a fourteen-year-old boy in 1945. Ever since, with the exception of two years' service as a US Marine, he kept fishing according to his Nisqually tribal laws and traditions, regardless of state law, which he believed he could do under the Treaty of Medicine Creek. In all, he was arrested, and often jailed, some fifty times. More and more, he became a public figure, speaking out publicly against the state and imploring all Washingtonians to save the salmon.

The newspapers and television stations loved his passionate and riveting speeches, plainspoken, humorous, and filled with traditional tribal knowledge about salmon and their importance to tribal Indians. His charisma and emphasis on bringing people together to conserve the salmon runs resonated with the public at large. He had an uncanny sense for the best legal and political results and benefited from long conversations with Hank Adams.

Billy Frank Jr. would be a major figure in the ongoing tribal, federal, and state actions in salmon management until he passed away in 2014.

In addition to the organized "fish-ins," many individual tribal members had long refused to obey state orders on the ground that the state agencies and courts were violating their treaty fishing rights. These individual Indians stood up and were arrested, jailed, and sometimes beaten. One group of tribal members, shown here, became known as the "Getting Arrested Guys" or the "Renegades." They are, from left, Jack McCloud, Don McCloud, Billy Frank Jr., Neugen Kautz, Herman John Jr., and Al Bridges. *Courtesy of the Washington State Archives.*

During one of our many conversations, he said, "I used to be a getting-arrested guy. Now I'm a policy guy." That transition began in the early 1960s.

In the Pacific Northwest and across Indian country nationally, there was recognition that Black people in the South had made progress through peaceful demonstrations, sit-ins, and other activist tactics. Ramona Bennett, for example, recognized that the civil rights movement had created a national atmosphere that could be favorable to Indians: "We rode the wave of the Civil Rights Movement." Tribal people, though, including Bennett and Janet McCloud, were uncertain about following the Black civil rights approach. They reasoned that Indian tribes and Black people had different goals: Black people wanted equality and assimilation while the tribes wanted, not assimilation, but recognition of the treaties, tribal sovereignty, and strong reservations, places where tribal governments and citizens could administer justice and protect their land, fishing and hunting rights, cultures, and traditions.

The fishing people basically accepted a middle ground on activism based on the premise that civil disobedience was required but that it should be an Indian, not a Black, approach. These were sensitive issues among all tribes. Many older Indians and Native organizations were uncomfortable with demonstrations, sit-ins, and other such tactics. NCAI, for example, at the time was generally opposed to "demonstrations," fearing that they might create the image of tribes as radicals. Some tribal leaders, including several in northwestern Washington, felt the same way. As for the fishing rights advocates, with the local SAIA, the national NIYC, Adams, and Wilkie, the leading voices on strategy all working together, they believed they had to be more affirmative but it had to be done in a distinctive Indian way. They would not do sit-ins.

Instead, they invented "fish-ins." To be sure their message would be heard, and to get full media attention, they notified the state agencies and the press of their fish-ins. The first fish-in would be held on March 1, 1964, on the Puyallup River and the second on March 2, on the Nisqually River. On March 3, they would hold a march on Olympia to present their issues to the governor and state legislature.

The fish-ins worked as planned. The public turnouts were in the hundreds. Most of the media reporting, which drew front-page and top-of-the-broadcast TV coverage, was sympathetic to the Indians, describing violent arrests of Indian fishers, who offered no resistance, just dead weight, as they were hauled up rocky hillsides to the police wagons. The media coverage was especially extensive at the first fish-in, on the Puyallup: Adams and Wilkie had arranged for Hollywood star Marlon Brando to attend. Brando pitched in by helping to haul in a net full of salmon. The officers made many arrests, including Brando, for illegal fishing. A higher-up, knowing that the Brando arrest gave the state a bad name, ordered the officers to release Brando from jail, which they did a few hours after the arrest. Later the charges were dropped.

After the two fish-ins, some 1,000 Indians held a march on Olympia, with Marlon Brando in tow, to protest state actions against Indian treaty fishers. Including members of the public, the total attendance was estimated at 2,000 to 5,000. It may well have been the largest gathering on tribal issues ever convened in the state of Washington up to that date. NIYC leader Clyde Warrior, Ponca of Oklahoma, gave a fiery speech, calling the state treatment of Indian fishers and their families "an indignity to the human spirit" and "the worst kind of discrimination." Hank Adams also spoke, offering a specific set of policy issues, proposing, for example, that the governor create an advisory board of Indian people to make recommendations on Native American policy issues.

Governor Rosellini did agree to meet with Adams, Wilkie, other Native leaders, and Brando and Warrior. The meeting, which lasted four hours, ended with the governor agreeing to some of the recommendations, including Adams's advisory board issue, that the Indians had presented to him in a memorandum. The governor had been generous in giving the Indians so much time, but his remarks to the crowd outside after the meeting with the Indians showed that he held little regard for Indian treaty fishing. The state, he argued, "could not condone a new [threat] in the form of an unregulated or uncontrolled fishery by Indians at such places as they alone shall choose. . . . Without such regulation," he asserted, "the Pacific salmon would be as rare as the dodo bird."

After the Olympia gathering, with the treaty fishing issues now much more in the public eye, the tribes accelerated even more of their efforts to create a broad-based legal capability to protect their treaty fishing. They drew in many attorneys. Initially, the only tribe with a tribal lawyer was the Makah, with Al Ziontz. With money raised mostly by fish bakes, SAIA and fishers brought in Jack Tanner, an attorney in Tacoma and, as an African American, president of the regional office of the National Association for the Advancement of Colored People (NAACP). An able attorney who later would be named a federal district court judge, Tanner worked conscientiously on treaty cases and brought in three American Civil Liberties Union attorneys. With the new visibility of the Indian fishers, and the civil rights implications of their cause, other local attorneys were volunteering pro bono help. By 1966, the ACLU was also providing attorneys to defend Indians involved in the fish-ins.

Help also came from the federal government. As of the mid-1960s, George Dysart had been in the Interior Department Solicitor's Office in Oregon for several years. This was still the termination era and federal attorneys had little interest in Indian law at the time. But Dysart was assigned to some Indian matters, committed himself to the field, and became arguably the most knowledgeable person about Indian law in the country. Dysart was quiet and understated, humble, really, but when he was right on something, he would announce his position firmly. He had followed the Indian fishing controversy closely for years and noticed how many more Indian fishing issues were landing on his desk. He carefully researched the powers of the states to regulate treaty fishing and concluded that states had very limited authority, far less than the states claimed. George Dysart, without an ounce of flamboyance, just an excellent lawyer with carefully developed views, would become one of the most important federal officials on Indian law through the end of the century.

Tribal leaders, knowing the United States' trust obligations to tribes, wanted more federal support for their rights under federal treaties and urged Dysart to bring the case. Dysart knew Sid Lezak, the activist United States Attorney for Oregon, and the two discussed the tribal fishing situation more and more regularly. During the mid-1960s, there were no overarching cases, and the Northwest treaties issues were being played out in state courts through the waves of arrests and prosecutions of individual Indian fishers. While the tribes had an increasing number of lawyers, most of them were pro bono private attorneys, diligent and enthusiastic but with little knowledge of Indian law.

To get at the problem, Dysart and Lezak took an idea back to the Justice Department in Washington, DC: authorize Justice Department lawyers to carry out the government trust responsibility to Indians by representing treaty fishers being prosecuted in state courts. The idea took. In April 1966, the Department of Justice did authorize assistant US attorneys to defend tribal fishers in state courts. It definitely helped: the prosecutions were many, but the US lawyers made a difference. Also, it marked a growing federal commitment in the combat over treaty fishing.

In 1967, the Legal Services Program was founded in Seattle under the Congressional War on Poverty that provided free legal services to low-income groups and people. John Sennhauser, an expert Indian lawyer, represented several tribes and members on treaty rights issues without any cost to them.

The influx of attorneys was a good step forward, but the current system, such as it was, of individual battles in state courts would never lead to a full, fair, and controlling overarching body of federal law that, among other things, would specify the nature of state law over Indian treaty fishing in the Pacific Northwest.

Dysart and Lezak both agreed that what was needed was major lawsuits brought by the United States in federal courts in both Oregon and Washington, since the legal issues over Stevens treaty rights were so similar in both states. This would mean getting wholehearted support at the highest levels of both the Department of Justice and the Department of the Interior, as well as the White House.

Neither Lezak nor Dysart could bring a lawsuit alone. The Interior Department does not litigate departmental issues—only the Department of Justice can do that. The Interior Department, though, can submit a litigation request to the DOJ to sue on behalf of the Interior. This meant that George Dysart had to get to work, which he did. He knew that it would be a big ask for the United States to bring suits against two states on behalf of nonfederal parties (tribes) involving highly controversial statewide issues. Dysart consulted with Lezak, Owen Panner, Jim Hovis, and Al Ziontz, attorneys for the Warm Springs, Yakama, and Makah tribes, respectively. They also got input from Hank Adams and tribal leaders. There was broad agreement on the strategy. The actual drafting was done by Dysart, who put together the litigation request from the Interior Department to the DOJ. The most distinctive part of the litigation request was a lengthy, informative, and well-presented history of state violation of Indian fishing rights in the Pacific Northwest. No immediate action was taken on the litigation request in Washington, DC.

The breakthrough came down in Oregon first. In the summer of 1968, as part of the extensive crackdowns by Oregon and Washington, state officers arrested thirteen Yakama fishers, including David Sohappy, for fishing on the Columbia River with gill nets contrary to state law. Sohappy's family had a long history of fishing the Columbia. An Army veteran, Sohappy wore his hair in a long braid and was convinced that the state arrests violated the treaties and the religion that had been passed down through his family for generations.

The individual Yakama tribal members filed a lawsuit, *Sohappy v. Smith*, against Oregon State Fisheries officials to enjoin the arrests. Dysart saw this as the opportunity. He thought that the policy of allowing Justice Department lawyers to defend individual Indian fishers in state court was a necessary first step. But, as he saw it, "You're in state court and treaty fishing is a federal question, so it ought to be in federal court." The state court cases against individual Indian fishers in particular places and circumstances were inadequate vehicles for demonstrating the magnitude of the overall state efforts against Indian treaty fishing. When it came to issuing the necessary, bold, and perhaps unprecedented injunctions against the states' attacks on treaty fishing, federal judges, with their lifelong appointments, would be much more likely to rise above local political opposition than elected state judges. Dysart urged even more strenuously that the litigation request be granted and applied in the Oregon litigation on the Columbia River, which presented the perfect opportunity.

Traditional Yakama fisherman David Sohappy brought a federal court lawsuit that would lead to historic court rulings in Oregon and Washington. Photograph © by Jacqueline Moreau. *Courtesy of Jacqueline Moreau, photographer.*

While there was "opposition from several Justice and Interior Departments attorneys who, Dysart said, believed that states had almost complete discretion in regulating treaty Indian fishing," most high-level federal attorneys and officials had moved beyond such termination-era thinking. The two departments approved litigation to be brought by Lezak on behalf of the United States against the state of Oregon over the controversy on the mid-Columbia River currently in court in *Sohappy v. Smith.*

Lezak and Dysart were now free to bring the suit that the two of them had envisioned for months. On September 15, 1968, they filed *United States v. Oregon* in federal district court in Oregon with the United States acting as trustees on behalf of the four tribes with treaty rights on the mid-Columbia River: the Warm Springs, Umatilla, and Nez Perce of Oregon and the Yakama of Washington. They requested expansive injunctive and declaratory relief, including a court-ordered tribal "fair and equitable share" of all fish harvested by tribal members at their "usual and accustomed" off-reservation fishing places.

Then, as planned by the federal attorneys in discussions with tribal lawyers Owen Panner and Jim Hovis, the tribes immediately filed on their own behalf and were recognized as full parties in the litigation. The federal and tribal complaints raised new and compelling arguments in both Indian and natural resources law. *United States v. Oregon* was soon consolidated with *Sohappy v. Smith* because the issues in both cases were so similar. And perhaps most of all, the tribes and their fishermen now had the prestige and resources of the United States of America behind them in this case where the plaintiffs were asking for unprecedented relief, including the central idea of a tribal share of the world-renowned Columbia River salmon runs.

It might seem that the tribes had come up against an unfortunate judge in this Oregon case—and, as well, in Western Washington, where *United States v. Washington* would soon be filed in Judge Boldt's court on essentially identical treaty law.

District Judge Robert Belloni, who was assigned to the consolidated *Sohappy v. Smith* and *United States v. Oregon*, was raised in small towns in Coos County on the southern Oregon coast. "I grew up with commercial fishermen—they're my best friends—and sportsfishermen." He kept contact with them all of his life. He belonged "to a little golf club in Newport, about a quarter of the members are commercial fishermen." Could he be biased, even if unconsciously, in favor of the commercial and sport fishermen who were so loudly and effectively urging the state to crack down on Indian fishing?

The answer was that the Oregon tribes, and the Washington tribes

Judge Robert C. Belloni.
Courtesy of the Oregon Historical Society.

a year later, had definitely not been assigned to judges who would be influenced by their personal relationships or general views about the law. They would be appearing before the kind of judges who are so admired for being at the very heart of American justice at its best—judges who, difficult though it sometimes would be, put aside all personal concerns and general professional views; look specifically and only at the particular cases in front of them; open-mindedly examine the facts of those cases; and work earnestly to determine the laws that govern those cases. That classic idealism and professionalism was never carried out more vividly than by Judges Robert Belloni and George Boldt. The moments that Judge Belloni and Judge Boldt were assigned to the cases turned out to be two of the most decisive moments in all of the wide-ranging historic litigation that would follow.

When Judge Robert Belloni sat down to decide *United States v. Oregon*, the existing decisions gave him little help. The main exception was the 1905 *United States v. Winans* case, written by Justice Joseph McKenna, which blocked attempts by local citizens to deny fishing rights to Yakama fishermen. *Winans*, still foundational to Indian and natural resources law, offered a powerful explanation of the reserved rights doctrine, explaining how tribes possessed fishing and water rights before the treaties and kept—or "reserved"—them in the treaties. To explain why tribes would have pressed so hard for their fishing rights at treaty time, Justice McKenna issued an arresting, much-quoted assessment of the centrality of Indian fishing to Native cultures, writing that salmon were "not much less necessary to the existence of the Indians than the atmosphere they breathed."

It is understandable that previous judges had given Judge Belloni only limited help because the tribes and United States raised overriding issues in wildlife and Indian law at a time when both fields had long lain dormant and were now right on the front edge of comprehensive reevaluation and reform. Modern fisheries law and environmental law were just beginning to evolve. Tribal governmental authority, the sovereignty announced by Chief Justice John Marshall in *Worcester v. Georgia*, had been largely ignored by the courts and Congress; when Judge Belloni ruled, the word *sovereignty* hadn't been used with respect to tribes by the Supreme Court in the twentieth century, but that was about to change.

Today we know that regulation of complex public fisheries regimes is evaluated in terms of fishing rights of individuals, group shares of fisheries, government regulation of harvests, and management of water and land habitat to assure sustainability. Pre-Belloni cases dealt mostly with rights of individuals under state law. As for a tribal share of the fish, no case had ever explored, either way, whether the courts should declare such a share and, if so, how large. On state regulation, the courts had addressed the issue only rarely and unhelpfully.

In July 1969, Justice Belloni responded with the opinion that continues to be celebrated by cutting through the existing confusion and presenting the case in the context of traditional Indian law and the demands of an emerging new era in public natural resource and wildlife law. He recognized that the treaties must be read to reflect the intent of the tribes and required strong protection of tribal off-reservation fishing rights. He ruled, which had never been done before, that tribes must have a specific share of the salmon resource. He did not put a number on it but called it a "fair share." As for the case as a whole, he knew that his decision would have to be employed in a real and complex world on real rivers, on specific runs in particular areas at designated times; he declared that the court would keep continuing jurisdiction to resolve continuing conflicts, a judicial remedy rarely used at the time. That continuing federal court jurisdiction in *United States v. Oregon* remains in force today.

Judge Belloni also clarified and defined, as had never been done before, the truth about the state's absolutist arguments to regulate tribal treaty fishing rights based on state police power and the right of the state to regulate for "conservation." He recognized that the state could regulate tribal fishing when "necessary" for "conservation," which had become a slogan to justify the state's century-long harassment of tribal fishers. He emphasized, however, that legal "necessity" and "conservation" had very different definitions than the state of Oregon claimed. Instead, this regulatory authority is narrow: the state *"may use its police power only to the extent necessary to prevent the exercise of that right in a manner that will imperil the continuing existence of the fish resource."*

Judge Belloni then thoroughly, and with great clarity, debunked the state's assertion that the current state policy was solely aimed at conservation of the fishery resource. Instead, he wrote, a key state objective was to allocate the resource to satisfy two powerful user groups—the commercial fishing industry and the sport fishing community. He explained in real-world terms how the Oregon system worked. Oregon has "divided the regulatory and promotional control between two agencies—one [the Game Commission] concerned with the protection and promotion of the fisheries for sportsmen and the other [the Fish Commission] concerned with protection and promotion of commercial fisheries." The regulations of these agencies, as well as their extensive propagation efforts, were designed "not just to preserve the fish but to perpetuate and enhance the supply for their respective user interests." This determination to meet the interests of these user groups, and promote them, without any concern about a tribal share, he held, amounted to discrimination against tribal treaty rights and violated overriding federal law.

This piercing observation, which explained in human terms the true basis of asserted state regulation, underlay his entire opinion. Each of Judge Belloni's holdings in *United States v. Oregon* was adopted by Judge Boldt, who added a definition of "fair share" to mean 50 percent. Judge Belloni's reasoning and rulings were also central to the Ninth Circuit, the US Supreme Court, and many decisions in other states.

There definitely was an aftermath. In 2002, I interviewed Federal District Court Judge Owen Panner in his chambers in Portland; Panner had been attorney for the Warm Springs Tribe for two decades before his appointment to the bench. Panner and Belloni had known each other back when Belloni tried *United States v. Oregon* and they became especially close after they both served on the federal district court for Oregon. I asked Judge Panner about the criticism that Judge Belloni received after rendering his opinion. The media reported extensive and angry public opposition to it. The commercial fishing interests fueled the fire. The sport fishermen were probably even more effective. The nonprofit Association of Northwest Steelheaders had articulate and hard-hitting representatives and wide influence with the media. Judge Panner was emotional about that onslaught on Indian rights in general. But he teared up, and took a long pause, when he explained how hard it was on his friend:

> [T]he case took a toll on Belloni. I know how much he worried about
> it. He lost a lot of friends, commercial fishermen down on the coast.
> He took a lot of abuse. That decision couldn't have happened without a
> federal judge who could put up with that kind of static and not have to
> worry about being reelected.

David Getches and John Echohawk having a discussion at the Native American Rights Fund offices in the 1970s. Both joined NARF as young men at its inception in 1970. Getches was NARF executive director and a lead attorney for tribes during the Boldt trial. He later was named dean of the University of Colorado Law School and became recognized nationally and internationally as a prominent scholar on Indigenous water and sovereign rights. Echohawk, Pawnee, also joined NARF in 1970 and has served as NARF executive director since 1977. Widely respected, he serves on many nonprofit Native American and conservation boards. Among his many awards, he was named one of the hundred most influential lawyers in the United States by the National Law Journal. *Courtesy of the Native American Rights Fund.*

8 The Buildup to the Boldt Decision

"Tribal fishermen were 'in dire need of a case to end all cases.'"

The 1969 Belloni Decision took Oregon off guard. No one expected it. The case had been closely watched up in Washington. While the Oregon decision did not apply there, Washington State officials and commercial and sport interests issued warnings that the Belloni Decision discriminated against non-Indian fishers and would be economically destructive, and the Oregon ruling should not be imported to Washington.

Indian country was elated by the Belloni Decision. At long last, after so much turmoil, Oregon Indians celebrated the full and official recognition of their treaty rights as they understood them. Washington tribes uneasily watched the Oregon case. When the ruling came down, tribal leaders quickly made it clear that they expected to achieve equal or perhaps greater legal protection of their treaty rights from federal courts in Washington.

Tribes who didn't have staff attorneys, knowing that Belloni-type litigation would likely go forward in Washington, began recruiting lawyers. The Quinault Indian Nation retained Michael Taylor and the new Evergreen Legal Services firm assigned John Sennhauser to represent the Muckleshoot, Sauk-Suiattle, Skokomish, and Stillaguamish Tribes. Hank Adams, learning of the founding of the Native American Rights Fund, the first national Indian legal services program for Indian litigation, requested help from NARF for the Nisqually and David Getches, NARF executive director, joined in the lawsuit. He also acted as general counsel with John Sennhauser, of Evergreen Legal Services, in representing the four tribes. All of these lawyers were young, with just a few years of experience but they all dove into it, immersing themselves in Indian law, which was not yet being taught in law schools, and worked long hours. Opportunities to represent minority people had been few and far between, but by the late 1960s, civil rights positions were beginning to open up in government offices and the new public interest firms. The young lawyers were thrilled at the idea of participating in what would become the Boldt Decision.

Al Ziontz, David Getches, and the other tribal lawyers knew that the best strategy was to replicate the *United States v. Oregon* procedural approach, with the United States bringing the suit as trustee for the tribes, who would then intervene in the case as full parties. The federal officials out in Washington were promising. George Dysart had shown that he would take action to protect Indian treaty rights. Stan Pitkin, the United States Attorney for Western Washington, had just been appointed, but the idealistic and energetic Pitkin had already taken on many controversial prosecutions, earning the moniker "one man against city hall." He was known to believe that the state may often have been overly aggressive on tribal fishing rights.

After the meeting with tribal leaders and lawyers, Pitkin and Dysart agreed that a litigation request should be made to the Justice Department office in Washington, DC, to allow Pitkin to file. The request, written by Dysart, went back East in the midsummer of 1970. It might seem that approval would be harder to get than the one for the Columbia River. Now it was the Richard M. Nixon, not the Lyndon B. Johnson, administration. Litigation requests often moved slowly.

By early September, however, everything came together. The state actually accelerated its crackdowns on tribal fishing. Stan Pitkin was convinced that tribal fishermen were "in dire need of a case to end all cases." Nixon was becoming one of the most effective presidents for Indians ever. Public sympathy for Indians was on the upswing. Nixon's White House staff included "loyal opposition" voices such as Brad Patterson, Len Garment, and Bobbie Greene Kilberg, all supporters of tribes and influential on tribal issues. On July 8, 1970, Nixon issued his much-heralded "Special Message on Indian Affairs" in which he

Judge Boldt swearing in Stan Pitkin as US Attorney for the
Western District of Washington in 1969, accompanied by Pitkin's
wife, Anne. *Courtesy of the Museum of History and Industry, Seattle,
Image no. 2000.107.141.36.02.*

addressed Congress and called for an end to termination and a new era
of "self-determination" for tribes. The next day, he hosted Hopi leaders
at the White House—in his message to Congress he had called for a
return of the Hopi Tribe's sacred Blue Lake—and the *New York Times*
carried a front-page photograph of the occasion.

Then, on September 9, 1970, as reported here in chapter 1, the military-style force of seventy-five state and Tacoma officers in riot helmets
and carrying guns, clubs, and tear gas carried out one of the most explo-

Stuart Pierson.
*Courtesy of Northwest
Indian Fisheries
Commission.*

Barbara Lane with, from right, Billy Frank Jr., Gilbert King George,
and Ed Johnstone at the premiere of the film *Back to the River* in 2013.
Courtesy of Northwest Indian Fisheries Commission.

sive and violent raids in memory on tribal fishers and families on tribal fishing grounds on the Puyallup River. The ugly confrontation went on national television. Stan Pitkin, in the crowd as an observer, was hit with tear gas. The White House had had enough. The litigation request was approved and, on September 18, 1970, nine days after the violence, Stan Pitkin filed the complaint in *United States v. Washington.*

Pitkin, who would not be trying the litigation himself, but knowing that this would likely be one of his biggest cases, placed a priority on bringing in a first-rate trial attorney. On February 17, 1971, Stuart Pierson, in his early thirties, arrived in Seattle. A law graduate of Duke University, Pierson had successfully handled several difficult civil rights cases in the South as a trial attorney in the Civil Rights Division of the Justice Department. As Special Assistant United States Attorney working full-time on *United States v. Washington,* his trial experience meshed perfectly with Dysart's deep knowledge of the Indian treaty issues.

The attorneys on the tribal side agreed that the first order of business was to retain an outstanding expert witness, a person of stature who would be able to process all historical and anthropological data and present it in an organized, definitive, and highly sophisticated fashion for the court, media, and general public. This by itself would be an expensive undertaking, difficult if not impossible for the impoverished tribes to absorb. It was an early affirmation of the value of coordination with the Justice Department, which would be assuming those expenses.

The lawyers conducted an extensive search among academics in the Pacific Northwest and the name that came up most often by far was Dr. Barbara Lane, a Canadian on the faculty at the University of Victoria in British Columbia. As it turned out, the decision to hire Dr. Lane enriched nearly every part of the sprawling litigation that was just getting started.

From the beginning, the assignment of the case to Judge George Boldt scared the Indian attorneys. This case would be tried by the court, not a jury, so the judge would be all-important.

Judge Boldt was a conservative jurist, a law-and-order judge who handed out tough sentences to criminals. Most notably, in December

1970, the Vietnam protesters called the "Seattle Seven" were charged with inciting to riot. When they disrupted the trial, Judge Boldt declared a mistrial—and then charged them with contempt of court and sentenced some of them to a full year in jail and others to six months, with no time off for the upcoming Christmas vacation. The Washington tribes wondered, "We are protesting government action—will he be fair with us?" To make matters worse, a local press report quoted Boldt as having said, before he was assigned to the case, "I don't want to hear about any more of these damned Indian fishing cases." It later developed that, while it was true that he said those words, he was probably expressing dissatisfaction with the intensity and number of state raids and arrests.

The concerns of tribal people and their attorneys gradually lessened as they saw Judge Boldt administer the case. That process began when he called an early meeting with attorneys soon after the filing of the complaint. At the meeting, Judge Boldt wanted to hear, first, from the federal and tribal attorneys about how they saw the case proceeding. Stuart Pierson and David Getches both emphasized one point: this litigation should produce a full record that would present all historical and anthropological information before the court.

To the delight of the plaintiffs, Judge Boldt agreed with this. Over his long career he had presided over many large cases and had even been a coauthor for a manual on complex federal litigation. He seemed to suggest that he understood how the Indian fishing issue had become a disruptive controversy in the Pacific Northwest and welcomed the opportunity to help bring order to it.

From beginning to end, the federal and tribal lawyers worked together closely, but differences did come up. Initially, Pierson and Dysart believed that Judge Boldt should reaffirm the Belloni Decision by adopting the tribal "fair and equitable share" of the fishery and recognizing the state's right to regulate Indian fishing when "reasonable and necessary." The initial federal opinion also included the belief that tribal fishing included only subsistence, not commercial, uses. Over the next three years, these positions would gradually evolve. For example, within a few months, Dr. Barbara Lane learned of the federal view on commercial fishing and was troubled by it. Her research showed that long ago tribes had developed mature and elaborate markets that were in place at treaty time. When George Dysart reviewed her findings, he agreed with her that tribal fishers, like white commercial fishers, should have the right to sell fish.

A year into this full-bore trial preparation, which was about as demanding as even large cases can get, everyone associated with *United States v. Washington* was taken aback by a completely unexpected surprise. One of President Nixon's top priorities was to bring down the surging inflation rate. His program included a Federal Pay Board that would oversee a number of measures including wage and price freezes. He reached out to Judge Boldt to chair the Pay Board and move to Washington, DC. Judge Boldt accepted and took leave from his cases on October 30, 1971. Judge William Goodwin, one of the judges in the Western District of Washington, was appointed to serve until Judge Boldt returned. Attorneys for the tribes had become much more comfortable with Judge Boldt and did not know what to think.

It didn't take long to see the difference between the two judges. The high-intensity pace of trial preparation had been driven by Judge Boldt, who pressed all attorneys to build a complete record of all current and historical circumstances on treaty fishing in northwestern Washington through expert witness testimony, depositions of all relevant people, and responses to written interrogatories. He held regular meetings with counsel to gauge and ensure progress. He had not set a trial date before he left, but he made it clear that he would not countenance any delays and that he expected all attorneys to be fully prepared.

Judge Goodwin was different. There is no indication that any attorneys, on either side, objected to any of his rulings, so that was not a problem. But the pace slowed. He did not throw himself into the case

the way Judge Boldt had. In late 1972, after about a year, Judge Boldt
finished up his work on the Pay Board and came back and resumed his
place with *United States v. Washington*.

The tribes were relieved, believing that they benefitted from a judge
who had a total command of all of the circumstances of this long and
complicated saga. Upon his return, Judge Boldt called for a meeting of
all attorneys in his chambers. The meeting went well—the judge was
energetic and seemed to be looking forward to working on the case. The
tribes welcomed him back. There was an omen: Stu Pierson noticed, on
the judge's desk, a copy of Vine Deloria's book *Custer Died for Your Sins*.

The state faced obstacles, not of its own making, in *United States v. Washington*. When *United States v. Oregon* was handed down in July 1969,
Washington state attorneys knew that a federal and tribal suit of similar
or greater magnitude would be filed against their state. The Belloni Decision had been handed down quickly with little expert testimony. The
Washington state attorneys learned that the tribes had already retained
noted anthropologist Dr. Barbara Lane, who specialized in tribes of the
Northwest, and could see that expert witnesses would also be essential
for the state's defense. That turned out to be a big problem for the state.

Administrative records of the day for the Department of Justice and
fisheries agencies lodged in the Washington State Archives show that
two anthropologists bluntly declined to take on the task. One of those
anthropologists, Professor Angelo Anastasio of Western Washington
State College (now University), offered several names but made it clear
that anthropologists have qualms about testifying against tribes: "[M]ost
anthropologists are reluctant to work without tribal approval because
they feel they would be closing sources of information that would be
available to them in connection with their research. . . . [A]n anthropologist tends to form bias strongly in favor of tribes . . . which they are
studying due to the nature of their work."

The state of Washington could never overcome this disadvantage, which plays out in various ways, sometimes unfairly, in litigation in many areas of law—medical malpractice litigation is an example—where expert testimony is at a premium. In *United States v. Washington*, Dr. Lane, fair-minded, deeply knowledgeable about Northwest tribes, and articulate, was a star witness. The state finally retained Dr. Carroll Riley, a distinguished anthropologist at Southern Illinois University, who had little knowledge on Northwest tribes and had done no research that touched on them at all in the past twenty years. So there was no semblance of a "battle of experts." In the end it probably made little difference. After all, Dr. Lane was acknowledged as the leading anthropologist on the culture and history of the Northwest tribes. Her exhaustive and careful reports were convincing to Judge Boldt and the appellate court judges who later ruled on the case.

In addition, the state's position was undermined by the upsurge of federal Indian law, which reshaped the field during the 1960s and 1970s. This revival was based on Supreme Court decisions by Chief Justice John Marshall, *Cherokee Nation v. Georgia* in 1831 and *Worcester v. Georgia* in 1832, which laid down the foundations of Indian law. *Cherokee Nation* ruled that the United States had a unique trust relationship with tribes that compelled the federal government to act as a trustee for tribes and individual Indians. *Worcester* held that that Indian tribes are independent sovereign governments protected from most state laws. But those dominant cases lay mostly dormant during the century-long suppression that followed the treaties. The tribes had little ability to go to court and they were so inactive that outside forces had little reason to go to court. There were other older cases, including the *United States v. Winans* decision of 1905 on salmon, that stood for strong tribal sovereignty and treaty rights.

The civil rights era, launched by *Brown v. Board of Education* in 1954, and imprinted on the national consciousness during the 1960s, provided the tribes an engaged judiciary, public support, and legal services attorneys who could articulate a new brand of Indian law to the courts, federal agencies, and Congress and even revive the foundational cases.

This change in American Indian law and policy had a highly specific and dramatic impact in the Northwest.

Because of this, *United States v. Washington* was a much stronger case for the tribes when it went to trial in late 1973 than when it was filed just three years earlier.

When President Richard Nixon entered office in 1969, radical termination policy was still in place, standing for the pullout of treaties and the federal government in favor of state rather than tribal authority across Indian country. With termination becoming more suspect on Capitol Hill and across the country, on July 8, 1970, President Nixon sent a transformative joint message on Indian Affairs to Congress, proposing a fundamental realignment of the federal, tribal, and state relationship. He flatly proclaimed termination to be "wrong" and "morally and legally unacceptable" and urged Congress to reject termination and replace it with sweeping "self-determination" legislation, which he described in detail. Self-determination quickly became the desired objective for federal Indian law and policy; Judge Boldt would soon adopt the phrase in his decision to recognize tribal governmental authority over salmon fishing.

In 1973, when the attorneys were immersed in preparation for trial in front of Judge Boldt in August, the US Supreme Court handed down three major Indian law decisions. *McClanahan v. Arizona State Tax Commission*, on March 27, decided whether states could assess income taxes against reservation Indians. The Supreme Court cast a broad net, clarifying the fundamental principles governing the critical issue of state regulations of tribes and individual Indians. The court began by finding that "the policy of leaving Indians free from state jurisdiction and control is deeply rooted in the Nation's history." The opinion, authored by Justice Thurgood Marshall, then turned to *Worcester v. Georgia* and recognized the sovereignty of tribes and its "tradition of Indian independence." The *McClanahan* Court unanimously struck down the Arizona tax. It was the first time that the Supreme Court had used the term *sovereignty* with respect to Indian tribes in the twentieth century.

On June 11, 1973, the Supreme Court issued its opinion in *Mattz v.*

Arnett. It had direct ramifications for *United States v. Washington*. In addition to Washington and Oregon, all the other western states were treating Pacific salmon fishing and hunting by Indians in the same manner as the two Northwest states. While grudgingly accepting tribal law on the reservations, these states viewed tribal off-reservation fishing and hunting in terms of combat, with the states determined to fight Indian fishers and bring them under state law.

Mattz came up in California. State agents arrested and confiscated the nets of Raymond Mattz, a Yurok tribal member and a lifelong salmon fisher on the lower twenty miles of the Klamath River, who was fishing at the traditional family fishing site near Brooks Riffle. California law prohibited the use of gill nets to harvest salmon, and Mattz was gill-net fishing. The Lower Klamath hardly felt like a reservation in the 1970s. Much of the land had been acquired by non-Indians and the white population far exceeded that of the Yurok. The tribe was mostly inactive at that time.

Raymond Mattz objected and, represented by Lee Sclar, an experienced litigation attorney from California Legal Services, with Harry Sachse of the US Justice Department joining as amicus curiae, took it to the Supreme Court. The question was whether the reservation and its protection of treaty fishing rights still existed.

From the earliest days, when the new arrivals came to the area where the Klamath River reached the Pacific Ocean, new settlers and developers wanted the Yurok tribal homeland on the Lower Klamath River. In addition to the large and reliable annual salmon runs, including ample king salmon, timber companies had no doubt about the commercial value of the gigantic old-growth Douglas fir, sequoia, and redwood forests. In 1855, President Franklin Pierce declared a two-mile-wide strip of land enveloping the twenty miles of the Lower Klamath to be a long and fairly narrow reservation. But that encompassed most of the Yurok's homeland.

The legal record in *Mattz* was extensive and confusing in the extreme. Two presidents, several Congresses, and uncountable numbers of administrative agencies and officials weighed in on the termination or survival of the Yurok Reservation. Certainly, the development interests acquired a large amount of Yurok land but most Indian reservations can and do have private inholdings with tribal sovereignty extending to the borders of the reservation.

Justice Harry Blackmun, speaking for a unanimous court, applied special rules of instruction on protection of tribal rights, stating that there must be a "clear indication of Congressional purpose to terminate," which did not exist at Yurok. The *Mattz* court held that the Yurok Reservation was still in place and that Raymond Mattz could continue fishing for salmon in his traditional ways at the family spot at Brooks Riffle.

As is common with judicial decisions, *Mattz* was not directly on point with *United States v. Washington* but, as it was well understood at the time, it showed that the current Supreme Court was protective of tribal rights in general and tribal treaty rights to fish and hunt in particular.

So, starting with the Belloni Decision in Oregon just four years earlier, the ground had steadily shifted in favor of the United States and the tribes.

Now Judge Boldt would rule on the many issues and dimensions of tribal and federal regulation of Native treaty fishing rights. He would be basing his decision on the most comprehensive record of history, facts, witness and expert testimony, and attorney briefings ever presented in any court on these matters.

9 The Trial

"Today the Indian fishing right is very much alive,
but it is in chains, and we ask this Court to emancipate
those fishing rights. . . ."

Judge Boldt set the trial, which would go for an unknown number of weeks, for August 27, 1973. Attorneys and clients knew this trial was coming even before the complaint was filed in December 1970 and had already put in considerable work before then. The demands of the case intensified after the filing and the action became frenetic during the year before trial. All parties were well prepared when the moment came.

Tribal people were fearful. To them this case was about a way of life that went back thousands of years—forever, really. Salmon fishing and all that it stood for mattered to them tremendously; it was at the heart of what it meant to be Indian. The state meant to take it away. Would Indians be treated fairly in this trial that could debilitate or bring an end to their way of life?

The commercial fishing industry also had a lot to lose. It was taking over 90 percent of the salmon, while the tribes were harvesting 3 to 6 percent, just as they had for decades. Going into the trial, industry leaders did not expect the tribes to be awarded 50 percent of the catch. That number had been floated, but the lawyers for the United States had asked for only a "fair share" as Judge Belloni had ruled. That was less threatening than 50 percent, but if Judge Boldt did find for the tribes, whatever amount he ordered was going to come mostly out of the current commercial harvest.

That didn't affect just "the industry." In addition to the corporations, individual commercial fishers would be directly hit. So would their families and the fishing communities, mostly on the coast, where the fishing boats were docked and went out for the harvesting.

The sport fishers took many fewer fish than the commercial fishers, but hundreds of thousands of people got salmon fishing licenses annually. In particular, hook-and-line fishers revered steelhead fishing, whether from shore, their own boats, or the crafts of sport fishing guides. To them, the tackle-busting, high-leaping steelhead was an icon, a magical being that gave special life to Northwest rivers. Increasing Indian fishing would mean reducing some non-Indian sport fishing.

United States v. Washington also was getting attention from the general public, not nearly as much as it would after the decision was handed down, but the trial was one of those court cases that people knew about and kept their eyes on. People variously worried about the impact on the economy, whether Indians would be treated fairly, and whether special tribal rights were justified or amounted to reverse discrimination.

Whatever specific views people had, at least the overall setting for the *United States v. Washington* trial exemplified the kind of dignified and solemn atmosphere that we expect when our most important challenging decisions are being addressed and resolved.

The trial was held in a classic federal courtroom in Tacoma's historic Court House Square Building at 1102 A Street, a handsome stone and brick structure, a full block long, constructed in 1910. Upon entering the courtroom by the door at the south end, a person is captured by the spaciousness. The judge's bench is about thirty-six feet away. East to west, the room is equally wide. The ceiling is two stories high. There are three tall wide windows on each side, with the Puyallup River flowing by on the east, where the jury box is located. For spectators, there are two parallel rows of seats that can accommodate about fifty visitors. The floor is marble tile and the furniture and wood surfaces are a warm light oak.

Judge Boldt, always wearing a bow tie with his robe, was a stickler for civil, courteous, and respectful proceedings. He made a point of not raising his voice and lawyers, witnesses, and others automatically did the same. Occasionally, given the size of the room, witnesses and even a few attorneys would be too soft-spoken for the court reporter, but a polite request from the judge to speak a bit louder would be successful. Judge Boldt expected lawyers to avoid personal conflicts with attorneys on the other side. A review of the transcripts shows that there was virtually no carping, quibbling, grousing, and such, much less broadsides, among attorneys during the three-week *United States v. Washington* trial. This would be a trial to the court, with no jury.

Judge Boldt gave all attorneys and witnesses a lot of leeway. He regularly admitted testimony, despite objections, noting that he would weigh the testimony for its value. "Every witness has a right to explain his answer if he chooses," he would say when permitting a witness to give an extensive, and sometimes rambling, answer. Very few exhibits offered by attorneys were rejected.

The first day of trial was dedicated to opening statements by the attorneys. They mostly kept their cards close to their chests. The trial would produce testimony, and cross-examination, from many witnesses and numerous exhibits as well. Also, the Supreme Court opinion in *Department of Game of Washington v. Puyallup Tribe* was expected to come down in the next several weeks on the reach of state regulation and the state's argument that it should have "reasonable and necessary" power to control off-reservation treaty fishing. The Supreme Court's opinion could possibly go into other matters. With so much uncertainty, the lawyers—especially those for the United States and the tribes—left the full expression of their positions to final briefing and argument after the trial.

As many as ten different attorneys for the plaintiffs participated at various points during the trial, but Stuart Pierson, David Getches, and

Al Ziontz were the most active. On the state side, Larry Coniff and Earl McGimpsey represented the Department of Game and the Department of Fisheries, respectively.

In his opening statement, Special Assistant US Attorney Stuart Pierson recommended, on the issue of a tribal share, that Judge Boldt adopt Judge Belloni's "fair share" allocation to tribal fishers. He argued that the state should be allowed to reevaluate tribal fishing only in the limited circumstances when it "threatens the preservation of the runs." Pierson believed that testimony would show that the tribes held a "deeply-felt duty . . . to preserve the resources for future generations" and that "this respect for the resource has been at least as effective in preserving it as the State's regulation of non-Indian fishery."

David Getches of the Native American Rights Fund spoke second and, like Pierson, asserted that tribal rights included commercial, as well as subsistence, uses. He offered a broad perspective:

> Not far from where this courthouse now stands, approximately one hundred twenty years ago, the first of several treaties negotiated by the United States of America with Indian tribes was signed. It was language within that treaty concerning fishing rights that this trial is all about. . . . One party comes with a right secured under the supreme law of the land reserved by them one hundred twenty years ago. The other party comes with rights that are really privileges, privileges that run from the state to the fishermen. . . .
>
> Today the Indian fishing right is very much alive, but it is in chains, and we ask this Court to emancipate those fishing rights, and in doing this we don't ask the Court for any radical judicial legislation.

Al Ziontz, a Seattle attorney, argued that the state should have no regulatory authority over the tribes:

> The rule of law we submit that the Court must conclude is that the treaty right is a federally reserved right which in no [ways] may be regulated, governed or in any way infringed upon by State authority.

If [the state's position] were to become the law, the settled law of the
land, it would be an exception, an anomaly to the entire body of treaty
law, which in no way yields to the State the right to regulate or infringe
on a federally established treaty right, which under our constitution is
dominant over State law.

Larry Coniff, assistant attorney general, representing the Department
of Game and the most combative of all of the lawyers, argued that the
tribes did not reserve any treaty rights at all:

If there is such evidence of such an exclusive right, then I would ask the
Court to carefully review the evidence in this record and ask the question,
first, then why after one hundred twenty years has it just been discovered?
Two, if it really exists at all.

The other state assistant attorney general was Earl McGimpsey, who
represented the Department of Fisheries. Under Washington law and
procedures the two agencies were separate and independent of each
other as of 1932. The two attorneys could and often did make conflicting
arguments. McGimpsey agreed with Coniff that tribal rights covered
only fish harvested for subsistence, not commercial uses. McGimpsey,
unlike Coniff, assumed that the treaties did confer off-reservation rights.
McGimpsey, and the Fisheries Department, did agree to a tribal "fair
share," as found by Judge Belloni. McGimpsey presented a detailed
model to identify a fair share that would mostly be determined by the
state. McGimpsey presented his approach, understandably, based on
his pride in the scientific expertise of the state, in a direct, fair-minded
manner that did not involve any attack on, or dismissal of, Indian fishing
rights.

The attorneys and Judge Boldt all saw the case as resting upon two time
frames: the time of the treaties and modern times. What promises were

made in the treaties? How could they be fulfilled a century and a half later with many more people and institutions and with an embattled Pacific salmon resource that everyone wants to see conserved?

Judge Boldt, with his long experience in hearing and deciding large and complex civil litigation cases, knew that a full and fair understanding of the stakes in *United States v. Washington* would require an overwhelming array of factual information. He knew that none of the dozens of existing tribal fishing rights cases had developed comprehensive factual records, either about the nineteenth-century treaty negotiations or the biological, economic, and social state of the modern fisheries.

At the end of the first day of trial, Judge Boldt spoke to this overriding concern about creating a truly full record.

> At the first pretrial conference with counsel in this litigation back in 1970, I expressed the hope that at long last the case had been brought in the federal court in which all parties having or claiming interest in fishing and fish rights, both Indians, and non-Indians had been brought. . . .
>
> . . . To the best of my capacity and experience, I will render a decision that when reviewed by the Circuit Court and the Supreme Court, as I expect and hope will be the case, that we may have provided all of the information that is obtainable on these questions. . . .
>
> It is an awesome task to undertake, but compensation, of course, for all of us, myself included, is to know that we have a tremendously interesting case. . . . You may be sure, to the utmost of my ability, I will give every moment of my time to this case to the exclusion of other matters until we have concluded this first phase of the trial of the issues in the case.

Dr. Barbara Lane, who would become the most important witness in the trial, grew up in British Columbia and obtained a BA and MA from the University of Michigan, then earned a PhD in anthropology from the University of Washington in 1953 with her doctoral dissertation entitled

"A Comparative and Analytic Study of Some Aspects of Northwest Coast Indian Religions." She had long been fascinated with the Indigenous peoples of Canada and America and began doing fieldwork with Northwest Indians in 1948. She taught at several schools, including the Universities of Washington, British Columbia, and Victoria, and Western Washington State University. Her real interest was field research with Indian people, which she much preferred to teaching. She loved research but found that, rather than publishing in academic journals, working directly for tribes in producing expert reports and testimony in court cases was much more fulfilling. Her husband, Robert B. Lane, was an anthropologist, and they collaborated on many projects, including *United States v. Washington*.

The Lanes' daughter Melia Lane-Kamahele, a cartographer and management assistant with the National Park Service in Hawaii, recalled the life of the Lane family: "The piece to understand is that the partnership with my father, over fifty-two or fifty-three years of marriage, was really critical in supporting what my mother was able to do. My dad taught for many years at the University of Victoria. He worked to support my mom.

"She worked eighteen to twenty hours a day. The house was a house, but also an office, a research center. My mom had staff, the whole thing. Jen, my mom's right-hand person, worked with her for twenty-five years.

"Work was the norm in our house. The dining room became the Boldt room. The living room was another tribe's files. As the kids moved out of the house, their rooms became even more file rooms. Eventually my parents bought another house across the street for files and the research collection to expand the workspace.

"People would disappear into the basement offices for hours and hours. David Getches, Billy Frank, came in and out all the time. Lots of people came through our house. I have very fond memories of David Getches. He was at the house a lot. I remember these tweed jackets he wore and he carried a beautiful leather briefcase."

Neil Vallance, an anthropologist and attorney in Victoria, BC, studied under Drs. Barbara Lane and Bob Lane at the University of Victoria and continued the relationship as an independent researcher for Canadian First Nations. He said, "I had a very close relationship with the Lanes after I got into grad school. They were some of the first people to set themselves up as independent contractors as consultants for First Nations issues. They made a deliberate decision to separate themselves from academia. And they devoted themselves full-time to working with Native Americans beginning in the '70s—that became their life from then on." Vallance continued:

> The Lanes' home had an incredible library. They had an enormous collection in their home. Barbara taught me everything I knew about serious research. She was a bulldog and left no stone unturned. I worked for her doing research on a First Nations claim and a Native American group in Hawaii. Barbara was very tough, determined, did matter-of-fact research. She was blunt and plainspoken, tough as nails. Judge Boldt respected her enormously; and there was a certain amount of affection as well. She was a superstar witness, no grandstanding. She took her duty very seriously. She was scrupulous, never one to overclaim or overstate things, no speculation. She didn't have the greatest sense of humor and took things very seriously. She was never one to do anything to be misconstrued, no errors by omission or anything like that. Her ethics were amazing.

For evidence at trial, Dr. Lane produced original research, the equivalent of a good-sized book, consisting of "anthropologist reports on the individual tribal plaintiffs in *United States v. Washington*." These reports examined the identity, lives, and fisheries of each tribe. She then wrote a forty-three-page summary report, "Political and Economic Aspects of Indian-White Culture Contact in Western Washington in the Mid-19th Century," in which Dr. Lane built upon the individual reports as well as broader anthropological research to understand the full picture of the negotiation of the treaties. The summary report also addressed how these traditional tribal lives and values have survived into modern times. These reports are all based on Dr. Lane's prodigious and unprecedented research campaign to locate virtually all written sources and, as well, her interviews with leading academics, many of whom offered their personal files and notes. This body of work by Dr. Lane for the Boldt Decision is considered today to be a leading source for academic research about Northwest tribal life, culture, and history. The research, along with Dr. Lane's testimony at trial, was plainly very influential to Judge Boldt, who apparently read the reports in their entirety.

Dr. Lane presented testimony on both of the two eras, treaty time and contemporary time, that lay at the heart of the litigation. The time of the treaties underlay the whole case, for any tribal rights established in the treaties, especially in this case, the tribal "right of taking fish . . . in common with the citizens of the territory," would be the supreme law of the land, binding upon the state. Treaties are bilateral agreements and, when terms are ambiguous or otherwise hard to understand, judges will look to the intent of the United States and the tribes. Because the treaties were written in English, the United States was the more powerful party, and because the United States is recognized as having a trust obligation to the tribes, the courts have developed rules of construction requiring that ambiguous treaty language must be liberally construed in favor of the tribes.

As for the contemporary time period, a great amount of testimony at trial would address current questions of modern concerns—federal, state, and tribal fisheries management and enforcement; health of the salmon runs; and sustainability of the runs. These issues were mostly beyond Dr. Lane's expertise. But the state, especially the Department of Game, raised a number of arguments that would be addressed by tribal witnesses and by Dr. Lane as well: Haven't the tribes abandoned their ancestral ways? Why did they wait 120 years to raise these asserted treaty rights? Can current Indian people be allowed to testify, based on so-called traditional oral history, on events that took place long before they were born, all the way back to treaty time? And how can these small, weak tribal governments be trusted to have any kind of active role whatsoever in modern and highly technical fisheries resource management?

In her written reports and under cross-examination, Dr. Lane presented, in plain and precise language, always supported by reliable sources, a broad range of observations about historic and contemporary Indian people and tribal societies relevant to the issues in *United States v. Washington*. Some of her opinions clashed with stereotypes of Indian societies, held by many non-Indian Americans, but rang true to anthropologists, historians, and non-Indians who had substantial knowledge of these tribes.

As to the importance of salmon at treaty time, Dr. Lane testified that, to the Northwest tribes, salmon was "the main food source, both in bulk and importance." Here is one example of "importance" she looked to:

> The first-salmon ceremony . . . was essentially a religious rite to ensure the continued return of the salmon to the area. The symbolic acts, attitudes of respect, and concern for the well-being of the salmon reflected a wider conception of the interdependence and relatedness of all living things which was a dominant feature of native world view.

She addressed commercial trade among Indian groups before the treaties as "very important, extensive, and covering a wide area." The trade was done "in order to acquire food stuffs, raw materials, and manufactured goods not available locally. The trade involved both basic necessities and luxuries of native life. The variation in local habitats is an important factor in understanding the native economy." By "extensive," she meant commercial trade:

> from the interior tribes across the mountains to tribes on the Sound, . . . and in the opposite direction, trade from the west coast of Vancouver Island through the intermediary of the Makah middlemen all the way down to the Columbia River to trading posts like Astoria . . .

Dr. Lane explained how the use of the Chinook Jargon made it difficult to construe the meaning of specific terms in the treaties:

Chinook jargon, a trade medium of limited vocabulary and simple grammar, is inadequate to express precisely the legal language embodied in the treaties. Its inadequacy was commented upon by both Indians and non-Indian witnesses to the treaty negotiations.

On the treaty term providing for the tribal off-reservation fishing right to "fish in common with the citizens of the Territory," Dr. Lane was certain that both sides to the treaty intended that "in common with" was meant to "secure to the Indians what they already had."

The state attorneys attempted to show that, both historically and contemporaneously, Northwest Indians had little or no effective governance. On several occasions, the state attorneys took positions that diminished or denigrated the nature of tribes in the past and present. On cross-examination of Dr. Lane, for example, attorney Coniff asked this question:

The defendants contend that, at the time of the signing of the treaties the Indians did not have any method for enforcing any rules regarding their conduct other than unstructural familial obligations.

I wonder if you could give us your opinions on whether there existed other such controls, and how they might work?

Dr. Lane testified:

Yes, there were certainly other social controls. The Indian societies in the case area were well ordered societies, which were not in any state of anarchy at the time the whites came into the area. . . . They had the kinds of social controls that anthropologists are quite familiar with, but which are sometimes a little difficult to explain to people who are used to court systems and police systems and formalized chieftainships, et cetera. This was not a society that had any of these attributes, but there were very effective means of social control. Some of them were supernatural and some of them natural, using these arbitrary categories in the way that I think are generally understood by people.

Ridicule and ostracism or holding someone up to public opprobrium,

shame were all very effective, and widely used means of keeping people
in line . . . [T]his I might add is one of the facets of C'Salish culture which
persists today and I have been at public gatherings in which a wrongdoer
was held up to public lecture in front of several hundred assembled guests
at a long house.

The state attorneys attempted to show that, at treaty time, Indians
were experiencing "rapid cultural decline." Since then, the attorneys
attempted to show, tribes had undergone an "acculturation" that meant
that the importance of salmon to modern Northwest Indians had greatly
diminished. Regarding the treaty era, Dr. Lane replied:

> I don't believe that the culture was rapidly declining [at treaty time],
> they were not declining into nothing, they were taking on aspects of the
> introduced culture. . . . At treaty times, I think the documentary evidence
> is abundant that Indian people were doing things like taking on the
> wearing of European clothes, they were using some introduced European
> foods, like bread, flour, coffee, tea, sugar, molasses, items of this sort.
>
> Similarly, the whites in this territory were eating salmon, Pacific
> salmon, which they had never eaten before. They were starting to wear
> Indian moccasins because they didn't have facilities for making shoes, no
> shoe factories. They tried to make shoes and it was a pretty sorry job. It
> was easier to take the Indian items of dress.
>
> They were using Indian mats to keep the wind out of the chinks in their
> log cabins, they were lining walls with mats in the fashion of the Indians
> in their cedar slab houses. They were lighting their homes with fish oil
> lamps from oil gotten from the Indians. They were taking on a number
> of items of Indian culture, just as the Indians were taking on a number
> of items of white culture. . . . So both cultures were borrowing both ways
> from one another.

Regarding the contemporary place of fishing in Indian life as compared with treaty time, Dr. Lane believed this:

For many Indians, fish continue to provide a vital component in their diet. For others, fish is not a necessary dietary item although it remains an important food in a symbolic sense. ... Few habits of human beings are stronger than dietary habits and their persistence is usually a matter of emotional preference rather than nutritional need. For many Indians, salmon remains important in an economic, nutritional, and symbolic sense.

Historically and to the present day, taking, preparing, eating and trading fish have been important functions in Indian communities. As such, fishing provides a basis for cultural identity and a cohesive force in Indian society.

During his lengthy cross-examination, Coniff, one of the state's attorneys, undoubtedly realizing that the state's case might well be fatally wounded if Dr. Lane's testimony were broadly accepted, asked if her testimony were "historical fiction" or "overformalized":

Q: You don't feel that you yourself have any problem in terms of overformalizing from the data that you have had available to you?

A: Well, this is always a problem. I have tried to be overcautious, since I am extremely sensitive to the problem.

Q: So your answer is that you do not believe that you have overformalized any conclusions that you have reached?

A: No, I do not think so, or I would not have done it.

On cross-examination, the state attorneys made little or no headway in correcting Dr. Lane's testimony or showing errors in it. She put forward her conclusions in a careful, low-key way. She never exaggerated; if a finding was based on a thin or conflicting historical record, she said so. She was ever ready to bring into court a specific source from her trove of research documents.

The defendants' expert witness, Dr. Carroll Riley, was an anthropologist on the faculty at Southern Illinois University Carbondale. Dr. Riley was a respected academic. Most of his work was on anthropology and archaeology in the American Southwest. He had never specialized on Northwest tribes and had not done any fieldwork with Northwest tribes since the 1950s. He was asked about his view on whether those tribes' "desire to fish as they did traditionally evidenced a continuation of their culture and way of life"; he responded with this:

> Since I have not worked with the Indian population since the 1950s, and since I know very little except what I read in the newspapers, of subsequent movements, of political movements by Indians in this area, I don't think I would be competent to answer that.

Judge Boldt was losing patience with Dr. Riley, who was notably resistant and defensive during much of the cross-examination. The judge finally gave a stern warning, the tenor of which was not directed toward any other witness or attorney during the entire trial:

> I don't know why you hesitate to answer simple questions of this kind, Doctor. It is disturbing me. . . . If you persist in appearing to dodge questions, answer to questions of this kind, it will bear heavily on my appraisal of your credibility, and I might as well say so right at this moment.

The tribal attorneys called twenty-nine witnesses from the eleven tribal plaintiffs to testify. Mostly tribal elders, they told stories, sometimes in their own languages, about their people, cultural values, salmon, the treaties, and state regulation. There seems to be general agreement among court observers that Judge Boldt was moved, and often rapt, during much of Native peoples' testimony.

One example was Lena Hillaire, Puyallup-Skagit, eighty-three years

old at the time of the trial. Like several of the tribal witnesses, she wore
traditional regalia and moccasins.

> [T]he first agents was really mean to our Indian people. They used whips
> on them, because they couldn't understand Christian work.
> They start licking them, slapping the old Indians in the face. Oh, they
> were mean, and Woods, he was the first superintendent. . . .
>
> Our leaders was really bad. If we had got good government men we
> would never have this trouble right now. That is true, but our people were
> not—they took us for animals, and it was not right.
>
> Now, we have a hard life, my people have a hard life. I seen them
> whipped, and I would jump up and cry. I felt so bad, you know, the way
> they would treat them, and then Dr. Woods at Neah Bay, he put on
> harness here, and he would go and lash the Indians like that. . . .

Then I got a petition, because I had a lot of white people help me, and we got him out of there, and we got an Indian, Mr. Dodds to take over.

On cross-examination of Indian witnesses, the defendant attorneys regularly addressed Indian culture in past and present times. This included a focus on whether they have become "Americanized" or "acculturated" with the result that the tribes' main interest in establishing treaty rights was economic. Attorney Coniff of the Game Department was especially adamant on the loss of culture. At trial, Mr. Coniff, in questioning Forrest Kinley, Lummi, suggested that Mr. Kinley believed that the tribes' objective in the treaty rights litigation was establishing an economic goal. Mr. Kinley responded:

I don't think that this is the prime interest. I think that you take a look at your own track record towards Indian people, that throughout the history of the United States, that the United States government and the non-Indian has tried to build a glove to put us into, that they have tried to make farmers out of us, they have tried to make executives out of us, and various other things, and they have tried to fit us into them, and we haven't been able to fit into any of those programs because there is a cultural value difference between what you value and what I value as an Indian, and I think that you can see the change that is being done now, that our people have lived with nature, and now you take this ecology and everything else, that they finally realized that we did have something, and you have turned around and you are trying to follow some of the ideas that we tried to present to you years ago.

So I think that not only [do] we need an economic base [and also] the type of work that we do that we enjoy and our people enjoy hunting and fishing, and they respect, you know, nature itself.

Regularly, as with Mr. Kinley, Indian witnesses seemed comfortable with the historical progression that pretreaty Indian culture had been changed, but not lost, over time. Joseph Andrews, Skokomish, put it this way:

Lummi Tribal Chairman Forrest "Dutch" Kinley (with hands in his pockets) at the
Lummi salmon hatchery. Kinley was a major tribal leader among the Northwest tribes
during the early years of the fishing rights movement. Among other things, he served as
chair of the charter committee that created the Northwest Indian Fisheries Commission
in 1974. *Photograph courtesy of the Kinley family.*

Q: Now, what differences do you see in the younger generation?

A: Well, they are getting educated and they seem to be going out and
finding different methods of securing a living.

Q: Would you say that the younger members are more Americanized
than your generation?

A: Well, they can't lose their identity as an Indian, but their ways are
changing, yes.

Q: And do you notice any difference in younger tribal fishermen than
you do in the older tribal fishermen?

A: No.

Many Indian witnesses referred to the treaties and promises made at those negotiations. Lena Smith, Stillaguamish, talked about information she received from her grandfather, who participated in the treaty negotiations: "Well, once when my grandfather was picked up for fishing and put in jail, we went to the jailhouse, and they were talking about the treaty. Isaac Stevens said to our chiefs that if there was a river or a creek where the Indians fished before, they could fish there after the treaty." Hilary Irving, a Makah Tribal Councilmember, objected to state regulation of his tribe's treaty fishing right "for the simple reason your treaty says that we can fish as long as the tide went out and came in."

Billy Frank Jr., who testified for several hours, went into detail on current Indian culture, discussing ceremonial meals, songs, and dances. Frank also addressed state regulatory practices. He had suffered multiple arrests since the 1940s, often including seizures of his catches, canoes, and nets. He brightened the courtroom during cross-examination by offering his testy reference to state regulation of Frank's favorite winter chum salmon runs on the Nisqually River:

Q: And is it my understanding that off-reservation fishing at the time that the chum are running is prohibited by the State?
A: Well, I have been in jail enough times to say it probably is.

Late in the trial, when most of the testimony had been heard, the shape of the case had become clear. Definitive testimony came from Dr. Lane and it covered a large part of the facts. The other most important body of information came from the twenty-nine tribal witnesses. It was a surprisingly high number, but the plaintiff attorneys believed that the testimony, which was not coached, would be broadly accepted as authentic and compelling. That proved to be true. Undeniably, some cultural ideas and practices had been changed, even lost, since the treaties. But salmon and the elaborate relationship between these Indian people and salmon remained vivid, alive, and lastingly important.

The tribal attorneys also decided to call Indian witnesses who would address an additional notion: the ambition of tribes to regulate their own members and to engage in salmon management. This matter was steadily becoming of greater importance to the attorneys, clients, and Judge Boldt, ever since the case had been filed and especially during this trial.

Suppose Judge Boldt were to rule that the treaties reserved to the tribes a "fair share" of the fish, whether 50 percent or some other formulation. By the 1970s, wildlife policy, certainly including salmon, was based on resource management by governments. To date, all management of salmon in the state of Washington was done by two governments, primarily the state and also the United States. Tribes had always been acknowledged as sovereign governments for the purposes of negotiating treaties and exercising jurisdiction over their own members (and in some circumstances over non-Indians as well).

To be sure, actual tribal governmental authority had been weakened for over a century by federal assimilation policies and aggressive regulatory actions. Still, as of September 1973, tribal sovereignty remained in place as a matter of federal law.

Just suppose Judge Boldt were to find that the tribes did have the right to harvest a large part of the salmon runs. Suppose he knew that he should decide on how this new arrangement would be managed. At the moment, two governmental managers were doing all of that work. Should a third governmental salmon resource manager be recognized?

The tribal attorneys, who worked ever more closely together as the case neared a decision by Judge Boldt, strategized about this. They knew that the law could support tribal management as a legal matter but it had to be done right. Could tribes effectively take on these management duties? There was support, they reasoned—Dr. Lane's research showed this. Tribes had always managed salmon through unwritten but widely understood conservation polices for thousands of years. Some modern tribes had adopted formal salmon management policies and systems, with written regulations and management departments.

When it came time to identify witnesses, the attorneys selected four representatives of the Quinault Indian Nation for their last witnesses. The idea would be to show, through the Quinault example, how fully successful tribes can be as natural resource managers. The Yakama Tribe had a comparable regime. The other plaintiff tribes had less-developed systems, but the plaintiff attorneys contended that the Quinault experience showed what tribes can accomplish in terms of managing salmon resources, including regulation of their own tribal members.

The Quinault witnesses presented the tribe's salmon regulation experience in chronological order.

Horton Capoeman, who was sixty-eight years old, had lived on the Quinault Reservation his whole life, except for military service in the Army. He spoke Quinault as well as English. A fisherman since he was eighteen, he was a member of the Quinault government body, the tribal Business Committee, for thirty years and was a tribal judge for ten years in the 1940s and '50s. His grandfather told him that the chiefs regulated tribal fishing. Family members "had their supply of fish, then traps were lifted, and the fish were allowed to go [up the river]."

In 1925, the Quinault Business Committee had adopted written regulations. Patrolmen were hired to enforce the regulations. The committee closed several rivers to fishing—the Raft, the Moclips, and several tributaries. The committee allowed non-Indians to fish under tribal permits on the Quinault River and scenic Lake Quinault in the Olympic range. On two occasions, the committee had to close Lake Quinault to fishing due to poaching and other violations by non-Indians and also some Indians. "It had to be done in order to bring them back to their senses."

Under the 1925 regulations, the Business Committee also banned two harvesting methods—drift nets and monofilament nets—that threatened the sustainability of the salmon runs. Both of those nets, Mr. Capoeman explained, have the potential to "wipe out a whole school of fish, wipe out the river clean with them."

For violations of the regulations, the net would be removed for one week; for the second offense, it would be three months; and for the fourth offense, it would be removed for the full season. "That would have been quite a loss to a fisherman. So, very few of them violated it," but when a patrolman brought a report to the committee, "we took action on it." When Mr. Capoeman was asked if he had ever, as a judge, decided to have a net taken out, he replied, "Well, absolutely." At the end of his testimony, Mr. Capoeman was asked if he thought the Quinault Indian Nation could regulate their own members off-reservation. He answered, "I believe they could."

The next witnesses held the two highest Quinault governmental offices on these issues: Joe DeLaCruz, Quinault tribal chairman, and Guy McMinds, director of the Quinault Resource Development Project.

Joe DeLaCruz, born in 1937, grew up on the reservation, fishing with his grandfather. After high school he enlisted in the Army and studied at the University of Portland for several years. He worked for the federal government in Portland until 1967, when tribal leaders recruited him as the tribal business manager. By the time of the Boldt trial, he was in his third year as tribal chairman, widely respected on the reservation and nationally, and was described by the *Seattle Times* as a "giant cedar of a man." He later served for twenty additional years as chairman until his death in 2000 and hold important regional and national offices, including president of the National Tribal Chairmen's Association and president of the National Congress of American Indians.

Guy McMinds, a generation younger, was able to attend college in the field that he most cherished: fisheries science. After serving in the Army, he obtained a bachelor of science degree at the University of Washington in 1966. He was considered a star student, and a professor recommended him for good jobs. During school and afterward, he worked for the federal Bureau of Sport Fisheries and Wildlife and for the

Washington Department of Fisheries as a fisheries scientist. He soon got to work specifically on Quinault matters. In time, he joined the natural resources staff at Quinault.

In the late 1960s, then-Tribal Chairman Jim "Jug" Jackson, Joe DeLa-Cruz, and Guy McMinds, consulting with a University of Washington professor, began work on an expanded, comprehensive management system to bring all tribal natural resources, including fisheries, timber, and razor clams, under one ecological unit. By the time of the Boldt trial, the tribal fisheries staff had five professionals with degrees in fish biology, four trained fisheries technicians, and eight full-time tribal member assistants. The tribe continued to consult with university professors. In addition to fisheries management, the tribe operated the Quinault National Fish Hatchery. The total annual fisheries budget was about $2 million with funding from the tribe, about 25 percent; federal, about 50 percent; and private foundations, about 25 percent.

As for enforcement, the tribe had four full-time patrolmen and twelve people sworn in as auxiliary police. The tribal court had two full-time judges. The court heard violations of the tribal code by Indians and non-Indians as well.

The tribe, however, faced a major barrier to good fisheries management dating back to the late 1800s. The 200,000-acre Quinault Reservation is magnificent by any standard. It has twenty-six miles of ocean coastline. The Quinault River heads in the Olympic Mountains and surges down the central part of the reservation. Most of the reservation is lush rain forest, mostly western red cedar, giant trees rising to canopies two to three hundred feet high. The forests, with their rich, spongy soils, provide for perfect watershed conditions for the Quinault River. These forests also contain some of the most valuable commercial timber in the world.

A generation after the treaty, the 1887 General Allotment Act opened the Quinault Reservation to settlement, transferring large blocks of tribal land to tribal members, held in trust by the Office (now Bureau) of Indian Affairs. In a classic case of captured agencies, the timber companies went straight to the BIA to harvest the timber on the allotments.

Joe DeLaCruz at a Quinault picnic in 1976. *Courtesy of Larry Workman, Quinault Indian Nation.*

Guy McMinds. *Courtesy of Larry Workman, Quinault Indian Nation.*

The BIA left the logging—almost all clear-cutting—to the timber companies. The damage was ruinous to the watershed. In many places, there were open lands—former forests, now slash: downed timber, limbs, and woody debris—as far as the eye could see. The river and tributaries paid a high price, and the salmon runs declined from the soil erosion and stream blockages. David Martin, who later served on the Business Committee, described it this way: "When I came back after forestry school, looking at it from a forester's perspective, the devastation was horrendous. How can you articulate it without being there, being hit with it? You could never see ground for acres and acres. There were huge piles of slash—hemlock, spruce, cedar. You could walk on top of it for miles, practically, in some areas."

As DeLaCruz explained at trial, the tribes went to the BIA and to court many times to stop the logging. In 1955, tribal leaders sought relief from Congress, but to no avail. The tribes had four suits pending at the time of the Boldt trial.

The final Quinault (and tribal) witness was Brian Allee, about to receive, later in the year, his PhD in fisheries from the University of Washington. He had worked on a number of fisheries projects during his university career and spent the past two years as a fisheries scientist for the Quinault. It was clear from his testimony that he believed in both doing book research and getting out on the ground to examine specific watershed conditions.

One of the key defense arguments was that tribes were not, at the time of the trial, and could not become, capable salmon managers. Quinault attorney Michael Wagner asked Allee to address an opinion of state witness J. E. Lasater, a biologist and one of two assistant directors of fisheries at the state fisheries department. Lasater had testified that the Quinault River runs had declined due to overfishing and the tribe's inability to manage the fishery. He based his conclusion on catch statistics between 1935 and 1973.

Allee believed that more and better data was available. He was able to take catch numbers back to 1910. More importantly, Allee looked beyond numbers to specific conditions on the upper Quinault River. In addition to an academic report by F. A. Davidson and J. T. Barnaby, the federal fish hatchery kept records on Quinault River conditions from 1914 to 1946. Those reports indicated that "the Quinault River around the turn of the century was confined to one channel . . . heavily timbered on either side. . . . Subsequent to the logging activity in the upper Quinault, this river then meandered." Pointing in court to a map, Allee showed how the logging affected the river. "You can see the sort of meander and the S-shaped patterns that it has adopted." This is called "braiding" of a stream. Allee added: "This sort of picture illustrates the instability of the Upper Quinault, the fact that the channel can shift in a sort of fluctuating situation based on the flow. What I would like to show here is that in a given year with high rainfall—by the way, this is an area that has 122 inches of rain on an annual basis . . . one of the highest in the States. . . . So it is a rather violent situation. The [federal] hatchery superintendent related in 1922 that during the last twenty years, the Upper Quinault River in the spawning area of the sockeye salmon has been devastated, absolutely devastated [by the BIA logging regime]."

At the end of Allee's testimony he was asked, biologically speaking, whether the Quinault tribe could manage a fishery either on or off the reservation. Allee had worked for the tribe full-time for two years and had lived on the reservation during that time. He worked closely with Indian people and the Business Committee. He replied, "Well, I think it's very possible for the Quinaults to manage their resource based on the sort of programs that we are developing on the reservation. I don't think it's at all preposterous that Indian people could do that sort of thing, to hire technical assistants, to have cooperation from the university college of fisheries, and Fisheries Research Institute, to attempt to understand, with a fair degree of sophistication and precision, the total run."

At the end of the day, Judge Boldt made a comment of a kind he rarely offered: "Thank you very much, Mr. Allee. I'm glad to have had the opportunity to have heard this portion of your testimony. It will give me a better basis for judging you, having heard you in person."

With all of the evidence submitted by September 18, the only step left in the trial was closing arguments. Judge Boldt had set them for December 10 both to give the attorneys time to file their final briefs, and, hopefully, to receive a decision from the US Supreme Court in *Department of Game of Washington v. Puyallup Tribe* (*Puyallup II*), dealing with state jurisdiction over off-reservation treaty fishing rights, and much-awaited out in the Pacific Northwest. The case involved the Washington Supreme Court's adoption and use of a standard, originally proposed by the Department of Game, for regulation of off-reservation treaty fishing so the state could regulate when "reasonable and necessary for conservation." This long-standing *Puyallup* litigation over the extent of state jurisdiction over tribal treaty fishing started in Washington state courts in 1963 and eventually went up to the US Supreme Courts three times.

In *Puyallup Tribe v. Department of Game of Washington* (*Puyallup I*), decided in 1968, Justice William O. Douglas wrote a short, shallow, and confusing opinion about the state's "reasonable and necessary" standard for state jurisdiction. The *Puyallup I* opinion suggested, but did not decide, that such a standard might apply to treaty fishing. The US Supreme Court remanded the case back to the Washington Supreme Court for a detailed explanation of the meaning of the state's standard.

At first glance, the words "reasonable and necessary for conservation" might seem to be harmless, technical, and bureaucratic language. That was not the case here. The state administrators were on a crusade to bring tribal fishing under its control. They believed—some out of professional conviction, some out of political or racial inclinations—that "conservation" was a top-rung value and that only state wildlife officials, not the tribes, were best equipped to uphold and protect the runs. The state officials knew, and so did all of the lawyers, that "reasonable and necessary" were terms designed to establish broad state administrative authority, code words for directing courts to uphold agency decisions.

"Conservation," standing alone, is a very broad term. State officials could construe it to mean almost anything that would negatively affect salmon. But these are federal treaty rights and such broad state authority over them was incongruous at best.

The possibility of "reasonable and necessary for conservation," as put forth in *Puyallup I*, stuck in the craw of the tribal lawyers. They wanted to undo it in *United States v. Washington* if they could. The well-respected Professor Ralph Johnson of the University of Washington wrote a scathing law review article in 1972 criticizing the "reasonable and necessary" test. In his article, Professor Johnson wrote this:

> No valid basis for the existence of such state power can be found. The Constitution of the United States provides that treaties are the "supreme law of the land." Because agreements with the Indians are treaties, the Indians are not subject to state regulation unless the treaty so provides or unless Congress so legislates.

Johnson's article was read widely by people connected to the Boldt case, and as well by the general public, which became ever more aware of the case as the trial date loomed. The demonstrations and fish-ins continued.

The high court did release its much-awaited opinion in *Puyallup II* on November 19, 1973, after all the evidence in *United States v. Washington* had been submitted but before closing arguments. Without doubt, *Puyallup II* favored the tribes. State Game Department regulations, approved by the Washington Supreme Court, prohibited net fishing for steelhead by tribal fishers on the Puyallup River but allowed hook-and-line fishing by non-Indians on the Puyallup. The US Supreme Court vacated because the regulations were not "conservation" but, rather, "discrimination." Justice Douglas authored the *Puyallup II* opinion but did not apply the "reasonable and necessary" test, which effectively removed the inappropriate language in *Puyallup I* from US Supreme Court jurisprudence. *Puyallup II* also found that the state's right to regulate treaty fishing for "conservation" is very narrow, existing only to protect against species eradication.

The state attorneys just shook their heads. This was the fifth significant decision against them since *United States v. Washington* was filed three years earlier, along with federal protribal policy and legislation such as "self-determination." It's rare in the extreme to have law evolve so quickly and pointedly. Lawyers on both sides were cautious in front of Judge Boldt about their use of *Puyallup II*. It was so new. It had an enigmatic quality about it. But it was there.

The briefs and positions at oral argument were well prepared and businesslike.

The state forcibly argued that 50 percent, or any high percentage, of the fishery should not go to the tribes. Nothing like that had been discussed at the treaty negotiations. Isaac Stevens and his team—and leaders back in Washington, DC—would never have agreed to such a thing. To them, the future in the Northwest would be American and the treaties were being negotiated primarily to protect present and future American settlers. The tribes, the state attorneys argued, knew that.

The state continued to emphasize broad policy power over wildlife. It had the scientific and administrative expertise; the tribes were not equipped to take on such resources management responsibilities. Whatever share of the resource would be awarded to the tribes, the state must make the difficult resource management decisions, and the agencies would protect the fish and be fair with the tribes.

The tribes were all together on the 50 percent share. Dr. Lane did not believe that the tribal negotiators were thinking in exactly those percentage terms; they did, though, want to be able to fish, hunt, and gather in the way they had at treaty time.

In their final briefs and at closing arguments, the tribal lawyers gave a more pronounced emphasis on tribal governance and sovereignty. The tribes were governments and should be recognized as such in the overall management regime that would be employed in the future.

Judge Boldt ended the proceedings with these words:

> I hope that out of all this effort and expense that we will be able to come
> up with something that will at least be a beginning in resolving once and
> for all these grievous problems that have plagued the people of this area
> for many, many years. Whether it turns out so, of course, time will tell.
>
> At least we will have made a contribution in one way: there will be
> a source of material upon which others may base studies, rulings, or
> whatever, such as has never been assembled before on this particular
> subject matter.

Judge George Hugo Boldt. *From the News Tribune.* © 1974 McClatchy.
All rights reserved. Used under license.

10 The Boldt Decision

"That judge, he made a decision, he interpreted the treaty, and he gave us a tool to help save the salmon."

Judicial opinions are hardly an art form. A formal opinion, by a single judge or a multijudge appeals panel, is written to explain specific, and often technical and complex, court cases. The primary audiences are the parties to the case and future judges, attorneys, and legal scholars interested in points of law. No judge likes to be overruled and so lower-court judges always have future reviewing courts in mind. Judges take the opinions seriously. Some work hard, not just to explain why the opinion is the right legal result, but also to articulate the court's reasoning in a well-organized and clear way, free of unnecessary legalese. Still, these are not page-turners.

In major public cases, while the general populace will not be reading the opinion, the judges know that the media, interest groups, and teachers will translate and boil down the opinion for public consumption and understanding, so judges may occasionally employ catchy or memorable language. Just over a century ago, Justice Oliver Wendell Holmes wrote his famous explanation of the limits on speech: "the most stringent protection of free speech would not protect a man in falsely shouting fire in a theatre and causing a panic." More recently, Justice Potter Stewart said he could not define pornography but "I know it when I see it." There have been examples of this in Indian law. Justice Hugo Black wrote, in a case involving an arguable treaty abrogation, that "great nations, like great men, should keep their word." In *United States v. Winans* in 1905, the first Supreme Court case on Pacific Northwest treaty fishing rights, Justice

Joseph McKenna explained that salmon "were not much less necessary to the existence of the Indians than the atmosphere they breathed."

George Hugo Boldt, such a classic, careful, traditional judge, surely never considered any such dramatic language. This was the most important case of his career, but he would put it down plain word by plain word, sentence by sentence, paragraph by paragraph.

Yet, as a man who understood complex federal civil litigation as well as anyone in the country, he was bold and courageous in deploying an array of judicial tools and prerogatives in a manner rarely seen. The terrain was so complex. So many rivers, bays, and ocean fishing sites. So many commercial fishers, sport fishers, tribes, and state and federal agencies. So many salmon runs in decline. Judge Boldt both decided the legal rights of the parties and also designed an elaborate system for the management of those rights long after his decision of February 12, 1974. Judge Boldt, too, would need to have an understanding of the northwestern Washington communities as well. Even more, he would have to understand the future as well as the past. What would it take to set up a system that would endure over time? For a judge in major public complex federal litigation, that is often the question.

In the introductory pages of his opinion, Judge Boldt put forth the essence of his ambitious vision for addressing the case: that the bitter struggle over treaty fishing rights had gone on for too long; that it afflicted society in the Pacific Northwest; that opportunities for settlement and healing, of which this was one, should be seized; and that a fundamental need was to create an expansive factual record to work from in staking out a fair, reasonable, and collaborative program to address the future. With all that in mind, he wrote this:

> For more than three years, at the expenditure by many people of great time, effort and expense, plaintiffs and defendants have conducted

exhaustive research in anthropology, biology, fishery management and other fields of expertise, and also have made extreme efforts to find and present by witnesses and exhibits as much information as possible that pertains directly or indirectly to each issue in the case. . . .

It is believed considerable historic and scientific information never before presented in a case involving treaty rights is now recorded and may prove of value in later proceedings in this case and possibly in others. . . .

The ultimate objective of this decision is to determine every issue of fact and law presented and, at long last, thereby finally settle, either in this decision or on appeal thereof, as many as possible of the divisive problems of treaty right fishing which for so long have plagued all of the citizens of this area, and still do.

Those words displayed his belief in the importance of this conflict. The package that was his opinion gave other indications as well. The document, which was 102 pages long, began with a detailed table of contents and set forth a complete table of all court cases cited, two devices rarely seen in court decisions. The ruling was dated February 12, President Lincoln's birthday. Judge Boldt did that intentionally, not to draw attention to himself, but to honor the magnitude of the legal and societal issues.

Tribal Culture

Overall, the Boldt Decision dedicated the most space to tribal culture, past and present. Those matters were unfamiliar to most of the legal community and the citizenry at large. Judge Boldt knew they had to be put forth in an authentic, understandable way if, as he had come to believe, those cultural matters were the key to understanding the past and present meaning of the high federal laws—the treaties—that the United States and the tribes were asking him to enforce.

In his opinion, he began his findings of fact on Indian culture by evaluating the expert testimony on both sides. During the pretrial proceedings, he had emphasized to the attorneys more than once his conviction that he expected them to put together the most extensive factual record on Indian culture ever produced in litigation. Many witnesses testified on that from the stand and expert witnesses presented piles of written reports as well as testimony in open court. And, as noted, Judge Boldt did believe that the factual record on Native culture, traditions, and life met his expectations.

The judge rendered a direct and blistering evaluation on the experts:

> The anthropological reports and testimony of both Dr. Barbara Lane and Dr. Carroll Riley have been thoroughly studied and considered by the court. In so doing, the court has noted the nature, extent and duration of field work in the case area and academic research. During trial constant observation was made of the attitude and demeanor of both experts while on the stand as witnesses, and the substance of their testimony has been carefully evaluated. Allowance for the criticism by defendants that some of Dr. Lane's conclusions are "over formulated" has been made in evaluating her testimony in every instance where the criticism might be applicable. Based upon these and other factors, the court finds that in specific facts, the reports of Dr. Barbara Lane, Exhibits USA-20 to 30 and USA-53, have been exceptionally well researched and reported and are established by a preponderance of the evidence. They are found to be authoritative and reliable summaries of relevant aspects of Indian life in the case area at and prior to the time of the treaties, including the treaty councils, Indian groups covered by the treaties, the purposes of the treaties and the Indians' understanding of treaty provisions. In these particulars, nothing in Dr. Lane's report and testimony was controverted by any credible evidence in the case. Dr. Lane's opinions, inferences and conclusions based upon the information stated in detail and well documented in her reports, appeared to the court to be well taken, sound and reasonable. In summary, the court finds that where their testimony differs in any significant particular, the testimony of Dr. Lane is more credible and satisfactory than that of Dr. Riley and is accepted as such except as otherwise specified.

Dr. Lane's report on traditional life among the treaty tribes was straightforward and nonromantic. Judge Boldt's characterizations were the same, as seen in these findings on major points:

[One] common cultural characteristic among all of these Indians was the almost universal and generally paramount dependence upon the products of an aquatic economy, especially anadromous fish, to sustain the Indian way of life. These fish were vital to the Indian diet, played an important role in their religious life, and constituted a major element of their trade and economy. Throughout most of the area salmon was a staple food and steelhead were also taken, both providing essential proteins, fats, vitamins, and minerals in the native diet. . . .

The major food sources of the Northwest Indians were the wild fish, animal and vegetative resources of the area. . . .

The first-salmon ceremony, which with local differences in detail was general through most of the area, was essentially a religious rite to ensure the continued return of salmon. The symbolic acts, attitudes of respect and reverence, and concern for the salmon reflected a ritualistic conception of the interdependence and relatedness of all living things which was a dominant feature of the native Indian world view. Religious attitudes and rites insured that salmon were never wantonly wasted and that water pollution was not permitted during the salmon season.

His detailed analysis of life common to all treaty tribes also spoke to commercial trade in salmon:

At the time of the treaties, trade was carried on among the Indian groups throughout a wide geographic area. Fish was a basic element of the trade. There is some evidence that the volume of this intra-tribal trade was substantial, but it is not possible to compare it with the volume of present day commercial trading in salmon. Such trading was, however, important to the Indians at the time of the treaties. In addition to potlatching, which is a system of exchange between communities in a social context often typified by competitive gifting, there was a considerable amount of outright sale and trade beyond the local community and sometimes over great distances.

Judge Boldt also explained the role of tribal commerce at treaty time: "Those involved in negotiating the treaties recognized the contribution that Indian fishermen made to the territorial economy because the Indians caught most of the non-Indians' fish for them, plus clams and oysters."

Each of the fourteen plaintiff tribes also had their own individual histories and practices. As a result, in addition to Judge Boldt's account of the tribes' common values and practices, in one of the most distinctive aspects of his opinion, he offered short, tight, and informational histories and present status of each plaintiff tribe. In doing this, he looked primarily to Dr. Lane's thick package of detailed summaries of each tribe's history and current status.

This more granular information helps to give depth and perspective to the broad common values and understandings held by all of the tribes at treaty time and how, during the century and a quarter since treaty time, they were impacted by non-Indian economic development, European diseases, state regulation, and federal policies.

The histories of individual tribes also showed how the modern tribes had many different circumstances by the time of the litigation. To take just one area, the tribes were very diverse in terms of their current connections to the harvest of salmon. While all of the tribes continued to fish for and value salmon, some tribes had robust fisheries staffs and harvesting operations and a few tribes had only a small number of members fishing. The Quinault, Lummi, and Yakama had elaborate, formal regulatory systems, while several others had adopted written regulations, but some tribes had not yet acted. These matters of fact about tribal capabilities would be critical to Judge Boldt because in his opinion, he would be putting in place a comprehensive regime for management of Pacific salmon, in which tribal self-management would be an important part.

Taken as a whole, Judge Boldt's findings of fact on tribal culture, a pervasive issue in *United States v. Washington,* show a confident reliance on the federal and plaintiff tribes' case. This applies to the expert testimony but he also was plainly impressed by the testimony and demeanor of the many tribal witnesses. While the judge relied little, if at all, on the state's arguments on tribal culture, he did, as discussed below, value experts for the state in addressing issues of resource management.

The Treaties and State and Tribal Shares of the Fishery

The tribal share of the fishery had always been the most explosive aspect of *United States v. Washington.* Going into Judge Boldt's court, the tribes were taking about 5 percent of the salmon harvest, the commercial fishers around 90 percent, the sport fishers the rest. The idea of a numeric Indian share of the fisheries had never been ruled on by any court before Judge Belloni had announced his "fair share" formula just a few years before the Boldt Decision. All of the parties, including the user groups and the state and federal agencies, knew what a high number for the tribes could mean. The stress in the courtroom was palpable. Nonetheless, before the trial, the idea of major cutbacks to industry and sport fishers had not yet raised any significant alarm among the media or citizenry. People knew that an "Indian fishing rights" case was in court and some people took one side or the other on that general notion, but the case was complicated and moved slowly. There was almost no talk about a ruling that could have a major impact on the Pacific Northwest economy.

In his opinion, Judge Boldt walked through his reasoning on the tribal and state shares of the fisheries. Treaties were contracts between two parties, the United States and the tribe. The governing law came down in a uniform line of decisions from Chief Justice John Marshall up through US Supreme Court rulings handed down just a few years before Judge Boldt wrote his opinion. Because these treaty negotiations were conducted and written down in the English language, the terms must be understood as the tribes understood them. In *United States v. Washing-*

ton, the treaties were explained to the tribes in the highly problematic Chinook Jargon. The key treaty words (as described in chapter 5, Treaty Time) were that the tribes were guaranteed "the right of taking fish at usual and accustomed places and is further secured to said Indians in common with all citizens of the Territory."

In giving meaning to the "in common with the citizens" language, Judge Boldt gave a great amount of his time to this issue and settled on an approach that he believed was right—and continued to believe it was right after the opinion was made public. He noted that Governor Isaac Stevens had made promises to the tribes that their off-reservation rights would be absolutely protected. His most trusted advisor, George Gibbs, had told Stevens that he would have to guarantee those rights; otherwise, the tribes would probably refuse to sign. Stevens made many assurances to the tribes, including at the Point No Point treaty negotiations: "Doesn't a father give his children a home. . . . This paper secures your fish. Does not a father give food to his children?" Dr. Lane concluded that the "in common with" language meant that the tribes could continue to fish as they always had, without any restrictions. Public dictionaries of the mid-1850s defined "in common with" as meaning "equal."

Judge Boldt included these passages in describing his ruling on "in common with":

> There is no indication that the Indians intended or understood the language "in common with all citizens of the Territory" to limit their right to fish in any way. For many years following the treaties the Indians continued to fish in their customary manner and places, and although non-Indians also fished, there was no need for any restrictions on fishing. . . .
>
> All of the evidence . . . in the record [shows] that the treaty Indians pleaded for and insisted upon retaining the *exercise* of those rights as essential to their survival. They were given unqualified assurance of that by Governor Stevens himself without any suggestion that the Indians' *exercise* of those rights might some day, without authorization of Congress, be

subjected to regulation by non-Indian citizens through their territorial or state government. . . .

By dictionary definition and as intended and used in the Indian treaties and in this decision "in common with" means *sharing equally* the opportunity to take fish at "usual and accustomed grounds and stations"; therefore, non-treaty fishermen shall have the opportunity to take up to 50% of the harvestable number of fish that may be taken by all fishermen at usual and accustomed grounds and stations and treaty right fishermen shall have the opportunity to take up to the same percentage of harvestable fish, as stated above.

The opinion also concluded that tribal treaty rights included commercial harvesting. In addition, the 50 percent share applied only to tribal off-reservation fishing. Since, because the treaty expressly provided for "exclusive" tribal rights on the reservations, as opposed to "in common" rights off-reservations, the tribes were entitled to 100 percent of the fish taken on the reservations for subsistence and cultural and religious purposes.

It was, to put it mildly, a bold opinion on these issues and many others as well. There would be much more to be told in the courts, in the state and federal agencies, and out on the streets and waters.

The Treaties and State Regulation

Another top-rung issue in *United States v. Washington* was the nature and extent of state regulation of Indian fishermen. State fisheries officials and lawyers covet the state police power put forth in the US Constitution's Tenth Amendment: "The powers not designated to the United States by the Constitution . . . are reserved to the States."

Courts have broadly defined state police power as the right to enhance the general welfare by regulating and protecting health, safety, and morals. State legal control over wildlife, including hunting and fishing, is one of the police powers. As a result, states do exercise most authority over fishing within their borders. It is different, though, when federal laws involving fishing rights are involved and the tribes hold specific treaty fishing rights. The states and their influential supporters had long argued that, while the tribes do have some rights, the state police power allows substantial actions against tribes when "reasonable and necessary for conservation." Washington state courts agreed and struck down many tribal harvests.

When the tribal legal team assembled after filing the complaint and began putting their ideas together, none, save for George Dysart, would call themselves "experts" in Indian law. That would change quickly as Al Ziontz and the energetic young legal services attorneys threw themselves into *United States v. Washington* and Indian law generally. Their research found strong support for the idea that state regulation of a federal treaty right would run directly contrary to congressional power in the Treaty Clause and in the Commerce Clause "to regulate commerce . . . with the Indian tribes." The treaties would trump state police power over wildlife.

The Indian leaders, Hank Adams, Janet McCloud, Billy Frank Jr., and others had many meetings with their attorneys. They had experienced the real world of state shutdowns of Indian fishing. The state courts gave the agencies, upheld by state judges, virtually untrammeled authority over Indian fishing; this was based on the "reasonable and necessary" provision in their codes. The tribal leaders knew how the relentless prosecutions had battered the lives of Indian people. To the tribal leaders, the 50 percent share issue was of course critical, but equally as much, the state regulation needed to be stopped.

The tribal attorneys moved cautiously. In their early submissions to Judge Boldt, they raised the argument that the state lacked any authority over treaty fishing but did not press it. As the case moved on, the US Supreme Court opinions that kept coming down made the tribes' argument against all, or mostly all, state power over Indian treaty fishing even more forceful.

Then came the breakthrough. While *Puyallup II* was issued in November 1973, after the taking of evidence in *United States v. Washington*, final arguments in front of Judge Boldt took place on December 10. Now, with *Puyallup II* in place, the plaintiffs could make an argument that states had no authority whatsoever over treaty fishing rights. Judge Boldt issued strong praise for their efforts, writing that the federal and tribal attorneys "have submitted well researched briefs and vigorous oral arguments in support thereof."

Judge Boldt denied the plaintiffs' sweeping contention that the state had no jurisdiction whatsoever. But, in a landmark victory for the tribes, looking to *Puyallup II* and other cases, he ruled that state regulation existed in only one very narrow instance: when it was reasonable and necessary for "conservation," which he defined specifically as "perpetuation of the fisheries species." He emphasized the limited reach of this conservation: all state officers "must understand that the power to [regulate Indian treaty fishing] must be interpreted narrowly and sparingly applied, with constant recognition that *any* regulation will restrict the exercise of a right guaranteed by the United States Constitution." He added, "This [state police] power does not include the power to determine for the Indian tribes what is the wisest and best use of their share of the common resource."

So roughly 50 percent of the fisheries, non-Indian commercial and sport fishing, would be regulated by the state under its police power. What of the tribal 50 percent share? Would it perhaps be federally regulated? Would it go unregulated? What would be the tribal role?

Tribal Sovereign Self-Management

Tribal rights and state police power rights had been so hotly contested that they captured most of the public attention leading up to the trial. At the same time, everyone agreed that conservation of the salmon runs had to be given top priority. The numbers and health of the salmon had diminished since treaty time and remained fragile and sometimes in decline on most rivers. Judge Boldt was keenly aware of this from the beginning and gave a lot of attention to environmental health. After all, the parties in front of him—federal, state, and tribal fisheries management programs—played the major roles in the conservation of Pacific salmon in the Northwest.

Fisheries management programs set seasons, prescribe the allowable size and number of fish to be taken, identify allowable fishing equipment, and issue closure of fishing grounds when necessary. They make the essential decisions on *escapement*, the number of returning fish that must be allowed to escape harvesting and be available for spawning and ensure sustainability of the run. Management programs, which have increased in size and sophistication over time, conduct research on all manner of scientific, social, and economic matters. Good salmon conservation depends upon these management programs.

Starting with Washington statehood in 1889, the great bulk of salmon management power was exercised by the state and, to a lesser degree, federal agencies. The tribes had always regulated their members informally and by the 1970s, several tribes had developed management systems. Still, in terms of real-world sovereign management authority over fisheries, the state and federal governments exercised nearly all management authority.

The United States, joined by the tribes, filed *United States v. Washington* because they believed that the state had abused its regulatory authority with respect to the tribes. Initially, the parties saw the case in terms of shares and state regulatory authority. As the case moved closer to trial, the tribes came to believe that those two sources of management authority—state and federal—large though they were, did not capture the larger notion: that *US v. Washington* should call for full recognition of tribal sovereignty over tribal fishing. To the tribal attorneys, and certainly to the tribal leaders, it was essential that *US v. Washington* would call for Pacific salmon to be managed by three sovereigns, not two.

After the trial and all lawyers' arguments were completed, Judge Boldt turned to writing his opinion. By then he probably had decided that the tribes were entitled to a 50 percent share. But that didn't answer the burning question: who will *regulate* the harvesting of the tribe's 50 percent share—half of the entire fishery!—and assure good environmental practices so that the salmon will have healthy sustainable runs?

Judge Boldt came forth with a highly innovative approach that had never been tried before. He must have been working his idea through his mind continually, especially as he intently watched and listened to the many Indian people who took to the witness stand.

As he pointed out, Congress and the federal agencies had shown no intention of taking on that management of tribal fishing and, as Judge Boldt understood the law, the treaties did not allow for virtually any state regulation of tribal fisheries. He explained his thinking: "Ever since the first Indian treaties were confirmed by the Senate, Congress has recognized that those treaties established self-government by treaty tribes." He accurately recognized that, during the century after the treaties, Congress did limit tribal authority. But he gave examples that, especially in the decade leading up to his opinion, Congressional legislation "has definitely been in the contrary direction." Referring to the almost tangible swell of statutes, presidential actions, policies, and court cases supporting tribal sovereignty and self-determination that he and others saw and felt right up through the trial, he wrote this:

> These measures and others make plain the intent and philosophy of Congress to increase rather than diminish or limit the exercise of tribal self-government. . . .
>
> The philosophy of Congress referred to above and the evidence in this case as a whole clearly indicate to this court that the time has now arrived, and this case presents an appropriate opportunity, to take a step toward applying congressional philosophy to Indian treaty right fishing in a way that will not be inconsistent with *Puyallup I* and *Puyallup II* and also will provide ample security for the interest and purposes of conservation.

In his decision, Judge Boldt set out a detailed set of qualifications and conditions that, if met by individual tribes, would entitle those tribes to qualify for self-regulation. Judge Boldt would rule, after tribal proposals and hearings, on whether individual tribes' qualifications showed that the tribe would accept and abide by the requirements. The required qualifications and conditions included competent and responsible tribal leadership, a well-organized tribal government that could adopt and apply tribal off-reservation fishing regulations, trained personnel to police enforcement of the regulations, well-qualified experts in fisheries science and management, official tribal membership rolls and individual tribal membership cards, and full fish catch reports.

As for particular tribes, Judge Boldt made a formal fact finding in his opinion based on "uncontradicted evidence" that the Quinault and Yakama Tribes met the standards and would be able to exercise sovereign self-management. He added that "the evidence indicates several other plaintiff tribes have capacity for, and are not far from, achievement of the same status, which potentially is within the capability of every plaintiff tribe."

This tall and unprecedented order on sovereign tribal self-government would now have to be upheld by higher courts and proven that it works in the real world, out on the waters.

Conservation and Comanagement:
A New Framework for the Future

Judge Boldt had no illusions about the challenges that lay ahead. At the moment he released his order, management of fisheries in northwestern Washington was a mess. The state and the tribes sometimes talked, but rarely. The two state agencies often disagreed with each other and the Department of Game was effectively a rogue agency when it came to tribal rights. The United States contributed valuable scientific research, supported the tribes in court, and gave management advice to both the state and the tribes, but did not otherwise directly engage in fisheries

Judge Boldt. *From the News Tribune.* © *1968 McClatchy. All rights reserved. Used under license.*

management. There was no jointly accepted data on such basic matters as fish health, total catches, or escapement so as to assure sustainability.

The task of creating and carrying out an effective fisheries management system for northwestern Washington, based as it was on new and untested requirements such as 50 percent shares and fisheries sustainability, was taxing to begin with. It was made all the more demanding because it needed to be carried out on a water and land environment reaching approximately eighty miles west to east and seventy-five miles north to south, encompassing ocean and mountain territory as well as terrains of rivers, lakes, and land. Fishers ranged from domestic and foreign trollers to commercial, sport, and Indian fishers on many hundreds of low-elevation rivers, lakes, and tributaries, all the way up to Native dip-net fishers in low and high mountain areas.

This was anything but static. The salmon are mostly in motion. The health of individual runs may be stable, increasing, or diminishing. Conditions in most places change year to year due to weather, economic development, or other factors.

Judge Boldt knew from the early days of pretrial discovery that the legal rights, however they would be decided, would have to be fulfilled within a fisheries management system. He directed the parties to provide him with all aspects of fisheries management. The experts and attorneys for all sides produced a prodigious amount of information, which the judge devoured, in the form of statistics, reports, and testimony, including facts that they could agree on. During the trial he often emphasized his debt to the many experts who came forth. On the second page of his opinion he spoke to the quality of the fisheries research, singling out the lengthy Joint Biological Statement on fisheries management. "The Joint Biological Statement, . . . jointly proposed and admitted in evidence as agreed facts applicable as indicated therein, was prepared by and agreed to by highly qualified experts employed by and representing both plaintiffs and defendants and is of exceptional importance and practical value." In the opinion, he included a detailed section, "General Fisheries Conservation and Management," based on the Joint Biological Statement, trial testimony of fisheries experts, and his own research to provide specific guidance to the parties in implementing his decree.

Judge Boldt had always believed difficult legal issues were best resolved by the parties sitting down and negotiating. He saw that this was missing in the years leading up to the filing of *United States v. Washington.* He became convinced, based on his own experience, his reading on fisheries science, and discussions with fisheries science professors at the University of Washington, that "fisheries management is a social science. We're managing people. If we manage people properly, the fish will take care of themselves." This required people to work together.

At many points, then, during pretrial and continuing into the trial and the opinion, he urged the parties to attempt to find common ground and in his court opinion he adopted procedures that might lead, over

time, to people working together. Ultimately, he hoped that the three
sovereigns would negotiate, and finally adopt, a comprehensive comanagement fisheries system. He was not remotely naive about this. He
knew it would take years. But he believed it could be done. As a man
who understood complex federal litigation and the powers of judges as
well as anyone in the country, he put forth a bold and courageous and
largely unprecedented opinion that called for cooperation on fisheries
long after February 12, 1974.

Judge Boldt knew all too well that the parties had a long record of failing
to work together cooperatively. Further, even if they did begin to cooperate, the far-reaching case area held so many runs, so many rivers, and
so many changing circumstances that devising and enforcing a system to
assure 50 percent shares and effective three-sovereign management could
not possibly be done without disputes that needed to go to court. The
Boldt Decision, in other words, was a final resolution in some respects
and a beginning point as well.

   The Boldt Decision included a number of orders, relating to court
administration, that set in motion what still needed to be done. He took
continuing jurisdiction to address disputes "for the life of this decree."
Continuing jurisdiction is ordered only rarely, then and now. Federal
courts aim to resolve most cases efficiently and produce final results,
but a small number of cases, mostly complex public cases—school desegregation and prisoner rights are examples—call for quick access to
the courts after a decree is handed down. Judge Belloni already had kept
continuing jurisdiction in the Oregon treaty fishing rights cases involving
new legal standards and parties with a history of not working together
well. Continuing jurisdiction meant that the court would remain available postdecree until the litigation is formally concluded, which, half a
century later, has not yet occurred.

   Judge Boldt also ordered a new apparatus for hearing continuing disputes in *United States v. Washington.* There would be a technical advisor, other experts, and an advisory committee on treaty rights fishing. With disputes expected to be numerous and immediate, Judge Boldt made a point of naming Professor Richard Whitney, a fishery scientist at the University of Washington, to the key position of technical advisor on the same day he issued his opinion.

The post-trial system called for parties to attempt to settle disputes but, if they could not reach an agreement, they could file with the court a "request for determination." The judge could rule on the request or refer it to the technical advisor, Professor Whitney. The technical advisor had authority to summon witnesses, take evidence, and hold hearings. He could also consult with the technical experts or the advisory committee. The technical advisor would then make a recommendation, which could be appealed to the judge. As was expected, Judge Boldt made good use of his technical advisor.

Judge Boldt also ordered the federal, tribal, and state parties to work together. Specific requirements included these:

> The biologists of defendants and . . . the tribes shall meet to formulate
> general principles . . . to be flexibly applied in the adoption of specific
> fishing regulations. The parties shall exchange all available data
> concerning size, timing, and condition of fish runs in the case area and
> the current level of harvest and escapement.

State agents had often seized the nets, canoes, and other gear of Indian fishers. Judge Boldt had declared some raids unlawful and directed the state to use its best efforts to locate gear seized and return it to the tribal fishers. The hearings for declaring tribes as self-managers began soon after the decision was handed down.

On February 12, 1974, the Boldt Decision made a big splash. John Echo-hawk, the longtime executive director of the Native American Rights

Fund, is as knowledgeable as anyone about Indian country. He emphasizes how the Boldt Decision lifted spirits and brought hope out to the
reservations nationally: "In the 1960s there was a general belief in the
public that treaties were ancient history, not the supreme law of the
land. Our wish became true. The tribes got what they were advocating
for. People knew about it right away. The treaties were acknowledged as
the law. The Boldt Decision was the first big win for the modern tribal
sovereignty movement. The Boldt Decision was very well received and
widely celebrated in Indian country." Otherwise, some people applauded
it and others thought it went way too far, but all across the Northwest,
and in other parts of the country as well (including the *New York Times*),
there was no doubt about its importance. Still, on that decision day, the
Boldt Decision could not be called "historic" or "great." Nothing had
happened yet out on the ocean and rivers. The Ninth Circuit Court of
Appeals or the US Supreme Court could overturn or weaken it. Right
away, powerful figures decided it was time to go to Congress, which
could abrogate the Boldt Decision completely.

To be sure, the Boldt Decision was formidable on its face. An able,
careful, and conservative judge had put down words that invoked the
highest powers of the federal judiciary and vindicated the cherished
rights of a small group of dispossessed peoples. But could it hold?

11 Rebellion

"It was like a *city* out there."

The judicial review by appellate courts of the Boldt Decision went forth quickly.

The case first went on appeal to the Ninth Circuit Court of Appeals. A three-judge panel of Judges Herbert Choy, William Goodwin, and James M. Burns unanimously upheld Judge Boldt's decision and affirmed that sweeping opinion, point by point, with only minor exceptions. Judge Burns, a district court judge sitting on the appellate panel by designation, wrote a most interesting concurring opinion. A conservative jurist, he generally objected to cases where judges took continuing jurisdiction: "I deplore situations that make it necessary for us to become enduring managers of the fisheries, forests, and highways, to say nothing of school districts, police departments, and so on." Judge Burns agreed, though, that Judge Boldt was correct in ordering continuing jurisdiction here: "The record in this case, and the history set forth in [other Northwest tribal fishing rights cases], make it crystal clear that it has been recalcitrance of Washington State officials (and their vocal non-Indian commercial and sports fishing allies) which produced the denial of Indian rights requiring intervention by the district court. This responsibility should neither escape notice nor be forgotten."

The state and several other parties then petitioned the US Supreme Court for a writ of certiorari to overturn the two lower-court decisions. There is no general right to appeal to the Supreme Court. Instead, parties must file for a writ of certiorari, which is discretionary with the court. The court denies most certiorari petitions. A decision to deny certiorari does not mean that the court agrees with the lower court. Instead, denial

simply means that the lower-court decision stands and is final throughout the geographical limits of the lower court, the Ninth Circuit in this
case.

On January 26, 1976, just eight months after the Ninth Circuit opinion,
the Supreme Court denied the writ of certiorari. While this denial did
not mean that the Supreme Court approved of the lower-court opinion,
it did make the lower-court opinion the final, binding law throughout
the Ninth Circuit, which of course includes Washington. The Boldt
Decision, subject to the minor adjustments by the Ninth Circuit, was
fully and finally the "supreme law of the land" in the state of Washington
under the US Constitution's Article VI, Clause 2, meaning that valid
federal laws, including treaties, override, or trump, conflicting state laws.

But it had long been clear that the zealous, often angry detractors of
Judge Boldt, tribal rights, and federal supremacy over state law were not
going to be satisfied by federal court rulings. The ink had barely dried
on Judge Boldt's signature when non-Indian fishers and some state officials broke out in open disdain of the court's rulings. So, too, with the
highest court's final order, denying a writ of certiorari, solid though it
was in constitutional law.

This open defiance of federal law, so reminiscent of the events in
the American South, would continue for five explosive years until the
Supreme Court finally decided that it had to step in and render its comprehensive ruling on the merits.

Snap phrases denigrating the Boldt Decision immediately sprang up
in conversations and on bumper stickers: "Nuts to Boldt," "Can Judge
Boldt—not salmon," "Screw Boldt." The leaders of the Northwest Steelheaders Council of Trout Unlimited said, "I had no idea an objective

adult could turn 180 degrees away from the state and effectively give the resources to the federal government" and "I was stunned. . . . I've been besieged by phone calls from irate sportsmen. . . ." Another steelhead fisherman wrote that "I was flabbergasted, it seems so preposterous . . . [Judge Boldt] has stripped the Game Department of all but a mere thread of its regulatory power, leaving no experienced agency or body to protect and manage the resource. . . ."

Commercial fishermen also forcefully criticized the opinion. Some state officials fueled the opposition. Early on, state attorney Larry Coniff argued that "there should be a blanket ban on off-reservation Indian net fishing for steelhead because commercialization was incompatible with conservation of that species." A week after the decision, Carl Crouse, director of the state Department of Game, said that the department would

Sport fishermen put forth this open-water protest against the Boldt Decision.
Photograph by Matt McVay. *Courtesy of Matt McVay, Seattle Times, 1978.*

Commercial fishermen marched on the Washington State Capitol Building in Olympia in 1975. *From the News Tribune. © 1975 McClatchy. All rights reserved. Used under license.*

appeal the decision and added that "if the Boldt Decision is allowed to stand, recreational steelhead fishing 'no longer will be meaningful.'"

Make no mistake: the impact on non-Indians was great, especially for commercial fishers. While steelhead and salmon sport fishers would see a modest reduction in total takes, most of the 50 percent tribal share would come from the commercial industry. Over time, even with the progressive state and federal programs that would ease the transition, individual commercial fishers, their families, and communities would all be affected.

Not all of the objections to the decision were based on concerns about fisheries per se. Some of the sport and commercial advocates, and numbers of citizens at large, saw the treaties as creating reverse discrimination that was unconstitutional or just dead wrong and unfair. Ironically, some objectors adopted the language of the civil rights movement, seeing themselves—who did not have the kind of rights that Indians had—as "second-class citizens" denied "equal rights."

While these concerns about racial equality resonated with some members of the public, as a matter of law these rights are governmental, not racial or individual rights. The fishing rights were established in the United States treaties with sovereign tribes, which held the rights. The sovereign tribal governments then authorized individual tribal citizens to fish under conditions covering their citizens, much like the state of Washington issues licenses to individuals. These rules of federal Indian law are complex and, understandably, not known among the general population, especially at that time.

So the Boldt Decision came to a Washington society that had little concept of the history, law, and constitutionalism that led Judge Boldt to rule as he did. As for the top state officials, it was their right to diligently appeal the Boldt Decision and get it overruled or modified—or, perhaps, to achieve a favorable settlement. They all worked hard to be successful in the appeals process. They needed to be perfectly straight with the public and not confuse, mislead, or inflame it.

Governor Daniel Evans, who served for three full terms from 1965 through 1977, did walk that line. Like Judge Boldt, Evans believed that there was a great deal of confusion and emotion about this case and that the ideal was for the opposing sides to come together and find common ground among the state, the tribes, and the various interest groups. He strongly disapproved of the "many mass protests that got out of hand." In his autobiography, he alluded to the remarks of two state senators. One charged, at a demonstration at the capitol steps, that George Boldt was "a senile judge, almost eighty years old," who had "completely demolished the fishing industry of our state." The other senator asserted that the Boldt Decision "tears this state wide open." Governor Evans was clear about it: "that was precisely what we didn't need."

Governor Evans is widely praised for his leadership and fairness as governor. A University of Michigan study in 1981 named him "one of the ten outstanding Governors in the twentieth century." As one example of Evans's understanding of federal and state law, when Judge Belloni issued his 1969 opinion recognizing extensive tribal treaty rights in Oregon, Governor Evans announced that Washington also was bound by that opinion. Bill Wilkerson, director of the Department of Fisheries in Washington in the early 1980s, accurately said that Evans was "one of the greatest leaders in the history of this state and was probably as big a supporter of the tribes you possibly could have had during that time, 1965 through 1977." Evans, who was determined to understand the circumstances of all of the parties in the fishing dispute, stated, "I discovered how intensely all fishermen (commercial, sport, and Native) felt about these amazing fish." He understood how the Boldt Decision "radically changed economic circumstances" of commercial fishers. He "also heard from tribal leaders deeply concerned about the future of salmon runs and the need to protect habitat in Puget Sound streams and rivers. . . . From wise leaders like Billy Frank, Jr., I began to learn about the importance of salmon, not only as a source of food, but as a spiritual part of tribal rituals and history."

As might be expected, numbers of lower-level state employees, long opposed to tribal fishing rights and sympathetic to the outbursts against the Boldt Decision, did not toe the straight and narrow. When Judge Boldt issued closures of non-Indian fishing, it was incumbent upon the state, through state attorneys and the fishers' agencies, to carry them out. But when non-Indian fishers violated the court orders—and there were violations galore—the Departments of Game and of Fisheries regularly refused to enforce the orders. On the relatively few occasions when the departments did seek enforcement, local judges, ignoring their oaths of office, often dismissed the charges.

The *Washington Post* explained the situation, writing that "Washington state legal officials refused to enforce Boldt's order. They instead denounced the judge, and encouraged fishermen to believe his decision upholding treaty rights was capricious and unlikely to stand up on appeal." Professor Fay Cohen referred to comments made by Assistant Attorney General Jim Johnson, one of the most vocal critics of Judge Boldt. In emotional rallies of commercial sport fishers, Johnson called the Boldt Decision "morally reprehensible" and predicted that "as far as we are concerned the tide has turned and as I say it shall be overturned." Professor Cohen accurately concluded this: "Buoyed by this attitude, it is little wonder that many non-Indian fishermen failed to respect the decision, now federal law, and that an 'outlaw fishery' ensued."

Mammoth outlaw fishing raged for years after the Boldt Decision. Attorney and later Federal District Court Judge Jack Tanner wrote that "despite an 'extensive commitment of both man-hours and equipment' by the federal government, . . . 'it is obvious that the federal enforcement effort is unable to control the rampant and wanton rape of the (salmon) resource by virtue of illegal fishing.'" A state Fisheries official reported, "There has been so much illegal fishing on the faltering coho salmon run in Puget Sound in recent nights that the State Fisheries Department is unable to stem it alone. Our guy working out of Seattle north toward Possession Point didn't even get to Possession Point, he was writing so many tickets." Mike Grayum, a scientist with the United States Fish and Wildlife Service at the time, witnessed how blatant illegal fishing was. His superiors asked him to estimate how many vessels were out on the water in Puget Sound at night, when non-Indian illegal fishing was known to be at its height. He got a boat and a night vision scope, but didn't have any luck making an estimate. There were so many boats and nets that he couldn't maneuver without running into a net and there were so many lights that he couldn't use his night vision scope. He explained: "It was like a *city* out there."

No estimate has ever been made of the total number of fish lost to the tribes through outlaw fishing. Still, some of the reports of specific incidents provide a sense of it. The state's report for 1977 on commercial fishers, for example, concluded this: "David C. Pratt, [Fisheries Department] biologist, produced a document indicating that commercial fishermen licensed by the state took more than 182,700 salmon illegally [in 1977], including nearly 110,000 chum salmon. The total illegal catch came to nearly 1.8 million pounds of fish." As for 1976, state biologists "estimate that more than $1 million worth of fish have been caught and sold illegally this year on Puget Sound."

The disturbances went beyond illegal fishing. Boldt opponents took out their anger on individual Indians. They rammed Indian boats, cut Indian fishing nets, slashed vehicle tires, and fired bullets at tribal members. Lummi fishers were shot at by snipers on at least three occasions. In one case, the target was a fourteen-year-old boy. The violence was sometimes leveled at state officials. Jim Tuggle, an officer in the Fisheries Department, recalled a frightening scene at an area closed to non-Indian gill netters to allow for tribal net fishing. The Fisheries Department sent out boats to enforce Judge Boldt's closure:

> Initiated by a few hotheaded gillnetters, multiple assaults against officers occurred as small patrol boats were rammed repeatedly by much larger and heavier gillnet boats. Shouts from enraged fishermen could be heard on the radio urging their cohorts to sink the patrol boats and kill the officers. Patrol boats were maneuvered quickly to avoid sinking and certain disaster. Despite attempts to avoid collisions, gillnet boats still managed to ram the much smaller patrol vessels. The confrontation became so violent that the US Coast Guard dispatched a cutter and the commander of that vessel, Chief Bob LaFrancis, ordered the bow-mounted 50-caliber machine gun uncovered, loaded and manned. No

This violent arrest was carried out by state officials against Puyallup fishermen at a traditional tribal fishing site in 1977. *Tacoma Indian News, vol. 1, no. 5, January 13, 1977.*

closed season gillnet fishing arrest took place that night, but if it were not for Chief LaFrancis' decisive actions, several Fisheries Patrol Officers might have died that night—and perhaps some gillnetters as well.

Angry non-Indians attacked individual fishers and their families. Georgiana Kautz, Nisqually, reported this: "Later when we started fighting about the Boldt Decision, those people wanted to hurt us bad. They'd carry these long flashlights. They took everything from us—our boats, our nets. We would be starving but they didn't care. We've had to fight continually." Among many others, Cathy Ballew, Lummi, endured similar cruelty: "I remember some of those fishermen yelling at us on the docks. We got gunshots in our boat. We'd get boulders thrown in our nets. They would ride around the reservation and shoot at houses. They would steal our dogs. One time near Christmas, white fishers came to our house with shotguns and threatened to shoot up our house. There was a [bullet] hole in my grandmother's door and it went very close to where my grandfather used to sit in his chair! That is the kind of lifestyle we had to live with after the Boldt case. I remember a lot of white people coming by to look at us down at the river. I don't know why." For years, every Indian family had to endure these abuses and be constantly on guard for the next indignity. State prosecutors brought few charges.

While attacks on individuals and their property were largely beyond Judge Boldt's jurisdiction, he was determined to address the chaotic defiance of his orders. As a main element in addressing the rising tide

Tribal members also had their protests, but that was later, as shown here in 1982, when the Boldt Decision was not being fully implemented due to the opposition of the state and its supporters. *From the News Tribune. © 1982 McClatchy. All rights reserved. Used under license.*

of conflicts, he wanted to make extensive use of a technical advisor. He considered many people.

Both the tribes and the state Fisheries officials regularly looked to the School of Fisheries at the University of Washington for scientific and management advice. Professor Richard Whitney was well known to both sides for his expertise and the open, fair-minded way he viewed fisheries issues. His job at the university allowed him to conduct important research and, as well, have back-and-forth relationships over management and sustainability matters with fisheries agencies and tribes. A devoted teacher, he became a mentor of Guy McMinds, Quinault, during the late 1960s, when McMinds was the only Indian fisheries scientist student at the university.

Even before his decision was released, Judge Boldt made it known that he intended to name a technical advisor whom he could rely upon when disputes came up. McMinds nominated Whitney for the position. Several people were nominated and apparently no one had objections to Whitney. Whitney let it be known that he was less than enthusiastic, saying "I already had the perfect job." Then Guy McMinds went to the dean of the Fisheries College and "went over my head," as Whitney described it, and the dean said "Dick, I think you should agree to be nominated."

A few days later, Judge Boldt called Whitney and invited him to come down to his courthouse office in Tacoma. Whitney asked him when they should meet and the judge replied, "Would you be available this afternoon?" He did drive down to Tacoma and was pleased at how polite, relaxed, and nonpushy the judge was. In his own mind, Whitney still wasn't sure, but when the judge asked him directly if he would accept the position, he found that his only thought was, "How can you say 'no' to a federal judge?"

During the trial, while the issues were large, the disputes had taken place in orderly courtroom proceedings. Now, especially with the outlaw fisheries, the legal landscape was tumultuous, with many high-stress hearings and ticketing and arrests by state and federal enforcement officials.

University of Washington Professor Richard Whitney, widely admired for his expertise and fairness, was a major and constructive figure over the course of two decades in the state-tribal conflicts over salmon. *Courtesy of Northwest Indian Fisheries Commission.*

Further, and mostly separate, were disputes over setting tribal and state shares for the hundreds of major runs on the numerous rivers. These were mostly scientific determinations. For example, a big part of the task was, when the adult fish were still at sea, to try to figure out how many fish there were in a particular run. The state-licensed commercial and sport offshore fishermen had first crack at the run, but the larger the run, the more salmon the nontribal fishers would get. The size of these runs was a science-based technical determination and there were many disputes over these determinations. Sometimes the scientists had historical data that could be a basis for estimating the size of runs. These estimates often required quick action, sometimes when the incoming runs were nearing the offshore boats.

Judge Boldt soon decided that he could bring Whitney in for many of these disputes. In November 1974, he issued an order that "whenever a fisheries problem arises, the party must go first to Whitney for discussion and counsel." This was a useful device and made the judicial process more efficient. In some situations, these discussions resulted in settlements. The parties still had the right to go to the judge, but Whitney could brief him and often made the judge's decision easier.

But the number of disputes steadily rose and more was needed. In

October 1975, Judge Boldt went beyond judicial efficiency and issued his landmark order establishing the Fisheries Advisory Board. This order would also plant the vision of the original 1974 Boldt Decision: communication and collaboration between the state and the tribes and reducing the need for adversary proceedings.

The FAB order required that all future disputes must be heard by the board before going to the judge; the only exception was for emergencies that would "threaten serious harm to the resource." The board had three members. Whitney was the nonvoting chair. The other two seats were rotating: for every dispute, Whitney would name two members, one from the state and one for the tribes. The three members would engage in discussions, often informal, with Whitney moderating. Spectators were allowed but could not speak unless permitted by the board. If the tribal and state members reached agreement, the dispute was resolved.

If they reached an impasse, they could then file in court, but Whitney would make a recommendation to the judge. Whitney, perhaps being a little hard on himself, described his influence: "I could make a recommendation to the court. As it turned out, both parties were afraid of me being a loose cannon and making recommendations that they did not agree with. That was a stimulus to reach agreements. I would let them know in advance what my recommendation would be."

The FAB order was a heralded success. From 1975 through 1979 (the life of the order), an estimated 72 percent of disputes were settled and never reached Judge Boldt's courtroom. Clients, lawyers, and scientists began working together as never before. Looking back, it is evident that the FAB process marked the early beginnings of the federal, tribal, and state comanagement of Northwest fisheries, envisioned by Judge Boldt, that emerged in the mid-1980s and remains solidly in place today.

If the federal court proceedings were moving in consistent and progressive ways during the mid-1970s, the same cannot be said of state judges.

For decades, Washington state courts had been handing down decisions on tribal treaty rights that belittled tribal rights, often in defiance of settled federal law. Now the state and non-Indian fishing interests stridently argued to state courts and the public that the 1976 ruling denying certiorari was not enough: because of the importance of these issues, therefore, Washington citizens were entitled to a full US Supreme Court opinion on the validity of the Boldt Decision. Illegal fishing steadily increased. Then, in June 1977, the Washington Supreme Court ruled in *Puget Sound Gillnetters Association v. Moos* that the Boldt Decision was void because the United States had no authority over Indian fishing. State agencies, therefore, could not allocate fish to tribal fishers under orders issued by Judge Boldt. The *Puget Sound Gillnetters* opinion, which ran directly contrary to settled federal law, was written by Justice Hugh Rosellini, whose unwavering contempt for Indian rights had been evident for all of his twenty-two-year tenure on the bench.

News of the bombshell opinion spread throughout the ranks of fishing rights opponents. Now, according to the state supreme court, there was no longer any "illegal fishing," so long as the state Fisheries Department opened areas for fishing, which it promptly did. Violations of Judge Boldt's orders spiked even higher. The tribal catch plummeted. Senator Warren Magnuson and President Jimmy Carter both expressed discomfort with the war on the water, with shots being fired and boats being rammed.

Judge Boldt fully recognized the severity of the problem. He took charge with an order of a magnitude that few trial court judges have ever reached. On August 31, 1977, he took over direct control of the fisheries. From then on, all fishing would have to be approved by his orders. Basically, he would regulate all fishing. Anyone violating his orders would face federal criminal citations for contempt of court. The federal departments of Justice, Interior, Commerce, and Transportation established a pool of interagency federal enforcement officers to carry out Judge Boldt's orders. Some outlaw fishing and violence did continue after the order, but they markedly diminished.

The non-Indian fishing interests opposing the Boldt Decision and their allies also went national. By the mid-1970s, tribes were winning court cases in many states and receiving support from the federal agencies. These victories raised objections based on special privileges, discrimination against non-Indians, and "super-citizenship." The earliest announcement of this national phenomenon came in a 1976 book, *Indian Treaties, American Nightmare*, by C. Herb Williams, a sports writer, and Walt Neubrech, chief of the Enforcement Division of the Washington Department of Game and longtime opponent of treaty rights. Williams and Neubrech emphasized the Boldt Decision: "This is dangerously close to dictatorship where all actions of the State of Washington are subject to the whim of a federal judge who enjoys a lifetime appointment and is not accountable to the people." They also made much of the impacts beyond the Washington state lines:

> 'It can't happen here,' is one of the most common reactions expressed across the United States when fish and game managers are first faced with Indian demands, petitions or law suits for unregulated fishing and hunting rights.
>
> Yet it is happening in state after state, as the courts grant special rights to Indians to take fish and game without regard for state conservation laws. The special rights also are being granted for water, timber, land and mineral claims.
>
> This attitude that, 'It can't happen here,' comes in part because demands of activist Indian groups are so incredibly vast they are not taken seriously at first.

The authors listed seventeen states where tribal advances were being contested.

Local and national groups opposing various tribal rights rose up and became active, including the Interstate Congress for Equal Rights and Responsibilities, Montanans Opposing Discrimination, and the Citizens Equal Rights Alliance. These organizations were dedicated and ambitious. For example, by 1977, in its first year ICERR had granted membership to fourteen organizations with similar interests in the state of Washington alone. These activists went straight to Congress and contributed to a change in attitudes, as Bill Richards wrote in the *Washington Post* in a 1977 article entitled "Hill Cools on Indian Affairs":

> When he was chairman of the Indian affairs subcommittee three years ago, Rep. Lloyd Meeds (D-Wash.) was known as something of a champion of the desires of the American Indian.
>
> 'At the time,' said Meeds, who no longer heads the panel, 'there was this feeling around the House that these were pretty good civil rights votes. Besides, no one was paying much attention to the Indians then.'
>
> In Meeds' Puget Sound district, they are paying plenty of attention these days. Indian demands for fishing catches equal to those of non-Indian fishermen based on a century old treaty—one upheld recently in federal court—have sparked what is close to open warfare among Meeds' constituents.
>
> Now, the seven-term congressman uses the word 'out-rageous' to describe Indian demands. Like Meeds, a number of former Indian supporters in Congress have begun to shy away from Indian issues, particularly since Indian land claims have begun to be filed in Eastern states and the controversy over conflicting Indian and non-Indian water claims in the West has grown.
>
> 'There's no question that a very substantial shift in feeling is under way, particularly where these claims are being felt,' Meeds said.

While tribes in the Northwest and nationally had continuing support in many governmental and political circles, this backlash would play an influential role in Indian affairs for at least a decade.

The most extreme proposal, the Native Americans Equal Opportunities Act, came from Washington Congressman Jack Cunningham in 1978. Among other things, it would abrogate all treaties, including fishing and hunting rights; within a year make Indians subject to all state laws including taxation; and eliminate tribal and individual property rights. This proposal, much like the discredited termination laws, did not provide for any compensation for the abrogation of their sovereignty or property rights. Numerous other bills would have extinguished or weakened water rights, abrogated water and land rights, and limited tribal self-governance rights and state regulation of off-reservation fishing rights. None of these or other similar bills passed. Congressman Cunningham's proposal never made it to a committee hearing. Still, they garnered publicity and made tribal efforts in Congress and governmental agencies more difficult.

In 1977, largely due to pressure from the Washington congressional delegation, President Carter announced the creation of the Federal Task Force on Washington State Fisheries. When announced, it was widely perceived as an influential effort that could lead to Congress revising the Boldt Decision or repealing it outright. The task force members, whose authority covered most of executive authority over Indian affairs, were the Secretary of the Interior, the Secretary of Commerce, and the US Attorney General. Washington Senators Henry Jackson and Warren Magnuson, both formidable leaders in the Senate, had pushed for Carter's action and would be heard. Jackson, a committed terminationist ever since he had arrived in the Senate a quarter of a century earlier, opposed the Boldt Decision. Magnuson would in time become a fierce advocate for the tribes. At this point, however, he was more moderate than Jackson but did have doubts about the Boldt Decision.

The Carter task force produced a fair amount of sound and fury, but ultimately ended up, after thirteen months, in a deadlock. A big part of that was due to the vagueness of the enterprise. President Carter's order contained no mission statement or indication of how federal power might be used. Most of all, it did not give even a hint as to whether the Federal Task Force should recommend changes to the Boldt Decision.

Right at the beginning, the three cabinet-level officials delegated their responsibilities to top administrators in their respective departments. This was an excellent group, balanced and knowledgeable, but they in turn subdelegated their responsibilities to a regional team of federal officials. The regional team members all had good reputations and experience in federal resources issues but not much depth in Northwest tribal treaty rights. They, too, also had no clear mission or ways to proceed.

The regionally led task force's elaborate, 490-page final plan, done over just thirteen months, was a mishmash. It tried to do too much, proposing sweeping and fundamental changes in the Pacific Northwest fisheries regime. In the end, neither the state, the non-Indian fishers, or the tribes could support the task force's report:

> Nobody liked the plan. The tribes, the fishermen's associations, and the state all rejected it. There were three major drawbacks from the state's point of view: too much federal involvement; failure to significantly alter the Indian and non-Indian sharing plan established by Judge Boldt; and failure to recognize the concurrent need for review of *US v. Washington* by the US Supreme Court.
>
> Commercial and sports fishermen felt that any acceptable settlement must: include US Supreme Court review of *US v. Washington*; base management on equalizing the sizes of the Indian and non-Indian fleets rather than upon other methods; and phase in distribution of the harvest more gradually.

The task force filed its final report in October 1978. With opposition from the immediate parties and lacking public support, no further action was taken.

The tribes had to defend themselves from abrogation proposals and accompanying insults during the post-trial period. They also took the time to step back and make fundamental short- and long-term changes to enhance their sovereignty, fisheries management capability, and influence of the Boldt Case area tribes as a collective group.

All of the tribes welcomed the Boldt Decision's provision that each tribe was "entitled to exercise its governmental powers by regulating the treaty right fishing of its members without any state regulation thereof." As noted in the Tribal Sovereign Self-Management section in chapter 10, The Boldt Decision, earlier in this book, to exercise this sovereign power under the court order, a tribe was required to show to the satisfaction of Judge Boldt that its government was qualified to carry out modern fisheries management. The conditions were demanding, requiring, for example, that a tribe must have extensive trained staff able to adopt and enforce comprehensive regulations, including well-qualified experts in fisheries science and management and trained enforcement officials. The judge found that the Quinault and Yakama Tribes had already met these standards; others were "not far from" the required status, and that qualification is "potentially within the capability of every plaintiff tribe."

The tribes not yet qualified jumped at the opportunity, which recognized tribal sovereignty in one of their most treasured areas. The opportunity was revolutionary: if all the tribes could achieve self-regulation, the tribes as a whole would be managing 50 percent of the northwestern Washington fishery, with the state regulating the other half.

The Interior and Justice Departments, having invested considerable resources in the litigation and, seeing themselves as trustees for the tribes, were supportive of the Boldt Decision's tribal self-regulation provisions from the beginning. They made funding for self-regulation a high priority. Within six months, $700,000 in federal money went out to the tribes to help support them in establishing more formal fisheries programs, including research and regulation. These and other early funds went to the Northwest Indian Fisheries Commission, the first intertribal organization formed by tribes around specific issues (today there are some one hundred intertribal organizations nationally). The NWIFC, formed at a meeting in Portland on May 1, 1974, then allocated funds to the tribes. The federal support continued, with some grants going to the NWIFC and some to individual tribes.

The NWIFC was effective from the beginning, with a strong board headed by Dutch Kinley, Lummi. Its role was to support tribal management of fisheries, with the tribes maintaining their self-governing authority. It quickly developed expertise and research in habitat protection and fisheries biology. It also served as a public relations voice for the tribes affected by the Boldt Decision. The NWIFC worked with the tribes on their petitions to Judge Boldt for self-management. Within just a few years, all Boldt Case area tribes were managing their own fisheries and members.

In early 1977, the Washington Supreme Court struck twice, launching two decisions announcing that the Boldt Decision violated the US Constitution or was otherwise invalid. Justice Hugh Rosellini, longtime advocate for state regulation over treaty fishing rights, authored both opinions. They were clumsily written and offered slender legal precedent.

Yet the real objective of the state government and its supporters was not to win the two cases in the state supreme court in Olympia. They wanted to use those decisions as footholds to induce the Supreme Court of the United States to rule on the Boldt Decision and overturn it.

Washington filed for writs of certiorari for both of the state supreme court cases. The state faced all manner of technical obstacles, starting with the fact that the US Supreme Court had already denied certiorari just two years before. But the Supreme Court's policy against allowing parties to get a second chance at certiorari was not absolute. Now there were legitimately different circumstances. There was now a direct split between the federal courts with authority in Washington and the state's highest court; the Supreme Court has always considered conflicts between state and federal courts as a top priority for granting certiorari. Further, in terms of widely publicized societal conflict, disobediences of federal court orders had reached a level of intensity equal to the heated civil rights conflicts in the American South. The state argued that the Supreme Court should grant certiorari and resolve the uncertainty.

The tribes fervently argued that the government, as trustee, should oppose certiorari. Several high officials in the Interior Department agreed with the tribes. Still, many leaders in Washington, DC, believed that a US Supreme Court opinion was in the national interest because it would blunt or eliminate the ugly regional chaos. It was up to Wade McCree, the Solicitor General of the Justice Department, to decide what positions the government would take before the Supreme Court. In the end, and of no small moment, the United States threw its weight behind granting certiorari.

On October 16, 1978, the US Supreme Court granted the writs of certiorari in order to issue a full ruling on both the cases.

12 The Supreme Court Acts

"Except for some desegregation cases, the District Court has faced the most concerted public and private efforts to frustrate a decree of a federal court ever witnessed in this century."

The energetic back and forth between parties out West and the Justice and Interior Departments continued after the strenuous lobbying on certiorari. Now, the Justice Department's Solicitor General had to decide what position to take on the merits and how to brief the case on behalf of the United States.

In carrying out Indian policy, federal officials sometimes face difficult questions when their trust duties to tribes may conflict with other national objectives. There is a long and checkered history with the tribes, especially in the earlier years, often receiving short shrift. In the Boldt Case, the Solicitor General, Wade McCree, did disagree with the tribes on the procedural issue of granting certiorari. Once the US Supreme Court agreed to hear the appeal, however, the Justice Department squarely put the prestige of the United States on the tribal side on the substantive issues. For example, the United States Brief on the Merits included this:

> The pledge given in the treaties, we believe, requires that Indian fishing at 'usual and accustomed grounds' be accorded special protection. In the circumstances now prevailing, that can only be done by allocating to treaty fishermen a discrete percentage of each fish run. The natural reading of the treaty provision fixes that share as 50%. That result, we believe, is confirmed by considering the reasonable needs of the treaty

tribes. Since experience has shown that the 50% allocation ordered does not exceed that standard, we conclude that it ought to be approved.

In addition to the 50 percent share, the United States' brief supported the tribal side on numerous other points as well.

Early on, for efficiency purposes, the Supreme Court consolidated three cases: the two Washington Supreme Court cases and *United States v. Baker*, a Ninth Circuit Court of Appeals case raising similar issues. Now, under the court's rules, there was just one consolidated case, under the title of *Washington v. Washington State Commercial Passenger Vessel Association*. That is quite a mouthful and even today lawyers and others groan about it, choosing to refer it as the *Passenger Vessel* case. So, technically, the Boldt Decision was not before the Supreme Court. But in the real world, it was very much at play. All of the three cases were reviewing various aspects of the Boldt Decision and virtually everyone—Supreme Court justices included—often referred to the proceedings as the Boldt Case, the district court opinion, or other shorthand terms describing the Boldt Decision. The Supreme Court case with the long and forgettable name, then, was actually about the Boldt Decision.

Oral argument took place in the United States Supreme Court Building (the "Marble Palace") on February 28, 1979, and it was a "hot bench," meaning that the court's questions—many interrupting the attorneys—came fast and furious. It was an impressive group of oral advocates. Washington's Attorney General Slade Gorton, who was an excellent appellate attorney, loved it. Unlike almost all state attorneys general, he himself argued all of Washington's cases before the United States Supreme Court. At argument, he persistently stuck to the state's position in its brief that the treaties did not provide for any numerical share, 50 percent or otherwise; the only tribal right was "equal" access rights to the fish on the ceded lands, as determined by the state as resource

In 1979, several tribal attorneys who did not participate in oral argument traveled to Washington, DC, to watch the argument in the *Passenger Vessel* case. This photograph was taken on the day of oral argument on the front steps of the United States Supreme Court Building. The attorneys, from left to right, are Bill Rodgers, Alan Stay, Mason Morisset, Al Ziontz (front), Tom Schlosser, and Steve Anderson.
Courtesy of Ziontz and Chestnut.

manager. Philip Lacovara, a talented and experienced DC attorney who previously served in Archibald Cox's Special Watergate Prosecutor's Office, represented the Associations of Non-Indian Fishermen. The lawyer for the tribes at oral argument was Mason Morisset. An expert in Indian law, he was a partner in Alvin Ziontz's Seattle firm and vividly articulated the antagonistic history between Washington and the tribes. Louis Claiborne, from the Solicitor General's office, was well known to the judges for his many appearances in Justice Department cases, including Indian matters. He disputed, with his typical eloquence, the state's position that the tribes reserved only a right of "equal" access to the ceded lands. According to Claiborne, a "mere" right of access, without a right to a portion of the fishery, would be "meaningless."

The court held a conference on March 2, just two days after the oral argument. These conferences are formal meetings where all justices meet among themselves to discuss cases before them. The court held several in the *Passenger Vessel* case. There are Supreme Court papers—handwritten notes and memos to all justices—from six of the nine justices. These documents present valuable insights into the court's deliberations.

At the March 2 conference, it was evident that neither side had made any breakthrough at oral argument. Most of the justices had not made up their minds.

By early June, though the justices had discussed the case several times in conferences, there still was no clear majority. Two broad camps had emerged and two justices stepped forward. Justice Lewis Powell, a gentlemanly Virginian and a Richard Nixon appointee, was a moderate with no ideological agenda. Powell favored the state's position that the treaties allowed only a right of access, nothing more. The other camp supported a wholesale affirmation of the Boldt Decision. Justice John Paul Stevens, in just his fifth year on the court, favored this approach. A moderate Republican appointed by President Gerald Ford, his thinking gradually evolved and by the early twenty-first century he was considered the leader of the court's liberal wing.

Powell and Stevens had circulated "memos," basically drafted court opinions. In order to bring specificity and make it somewhat more palatable to the other side, Justice Stevens clarified that the tribes' 50 percent share was a *ceiling* rather than a floor. Now the options were clearer but not all justices had decided.

Time was getting short. Supreme Court terms begin in October and end on the last day of June. In this case, the calendar was putting pressure on the justices since if the opinion were not completed and filed in June, it would have to be reargued in the next term. Then, on June 18, the conservative Chief Justice Warren Burger, recognizing the time pressure, proposed that the case be moved into the next October term. Justice Byron White had made the same proposal a few days earlier. On June 21, the chief justice, who had said little to date, wrote this: "John (Paul)

Stevens has done a 'noble' job but . . . developing a principled decision here is extremely difficult. I do not know whether time will help, but I join Byron in opting for reargument."

Justice Harry Blackmun, who favored the Stevens draft opinion that would uphold the Boldt Decision, then distributed an internal memo. Blackmun, a Nixon appointee from Minnesota, was expected to be a thoroughly conservative justice but his opinions became increasingly liberal over his time on the court. The Blackmun memo seems to have been the deciding factor in the court's decision to render an opinion during the current term rather than putting it over to reargument in the fall. Most of it is reproduced here in full because it has such subtle force and is emblematic of how the court sometimes sees its role in American society:

MEMORANDUM TO THE CONFERENCE:

I would like to weigh in with my comment about these cases. I sincerely hope they do *not* go over for reargument. It seems to me that the cases have been thoroughly briefed and fully argued and that the likelihood of any new enlightenment is meager. Also, we already have a number of other cases on the calendar for reargument.

It seems to me that John [Stevens] has done an admirable job of accommodating the views of those members of the Court who think some apportionment is required and who reject the 'equal access' approach. Indeed, his most recent amendments to his memorandum take into account many of the objections the State itself has made to the orders of the District Court.

One factor that disturbs me is that a postponement for reargument would exacerbate the civil disobedience aspect of the cases. Despite the previous denial of certiorari on some of the issues litigated again here, the District Court has had difficulty in attaining compliance with its orders. If we go to reargument, enforcement during the summer and fall will continue to be difficult. Almost all the recreational fishing takes place during the summer, and the State's Department of Game is the branch of state government that has been least willing to concede fishing rights to the Indians. The prospect of still more strife, caused by our uncertainty over the details of an order already being amended by the District Court, is not a happy one....

On June 22, Chief Justice Burger reversed course and circulated an internal memo stating "I have decided to vote against reargument. I now join John's modified draft." After taking the weekend to think it over, Justice White did the same. Justice Stevens had his majority.

The Supreme Court released its opinion on July 2, 1979, the last case to be decided in the October 1978 Term of Court. The six-member majority opinion was authored by Justice Stevens, joined by Chief Justice Burger, Justice Blackmun, Justice White, Justice Thurgood Marshall, and Justice William Brennan. Three justices dissented, Justice Lewis Powell, Justice William Rehnquist, and Justice Potter Stewart.

Leaving aside a few minor points, the court's ruling amounted to a full-blown approval of the Boldt Decision. It was not a matter of affirming the lower court result but using different reasoning, which often happens. Here, the Supreme Court not only affirmed virtually all of Boldt's specific findings but also cited or quoted from his opinion many times.

On the historical circumstances at treaty time, the Supreme Court found, quoting Judge Boldt, that the tribes all "shared a vital and unifying dependence on anadromous fish" and that "fish constituted a major part of the Indian diet, was used for commercial purposes, and indeed was traded in substantial volume." To underscore the deep and profound place of salmon in Northwest Indians' lives, the court looked to its own 1905 *United States v. Winans* case: the right to take salmon was "not much less necessary to the existence of the Indians than the atmosphere they breathed."

On the relationship between the tribes and the United States, the

The Burger US Supreme Court of 1975 with votes on the *Passenger Vessel* case. Front row left to right: Byron R. White (joined majority), William J. Brennan (joined majority), Chief Justice Warren Burger (joined majority), Potter Stewart (joined dissent), Thurgood Marshall (joined majority). Back row left to right: William H. Rehnquist (joined dissent), Harry A. Blackmun (joined majority), Lewis F. Powell Jr. (authored dissenting opinion), and John Paul Stevens (authored majority opinion).
Courtesy of the Collection of the Supreme Court of the United States.

Supreme Court, like Boldt, found that the tribes heavily relied upon the good faith of the federal government and that the United States promised, through its negotiators, that their treaty fishing rights would be honored. Isaac Stevens offered this assurance at the treaty negotiations: "Are you not my children and also children of the Great Father? What will I not do for my children and what will you not do for yours? Would you not die for them? This paper is such as a man would give his children and I will tell you why. This paper gives you a home. Does not a father give his children a home? . . . This paper secures your fish. Does not a father give food to his children?"

The Supreme Court and Judge Boldt agreed that tribal negotiators did not comprehend the meaning of English treaty words such as "in common with all citizens of the territory" and other terms in the treaties, and the Chinook Jargon was insufficient to communicate the exact treaty meaning. Nonetheless, as a matter of settled law, the intent of the tribes was central to the case. Dr. Barbara Lane's testimony, based on her extensive research, showed that the tribes did not specifically think of their share as being 50 percent; the tribes did, however, as shown in both the Supreme Court and Boldt opinions, have a common understanding of the treaties. The tribes believed, based on all factors, including the assurances of Stevens and other whites, that the treaties guaranteed the tribes "would forever be able to continue the same off-reservation food gathering and fishing practices as to time, place, method, species, and extent as they had or were exercising." In a lengthy passage, the Supreme Court also pointed to a number of other federal cases and factors showing that an equal share would be a fair representation of the tribal intent.

Despite its broad approval of Judge Boldt's ruling, the Supreme Court did disagree on a few points. Consistent with Justice Stevens's amendment to his memo during the post–oral argument period, the 50 percent share is a ceiling, not a floor, and the tribal share secures only a "moderate standard of living;" if that amount is exceeded, that tribe's share could be "modified." Also, the court found that if a tribe were to "dwindle to just a few members" or abandon its fisheries, the tribal share would be reduced or eliminated. After fifty years, neither the "moderate standard of living" nor the "dwindling to just a few members" has ever been acted upon by any court. Also, the Supreme Court reduced the number of tribal fish in two ways: contrary to Judge Boldt, the court found that fish harvested on-reservation and fish taken for ceremonial and subsistence purposes must be included in the tribal 50 percent shares. These adjustments reduced the tribal take only marginally.

More importantly, in its sweeping opinion, the Supreme Court went out of its way to give blunt assessments of how the state and its allies' disruptive conduct pervaded the entire case. That disruptive conduct compelled the court to articulate and uphold wide-ranging trial court powers that justified Judge Boldt's orders and would be available to future trial court judges if such conduct were to continue.

In addition to its broad approval of Judge Boldt's opinion on the various parties' treaty rights and obligations, the Supreme Court was also called upon to rule on the hundreds of trial court orders during the five years after the decision came down in February 1974. Rather than ruling on those orders one by one, the court upheld all of them because the district court was responding to the state's long pattern of conduct attacking tribal rights and federal court authority:

> When Fisheries was ordered by the state courts to abandon its attempt to promulgate and enforce regulations in compliance with the federal court's decree—and when the Game Department simply refused to comply— the District Court entered a series of orders enabling it, with the aid of the United States Attorney for the Western District of Washington and various federal law enforcement agencies, directly to supervise those aspects of the State's fisheries necessary to the preservation of treaty fishing rights. The District Court's power to take such direct action and, in doing so, to enjoin persons who were not parties to the proceeding was affirmed by the Ninth Circuit Court of Appeals.
>
> Because of the widespread defiance of the District Court's orders, this litigation has assumed unusual significance. We granted certiorari in the state and federal cases to interpret this important treaty provision and thereby to resolve the conflict between the state and federal courts regarding what, if any, right the Indians have to a share of the fish, to address the implications of international regulation of the fisheries in the area, and to remove any doubts about the federal court's power to enforce its orders.

At the very end of the opinion, the exasperated Supreme Court looked back and reemphasized the hard and fast supremacy of a valid federal law over a contrary state law on the same subject. The court admonished State Attorney General Slade Gorton, who "continues to argue that the District Court exceeded its authority when it assumed control of the fisheries in the State, and the commercial fishing groups [who] continue to argue that the District Court may not order the state agencies to comply with its orders when they have no state-law authority to do so." The court responded that "a brief discussion" shows that such assertions cannot be upheld:

> State-law prohibition against compliance with the District Court's decree cannot survive the command of the Supremacy Clause of the United States Constitution.
>
> The federal court unquestionably has the power to enter the various orders that state official and private parties have chosen to ignore, and even to displace local enforcement of those orders if necessary to remedy the violations of federal law found by the court.

In its last passage, the court, hopefully but firmly, addressed how governance and litigation of Northwest fisheries should proceed in the future:

> In short, we trust that the spirit of cooperation motivating the Attorney General's representation will be confirmed by the conduct of state officials. But if it is not, the District Court has the power to undertake the necessary remedial steps and to enlist the aid of the appropriate federal law enforcement agents in carrying out those steps. Moreover, the comments by the Court of Appeals strongly imply that it is prepared to uphold the use of stern measures to require respect for federal-court orders.

At the end of that last paragraph, the court offered a dramatic pronouncement, of a kind the Supreme Court rarely makes, that profoundly reminds all of us of the historic, national, and constitutional place of this controversy:

The state's extraordinary machinations in resisting the [1974] decree have forced the district court to take over a large share of the management of the state's fishery in order to enforce its decrees. Except for some desegregation cases [citations omitted], the district court has faced the most concerted official and private efforts to frustrate a decree of a federal court witnessed in this century. The challenged orders in this appeal must be reviewed by this court in the context of events forced by litigants who offered the court no reasonable choice.

Judge Boldt would not be overseeing the *US v. Washington* case after the 1979 opinion. Several months before, he had retired from his judgeship due to health. On the day of the Supreme Court opinion, he said he was "quite elated"—in fact, so much so that he said "I was quivering a little." He called the court ruling "a victory for justice." He made it clear that he had no regrets about retiring. It was time for others to take his place.

At first, it looked as though Judge Boldt's departure might mean a major change, but that was not to be. The federal judges of the Western District of Washington knew the importance of the Boldt Decision. From the beginning, Chief Judge Walter McGovern made sure that a judge would be assigned to handle the case, under the continuing jurisdiction of the district court ordered by Judge Boldt in 1974; those judges would also be assured of all resources necessary to manage the case. The successor judges who followed him have worked hard—because of the complexity of the case in the law books and out on the waters—and from 1979 through the present day have followed and enforced Judge Boldt's opinion and orders. Today, fifty years later, *US v. Washington* is one of the oldest continuing cases in both the federal and state court systems.

13 Comanagement
Eliminating Overfishing and Preserving Salmon Habitat

"Billy Frank started talking about real conservation, and growing the resource, and I thought he was making a lot of sense."

The 1979 Supreme Court ruling was, without question, a major event in the long-standing dispute over the Northwest fisheries. It received broad public coverage and most Washingtonians, whether directly involved with the litigation or not, assumed that Indian treaty rights were here to stay. The tribes had promptly moved ahead and successfully petitioned Judge Boldt for the tribal self-regulation status that he would approve when tribes met the criteria he set out. Immediately after the Boldt Decision, the Justice and Interior Departments put together major annual grants so that the tribes could establish full-scale tribal fisheries management capability. By the late 1970s and early 1980s, most of the tribes were operating substantial and effective fishery programs. Most importantly, by then the tribes had developed fisheries staffs—scientists, ecologists, hydrologists, fish health scientists, geneticists, pathologists, and others—roughly equal in quality and size to the state department staffs.

Still, as would be expected, there was resistance in some quarters. Staff in both the state Fisheries and Game Departments had doubts about tribal management. Some professionals thought that trying to comanage with tribal departments would just be too unwieldy. Others believed that the tribes were not capable of fisheries management. The state agencies had viewed Indian law and Indian people through the lens of litigation for over three decades and some agency personnel believed they should continue with lawsuits to chip away at tribal management authority.

By the early 1980s, the agencies continued the arms-length relationship with the tribes. The state of Washington filed several lawsuits in state courts, asserting state control of salmon management. There was no progress toward the comanagement envisioned by Judge Boldt and the US Supreme Court. Out on the bays and on the rivers, the runs and the catches were steadily declining.

Then things began to change. In 1981, Bill Wilkerson was named deputy director of Washington's Department of Fisheries. He was taken aback by what he saw. "We were still fighting the Boldt Decision. We were pretending like we had won even after the Supreme Court decision." A lawyer, Wilkerson thought otherwise: "I was trained to believe that the law was the law and it was the state's responsibility to implement it." "It was like a debating society in court. There was no sharing of data. The staffs didn't communicate. The adversarial process has its limits."

In 1983, the Director of Fisheries position opened up and the conservation-oriented Governor John Spellman, a Republican, appointed Wilkerson to the position. Wilkerson and Spellman came to agree that "what was needed was to end the fish war." By then, Wilkerson had spent a lot of time with the Nisqually's charismatic tribal leader Billy Frank Jr. Billy had a way with words and could articulate the tribes' focus on salmon rather than fighting the state:

Here's what I tell Indian people when I talk to them. I tell them I wish we were managing thirty years before Judge Boldt issued his ruling in '74. I wish we had co-management then. We might have been able to use the treaties and our professionals back when we really needed it.

But we do have that decision, and it gives us a chance. We're the advocates for the salmon, the animals, the birds, the water. We're the advocates for the food chain. We're an advocate for all of society. Tell

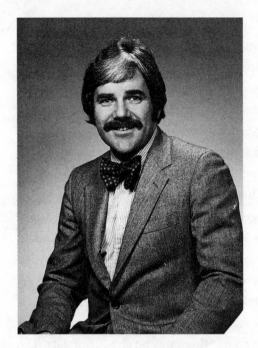

Bill Wilkerson was essential to ending the state-tribal combat that was expensive and causing the decline in the salmon runs. Judge Boldt was passionate about moving to the comanagement relationship between the state and the tribes that is still in place today. Wilkerson and Billy Frank Jr. worked tirelessly all across the state to instill that vision in the minds of the state government, the tribes, and the general public. *Susan Parish Photograph Collection, 1889-1990, Washington State Archives; AR-25501080-ph003669.*

them about our life. Put out the story of our lives, and how we live with the land, and how they're our neighbors. And how you have to respect your neighbors and work with your neighbors.

Frank and Wilkerson were seeing each other regularly and found that they both had the same basic view. Wilkerson put it this way:

We were making speeches all over the state at the time. Billy was saying "What good was a treaty right when all we were doing was fighting over a smaller and smaller resource?" And he started talking about the plight of the salmon. I thought we were supposed to protect the salmon. Our [state] statute was crystal clear—we were supposed to protect the fisheries resources of the state. We were more interested at that time in allocation than we were in conservation. We misused the term *conservation* for so long that we lost touch as a large state agency as to what conservation really was. Billy Frank started talking about real conservation, and

growing the resource, and I thought he was making a lot of sense. And
I started talking about it myself. Co-management was what Judge Boldt
was talking about. He thought the tribes should be involved in the management of the resource and that [the State] should be involved in the
management of the resource.

By 1984, public attention to comanagement had risen. A major court
case underscored the force of the Boldt Decision: in *Hoh Indian Tribe v.
Baldridge*, Judge Walter Early Craig, Judge Boldt's successor, ordered the
state, tribes, and federal agencies to negotiate a long-term comanagement
agreement for salmon. At the same time, the non-Indian fishing interests
were pushing for termination of tribal fishery rights through a proposed
state ballot initiative declaring that only the state, not tribes, could engage
in resource management. Standing for comanagement, Wilkerson and
Frank—both attractive, smart, experienced, and fair—were holding
meetings all across the state. They were being heard. Their message
was that the goal was not for one group or another to win. The critical
objective was to assure the health of the salmon: the state and the tribes
both had legal management authority. They also had the scientists and
leaders who could work together, always looking to broad community
acceptance, as comanagers of the salmon.

In response to the continuing conflict, a diverse and influential group
of organizations sponsored a two-day conference in 1984 on comanagement to be held at the Port Ludlow Resort, on the shore of the Olympic Peninsula looking out over Puget Sound. Governor Spellman sent
Wilkerson to represent the state at the conference.

Here was the beginning of true operational comanagement. At Port
Ludlow, the state and all Puget Sound tribes agreed to negotiate rather
than litigate in the future. The full specifics could not be done at Port
Ludlow but a year later they agreed to a detailed 42-page document,
the Puget Sound Salmon Management Plan of 1985. As of this writing,
that trail-blazing plan, revised and brought up to date every ten years,
is still in force.

The Puget Sound Salmon Plan, therefore, was a major step forward, but the tribes would need to go farther within Washington. The 1985 plan applied to only the state Department of Fisheries. At the time of the debate, logging on Washington's magnificent old-growth forests was at its highest pitch. The spotted owl and other Northwest forest species had been listed under the federal Endangered Species Act and the conflict generated national media attention. State forest lands, often pristine, were critical salmon habitat. Timber harvesting on nonfederal lands in Washington was regulated by the state and managed by the Department of Natural Resources. Other important forestlands in Washington were administered by the US Forest Service.

In early 1986, the tribes, environmental organizations, timber companies, and state officials decided to meet, again at Port Ludlow, to see if they could agree to DNR regulations on timber harvesting and salmon. After intensive negotiation covering nearly the full year, they did reach agreement.

The ambitious Timber, Fish, and Wildlife Agreement of 1987 mandated stricter state regulations to achieve sustainability of whole watersheds. The TFW Agreement emphasized the link between forest management and salmon by adopting the goal of assuring "long-term productivity for natural and wild fish" and other provisions. Interdisciplinary teams, with prominent tribal participation, would carry out on-the-ground review and evaluation of proposed harvesting and completed projects.

Implementing the TFW Agreement has been a challenging enterprise. It had to be done under state agency authority. There have been many meetings. State practices have improved but overall forest health is hard to measure. Still, the tribal participation has been active and productive and most people involved seem to agree that the program, while not revolutionary, has been worthwhile. In 2020, Lorraine Loomis, former chair of the Northwest Indian Fisheries Commission wrote this:

> In a bold move, NWIFC Chairman Billy Frank Jr. and [timber industry leaders] committed to find a way forward through cooperation. What

they found was a solution that not only protected fish and wildlife habitat but also ensured a healthy and sustainable timber industry.

Dozens of meetings between all parties led to the creation of the 1987 TFW Agreement that replaced conflict with a cooperative science-based management approach. Best available science would now "lead wherever the truth takes us," Frank said.

Today, those ideals embodied in law protect more than 60,000 miles of streams on 9.3 million acres of private forestlands across Washington. But it is the classic case of one step forward, two steps back. Growth, development and a changing climate are causing salmon populations to continue to decline because we are losing their habitat in other areas faster than it can be restored and protected.

Steve Barnowe-Meyer, speaking for the Washington Farm Forestry Association praised TFW, saying it was a "ground-breaking Agreement." Tulalip tribal leader Terry Williams's sardonic view probably represents the attitudes of most of the tribes: the TFW Agreement "is just another way that we can try to help influence the state of Washington to do things that will protect our interests."

Another relevant state agency was the Department of Ecology, responsible for managing water quality and water supply. Again, the interest groups engaged in arduous negotiations and came up with a collaborative approach, the Chelan Agreement of 1992. The agreement provided for tribal involvement. Western water law, however, is notoriously complicated and controversial. Attempts to provide for water conservation and instream flows to protect salmon ran into imposing legal and political protections of existing state private water rights for agriculture, hydropower, urban uses, and other purposes. The tribes have put in a lot of time and effort but reforms have moved slowly.

In 1989, the Centennial Accord Agreement between the state of Washington and all twenty-six tribes in the state was signed into law by Governor Booth Gardner and tribal leaders of each tribe. It was the first in the nation of its kind and has been carried out in similar terms in most

Lorraine Loomis, Swinomish, shown here with Governor Gary Locke, was one of
the first women to play an active role in fisheries management in the Northwest and
nationally. In 1974, inspired by the Boldt Decision, she went into salmon management
with her tribe and then with the Northwest Indian Fisheries Commission. Long
respected and liked by the tribes and the state, she was committed to comanagement
and for years was designated as the lead negotiator for tribes in the comprehensive
annual North of Falcon fisheries planning process. Loomis became one of the most
prominent figures in the field when she was named vice chair of the NWIFC in 1995 and
then succeeded Billy Frank Jr. as the chair of the commission when Frank passed on in
2014. Loomis passed away in 2021. *Courtesy of Northwest Indian Fisheries Commission.*

states with significant Indian populations. In the Centennial Accord,
the tribes and the states agreed to respect each other's sovereignty and
work together on common problems and opportunities. The Centennial
Accord has led to the development of new commitments including the
Millennium Agreement in 1999 and the Out of State Accord in 2004.
An annual three-day meeting is attended by state and tribal top-level
officials and staffers. Tribes and the state of Washington now collaborate
broadly on education, health, and natural resources.

Needless to say, the Centennial Accord Agreement and subsequent agreements do not solve all disputes. But governmental bodies in America—federal, tribal, state, county, and local—commonly have working agreements of various kinds with other governments. Some work well. Some don't. On the whole, this agreement in Washington over sovereignty between tribes and the state has been a success. Lorraine Loomis stated in a 2017 news article that "we are proud of the Centennial Accord because it recognizes and honors the best in all of us. It is a constant reminder that cooperation is key to a successful natural resources comanagement."

Necessary though this Washington-tribal cooperation was, even more needed to be done. The state and the tribes are far from the only parties in Puget Sound Pacific salmon management. Salmon do not stay put. They fan out into other jurisdictions. Salmon are born and then reproduce in Washington waters, spending years of their lives in waters of California, Oregon, Canada, and as far away as Alaska. Fish returning to their home rivers in Washington can be intercepted in those distinct jurisdictions. Hence, for example, the lawsuit brought by the Hoh, Quileute, and Quinault tribes over salmon harvesting in Alaska. Other nations and their citizens are involved in another way: foreign fishing fleets from Japan, Russia, and Canada operate in ocean waters off the Pacific Coast, where the United States has jurisdiction.

Salmon management, then, is extraterritorial. For many salmon runs, good environmental practices need to be in place in several federal, state, tribal, and international jurisdictions to ensure healthy migration and spawning.

Congress has always had the power to act but, for most of a century, failed to address the vexing institutional and international quagmire. It was bad enough back in the 1880s, when the hatcheries and high-intensity net fishing began to debilitate the runs. In an 1892 address to the

American Fisheries Society, Dr. Livingston Stone of the US Bureau of Fisheries declared that "the helpless salmon's life is gripped between the two forces—the murderous greed of fishermen and the white man's advancing civilization—and what hope is there for the salmon in the end?" President Theodore Roosevelt lamented in his 1908 state of the union address that "the fishermen of [Oregon and Washington] have naturally tried to take all they could get, and the two legislatures have never been able to agree on joint action of any kind."

By the early twentieth century, the realization set in that overfishing was not the only threat to salmon preservation. Habitat destruction caused by high-yield logging, large storage dams, and agricultural river diversions winched up the pressure on the salmon at least as much as the harvesting.

Congress finally came forward in 1976, when it passed the Fishery Conservation and Management Act. This breakthrough statute is often called the Magnuson-Stevens Act, representing the leadership of Washington's Senator Warren Magnuson and Senator Ted Stevens of Alaska, reflecting the seriousness of the Pacific Northwest fisheries as a national obligation. The purpose of the statute was to consolidate control over territorial waters in order to end overfishing, conserve fishery resources, and improve habitat.

The act created eight regional fishery councils off the East and West Coasts. The reach of the Pacific Fishery Management Council's jurisdiction is immense. Under federal law, states have jurisdiction out to 3 miles off their coasts. Then exclusive federal jurisdiction exists out from 3 miles to 200 miles. Washington and the Boldt Case tribes are affected mostly by the Pacific Fishery Management Council, which regulates the 3- to 200-mile area offshore of Washington, Oregon, and California. The Pacific fisheries council manages commercial, recreational, and tribal fisheries throughout its 3- to 200-mile ocean zone through plans developed after input from states, tribes, fishing communities, scientific research, and approval by the National Marine Fisheries Service. Congress intended that the Pacific Fishery Management Council would drive action under the statute and it has turned out that way.

From the beginning, the Pacific fisheries council's work was successful. Foreign fishing was cut back or eliminated. The act was well funded and early on the Pacific fisheries council built up an excellent staff and began putting in solid programs on conservation and habitat.

For three years, the tribes were brought in, but only as interested parties, not governments. The Supreme Court's ruling approving the Boldt Decision changed that. After Port Ludlow, Governor Spellman, now imbued with comanagement and understanding the tribes' treaty rights and management capabilities, nominated tribal members for one of the Pacific fisheries council's governing seats. Ever since then, there has been a designated tribal seat on the council. The council has several scientific and advisory committees and the tribes have members on virtually all of them.

Numerous initiatives have been adopted under the Magnuson-Stevens Act, always with state, tribal, and federal input, to update and improve the intricate interjurisdictional system. One major example is the United States–Canada Pacific Salmon Treaty of 1985. Both countries had legitimate problems. Pacific salmon from Canada's large and productive Fraser River migrate south to Washington, Oregon, and California and north to Alaska. Fish from America's Columbia River and Puget Sound go north to Canada. Each country wanted the other to limit overharvesting and conserve watershed habitat. Both countries acknowledged that joint management was necessary, but efforts dating back to the 1930s had made little progress until the treaty of 1985. It was an effective vehicle; through joint management, overharvest by one country of the other country's fish was controlled and habitat conservation measures were adopted in both countries. Significant revisions to the original treaty have been made in 1999, 2005, and 2018.

Tribes have been deeply involved in both the negotiation and the implementation of the United States–Canada Treaty. The treaty is administered by the Pacific Salmon Commission. One commission seat is held by a tribal member. Tribal members sit on the key panels and committees and are generally very active in all the commission's activities.

Perhaps the best way to comprehend the sprawling federal, tribal, and state program for fisheries management in the Pacific Northwest based on conservation, collaboration, and science, and the tribes' central role in it, is through an understanding of the North of Falcon process.

Falcon Point is on the far northern Oregon coast, just south of the Columbia River. Since the North of Falcon process is tightly linked to the annual meetings of the Pacific Fishery Management Council, with its astounding geographical reach, the North of Falcon and Pacific fisheries council annual meetings are the biggest and most influential events each year for Pacific Northwest fisheries.

The participants in the North of Falcon process, which dates back to the mid-1980s, are the states and tribes of Washington, Oregon, Idaho, and California that have harvesting authority over rivers where Pacific salmon runs migrate out to the Pacific fisheries council's 3- to 200-mile jurisdiction from California to the Canadian border. Harvests in Alaska are also included.

The states and tribes adopt their own collaborative regulations on inland waters, including harvesting requirements that assure the sustainability of the runs. Because the salmon are out in the ocean for so long under the Pacific fisheries council's jurisdiction, however, the states and tribes need to be assured that the offshore regulations will themselves assure sustainability. The Pacific Fishery Management Council has the same concerns about the regulations of the tribes and states. The two processes need to work together and they do.

Pacific salmon fisheries have huge economic and political impacts. Salmon are an esteemed delicacy in homes and restaurants. Fishing for salmon is a prized sport and a multifaceted tourist industry has built up around it. For all too long, the states had deferred to these interest groups and put few restrictions on commercial and sport fishing, causing declining salmon runs. There were few minimal limits on harvesting out on the ocean.

By the mid-1980s, however, a sturdy consensus emerged that healthy, sustainable runs, as defined by world-class science, come first. Then the politics of harvesting for food and sport can be addressed. Both the Pacific fisheries council and the tribes and states agree with that and reach their decisions in this very complicated endeavor based on the work of their scientists—many, many of them. Complex Endangered Species Act requirements play a critical role.

When the North of Falcon participants gather for their annual meeting in late March and early April, hundreds of people attend. The largest group is made up of scientists but many tribal leaders, administrators, and lawyers attend as well. Industry representatives, conservation organizations, and interested citizens also attend as spectators. The participants must achieve, in a long month, an almost indescribably ambitious—but necessary—objective: *to determine for the upcoming year, based on the best possible science, the conservation needs, especially for escapement, for every single fishery whose waters flow out to the Pacific from each of the North of Falcon states.*

These detailed annual forecasts can rely on data from many years of historical research but, as mentioned above, North of Falcon is now a year-round enterprise. The scientists for the Washington Department of Fish and Wildlife and the twenty tribes' comanagers, for example, build upon the historical record but also must collect current data on every fishery, conduct research, and share knowledge so that they have full up-to-date data for each annual meeting. The Washington comanagers also hold about thirty meetings every year across the state to hear from the public.

The other states and tribes also come up with individual forecasts of their conservation needs. Then all of the participants work together to present a total package to the Pacific Fishery Management Council.

At that point, the Pacific fisheries council will have developed preliminary forecasts of ocean conservation needs and allowable commercial and recreational fishing seasons and catch limits. Then all of the parties work to make adjustments and reach consensus on an overall inland and ocean management plan for the upcoming year. That plan is submitted to the US Secretary of Commerce for approval.

North of Falcon deliberations and negotiations aren't always pretty: there is such an expansive geography of land and water, there are so many runs, so much data, so much law, so many people, and so many opinions. But, for all the rabbit trails that might have been taken, the consensus decision-making process has been ultimately determined by a love of salmon, the fairness of professional leaders, and the opinions of excellent scientists. The results have been some of the most progressive fisheries policies adopted anywhere in the world.

There is no question about the prime leadership role of the tribes. In Washington State, comanagement is not a slogan: the tribes are full and equal partners with the state, just as Judge Boldt envisioned. The tribal and state scientific staffs are of the same quality and size, the two governments work jointly in gathering data from the streams. Especially, the state recognizes that the tribes have superb records on the streams and creeks where their reservations are located. The four tribes on the Olympic Peninsula have large resident staffs while the state has no offices out there; by agreement, the tribes do a heavier part of the data gathering on the peninsula.

Ron Warren, director of fish policy at Washington Department of Fish and Wildlife, reported that "almost everything we do at this department is with our fellow co-managers, the tribes." On its website, the department describes its "fierce" commitment to collaborating with tribes on North of Falcon:

At the core of the North of Falcon process is a fierce commitment to cooperation, fostering a solution-oriented environment that moves natural resource management, protection, and restoration efforts forward. Throughout the process, WDFW and tribal co-managers work together to prioritize salmon conservation, listen to one another's needs, seek solutions, communicate, use the best available science to inform decisions, and accurately document, share and react to important data.

Director Warren also described a personal satisfaction that outsiders commonly feel when working with tribes, especially on comanagement matters: "Nothing in my career has been as rewarding as being a co-manager with the tribes."

Professor Syma Ebbin of the University of Connecticut accurately described the revolutionary nature of sovereign tribal governments in overall fisheries management in the Pacific Northwest:

> The institutional restructuring that came about as a result of the shift to state-tribal co-management provided the Northwest tribes with the opportunity to become substantively involved in all levels of salmon management, from local to international. Tribes are active and formal participants in all management regimes encompassing their local salmon stocks. Additionally, they are active in all phases of salmon management: pre-season planning, in-season management and, to the extent that they occur, post-season evaluations.
>
> Tribes moved from having no seats at the table to having seats at all the relevant tables.

W. Ron Allen joined the tribal council of the Jamestown S'Klallam Tribe shortly after the Boldt Decision. He was named chair in 1979 and has served in that position ever since as a strong advocate for his tribe's land and fisheries rights. He also has been a regional and national tribal leader; among other duties, he was named a member of the board of the National Congress of American Indians in 1989 and has stayed every year since, with four of those years as NCAI president. *Courtesy of Debbie Preston, Nisqually Tribe Communications and Media Services.*

14 The Boldt Decision at Fifty

"Is there a future for wild Pacific salmon in the Pacific Northwest? There can be, but it is up to all of us concerned about these magnificent animals. . . ."

The fiftieth anniversary of the Boldt Decision falls on February 12, 2024. Rare though it is to step back and celebrate long-ago court opinions, especially of trial courts, the depth, breadth, and lasting impact of this particular judicial ruling makes this a fit time to assess its legacy.

As a starting point, the Boldt Decision, so daring, so controversial, and so impactful on a major economy, is fully in place fifty years later. Despite fierce resistance to the justice and civil rights of a small minority that Judge Boldt ordered, the Northwest tribes continue to receive their 50 percent share of salmon and other marine resources. Tribal leaders continue to see the decision as both a mainstay in their history and a paramount continuing asset. Ron Allen, chairman of the Jamestown S'Klallam Tribe since 1977, said this: "There is a saying for all our Northwest tribes: 'Every river has a people.' The Boldt Decision was an epic point in our history. It restored our peoples' right to our rivers and the salmon that is our cultural identity. The decision recognized that the treaties reserved our sovereignty and traditional practices for our people and grandchildren forever."

According to Fawn Sharp, longtime president of the Quinault Indian Nation and now president of the National Congress of American

After graduating from the University of Washington Law School in 1995, Fawn Sharp worked as staff attorney for her tribe, the Quinault Indian Nation. She then was elected president of the Quinault Indian Nation, serving for five terms, and is the current vice president. She also is now president of the National Congress of American Indians, the oldest and largest intertribal organization. Sharp is an expert in climate change, having written on that subject and put into law important advances at the tribal, state, national, and international levels. *Courtesy of Northwest Indian Fisheries Commission.*

Indians, "Judge Boldt had a way of seeing the treaty through our eyes. He was witness to our words, our traditional words and history. All of our Northwest tribes see the Boldt decision as foundational. I often wonder what standing we would have to protect the natural world and our environment if we did not have Judge Boldt."

Judge Boldt's vision of an expert, collegial state-tribal management system dedicated to conserving salmon also became a reality: The state of Washington and the tribes now conduct a mature and effective co-management regime, which was in place by the mid-1980s. For more than three decades, the state of Washington and the tribes have had professional fisheries management resources and staff, working closely together, that are about equal in quality and number. But there is much more.

Judge Boldt, ever future-looking, ordered continuing jurisdiction so that the courthouse doors in *United States v. Washington* would remain open. He knew that the federal court would be needed to address the many disputes that would be forthcoming in the combative legal and political atmosphere prevailing at that point. Hundreds of cases, large and small, were decided by Judge Boldt and successor judges under the continuing jurisdiction.

Perhaps the two most impactful decisions under continuing jurisdiction involved tribal rights to harvest shellfish and the existence of a so-called environmental right in the treaties.

As for shellfish, after the Boldt Decision came down, the tribes became convinced that their right to take "fish" on ceded off-reservation lands included shellfish. Long before the treaties, the tribes treasured such delights as oysters, clams (littleneck, razor, and geoducks), Dungeness crabs, and shrimp. In Washington, most shellfish are found on tidelands owned by non-Indians and the landowners, supported by the state, would not allow gathering of shellfish on their lands. They pointed to the "shellfish provision" in the Stevens treaties, wherein the tribal right to take "fish" was followed by this: "provided, however, that they not take shell-fish from any beds staked or cultivated by citizens." The landowners took that to mean that they had exclusive rights to the shellfish on their properties. They successfully kept the Indians off their tidelands, with the result that the tribes had been able to do little shellfish harvesting since the treaties. There was no existing law on the meaning of the shellfish provision.

Judge Boldt emphasized salmon in his opinion but did not address tribal rights to shellfish either way. The tribes and landowners negotiated but could make no progress. The United States and sixteen tribes brought suit in the *US v. Washington* continuing jurisdiction.

The initial Rafeedie opinion came down in 1994 (although the shellfish cases involved two opinions by Judge Edward Rafeedie and an affirmance by the Ninth Circuit Court of Appeals, in common parlance people refer to that body of law simply as the Rafeedie Decision). As a matter of the English language, the landowners' position—that the shellfish provision recognized their "staked or cultivated" beds as their exclusive property right—was entirely reasonable. But the tribal negotiators spoke only halting English. Judge Rafeedie looked to the original Boldt Decision and applied the special rule of interpretation for Indian treaties, two-party agreements in which the United States drafted the treaties and negotiated them in English, not tribal languages: "Ambiguities will be resolved from the standpoint of the Indians." Treaties should be read "in the sense in which the Indians understood them," and "in a spirit which generously recognizes the full obligations of this nation to protect the interests of a dependent people."

Judge Rafeedie seemed to have no trouble finding that shellfish were intended by the tribes to be "fish" under the treaties and that the tribal 50 percent share was generally applicable. He did hold, however, that the treaty provided for some landowner rights in areas "staked or cultivated by citizens." The parties to the treaty, he found, "intended only to exclude Indians from artificial, or planted, shellfish beds; they neither contemplated nor desired that Indians would be excluded from natural shellfish beds." Thus, 50 percent of the "natural beds . . . located on privately owned tidelands, are part of the tribal fishery."

The Rafeedie Decision also included a ruling that, in addition to tidelands, tribes had rights to fish in deep-water areas and that the right extended to all types of shellfish.

Judge Rafeedie, working with the parties, developed detailed orders, called Implementation of Shellfish Provisions, establishing procedures for shellfish gathering.

The shellfish rulings have proved to be of great importance to the tribes by clarifying that the Boldt Decision applies to many species beyond salmon. Tribes are entitled to harvest for shellfish throughout the Salish Sea and coastal waters where tribes gathered shellfish before the treaties. As for financial concerns, Dungeness crab and other commercial shellfish revenues now exceed those for salmon at a time when salmon are declining. The shellfish harvesting also provides a welcome amount for family meals and ceremonial occasions. Tribal members wear shells on clothing and use them in various other decorative ways. With shellfish, there is now a fuller package of the traditional values and practices that tribes have wanted to preserve in the treaties.

While the continuing jurisdiction has heard many weighty cases, the "culvert case," along with the Rafeedie Decision, is especially notable.

When the tribes filed their original complaint, they included a count alleging that the treaties provided for an "environmental right" preventing development that adversely harmed the salmon runs. Judge Boldt directed that the tribal "fair share" issue would be tried first and then the environmental right would be taken up as "Phase Two." In 1976, the United States and twenty-five tribes brought a case in continuing jurisdiction to establish the environmental right. Nine years later, the Ninth Circuit Court of Appeals ruled that the issue as raised was too general and needed to be decided in a "particular dispute." So the environmental right still had not been decided in court.

In 2001, the tribes and the United States did sue, again in continuing jurisdiction, on a particular dispute: the impact on salmon of culverts under state roads. A culvert is a tunnel carrying water under a road, so the road will not wash out. They are especially needed in the wet Pacific Northwest to stabilize roads from all manner of small rivers, streams, and runoff. The problem is that salmon in those waterways may need to go through one or more culverts on their runs out to the ocean and on their returning journeys back to their spawning grounds. Even culverts on small streams may have large amounts of salmon habitat above them. If culverts are properly designed, installed, and maintained, the salmon swim through them and prosper. But if culverts are not designed to proper fish passage standards and get broken down or are otherwise inadequate—in the case of salmon, scientists call them *barrier culverts*—whole salmon runs can be weakened or destroyed.

The evidence at trial showed that state culverts in northwestern Washington were causing significant damage to salmon passage. More than 800 culverts blocked access to "significant habitat." At the time of the trial, state culverts blocked access to 1,000 miles of streams, comprising almost 5 million square meters of salmon habitat. In 2013, Judge Ricardo S. Martinez issued a sweeping injunction giving the state seventeen years to correct the blocking culverts. The cost estimates ran up to one billion dollars.

The Ninth Circuit Court of Appeals affirmed the district court opinion. In this much-watched litigation, the court found in a comprehensive opinion that having sufficient salmon to sustain them was a purpose of the Stevens treaties and that "in building and maintaining barrier culverts within the Case Area, Washington has violated, and is continuing to violate, its obligation to the Tribes under the Treaties." Professor William Rodgers called it "a stunning ruling that forbids the State of Washington from destroying anadromous fish runs."

The controversial environmental rights case then went to the US Supreme Court in 2018. At oral argument, questioning centered on the breadth of the right: Even supposing there is such a right, it was recognized that many state actions do cause some environmental stress but many of these stresses are minor. What should the standard be—"substantial" stress, for example? The court was unable to agree on whether there should be such a test and how strict it should be. Justice Anthony M. Kennedy recused himself and did not vote. The other justices split four to four. The court's one-page order meant that the Ninth Circuit Court opinion would remain in force, but only in the Ninth Circuit.

Thus, the existence and extent of the environmental right isn't yet known. For the foreseeable future, the strong Ninth Circuit Court culvert opinion is the law throughout all Ninth Circuit courts in Washington, Oregon, California, Arizona, Nevada, Idaho, Montana, Alaska, and Hawaii. To the date of this writing, there have been no significant developments on these issues since 2018.

Treaty fishing rights also were protected in historic events on the Elwha River.

The Lower Elwha Klallam Tribe, discussed in chapter 2, had fishing rights recognized in the Boldt Decison. However, the rights of the Lower Elwha were not respected due to the construction of two dams in 1911 and 1926 on the Elwha River. These dams devastated the salmon runs and tribal cultures. For generations, the damage to the salmon, the tribes, and the environment was an outrage to many Washingtonians on the Olympic Peninsula and across the Northwest. The key to honoring the Boldt Decision rights was to bring the dams down. Nearly everyone, though, assumed that taking out the dams would be politically and legally impossible.

The Lower Elwha Klallam Tribe eventually took the lead, with supporting conservation organizations and other citizens groups, and succeeded in obtaining federal legislation authorizing complete removal of both dams. In 1992, the Elwha River Ecosystem and Fisheries Restoration Act was signed into law. The legislation authorized the Secretary of the Interior to acquire the dams and take action to restore the Elwha

River. The dam removal process began with a large and enthusiastic formal dam-removal ceremony on September 17, 2011, on the banks of the Elwha River.

This was the first major dam removal in American history. It was testament to Lower Elwha Klallam culture, sovereignty, treaty rights, and staying power. Lower Elwha Klallam Tribal Chair Dennis Sullivan explained it this way: "We are salmon people. . . . You take away the salmon, which happened since the dams . . . and you are removing part of our culture, our way of living, our survival. . . .

"Our elders—nobody would listen to them, their voices weren't heard—until the late 1960s. . . . It was unheard of to remove the dams. It took a lot of educating. Still today we are educating. . . . We are the protectors of the salmon. Salmon and us are like family to each other. We need each other. A lot of people who opposed are now in agreement that the [dams needed] to come out. That is how we won the battle, just by educating."

The legal principles in the Boldt Decision have been deeply influential beyond the state of Washington. As explained by Reid Peyton Chambers, a former law professor at University of California, Los Angeles, and a longtime practitioner and scholar, "The Boldt Decision has furnished a basic template for similar decisions in other states," including Oregon, Michigan, Wisconsin, and Minnesota. "The dramatic reallocation of fish resources to tribes in the Washington case that reached the Supreme Court in 1979 seems a remarkable and largely unblemished success."

Beyond the specifics of treaty fishing rights, the decision is a foundational case in the overall body of federal Indian law, including the unique and central issues of tribal sovereignty, the United States' special trust relationship with the tribes, and tribal treaty rights generally. University of Connecticut law professor Bethany Berger explained it this way:

The fishing rights battle helped kickstart the formal study of Federal Indian law in law schools, and contributed to the passage of regulations for acknowledgement of unrecognized Indian tribes. The struggle resulted in important legal victories, and had an incalculable impact on the modern resurgence of tribal sovereignty.

Historian Phil Dougherty looked back in 2020:

"The Boldt Decision," as it is commonly referred to, was one of the biggest court decisions issued during the twentieth century involving Native rights. While the decision itself dealt with tribal fishing rights, its affirmation of tribal sovereignty was more far-reaching and presented a huge (and unexpected) victory for Native Americans.

The Boldt Decision has also had influence internationally. In Canada, *Regina v. Sparrow*, the "cornerstone case" on First Nations' fishing rights, "mirrored the Boldt Decision." Other Canadian court decisions and policies were informed by Judge Boldt's work. While internationally the influence of the Boldt Decision has not been as direct as in Canada—and not to make too much of it—the decision has sometimes been noted as one of the many sources in the burgeoning recognition of Indigenous rights in several foreign countries. Australia is one example:

Australia has struggled to redefine its relationship with indigenous peoples. In adopting doctrines in the United States of America, Canada, New Zealand and other common law countries, Australia common law has belatedly moved from its traditional denial of legitimacy of claims by its original inhabitants toward the recognition of legally enforceable aboriginal rights.

The Boldt Decision also was looked to in the early development of the historic United Nations Declaration on the Rights of Indigenous

Peoples, passed by the General Assembly in 2007. "Spurring the process
... were diverse efforts to draw attention to human rights problems facing
Indigenous Peoples. Water conflicts were salient in this context. They
included 'fish wars' associated with the landmark 1974 Boldt Decision
in the Columbia River Basin. . . ."

As shown in earlier chapters, before comanagement in the mid-1980s,
the state of Washington effectively exercised full management control
over its salmon fisheries. It is now understood that overfishing was one
of two major causes for the declining salmon runs: the state basically
approved all requests from commercial and sport fishers for harvesting
licenses. The only exception was that the state set many barriers to tribal
fishing and made regular raids and arrests. There was only superficial
research on what needed to be done every year on every river to ensure
sustainability of the runs. Within just a few years, under state-tribal co-

Northwest Indian Fisheries Commission
Executive Director Justin Parker receiv-
ing a gift from Congresswoman Mary
Peltola, Yup'ik from Western Alaska,
both the first woman and the first Alaska
Native ever to represent the state of
Alaska in the United States House of
Representatives. Here, Peltola was head-
ing up a delegation of Alaska Natives
to meet with Pacific Northwest tribes.
*Courtesy of Northwest Indian Fisheries
Commission.*

Hokkaido, the northernmost island in Japan, is home to the Ainu, the Indigenous people of Japan. Inspired by the Boldt Decision, lawyers for the Ainu, whose fishing rights have been denied by the Japanese government, came to the United States to learn about Northwest tribal fishing rights. They found that Hokkaido and the Pacific Northwest have similar longitudes, environmental conditions, and native salmon runs. The Ainu began calling themselves the "Salmon People." The Ainu still face governmental opposition to the kind of rights that American tribes have, but they are actively working in the courts and legislature to improve the situation. As with other countries, the Northwest tribes and the Ainu have been making back-and-forth visits. Here, Nisqually Tribal Chairman Willie Frank III and Councilmember Chay Squally meet, at the Wa He Lut Indian School, with filmmakers from Japan visiting Northwest tribes as part of a documentary about Ainu people and salmon in 2022. *Courtesy of Northwest Indian Fisheries Commission.*

management with a strong scientific component, including the North of Falcon process described in chapter 13, overfishing was mostly eliminated on both inland and ocean waters.

The other great threat to the salmon runs was the age-old nemesis, habitat destruction. Starting in the 1980s and continuing to the present, Washington has made inroads on habitat problems under the comprehensive federal, state, and tribal resource management system described in chapter 13. Still, legal, political, and corporate barriers have too often blocked or slowed restoration of salmon habitat damage caused by dams, logging and grazing practices, agricultural and municipal water diversions, growth, and various industrial discharges that polluted the inland and ocean waters.

The immensity of salmon depletion has steadily become more serious than previously realized: the runs have continued to decline. For example, the American Fisheries Society reported a West-wide salmon "crisis" and made an early finding that more than a hundred salmon runs had a "high risk of extinction." The Endangered Species Act moved into salmon management. In 1991, the National Marine Fisheries Service granted a petition by the Shoshone-Bannock Tribe of Idaho and listed the imperiled Snake River sockeye run under the Endangered Species Act; it was the first listing in the Pacific Northwest. The NMFS continued its listings unwaveringly. Today, the ESA language—and reality—of salmon runs as "endangered," "threatened," and even "extinct" has become commonplace among state, tribal, and federal governmental officials and the Pacific Northwest citizenry at large.

Then, about a generation ago, the devastating impacts of climate change became fully apparent. Climate change is raising the temperature in both freshwater and marine environments, decreasing water quality for cold-water fish including salmon, changing flow regimes, and diminishing food sources and habitat in an exponentially compounding fashion. As the Washington State Recreation and Conservation Office rightly put it, "[Too] many salmon remain on the brink of extinction.

And time is running out. The climate is changing, rivers are warming, habitat is diminishing, and the natural systems that support salmon in the Pacific Northwest need help now more than ever."

Today, in spite of all the challenges, Washington as a place has built a truly imposing system—a movement, really—to carry out the state's universally held commitment to salmon protection and preservation. The effort, at once informal and organized, includes virtually all aspects of leadership and progress in the state: political leaders and government officials; new programs at the federal, state, tribal, and local levels; new and expanded nonprofit prosalmon organizations; conservation groups; sport fishing, guides and packers, and river groups; farm groups; corporate participation; churches; and academic and scientific personnel.

This movement has been extraordinarily successful. It is active and effective in political and legal matters. Also, a notable hallmark of this effort has been dozens upon dozens of programs to introduce the ways that individual citizens can help salmon protection in their own lives. As a result, untold members of the public have made sure not to ride bikes or off-highway vehicles in streams, rivers, or wetlands. Many have participated in hands-on programs to protect and restore estuaries and wetlands; reduced runoff from their lands; placed woody debris in stream corridors; pledged themselves to conserve water and avoid waste of water in all settings, large and small; and avoided using pesticides in gardens and lawns (in the Pacific Northwest you can see lawn signs that proudly declare "Salmon Friendly Lawn").

It is impossible to know whether the salmon preservation coveted so passionately by so many people, including Judge Boldt, can survive. I notice that virtually everyone involved agrees that the salmon are at risk but that few or none have gone so far as to argue that the salmon absolutely cannot survive. Recent studies hold out hope if the right decisions are made in the future. In *Wild Pacific Salmon: A Threatened Legacy*, fisheries scientist Jim Lichatowich and six of his colleagues put it this way:

If we are to leave future generations a legacy of wild salmon, it will require a major push by the concerned public to insist that management policies, activities and normal behaviors be changed. The public already suspect there is a need for change in how we manage and recover salmon. . . .

Is there a future for wild Pacific salmon in the Pacific Northwest? There can be, but it is up to all of us concerned about these magnificent animals to force a change in the status quo, to hold accountable the elected officials and public servants charged with salmon stewardship, and to join in and support those organizations who speak truth to those in power.

Professor Michael Blumm, who has written widely on Pacific salmon law, offered this in his 2022 book *Pacific Salmon Law and the Environment: Treaties, Endangered Species, Dam Removal, Climate Change, and Beyond*:

But salmon matter to people beyond those who harvest them. For many they represent a barometer of the environment, one of the best we have. For although salmon are tenacious in their fidelity to place, they've proved adaptable to changed river conditions, so long as the conditions are habitable. Although the law certainly has not demanded salmon habitability in the past, a challenge for the future is to require that the climate-changed world ahead will be habitable for the West's most iconic marine species. Existing laws will not ensure that habitability. There is much work ahead for those wishing to ensure salmon's future.

One of the most luminous contributions of the Boldt Decision over the past fifty years is its standing as a classic example of how much the rule of law can mean when it works right. The rule of law is said to be one of our nation's core values. But how does the rule of law work? As I write this, we Americans face a crisis over the rule of law.

The rule of law means that we—all people and all institutions—are bound to comply with valid laws. This is not a harsh notion but a compassionate one that builds safe, stable, and trusting relationships among governments and smoothly working communities. Needless to say, individuals and organizations often stray, out of pique, exasperation, bad judgment, or a conscious decision to break the law. Nonetheless, the rule of law has remained a sacred aspiration, an eternal part of the ideals that make us proud to be Americans. Overall, this may mean recognizing that sensitive, difficult circumstances can produce heartrending conflicts that require long, strenuous efforts by many parties if the rule of law is to be honored.

From the moment Judge Boldt handed down his opinion in 1974, it was unclear whether it could hold. Of course, this was rarely articulated in terms of the rule of law, but that is what it was.

There was a widely held view at the time that this official government action was wrong. People asked, What kind of law is an Indian treaty? It was vague. Nobody knew about it. It was considered outmoded, never designed to deal with modern commercial and sport fishing. People wanted to know, Doesn't the law protect good, honest, and valued businesses? There is no way to articulate the joy of steelhead fishing. Would the steelheading take be reduced, or seasons shortened or shut down entirely for non-Indians? And doesn't the law prohibit discrimination by race? And besides, how can one judge just tear society apart like this?

These people weren't racists. They were normal, fair-minded Washingtonians who just did not comprehend how the Boldt Decision made sense. The outrage in Washington over the Boldt Decision took the anger to a new level and reinforced objectors in Oregon, especially when Judge Belloni adopted the Boldt 50 percent share in *United States v. Oregon*. As described in chapter 11, Rebellion, for years refusal to obey federal law was supercharged in Washington and evident to a lesser degree in Oregon as well. Could the Belloni and Boldt Decisions hold?

Part of the answer came from the US Supreme Court in 1979. The court upheld the rule of law. The overt illegal fishing mostly ceased. But that didn't end the matter. Everyone knew that Congress could adjust or abrogate the treaty rights entirely. It could be done fairly and legally by paying off the tribes. In Washington, Senator Slade Gorton and Congressman Jack Cunningham did exactly that, trying to find some mechanism that would be acceptable to the public and Congress. But in the end—roughly the 1990s—the rule of law held, not just in the courts, but in Congress and the general public as well.

The story of why the rule of law, as embodied in *United States v. Washington*, finally held is complex and can't be addressed in detail here, but there are a few points to note. Washington's political leadership in the 1970s, 1980s, and 1990s, was exceptional: Governors John Spellman and Booth Gardner. US Senator Patty Murray. Dan Evans, who as governor and United States senator, recognized the legitimate interests of the tribes and worked with them, during the most difficult years. US Senator Warren Magnuson grew in office and came to believe to his depths that the treaties should be honored and that sovereign tribal governments were powerful tools in Pacific salmon conservation. Many nontribal people realized the salmon were in trouble and came to accept Judge Boldt's interpretation of the treaties. The idea of treaty abrogation dissipated. In ways not fully understood, the general public was willing to accept the new system. Hard though it often was, people on all sides came together to create systems that all could live with. Today, the treaty rights and tribal self-management are embedded in widely accepted comanagement systems. Again, there was no announcement that the rule of law held, and the public discourse didn't put it that way. But that is what happened.

Over time, the state and individual citizens took actions and made statements demonstrating that the treaties were always the law and the tribes were and are sovereign. As noted in chapter 13, Comanagement—Eliminating Overfishing and Preserving Salmon Habitat, Governor Booth Gardner initiated the idea of a statewide recognition of the relationship between the tribes and the state, then negotiated with tribal leaders to accomplish the Centennial Accord Agreement of 1989, recognizing the relationship between the state's sovereignty and the tribal sovereign governments. This agreement, the first of its kind in the country, was welcomed by the tribes. State officers returned to tribal fishers their nets, canoes, and gear illegally seized during the difficult years.

In 2014, the Washington State Legislature produced a statute that allowed tribal members, living and deceased, to clear their state criminal records if they were convicted of fishing violations during the "fish wars." The bill passed both houses virtually unanimously. State Senator Bob Hasegawa, representing the sentiments of both houses, said that "it is incumbent on us as a society to admit that we were wrong previously—and we are righting those wrongs." Johnson Meninick, Yakama tribal member, was finally able to vacate his great-uncle's 1917 conviction for illegal fishing. Meninick said, "[It] took 100 years to clear his name, but my sons and grandsons still fish there at Prosser [Reservoir]. We'll feel more comfortable fishing there now."

It took a great many tribal people to accomplish the justice and rights that flowed from the Boldt Decision, but Billy Frank Jr. was perhaps the most well-known advocate. He received many federal, state, and university honors, always saying, correctly, that honoring him really represented the work of all Indian people. On December 18, 2015, after enthusiastic passage of the act in both the US Senate and House of Representatives, President Barack Obama signed the act changing the title of the national monument at the mouth of the Nisqually River, the area Billy and his ancestors had called their homeland for so long. The wildlife refuge is now named the Billy Frank Jr. Nisqually National Wildlife Refuge.

Billy Frank Jr. passed on in 2014, prior to the declaration of the national wildlife refuge. His death was reported widely in the Pacific Northwest (his passing was front page news in the *Seattle Times* for three days afterward) and throughout the nation. His memorial service, which I attended as a speaker and pallbearer, on the Squaxin Island Reservation in rural Washington was attended by roughly 6,000 people. Overflow parking was impossible. The crowd was roughly one-half Native and one-half non-Indian. The governor, both United States senators, and

President Barack Obama and Billy Frank Jr. *Courtesy of Northwest Indian Fisheries Commission.*

five congressional representatives attended. In Washington, DC, flags were flown at half-mast in Frank's honor. President Obama sent a formal American flag to the family and in a press release stated, "Today, thanks to his courage and determined effort, our resources are better protected and tribes are able to enjoy the rights preserved for them more than a century ago." Bill Wilkerson, former Washington State director of fisheries, reflected, "I don't think there is probably any single leader in the history of our state who has been treated with greater respect than Billy was treated upon his death."

In 2021, the state of Washington once again paid high honor to Billy Frank Jr. The National Statuary Hall Collection is located on the first floor of the United States Capitol Building on Capitol Hill in Washington, DC. It is a grand gallery of a hundred statues of exemplary Americans, two from each state. In 2021, Governor Jay Inslee signed into law a bill replacing the statue of Marcus Whitman, an early pioneer, with a statue of Billy Frank Jr. The replacement was widely and passionately supported. The bill passed the state House of Representatives by a vote of 92–5 and the state Senate approved it by a 44–5 vote. At the signing ceremony near the Nisqually River, with many Indian people present, including Nisqually drummers and singers wearing hand-sewn regalia, the governor said this:

> We expect to send our best from the state of Washington to be memorialized in the United States Capitol in Statuary Hall. We can't send the Nisqually River or Mount Rainer, but we can send Billy Frank Jr.

It is no small thing when societies immersed in intense, long-standing public disputes over emotional and divisive issues find a way to come together and make the rule of law a working, real-world reality. It is even more rewarding when it moves beyond compromise to genuinely improved professional and personal relationships. The state and the tribes continue to have many disagreements and always will—their ultimate goals and beliefs differ. Nonetheless, the people of Washington, and Oregon as well, should be everlastingly proud of what their judges, political leaders, tribal leaders, and citizenry accomplished over the fifty years since the Boldt Decision.

Acknowledgments

This book has been in progress for a number of years. Shortly after work on it began, an interruption of three years occurred in order to be able to serve as Special Advisor to the Bears Ears Inter-Tribal Coalition in regard to the creation of the Bears Ears National Monument, proclaimed by President Barack Obama in 2016.

There are a great many people to whom a debt of gratitude is owed for their important contributions to this book.

Personal interviews were invaluable. Special gratitude to Ron Allen, Matt Belew, Nettsie Bullchild, Ron Charles, Cliff Cultee, John Echo-hawk, Billy Frank Jr., Mike Grayum, Phil Greene, Timothy J. Greene Sr., Darrell Hillaire, Chief Bill James, Jeremiah Julius, Larry Kinley, Melia Lane-Kamahele (daughter of Barbara Lane), Janine Ledford, David Martin, Phillip Martin, Guy McMinds, Rebekah Monette, Justin Parker, Virginia Riedinger (daughter of Judge Boldt), William Rodgers, Fawn Sharp, Steve Solomon, Russ Svec, Neil Vallance, Richard Whitney, Bill Wilkerson, and Alvin Ziontz.

Wholehearted appreciation to these colleagues who took time out of their busy lives to review the manuscript—the late John Hollowed, Mike Grayum, Ron Allen, and Fran Wilshusen.

Several law students served as research assistants and did fine work on this book, poring over legal transcripts and historical documents, scouring various libraries for important books and obscure sources. Their many comments and suggestions were very beneficial, as well their friendship. Deepest thanks to Tarn Udall, Chloe Bourne, Shelly Oren, Allison Hester, Lauren Goschke, Bridgett Murphy, John Rader, Zoe Osterman, Christina Warner, Eric Dude, Alana Martin, Taylor Schad, Siena Kalina, Kelby Welsh, and Charlotte Collingwood. Thank you also to Cynthia Carter, longtime faculty assistant, who came out of retirement and worked part-time to help with completion of this book.

There is immense gratitude for the generous support of the Northwest Indian Fisheries Commission. Justin Parker always had an open door for absolutely any question or need that came up. Also helpful were Willie Frank, Lois Allen, and Tony Meyer, among many others. Genuine gratitude and admiration go out to Kari Neumeyer, Gena Peone, and the rest of the amazing and devoted NWIFC team who worked tirelessly on the acquisition of images for this book. A special thank-you to Bruce Jones for his expert work on the maps.

The University of Colorado Law School has been supportive in every way for so many years. Everlasting gratitude to these deans for all of their help and collegiality—Phil Weiser, S. James Anaya, and Lolita Buckner Inniss.

A huge thank-you to the Wise Law Library at the University of Colorado Law School for their indispensable assistance in acquiring research documents, articles, and books—Jane Thompson, the late Matt Zafiratos, Michelle Pen, Jill Sturgeon, and Joan Policastri. Thanks to the University of Colorado's Norlin Library for the hundreds of books they provided for research. A special thank-you to Mary Whisner of the Gallagher Law Library at the University of Washington School of Law for being so helpful. A resource of special mention is the Tribal Voices Archive Project sponsored by Salmon Defense and the Northwest Indian Fisheries Commission that contains audio and video collections of tribal member perspectives from those who lived before, during, and after the Boldt Decision. Sincere thanks to Shaun LaBarre at the law school's Getches-Wilkinson Center for administering the accounts for research assistant funding and other valuable support. A hearty thank-you to the wonderful law school Faculty Coordinators team for their collective expertise and ever-cheerful attitudes in assisting in all kinds of ways.

Very high regard to these thoughtful, talented, and collaborative professionals at the University of Washington Press—Nicole Mitchell, Larin McLaughlin, Jennifer Comeau, Kris Fulsaas, and Molly Woolbright.

A dear thank-you to Henry Thayer, literary agent extraordinaire, for his sound advice and always being available.

Profound appreciation goes out to the many Northwest tribal members and others for sharing their personal experiences related to living through the challenging years leading up to and through the Boldt Decision. These important conversations hold deep meaning for this book.

Lasting respect to experts, colleagues, and friends whose shared knowledge, advice, and discussions have helped so much with this book—Dick Trudell, Billy Frank Jr., Alan Stay, Justin Parker, Ron Allen, Fawn Sharp, Willie Frank, John Echohawk, Bill Wilkerson, Gary Morishima, Mike Grayum, John Hollowed, Rick Collins, Sarah Krakoff, Kristen Carpenter, Matthew L. M. Fletcher, John Hughes, Michael Blumm, Laura Berg, Daniel Cordalis, Amy Cordalis, Monte Mills, and Ann Getches. All of the good information, camaraderie, and valuable time that you gave so generously is most sincerely appreciated.

There is such deep love and gratitude for the Wilkinson family for all of their support, care, time, help, and love during the writing of this book and always. Dearest Ann, Seth, Zahraa, Khalil, Meera, Philip, David, Samantha, Ellen, Calvin, and Ben—you are my heart.

Notes

1   Fury on the Puyallup River

1   **The Puyallup riverbank . . . provided the site of one of the most terrifying police raids.** *See, e.g.,* Lynda V. Mapes, "Fish-camp Raid Etched in State History," *Seattle Times* (September 6, 2010), https://perma.cc/9JCA-SRYN.

2   **Indians at the encampment fired four warning shots.** Gabriel Chrisman, "The Fish-in Protests at Franks Landing" (2008), Seattle Civil Rights and Labor History Project, University of Washington, https://perma.cc/583L-6NUB. This particularly informative article on the protests at Frank's Landing includes vivid accounts from both sides of the clash.

2   **Ramona Bennett . . . lived the violence that day.** Mapes, "Fish-camp Raid."

2   **They arrested more than sixty people.** *Id.*

2   **They dragged the fishermen up the rough, rocky riverbanks.** Chrisman, "Fish-in Protests."

3   **"the right of taking fish"** Treaty with the Nisquallys and other Tribes, December 26, 1854, 10 Stat. 1132, Article 3 (ratified March 3, 1855; proclaimed April 10, 1855), reprinted *in* Charles J. Kappler, *Indian Affairs, Laws and Treaties,* p. 662 (Washington, DC: Government Printing Office, 1904); Treaty with the Dwamish and other Tribes, January 22, 1855, 12 Stat. 927, Article 5 (ratified March 8, 1859; proclaimed April 11, 1859); Treaty with the S'Klallam, January 26, 1855, 12 Stat. 933, Article 4 (ratified March 8, 1859; proclaimed April 29, 1859); Treaty with the Makah, January 31, 1855, 12 Stat. 939, Article 4 (ratified March 8, 1859; proclaimed April 18, 1859); Treaty with the Qui-Nai-elt and other Tribes, July 1, 1855, 12 Stat. 971, Article 3 (ratified March 8, 1859; proclaimed April 11, 1859).

4   **"renegades" and "poachers"** Charles Wilkinson, *Messages from Frank's Landing: A Story of Salmon, Treaties, and the Indian Way,* p. 31 (Seattle: University of Washington Press, 2000).

5   "[T]his boat was coming at me and Bridges" *Id.* at p. 33.

5   "At the beginning, these guys had no idea" *Id.*

7   "this paper secures your fish" "Record of the Proceedings of the Commission to Hold Treaties with the Indian Tribes in Washington Territory and the Blackfoot Country, December 7, 1854–March 3, 1855," Records of the Washington Superintendency of Indian Affairs, 1853–1874, roll 26, M5, National Archives and Records Administration, p. 4; *Worcester v. Georgia*, 31 U.S. 515 (1832); *Cherokee Nation v. Georgia*, 30 U.S. 1 (1831); *Johnson v. McIntosh*, 21 U.S. 543 (1823).

2   The Salmon People

9   **The right to fish "in common with the citizens of the Territory."** Treaty with the Nisquallys and other Tribes, December 26, 1854, 10 Stat. 1132, Article 3 (ratified March 3, 1855; proclaimed April 10, 1855), reprinted *in* Charles J. Kappler, *Indian Affairs, Laws and Treaties*, p. 662 (Washington, DC: Government Printing Office, 1904); Treaty with the Dwamish and other Tribes, January 22, 1855, 12 Stat. 927, Article 5 (ratified March 8, 1859; proclaimed April 11, 1859); Treaty with the S'Klallam, January 26, 1855, 12 Stat. 933, Article 4 (ratified March 8, 1859; proclaimed April 29, 1859); Treaty with the Makah, January 31, 1855, 12 Stat. 939, Article 4 (ratified March 8, 1859; proclaimed April 18, 1859); Treaty with the Qui-Nai-elt and other Tribes, July 1, 1855, 12 Stat. 971, Article 3 (ratified March 8, 1859; proclaimed April 11, 1859).

11   **The North Pacific current . . . brings in moderate temperatures.** See generally Cliff Mass, *The Weather of the Pacific Northwest* (Seattle: University of Washington Press, 2008).

12   **The forest floors were a spongy wet mass of organic matter.** See generally Thomas A. Spies and Sally L. Duncan, *Old Growth in a New World: A Pacific Northwest Icon Reexamined* (Washington, DC: Island Press, 2009).

12   **The ocean awaited the young salmon.** See generally Thomas P. Quinn, *The Behavior and Ecology of Pacific Salmon and Trout* (Seattle: University of Washington Press, 2018); Cornelis Groot and Leo Margolis, eds., *Pacific Salmon Life Histories* (Vancouver, BC: University of British Columbia Press, 1991).

13   **Indian people today often say that their people were "rich" or "wealthy."** Suquamish Tribe, "Timeline, Pre-Contact" (2015), *Suquamish Tribe History and Culture*, https://perma.cc/MU4M-2BEJ; Melissa Peterson-Renault and the Makah Cultural and Research Center, *Makah Tribe History* (accessed April 19, 2022), Makah Tribal Council, https://perma.cc/2FM8-KGRX; *see also* Barbara Lane, *Anthropological Report on Makah Economy Circa 1855 and the Makah Treaty, US v. Washington*, Exhibit USA-21, pp. 17–29 (August 24, 1973); *United States v. Washington*, 384 F. Supp. 312, 364 (W.D. Wash. 1974).

13   Scholars regularly agree, describing the tribes of northwestern Washington as being "prosperous" or "wealthy." Scott Byram and David G. Lewis, "Ourigan: Wealth of the Northwest Coast," vol. 102, no. 2 *Oregon Historical Quarterly*, p. 147 (Summer 2001); R. Kent Rasmussen, "Northwest Coast," in *American Indian Tribes*, vol. 1, pp. 38–40 (Hackensack, NJ: Salem Press, 2000). Some scholars have questioned this. *See, e.g.,* June McCormick Collins, *Coast Salish and Western Washington Indians II*, p. 131 (New York: Garland Publishing, 1974).

14   The Pacific Northwest produced more protein per acre than virtually any place in North America. Eric O. Bergland, *Summary Prehistory and Ethnography of Olympic National Park, Washington*, pp. 34, 54 (Seattle: National Park Service, 1984); William C. Sturtevant, ed., *Handbook of North American Indians*, vol. 11, p. 338 (Washington, DC: Smithsonian Institution, 1978).

15   The Lummi villages . . . spoke the same Salishan dialect; employed the specialized technology of reef-net fishing . . .; and had similar societies, institutions, customs, and traditions. See the excellent history of the Lummis, Bernhard J. Stern, *The Lummi Indians of Northwest Washington*, p. 7 (New York: Columbia University Press, 1934); Barbara Lane, *Anthropological Report on the Identity, Treaty Status and Fisheries of the Lummi Tribe of Indians, US v. Washington*, Exhibit USA-30, pp. 2–3 (August 24, 1973).

15   Combat and even wars with other tribes *See, e.g.,* Wayne Suttles and William C. Sturtevant, eds., *Handbook of North American Indians*, vol. 7, pp. 456–457 (Washington, DC: Smithsonian Institution, 1990), which treats conflicts with other Coast Salish tribes as "occasional," but emphasizes major raids from the Lekwiltok Kwakiutl, an aggressive or "truly warlike" tribe from the north end of Vancouver Island; Debra L. Martin and David W. Frayer, eds., *Troubled Times: Violence and Warfare in the Past*, p. 289 (Amsterdam: Gordon and Breach, 1997), which concluded that "larger-scale conflicts," called "genuine warfare" . . . by Old People to distinguish them from raids, occasionally occurred, as when the Lekwiltok displaced the Coast Salish on the Northern Strait of Georgia and occupied their territory in the early 1800s: "Most conflict, however, was of a different nature, involving violent removal of property rather than hostile territorial acquisitions."

16   "Whale Story" Chief Bill James, Lummi tribal member, interview with Zoe Osterman, research assistant, Lummi Reservation, Washington, April 15, 2014.

16   "returning home" Jeremiah Julius, Lummi tribal member, interview with Zoe Osterman, research assistant, Lummi Reservation, Washington, April 14, 2014.

16   These large houses For the best description of Lummi houses, *see* Stern, *Lummi Indians of Northwest Washington*, pp. 31–32. *See also* Suttles and Sturtevant, *Handbook of North American Indians*, vol. 7, p. 462 (reporting one house

640 feet long); Julie Stein, *Exploring Coast Salish Prehistory: The Archaeology of San Juan Island*, p. 60 (Seattle: University of Washington Press, 2000).

16　**The society was stratified** See, e.g., Wayne Suttles, *Coast Salish Essays*, p. 17 (Vancouver, BC: Talonbooks, 1987).

16　**Obligations . . . to . . . fishers at other locations.** See Stern, *Lummi Indians of Northwest Washington*, p. 46.

16　**Depended upon this generosity** Suttles, *Coast Salish Essays*, pp. 19–21.

17　**Potlatching . . . allowed people in the lower classes to move upward.** *See, e.g.*, Suttles, *Coast Salish Essays*, pp. 23–25.

17　**Salmon was the most important food.** Daniel L. Boxberger, *To Fish in Common*, p. 13 (Seattle: University of Washington Press, 2000). On Coast Salish equally, see Suttles and Sturtevant, *Handbook of Northwest Indians*, vol. 7, p. 457.

17　**Expansive reef nets** See generally Stern, *Lummi Indians of Northwest Washington*, p. 43; Boxberger, *To Fish in Common*, pp. 16–17; Suttles and Sturtevant, *Handbook of Northwest Indians*, vol. 7, p. 457; Ann Nugent, *Lummi Elders Speak*, pp. 19–20 (Lynden, WA: Lynden Tribune, 1982); Don Welsh, *Semiahmoo Reef Net* (n.d.), https://perma.cc/E38S-5PAT (Welsh's dioramas show the sophisticated technology of reef-net fishing).

17　**Thousands of fish in a single day** Daniel L. Boxberger, "Ethnicity and Labor in the Puget Sound Fishing Industry, 1880–1935," vol. 33, no. 2 *University of Pittsburg Ethnology*, pp. 179–191 (Spring 1994).

18　**"like the blood in your veins"** Steve Solomon, Lummi tribal member, interview with Zoe Osterman, research assistant, Lummi Reservation, Washington, April 15, 2014.

19　**Makah language** Barbara Lane, *Anthropological Report on the Identity, Treaty Status and Fisheries of the Quileute and Hoh Indians, US v. Washington*, Exhibit USA-22, pp. 2–3 (August 24, 1973).

19　**Quileute . . . a "language isolate"** Suttles and Sturtevant, *Handbook of Northwest Indians*, vol. 7, p. 431; *see also* Lane, *Anthropological Report on Quileute and Hoh*, Exhibit USA-22, p. 3.

19　**The Makah considered halibut a greater delicacy than salmon.** Phil Greene, Makah tribal member, interview with Christina Warner, research assistant, Makah Reservation, Washington, August 9, 2014: "We did all the fisheries. . . . We weren't salmon people, though. . . . Our main fisheries were halibut, whale, and seal"; Russ Svec, Makah tribal member, interview with Christina Warner, research assistant, Makah Reservation, Washington, August 2014: "Salmon people isn't quite the right term for the Makah. They are much more than that."

19　**The Makah roofs were flat . . . [where] they dried and preserved the halibut.** Samuel Fallows, Edmund Buckley, and Shailer Mathews, *Hearst's Magazine: The World Today, July 1911–June 1912*, vol. 21, no. 1 (Chicago: Current Encyclopedia Co., 1912), pp. 795–796.

19   **The Makah . . . ocean hunt** Joshua L. Reid, *The Sea Is My Country: The Maritime World of the Makahs*, pp. 2119 (New Haven, CT: Yale University Press, 2015); Makah Cultural and Research Center, *The Makah Whaling Tradition* (April 4, 2019), Makah Tribal Council, https://perma.cc/B7ZD-RSF5.

21   **"The ocean made us rich"** Janine Ledford, Makah tribal member and executive director of the Makah Cultural and Research Center, interview with Christina Warner, research assistant, Neah Bay, Washington, August 12, 2016.

21   **The cultural and family connections with the Nootka tribes on Vancouver Island . . . The ocean landscape** See generally Reid, *The Sea Is My Country*.

21   **Accommodation was the rule.** See Suttles, *Coast Salish Essays*, pp. 23–25.

22   **Chief Tatoosh was ready for [Meares].** *See also* Tim Wright, "A History of Treaties and Reservations on the Olympic Peninsula, 1855–1898" (accessed April 19, 2022), *Center for the Study of the Pacific Northwest*, University of Washington, https://perma.cc/YTZ5-6GAA.

22   **"so surly and forbidding a character"** Richard W. Blumenthal, ed., *The Early Exploration of Inland Washington Water: Journals and Logs from Six Expeditions, 1786–1792*, p. 9 (Jefferson, NC: McFarland & Co., Publishers, 2004).

22   **To Tatoosh, the rules were so obvious** Reid, *The Sea Is My Country*, pp. 20–23.

23   **Western red cedar** See Stern, *Lummi Indians of Northwest Washington*, p. 14.

23   **Tensile strength . . . "of red cedar" . . . a breaking load of 425 pounds.** Hilary Stewart, *Cedar: Tree of Life to the Northwest Coast Indians*, p. 161 (Seattle: University of Washington Press, 1984).

24   **"The trees that supported the roof"** *Id.* at p. 61.

24   **A Quinault V-shaped weir system . . . is . . . 1,000 years old.** *See* Randall Schalk and Greg C. Burtchard, "The Newskah Creek Fish Trap Complex, Grays Harbor, Washington," pp. 2–17, Final Report prepared for US Army Corps of Engineers (Seattle District, PO Box 3755, Seattle, WA 98124) by International Archaeological Research Institute Inc. and Cascadia Archaeology, Seattle, Washington (October 2001).

24   **Canoed to the mouth of the Columbia River . . . a traditional Quinault journey.** Phillip Martin Sr., Quinault tribal member, interview with author, Taholah, Washington, June 24, 2014.

25   **"we would go to Celilo Falls"** *Id.*

27   **"we have always been here"** Cecelia Svinth Carpenter, *Where the Waters Begin: The Traditional Nisqually Indian History of Mount Rainier*, p. 13 (Seattle: Discover Your Northwest, 1994).

27   **Their largest village** Barbara Lane, *Anthropological Report on the Identity, Treaty Status and Fisheries of the Nisqually Tribe of Indians, US v. Washington*, Exhibit USA-25, p. 7–10 (August 24, 1973); Nettsie Bullchild, director of the Nisqually Tribal Archives and Tribal Historic Preservation Office, interview with author, Yelm, Washington, November 8, 2021.

27   **Every village was sovereign.** Lane, *Anthropological Report on the Nisqually*, Exhibit USA-25, pp. 1–10.

27   **"The Nisqually have always been a fishing people."** Nisqually Indian Tribe, "Culture" (2023), http://www.nisqually-nsn.gov/index.php/heritage/.

27   **"The Nisqually held the salmon in special esteem."** Lane, *Anthropological Report on the Nisqually*, Exhibit USA-25, pp. 1–10.

27   **Rainier, called Ta-co-bet by the Nisqually** Carpenter, *Where the Waters Begin*, p. 99.

27   **"The mountain was always there"** *Id.* at p. 23.

27   **"They visited the thermal springs"** Charles Wilkinson, *Messages from Frank's Landing: A Story of Salmon, Treaties, and the Indian Way*, p. 23 (Seattle: University of Washington Press, 2000).

28   **"The thunder of hundreds of horses"** Northwest Treaty Tribes, "Restoring the Cultural Importance and Healing of Horses" (March 31, 2021), https://nwtreatytribes.org/restoring-the-cultural-importance-and-healing-of-horses/.

28   **Salmon was the single most important food for the Nisqually.** *Id.*

28   **"Everywhere, in this part of the country"** Joseph G. Clark, *Lights and Shadows of a Sailor Life*, p. 222 (Boston, MA: B. B. Mussey, 1848).

28   **They also picked many kinds of berries.** Yelm History Project, "A Bountiful Harvest" (May 14, 2009), *Nisqually People and the River*, https://perma.cc/P73S-H8V8.

29   **Extensive use of fire** *See, e.g.*, Robert Boyd, *Indians, Fire, and the Land in the Pacific Northwest*, pp. 9–10 (Eugene: University of Oregon Press, 1999). Boyd's excellent and comprehensive book provides a full treatment of the extensive use of fire as a land management device in precontact times. He believes virtually every Native American tribe made substantial use of fire for land management.

31   **"the river wound through every aspect"** Lynda V. Mapes, *Breaking Ground: The Lower Elwha Klallam Tribe and the Unearthing of Tse-whit-zen Village*, p. 23 (Seattle: University of Washington Press, 2009).

31   **"People who lived up the river hunted"** Charles Wilkinson, "The Olympic Peninsula's Elwha River: Prisoner of History, Harbinger of Hope," in Mary Peck, *Away Out Over Everything: The Olympic Peninsula and the Elwha River*, p.71 (Stanford, CA: Stanford University Press, 2004).

31   **Salmon had a pervasive importance** Mapes, *Breaking Ground*, p. 27.

32   **"Some of the richest runs of salmon"** National Park Service, *History of the Elwha* (updated October 2, 2019), https://perma.cc/PQ6B-5NTA: "Ten different runs of anadromous (sea-run) fish made this pristine valley their home, including all five species of Pacific salmon, as well as native char (bull trout and Dolly Varden), winter and summer-run steelhead, and sea-run cutthroat trout."

32   **Everything depended on the gathering of food.** For an excellent treatment of the many implements needed in Indian fishing, *see* Hilary Stewart, *Indian Fishing: Early Methods on the Northwest Coast* (Seattle: University of Washington Press, 2018). On the architecture of Pacific Northwest canoes, *see, e.g.,* "Black Eagle" (accessed December 26, 2022), the Bill Reid Centre, Simon Fraser University, Burnaby, British Columbia, https://perma.cc/J5Q8-88VM.

33   **Storytelling** *See, e.g.,* Peter Goodchild, ed., *Raven Tales: Traditional Stories of Native Peoples* (Chicago: Chicago Review Press, 1991). Among the earliest collections of Northwest storytelling are Albert Reagan and L.V.W. Walters, "Tales from the Hoh and Quileute," vol. 46 *Journal of American Folklore*, pp. 297–346 (1933); Albert B. Reagan, "Some Additional Myths of the Hoh and Quileute Indians," vol. 11 *Utah Academy of Sciences, Arts, and Letters*, pp. 17 (1934).

33   **"Before Raven came"** For this version of the often-told story of Raven and light, *see* Glenn Welker, "How Raven Stole the Sun" (updated May 11, 2023), *Raven Stories*, https://perma.cc/D4CT-B8PU.

34   **Thunderbird . . . attacked the Mimlos-whale.** The conflict between these two summarized here is a common theme in Pacific Northwest storytelling. *See* Pacific Northwest Seismic Network, "Thunderbird Fights Mimlos-Whale" (accessed December 26, 2022), *Tales from the Hoh and Quileute*, https://perma.cc/6TSP-FCK6.; Reagan and Walters, "Tales from the Hoh and Quileute."

3   Natives and Europeans Collide

35   **Spanish leaders . . . worried about Russian and British initiatives . . . in the Pacific Northwest.** Edmond S. Meany, *History of the State of Washington*, pp. 17–39 (New York: Macmillan, 1909); Richard White, *It's Your Misfortune and None of My Own: A New History of the American West*, pp. 5–8, 32, 36 (Norman: University of Oklahoma Press, 1991); Oscar O. Winther, *The Great Northwest: A History*, pp. 21–25 (New York: Alfred A. Knopf, 1950).

35   **The first explorer to make landfall in the Pacific Northwest.** Meany, *History of the State of Washington*, pp. 15–16.

35   **Juan José Pérez Hernández . . . was the first . . . to make landfall.** Norman A. Graebner, "The Northwest Coast in World Diplomacy, 1790–1846," *in* eds. David H. Stratton and George A. Frykman, *The Changing Pacific Northwest: Interpreting Its Past*, p. 25 (Pullman: Washington State University Press, 1988).

36   **John Meares . . . was repulsed by Makah Chief Tatoosh.** Joshua L. Reid, *The Sea Is My Country: The Maritime World of the Makahs*, pp. 19–23 (New Haven, CT: Yale University Press, 2015); *see also* chapter 2, The Salmon People, in this book.

37 **Captain James Cook . . . traded . . . for . . . sea otter pelts.** *See, e.g.,* Earl Pomeroy, *The Pacific Slope: A History of California, Oregon, Washington, Idaho, Utah and Nevada,* pp. 13–14 (New York,: Alfred A. Knopf, 1965).

38 **Nootka Convention of 1790** *See* Graebner, "Northwest Coast in World Diplomacy," pp. 5–7.

38 **Last Spanish voyage** Warren L. Cook, *Flood Tide of Empire: Spain and the Pacific Northwest 1543–1819,* p. 900 (New Haven, CT: Yale University Press, 1973).

38 **The Europeans unwittingly brought killing diseases.** Elizabeth A. Fenn, *Pox Americana: The Great Smallpox Epidemic of 1775–82,* pp. 248–250 (New York: Hill & Wang, 2001).

38 **The two most authoritative sources** *See, e.g.,* Fenn, *Pox Americana,* p. 248–250; Robert Boyd, *The Coming of the Spirit of Pestilence: Introduced Infectious Disease and Population Decline among Northwest Coast Indians, 1774–1874,* pp. 34–37 (Seattle: University of Washington Press, 1999). These two books provide exceptional coverage of this difficult era in the Northwest. Fenn's Pulitzer Prize–winning book covers the epidemics nationally with solid treatment of the Northwest. Boyd's contribution offers a highly detailed, conservative analysis of the Pacific Northwest.

39 **"Old timers said that the sickness came from the south"** This account from Amelia Brown, member of the Tolawa Tribe of California, is located within the study by Richard A. Gould, *Archaeology of the Point St. George Site, and Tolowa Prehistory,* pp. 96–97 (Berkeley: University of California Press, 1966).

39 **"possibly the greatest demographic disaster"** William Denevan, *The Native Population of the Americas in 1492,* p. 7 (Madison: University of Wisconsin Press, 1976).

39 **The commonly accepted range of Native Americans** Russell Thornton, *American Indian Holocaust and Survival: A Population History Since 1492,* pp. 25–32 (Norman: University of Oklahoma Press, 1987).

39 **The Pacific Northwest Natives suffered** Boyd, *Coming of the Spirit of Pestilence,* pp. 262–268.

39 **"Variola's relationship to humankind"** Fenn, *Pox Americana,* pp. 5–6.

40 **"[A]t the extremity of the inlet"** George Vancouver, *A Voyage of Discovery to the North Pacific and Round the World,* vol. 2, pp. 241–242 (London: G. G. and J. Robinson, 1798).

40 **"The Small pox most have had"** Boyd, *Coming of the Spirit of Pestilence,* p. 30.

40 **Smallpox exploded over the land.** *Id.* at p. 22.

40 **"The smallpox has distroyed"** Meriwether Lewis and William Clark, *The Journals of the Lewis and Clark Expedition, Vol. 6, November 2, 1805–March 22, 1806,* Gary Moulton, ed., p. 285 (Lincoln: University of Nebraska Press, 1990).

40 **The contagions continued** Boyd, *Coming of the Spirit of Pestilence,* p. 22.

40 "the old historian of the [Squamish] tribe [of the Lower Fraser River]"
Cole Harris, *The Resettlement of British Columbia: Essays on Colonialism and Geographical Change*, pp. 7–8 (Vancouver: University of British Columbia Press, 1997); *see also, e.g.*, Boyd, *Coming of the Spirit of Pestilence*, p. 55.

41 **The European diseases wrought more** *See, e.g.*, Fenn, *Pox Americana*, p. 22.

41 **One tribal healing practice** *Id.* at pp. 24–25; David Lavender, *Let Me Be Free: The Nez Perce Tragedy*, pp. 1–20 (Norman: University of Oklahoma Press, 1992); Henry F. Dobyns, *Their Number Become Thinned: Native American Population Dynamics in Eastern North America*, p. 16 (Knoxville: University of Tennessee Press, 1983).

41 "the unfortunate Indians" Fenn, *Pox Americana*, p. 25.

42 "He assembled several of the chieftains" Washington Irving, *Astoria or Anecdotes of an Enterprise Beyond the Rocky Mountains*, Edgeley W. Todd, ed., p. 117 (Norman: University of Oklahoma Press, 1964). Robert H. Ruby and John A. Brown, *The Chinook Indians*, pp. 135–136 (Norman: University of Oklahoma Press, 1976), find it highly unlikely that the Clatsops and Chinooks were involved in the massacre of the *Tonquin* crew. The dispute seems to have been caused by the ship captain's poor treatment of a tribal elder. *See* Robert F. Jones, "The Identity of the *Tonquin*'s Interpreter," vol. 98, no. 3 *Oregon Historical Quarterly*, pp. 296–300 (Fall 1997). On "smallpox in a bottle" episodes at Astoria and elsewhere, see Boyd, *Coming of the Spirit of Pestilence*, pp. 45–46, 112–115.

42 "fatalism" Richard White, "The Treaty at Medicine Creek: Indian-White Relations on Upper Puget Sound 1830–1880," p. 8, MA thesis, University of Washington (1972).

43 **Russian and Spanish claims would all be extinguished by 1825.** Vine Deloria Jr., *Indians of the Pacific Northwest: From the Coming of the White Man to the Present Day*, p. 28 (Garden City, NY: Doubleday, 1977).

43 "Americans tended to be mostly whites" Deloria, *Indians of the Pacific Northwest*, p. 29.

43 "The first experience of the Indians with the Americans" *Id.* at p. 24.

44 "the Indians and the 'King George' men lived in comparative peace" *Id.* at p. 31.

44 **British traders tended to take Native wives.** Emma Milliken, "Choosing between Corsets and Freedom: Native, Mixed-Blood, and White Wives of Laborers at Fort Nisqually, 1833–1860," vol. 96, no. 2 *Pacific Northwest Quarterly*, p. 95 (Spring 2005).

45 **Fort Nisqually, founded in 1833** Clarence B. Bagley, "Journal of Occurrences at Nisqually House, 1833," vol. 6, no. 3 *Washington Historical Quarterly*, p. 179 (July 1915); Cecelia Svinth Carpenter, *Fort Nisqually: A Documented History of Indian and British Interaction* (Seattle: Tahoma Publications, 1986).

45   **Took an interest in the culture and customs** White, "Treaty at Medicine
Creek," pp. 11–12.

45   **"approach the Indians with a modicum of humanity"** *Id.* at p. 12.

45   **"Fort Nisqually became a place"** Cecelia Svinth Carpenter, *Stolen Lands: The
Story of the Dispossessed Nisquallies,* p. 3 (Tacoma, WA: Tahoma Research Service, 2007).

45   **Election in 1844 of James Knox Polk** *See* Eugene Irving McCormac, *James K.
Polk, A Political Biography* (New York: Russell & Russell, 1965); Charles A.
McCoy, *Polk and the Presidency* (Austin: University of Texas Press, 1960).

45   **"54–40 or fight"** McCoy, *Polk and the Presidency,* p. 563; Meany, *History of the
State of Washington,* pp. 132–137.

45   **Joint Occupancy Agreement of 1818** Treaty of 1818, 8 Stat. 248; Treaty Series
112 (1819). *See also* Robert E. Ficken and Charles P. LeWarne, *Washington: A
Centennial History,* p. 18 (Seattle: University of Washington Press, 1988).

46   **1846 treaty** James K. Polk, Treaty of Limits, Westward of the Rocky Mountains,
between the United States of America and the British Government (ratified on
June 19, 1846; proclaimed on August 5, 1846, in Washington). *See also* White, *It's
Your Misfortune,* pp. 76–77.

46   **The 1847 Whitman Massacre** *See* Narcissa Whitman, *The Letters of Narcissa
Whitman, 1836–1847* (Fairfield, WA: Ye Galleon Press, 1986); *see also* Thomas E.
Jessett and Miles Cannon, *The Indian Side of the Whitman Massacre* (Fairfield,
WA: Ye Galleon Press, 1969).

46   **Expansion-oriented politicians** *See, e.g.,* Clyde A. Milner, Carol A. O'Connor,
and Martha A. Sandweiss, eds., *The Oxford History of the American West,* p. 366
(Oxford, UK: Oxford University Press, 1994).

47   **1848 . . . Territory of Oregon** When news of the Whitman massacre reached
the United States capitol, Congress quickly passed the Act to Establish the Territorial Government of Oregon, to officially turn the region into a US territory.
30th Congress, 1st Session, ch. 177, August 14, 1848.

47   **Population of the Oregon Territory . . . 13,000** US Census Bureau, *The Seventh
Census of the United States: 1850* (Washington, DC: US Department of Commerce, 1853).

47   **1845 . . . Simmons Party arrived** Edmond S. Meany, "First American Settlement on Puget Sound," vol. 7, no. 2 *Washington Historical Quarterly,* pp. 138–142
(1916).

47   **Thurston "was an indefatigable promotor"** Senate Committee on Interior
and Insular Affairs, Jerry A. Callaghan, "The Disposition of the Public Domain
in Oregon," 86th Congress, 2d Session, pp. 31–32 (Washington, DC: Government Printing Office, 1960) [hereinafter "The Disposition"].

47   **"rightful occupants of the soil"** *Johnson v. McIntosh,* 21 U.S. (8 Wheat.) 543 (1823).

47   **Tribes retained their right of occupancy.** *See, e.g.,* Charles F. Wilkinson, *American Indians, Time, and the Law: Native Societies in a Modern Constitutional Democracy,* pp. 39–41 (New Haven, CT: Yale University Press, 1987); Felix Cohen et al., *Cohen's Handbook of Federal Indian Law,* 2012 ed., § 15.03, pp. 997–999 (New Providence, NJ: LexisNexis, 2012).

48   **1850 . . . Oregon Indian Treaty Act** Oregon Indian Treaty Act, ch. 16, 9 Stat. 437 (June 5, 1850).

48   **Oregon Indians universally hated the Oregon Indian Treaty Act.** *See, e.g.,* Terence O'Donnell, *An Arrow in the Earth,* p. 138 (Portland: Oregon Historical Society Press, 1992); C. F. Coan, "The Adoption of the Reservation Policy in the Pacific Northwest, 1853–1855," vol. 23, no. 1 *Oregon Historical Quarterly,* p. 7 (March 1922). Coan describes the "east of the mountains" policy as a "complete failure": C. F. Coan, "The First Stage of the Federal Indian Policy in the Pacific Northwest, 1849–1852," vol. 22, no.1 *Oregon Historical Quarterly,* p. 65 (March 1921).

48   **Willamette Valley tribes were . . . removed.** *See, e.g.,* Charles Wilkinson, *The People Are Dancing Again: The History of the Siletz Tribe of Western Oregon,* pp. 79–148 (Seattle: University of Washington Press, 2010).

48   **Donation Land Act** For an excellent discussion of the Donation Land Act, see William G. Robbins, "The Indian Question in Western Oregon: The Making of a Colonial People," *in* eds. G. Thomas Edwards and Carlos A. Schwantes, *Experiences in a Promised Land: Essays in Pacific Northwest History,* pp. 53–56 (Seattle: University of Washington Press, 1986). The act itself is found at ch. 76, September 27, 1850, 9 Stat. 496 (1850) [not codified].

48   **"came very close to meeting the classic homestead ideal"** "The Disposition," p. 34.

48   **Gold Rush** Leading authorities include Rodman Paul, *California Gold: The Beginning of Mining in the Far West* (Cambridge, MA: Harvard University Press, 1947), and J. S. Holliday, *The World Rushed In: The California Gold Rush Experience* (Norman: University of Oklahoma Press, 2015).

49   **Created the Territory of Washington** *See, e.g.,* Ficken and LeWarne, *Washington: A Centennial History,* pp. 26; Meany, *History of the State of Washington,* pp. 155–159.

4   Young Man in a Hurry

51   **His excellent biography of Stevens** Kent D. Richards, *Isaac I. Stevens: Young Man in a Hurry* (Provo, UT: Brigham Young University Press, 1990).

51   **High praise for his wartime advice and courage** *Id.* at pp. 53–70.

53   **The new president did put Stevens forward** *Id.* at pp. 95–97.

53   **Commander of the survey of the northern route for the transcontinental railroad** *Id.* at pp. 97–145. For a detailed account praising Stevens's role as head of the survey, see Paul D. McDermott, Ronald E. Grim, and Philip Mobley, *Eye of the Explorer: Views of the Northern Pacific Railroad Survey 1853–54* (Missoula, MT: Mountain Press, 2010).

54   **The Jeffersonian Ideal** *See, e.g.,* the classic exploration, Douglass G. Adair, *The Intellectual Origins of Jeffersonian Democracy* (Washington, DC: Lexington Books, 2000).

54   **"Those who labor in the earth"** Thomas Jefferson, *Notes on the State of Virginia*, Query XIX, p. 175 (1785). Jefferson put forth many of his ideas in this early work. *Encyclopedia Virginia* asserts that "many consider it the most important American book written before 1800": Robert Forbes, "Notes on the State of Virginia (1785): Summary" (updated May 14, 2023), *in Encyclopedia Virginia*, Virginia Humanities, University of Virginia, https://encyclopediavirginia.org/entries/notes-on-the-state-of-virginia-1785.

54   **The second titanic acquisition of western lands** *See* Paul H. Bergeron, *The Presidency of James K. Polk* (Lawrence: University Press of Kansas, 1987); Walter R. Borneman, *Polk: The Man Who Transformed the Presidency and America* (New York: Random House, 2009).

55   **John O'Sullivan . . . adopted a new term, "manifest destiny"** John O'Sullivan, editorial, *New York Morning News* (December 27, 1845).

56   **Companion legislation to the Donation Land Act** *See* chapter 3, Natives and Europeans Collide, in this book.

57   **"I have come here, not as an official for mere station"** *Washington Pioneer and Democrat*, December 3, 1853, as quoted in Richards, *Young Man in a Hurry*, p. 150.

57   **"We confidently assume that Washington Territory has . . . a model Governor"** *Id.*

57   **the "laying-out and construction of roads"** Hubert H. Bancroft, *History of Washington, Idaho and Montana*, p. 63 (San Francisco: The History Co., 1890).

58   **"it is almost impossible"** Richard White, "The Treaty at Medicine Creek: Indian-White Relations on Upper Puget Sound, 1830–1880," p. 52, MA thesis, University of Washington (1972).

58   **He met relentlessly . . . with influential locals.** Richards, *Young Man in a Hurry*, p. 151; SuAnn M. Reddick and Cary C. Collins, "Medicine Creek to Fox Island: Cadastral Scams and Contested Domains," vol. 106, no. 3 *Oregon Historical Quarterly*, p. 378 (Fall 2005); Richard Kluger, *The Bitter Waters of Medicine Creek: A Tragic Clash Between White and Native America*, p. 47 (New York: Alfred A. Knopf, 2011).

58   **The elaborate, highly praised final [railway survey] report** *See, e.g.,* McDermott, Grim, and Mobley, *Eye of the Explorer,* pp. 2–4, 19–24.

58   **Needed to get out to several roads . . . to understand their conditions** White, "Treaty at Medicine Creek," p. 52.

58   **This left little time for dealing with the tribes.** *Id.:* "he moved too quickly and under pressure from too many conflicting demands to give much time to the Indians, after the government, the settlers, and his own ambitions were satisfied. His attention was too diffused with his railway survey, his councils with more powerful tribes to the east, and with governing the territory, to devote much time to the local Indians."

59   **A "hurried" midwinter trip** *Id.*

59   **He also lacked knowledge of Indian people.** *See, e.g.,* Richards, *Young Man in a Hurry,* p. 178; Alexandra Harmon, "Indian Treaty History: A Subject for Agile Minds," vol. 106, no. 3 *Oregon Historical Quarterly,* p. 366 (Fall 2005).

59   **The railway survey expedition had scattered exchanges with Indians.** *See, e.g.,* Richards, *Young Man in a Hurry,* pp. 109–112.

59   **His advisor on tribal cultural matters . . . George Gibbs** On the life of Gibbs, see the very useful dissertation by Stephen Dow Beckham, "George Gibbs, 1815–1873: Historian and Ethnologist," PhD diss., University of California, Los Angeles (1969).

60   **Gibbs signed up with Stevens's railway survey.** *Id.* at pp. 122–126.

60   **A second aide on tribal matters . . . Michael Simmons** *See, e.g.,* White, "Treaty at Medicine Creek," p. 53; Reddick and Collins, "Medicine Creek to Fox Island," p. 378.

60   **His formal address to the territory's first legislative assembly** *See, e.g.,* Edmond S. Meany, *History of the State of Washington,* pp. 152, 162 (New York: Macmillan, 1909).

61   **The Native political structure . . . would require too many "tribes"** *See, e.g.,* Reddick and Collins, "Medicine Creek to Fox Island," p. 378; White, "Treaty at Medicine Creek," p. 55; Harmon, "Indian Treaty History," p. 366.

61   **"Simmons and Shaw wielded enormous power"** Reddick and Collins, "Medicine Creek to Fox Island," p. 379.

61   **The project closest to Stevens's heart was the railroad survey and report.** William Compton Brown, *The Indian Side of the Story: Being a Concourse of Presentations Historical and Biographical in Character Relating to the Indian Wars,* p. 84 (Spokane, WA: C. W. Hill Printing, 1961).

62   **The magnitude of this effort** On the transcontinental railway surveys, see generally William H. Goetzmann, *Army Exploration in the American West, 1803–1863,* pp. 262–337 (New Haven, CT: Yale University Press, 1959).

62   His report was "probably the most important single contemporary source" Robert Taft, *Artists and Illustrators of the Old West, 1850–1900*, p. 5 (New York: Charles Scribner's Sons, 1969); on the excellence of the project, see generally McDermott, Grim, and Mobley, *Eye of the Explorer*, pp. 97–145.

63   Congress's passage in 1862 of the Central Pacific and Union Pacific grant *See, e.g.*, Richard White, *It's Your Misfortune and None of My Own: A New History of the American West*, pp. 246–252 (Norman: University of Oklahoma Press, 1991).

63   "in no former equal period in our history" *See* George Manypenny, "Report of the Commissioner of Indian Affairs–Salt Lake City," p. 20 (1856); David H. DeJong, *Paternalism to Partnership: The Administration of Indian Affairs 1786–2021*, pp. 86–94 (Lincoln: University of Nebraska Press, 2022).

63   Manypenny, who wanted "a limited number of reservations . . . in a limited number of districts" *See* White, "Treaty at Medicine Creek," pp. 57–58; Washington State Acting Commissioner Mix to Stevens, August 30, 1854, National Archives and Records Administration.

63   George Gibbs, who had the best understanding . . . favored a different approach. Richards, *Young Man in a Hurry*, p. 198.

63   The governor . . . sent an inconclusive report . . . suggesting a large central reservation. White, "Treaty at Medicine Creek," p. 58.

5   Treaty Time

65   It had been a hard trip. Kent D. Richards, *Isaac I. Stevens: Young Man in a Hurry*, pp. 171–173 (Provo, UT: Brigham Young University Press, 1979).

65   "In closing this communication" Washington Legislative Assembly House of Representatives, *Journal of the House of Representatives of the Territory of Washington: Being the Second Session of the Legislative Assembly, Begun and Held at Olympia, December 4th, 1854*, p. 15 (Olympia, WA: Geo. B. Goudy, Public Printer, 1855).

66   Gibbs . . . played a major role in drafting and negotiating treaties. Richards, *Young Man in a Hurry*, p. 198.

66   The first order of business was to discuss the Blackfeet. Richard White, "The Treaty at Medicine Creek: Indian-White Relations on Upper Puget Sound 1830–1880," p. 59, MA thesis, University of Washington (1972); George Gibbs, secretary of the Western Washington Treaty Commission, "Record of the Proceedings of the Commission to Hold Treaties with the Indian Tribes in Washington Territory and the Blackfoot Country, December 7, 1854–March 3, 1855," Records of the Washington Superintendency of Indian Affairs, 1853–1874, roll

26, M5, National Archives and Records Administration Records [hereinafter Gibbs, "Record of the Proceedings"].

66   **Gibbs did submit a draft to the group.** Stephen D. Beckham, "George Gibbs, 1815–1873. Historian and Ethnologist," pp. 160–161, PhD diss., University of California (1969); on the December 10 meeting, see generally Richards, *Young Man in a Hurry*, pp. 184–185. Handwritten copies of the treaty minutes signed by George Gibbs are on microfilm; *see* Gibbs, "Record of the Proceedings."

67   **Chinook Jargon, a rudimentary device** *See, e.g.,* the opinion by Judge George Boldt in *United States v. Washington*, 384 F. Supp. 312, 330 (W.D. Wash. 1974). The literature on the Chinook Jargon is quite extensive. See generally Jim Holton, *Chinook Jargon: The Hidden Language of the Pacific Northwest* (San Leandro, CA: Wawa Press, 2004); Horatio Hale, *An International Idiom: A Manual of the Oregon Trade Language, or "Chinook Jargon"* (London: Whittaker & Co., 1890); George Gibbs, *Dictionary of the Chinook Jargon, or, Trade Language of Oregon* (New York: Cramoisy Press, 1863); George C. Shaw, *The Chinook Jargon and How to Use It* (Seattle: Rainier Printing Co., 1909).

67   **Shaw, as interpreter, had only a moderate grasp of the Chinook Jargon.** *See, e.g.,* SuAnn M. Reddick and Cary C. Collins, "Medicine Creek to Fox Island: Cadastral Scams and Contested Domains," vol. 106, no. 3 *Oregon Historical Quarterly*, The Isaac I. Stevens and Joel Palmer Treaties, 1855–2005, p. 379 (Fall 2005).

67   **"To a great extent, effective communication depends"** Edward Harper Thomas, *Chinook: A History and Dictionary of the Northwest Coast Trade Jargon*, 2nd ed., p. 53 (Portland, OR: Binford & Mort, 1970).

67   **"The way a word is spoken"** W. S. Phillips, *The Chinook Book: A Descriptive Analysis of the Chinook Jargon in Plain Words*, p. 6 (Seattle: R. L. Davis Printing Co., 1913). *See also* George Lang, *Making Wawa: The Genesis of the Chinook Jargon* (Vancouver: University of British Columbia Press, 2008); James G. Swan, *The Northwest Coast or, Three Years' Residence in Washington Territory* (Manhattan: Harper & Brothers, 1857; Seattle: University of Washington Press, 1969); Barbara P. Harris, "Chinook Jargon: Arguments for a Pre-Contact Origin," vol. 29, no. 1 *Pacific Coast Philology*, p. 28 (September 1994); Horatio Hale, *Ethnology and Philology* (Ridgewood, NJ: Gregg Press, 1968; first published 1846).

67   **"The right of taking fish"** Treaty with the Nisqually and other Tribes, reprinted in Charles J. Kappler, *Indian Affairs, Laws, and Treaties*, p. 662 (Washington, DC: Government Printing Office, 1904).

68   **Gibbs's remarkable report of March 1855** George Gibbs, *Indian Tribes of Washington Territory* (Fairfield, WA: Ye Galleon Press, 1972); Beckham, "George Gibbs," pp. 142–148.

69   "they require the liberty of motion" Gibbs, *Indian Tribes of Washington Terri-tory*, p. 29.

69   "the right of fishery" *Id.*

69   The tribes consistently made it clear that traditional fishing rights must be guaranteed. The Supreme Court made this point, after examining the records in the Stevens treaties negotiations, in *Washington v. Washington State Commer-cial Passenger Vessel Association*, 443 U.S. 658, 676 (1979): "During the negotia-tions, the vital importance of the fish to the Indians was repeatedly emphasized by both sides, and the Governor's promises that the treaties would protect that source of food and commerce were crucial in obtaining the Indians' assent."

69   "A large portion of their territory" Gibbs, *Indian Tribes of Washington Terri-tory*, p. 29.

69   Treaties as a "temporary expedient" with a "short lifespan" Alexandra Har-mon, "Indian Treaty History: A Subject for Agile Minds," vol. 106, no. 3 *Oregon Historical Quarterly*, The Isaac Stevens and Joel Palmer Treaties, 1855–2005, p. 360 (Fall 2005).

70   The commissioners agreed to get the word out to the tribes. Reddick and Collins, "Medicine Creek to Fox Island," pp. 380–381.

70   Simmons and Shaw advised the Indians *Id.* at p. 384.

70   Simmons and Shaw headed out to the tribal villages. *Id.*

71   Perhaps their main targets were Leschi and Quiemuth. Richard Kluger, *The Bitter Waters of Medicine Creek: A Tragic Clash Between White and Native Amer-ica*, p. 76 (New York: Alfred A. Knopf, 2011).

71   Americans had many contacts with [Leschi and Quiemuth]. Alexandra Har-mon, *Indians in the Making: Ethnic Relations and Indian Identities around Puget Sound*, pp. 88–89 (Berkeley: University of California Press, 1999); Charles Grainger as quoted in Ezra Meeker, *Pioneer Reminiscences of Puget Sound: The Tragedy of Leschi*, p. 459 (Seattle: Lowman & Hanford Stationery & Printing Co., 1905).

72   A group of settlers went out to prepare the site. Joseph Hazard, *Companion of Adventure: A Biography of Isaac Ingalls Stevens First Governor of Washington*, pp. 1015 (Portland, OR: Binford & Mort, 1952).

72   "carcasses of beef, mutton, deer, elk" *Id.*

72   "Thin temporary huts" Beckham, "George Gibbs," p. 160.

73   Stevens arranged for every Native leader to receive a "certificate of author-ity." *See, e.g.,* Drew Crooks, "Governor Isaac I. Stevens and the Medicine Creek Treaty, Prelude to the War in Southern Puget Sound," vol. 10 *Pacific Northwest Forum*, pp. 23–25 (Summer–Fall 1985).

73   "his flannel shirt open at the throat" *Id.*

73   James Doty . . . had the duty to prepare minutes but all that remains is a

brief, superficial ... three-page summary. *See* Gibbs, "Record of the Proceedings."

73   **"December 25th: The Programme of the Treaty"** Gibbs, "Record of the Proceedings," p. 5.

74   **"I could talk the Indian languages"** Crooks, "Governor Isaac I. Stevens and the Medicine Creek Treaty," pp. 23–25; Vine Deloria Jr., *Indians of the Pacific Northwest: From the Coming of the White Man to the Present Day*, p. 42 (Garden City, NY: Doubleday, 1977).

74   **more than 1,500 people, would move to a single reservation on Squaxin Island.** Reddick and Collins, "Medicine Creek to Fox Island," pp. 381–383.

74   **[Leschi] was a "horse" Indian who rode for hunting.** Meeker, *Pioneer Reminiscences of Puget Sound*, p. 248.

75   **"[H]e stood up before the Governor"** *Id.* at p. 242. *See also* Reddick and Collins, "Medicine Creek to Fox Island," p. 383.

75   **Signatures of both Leschi and Quiemuth appear on the treaty ... they may have been forged but that cannot be proved.** Kluger, *Bitter Waters of Medicine Creek*, p. 101.

76   **"the Great Father" and his "children"** Gibbs, "Record of the Proceedings," p. 5.

76   **"the treaty was then read"** *Id.* at p. 6.

76   **Two days after the ... Treaty Council concluded, George Gibbs and Frank Shaw ... examine[d] the Nisqually reservation.** Reddick and Collins, "Medicine Creek to Fox Island," pp. 368–388.

77   **The two men then went to the Puyallup reservation.** *Id.* at p. 389.

77   **Leschi tried to find ways to convey his distress.** *Id.*

78   **"Dick signed the treaty and then [later felt] like a fool"** Meeker, *Pioneer Reminiscences of Puget Sound*, pp. 244–245.

79   **Michael Simmons, James McAllister ... , and other locals made clear their belief that Leschi ... was likely to ignite hostilities.** SuAnn M. Reddick and Cary C. Collins, "Medicine Creek Remediated: Isaac Stevens and the Puyallup, Nisqually, and Muckleshoot Land Settlement at Fox Island, August 4, 1856," vol. 104, no. 2 *Pacific Northwest Quarterly*, pp. 86–87 (Spring 2013).

79   **"Should you meet any unusual or suspicious assemblage of Indians"** *Id.* at p. 275; Charles Mason, acting governor, to Charles Eaton, October 23, 1855, *in* "Message of the Governor of Washington Territory," (Olympia: E. Furste, public printer, 1857), https://www.loc.gov/item/09032153/.

79   **Eaton rounded up nineteen volunteers to bring in Leschi and Quiemuth.** White, "Treaty at Medicine Creek," pp. 71–72, 89–90; Lisa Blee, *Framing Chief Leschi: Narratives and the Politics of Historical Justice*, pp 162–163 (Chapel Hill: University of North Carolina Press, 2014).

79 **In military terms, it was not a major war.** Harmon, *Indians in the Making*, pp. 88; White, "Treaty at Medicine Creek," pp. 89–90.

79 **Stevens convened a conference, held at Fox Island.** Reddick and Collins, "Medicine Creek Remediated," pp. 80–98.

80 **[Stevens] came under considerable fire . . . in both the territory and Washington, DC.** *Id.* at p. 88.

80 **"the Governor's treaties had a great deal to do in fomenting this war"** Quoted in Swan, *Northwest Coast*, p. 428.

80 **Stevens promised to eliminate the two unusable reservations and replace them with two suitable reservations.** For descriptions of the reservations, maps, and the process making them available, *see* Reddick and Collins, "Medicine Creek Remediated," pp. 93–95.

81 **Stevens . . . described as "obsessed" with Leschi.** Reddick and Collins, "Medicine Creek Remediated," p. 87.

81 **They charged [Leschi] with the murder. . . . they tried him immediately.** On the trials and appeal, *see, e.g.,* Richards, *Young Man in a Hurry*, pp. 292–293.

81 **Quiemuth came in voluntarily. . . . he was stabbed to death.** White, "Treaty at Medicine Creek," pp. 115–116.

81 **"Whatever the future holds"** Blee, *Framing Chief Leschi*, pp. 96–97.

81 **"I do not know anything about your laws."** Meeker, *Pioneer Reminiscences of Puget Sound*, pp. 427–428.

81 **Leschi was correct on the law.** Ex parte Quirin, 317 U.S. 1, 31 (1942).

81 **"Leschi was a square-built man,"** Crooks, "Governor Isaac I. Stevens and the Medicine Creek Treaty," pp. 23–25.

82 **Washington Historical Court of Inquiry and Justice . . . found that justice had not been done.** Associated Press, "Indian Chief Hanged in 1858 Is Cleared," *New York Times* (December 12, 2004). For a full discussion of the 2004 proceeding, *see* Kluger, *Bitter Waters of Medicine Creek*, pp. 280–285.

83 **Mukilteo, meaning "good camping ground" in Salish** *See, e.g.,* Margaret Riddle, "Mukilteo—Thumbnail History," Essay 8422 (December 29, 2007), *HistoryLink.org*, https://perma.cc/M8G7-UH3M.

83 **Governor Stevens chose the area for . . . the Treaty of Point Elliott.** The subject has received excellent scholarly attention. The Center for the Study of the Pacific Northwest held a Sesquicentennial Conference to reassess the Stevens treaties, and treaty developments in Canada, with Point Elliott serving as the anchor treaty. *See* Alexandra Harmon, ed., "Introduction," *in The Power of Promises: Rethinking Indian Treaties in the Pacific Northwest*, pp. 8–11 (Seattle: University of Washington Press, 2008). In 2004, Washington State Ferries (WSF) planned to relocate the Mukilteo Ferry Terminal. The area was rich with Indian cultural resources and includes the treaty locale. An environmental

impact statement was required and WSF did a superb job of in-depth research, using many primary sources regarding historical use and the treaty proceedings. This surprising but exceptionally valuable source is Christian J. Miss et al., "Cultural Resource Discipline Report," *in* Northwest Archaeological Associates and SWCA Environmental Consultants, *Mukilteo Multimodal Project Draft EIS* (October 2, 2012, revised April 1, 2013), prepared for US Department of Transportation, Federal Transit Administration, and Washington State Department of Transportation, Washington State Ferries; available for download at https://perma.cc/A32J-JQJ8 [hereinafter Miss et. al., "Cultural Resource Discipline Report," *in Mukilteo EIS*].

83   **All ten [Stevens] treaties would be almost completely identical.** For the best description of this, and how the ten treaties can be thought of as a unit, *see* Harmon, ed., "Introduction," *in Power of Promises*, pp. 8–11.

83   **A large Native attendance. Estimates ranged between 2,300 and 2,500.** *See, e.g.*, Miss et. al., "Cultural Resource Discipline Report," p. 122, *in Mukilteo EIS*.

83   **Lummi, Duwamish, and other peoples arrived as early as five days in advance.** *Id.*

83   **"The canoes, filled with the natives, . . . was said to be imposing"** *Pioneer and Democrat* (Olympia, Washington Territory), p. 2 (February 3, 1855).

84   **The tribes transferred their Indian title to the most valuable part of northwest Washington.** Treaty with the Dwamish and other Tribes, art. 1, January 22, 1855, 12 Stat. 927 (ratified March 8, 1859; proclaimed April 11, 1859) [hereinafter Treaty of Point Elliott]. *See also* Harmon, "Introduction," *in Power of Promises*, p. 7.

84   **The total amount of land was about six hundred thousand acres.** Pauline R. Hillaire, *Rights Remembered: A Salish Grandmother Speaks on American Indian History and the Future*, p. 124 (Lincoln: University of Nebraska Press, 2016). The cession included part of the present counties of King, Kitsap, Snohomish, Skagit, Whatcom, Island, and San Juan. *See* Clarence Bagley, "The Point Elliott Treaty," vol. 22, *Washington Historical Quarterly*, pp. 247–250 (October 1931). The map in Harmon, *Indians in the Making*, p. 81, demonstrates the reach of the tribes' Point Elliott cessions.

84   **"My Children! You are not my children because you are the fruit of my loins"** *See* Gibbs, "Record of the Proceedings," Point Elliott Minutes, p. 22.

85   **"I look upon you as my father."** *Id.* at p. 25.

85   **"Now by this we make friends"** *Id.* at p. 33.

85   **"Today I understand your heart"** *Id.* at p. 26.

87   **"I don't want to say much, my heart is good."** *Id.*

87   **"I am happy at heart."** *Id.*

87   **Why did the tribal leaders react this way, given that they were about to sur-**

render such an expansive block of beloved traditional land? This is a main example of the subtleties and imponderables in the tribal-white relationship. Professor Alexandra Harmon has made an outstanding contribution in *Indians in the Making*, pp. 72–79.

87   **A major epidemic had hit the territory just two years before.** *See, e.g.,* Robert Boyd, *The Coming of the Spirit of Pestilence: Introduced Infectious Disease and Population Decline among Northwest Coast Indians, 1774–1874,* p. 162 (Seattle: University of Washington Press, 1999).

88   **In addition to land ownership, the treaty dealt with other matters.** Treaty of Point Elliott, art. 14.

89   **"I was at Muckleteoh when Gov. Stevens made the treaty with our people in 1855."** Miss et. al., "Cultural Resource Discipline Report," p. 133, *in Mukilteo EIS.*

89   **"In the Treaty my uncle Pat Kanim reserved the salmon"** *Id.* at p. 132.

90   **"Better sign and get something some other way."** Meeker, *Pioneer Reminiscences of Puget Sound,* p. 245.

90   **Isaac Stevens held his next [the Point No Point] treaty council.** On the Point No Point Treaty, see generally Jacilee Wray, ed., *Native Peoples of the Olympic Peninsula: Who We Are,* p. 68–71 (Norman: University of Oklahoma Press, 2002); Jerry Gorsline, ed., *Shadows of Our Ancestors: Readings in the History of Klallam–White Relations,* pp. 41–45 (Anacortes, WA: Empty Bowl, 1992).

90   **"long nose"** Edmond S. Meany, *Origin of Washington Geographic Names,* p. 221 (Seattle: University of Washington Press, 1923).

90   **An important fishing area for the S'Klallam** Ron Charles, Port Gamble S'Klallam Tribal Council Chairman and Tribal Historian, interview with author, Poulsbo, Washington, June 18, 2005.

90   **The vista is breathtaking. . . . Point No Point is located on the northern tip of Kitsap Peninsula.** Site visit by author, June 18, 2015.

90   **At Point No Point, he would obtain for the United States more than half of the peninsula, over a million acres.** Harmon, ed., *Power of Promises,* map on p. 4.

91   **The crowd of 1,200 Indians** Gibbs, "Record of the Proceedings," p. 1.

91   **Stevens gave his normal "Great Father" speech.** *Id.* at pp. 1–2.

91   **Stevens then "asked [the Indians] if they had anything to say."** *Id.*

91   **"I wish to speak my mind as to the selling of the land."** *Id.*

91   **"I do not want to leave the mouth of the River."** *Id.*

91   **Two others spoke strongly against the treaty.** *See* Nah-whil-luk (Skokomish chief), *id.,* and Hool-hol-tan, or Jim (Skokomish subchief), *id.*

92   **Several of the thirty-three Skokomish villages were within it, but the large majority were not.** *See* Wray, ed. *Native Peoples of the Olympic Peninsula,* map on p. 67.

92   **Two of the anguished voices at Point No Point were Skokomish chiefs.** *See*

Che-lan-teh-tat in Gibbs, "Record of the Proceedings," p. 2; Nah-whil-luk, *id.*

92   **Their villages, twenty-six for S'Kllalam . . . were up on the Strait of Juan de Fuca, seventy miles or more to the north.** *See* Wray, ed., *Native Peoples of the Olympic Peninsula*, map on p. 17.

93   **"Mr. F. Shaw, the Interpreter explained"** Gibbs, "Record of the Proceedings," p. 2.

93   **"the Treaty was read to you last night."** *Id.*

93   **"the Indians came up bearing White Flags"** *Id.*

93   **The three designated leaders, [one from each of the tribes], gave their support to the treaty.** *Id.*

93   **"Governor Stevens once more asked if they were satisfied to sign the treaty."** *Id.* at p. 4.

93   **By the time the US Senate ratified the treaty four years later** *See* State of Washington, Governor's Office of Indian Affairs, "Resources," Treaty of Point No Point (ratified on March 8, 1859; proclaimed April 29, 1859). On relocation of the Skokomish, *see* Wayne Suttles and William Sturtevant, *Handbook of North American Indians*, vol. 7, *Northwest Coast*, p. 171 (Washington, DC: Smithsonian Institution, 1990).

94   **[the S'Klallam] refused to give in . . . purchasing private lands and obtaining public domain parcels.** *See, e.g.,* Wray, ed., *Native Peoples of the Olympic Peninsula*, pp. 55–56. On Indian homesteads from public domain land, *see* Felix Cohen et al., *Cohen's Handbook of Federal Indian Law*, 2012 ed., p. 1076 (New Providence, NJ: LexisNexis, 2012).

94   **The [Chimakum] tribe . . . over the course of about two generations disappeared as a distinct tribal entity.** Suttles and Sturtevant, *Handbook of North American Indians*, vol. 7, *Northwest Coast*, p. 171.

94   **The Makah had received no formal notice.** Cary C. Collins, "The Water Is Our Land: The Di ya Treaty of 1855," vol. 104 *Pacific Northwest Quarterly*, p. 21 (Winter 2012–2013).

94   **The Quileute would not go to Neah Bay on such short notice.** *Id.* at p. 24.

94   **The Makah had refused to participate in the Point No Point treaty.** Joshua L. Reid, *The Sea Is My Country: The Maritime World of the Makahs*, pp. 135 (New Haven, CT: Yale University Press, 2015).

94   **The Makahs had suffered one of the deadliest smallpox epidemics, costing an estimated 40 percent of their people.** Boyd, *Coming of the Spirit of Pestilence*, makes several references to this major event; *see* pp. 161, 162 (map), 167, 264, 267, 302. On the 40 percent estimate, *see, e.g.,* Tim Wright, "A History of Treaties and Reservations on the Olympic Peninsula, 1855–1898" (accessed April 19, 2022), *Center for the Study of the Pacific Northwest*, University of Washington, https://perma.cc/YTZ5-6GAA.

94   **"this was the moment"** Reid, *The Sea Is My Country*, p. 135.

94   **"the most formidable navigators of any in the American territories"** R. R. Thomas, Indian Agent, report to J. Palmer, Superintendent of Indian Affairs for Oregon Territory (September 16, 1854) *in* Senate Exec. Doc. No. 1, 1854 Commissioner Report, 33d Congress, 2d Session, p. 449, https://digitalcommons.law.ou.edu/indianserialset/1057/.

94   **"the superior courage of the Makahs"** *Id.* at p. 450.

95   **"Since the maritime fur trade, Makahs had participated in making colonialism possible"** Reid, *The Sea Is My Country*, p. 129.

95   **Stevens invited Makah leaders to join him on the schooner R. B. Potter.** On this evening meeting, *see, e.g.,* Reid, *The Sea Is My Country*, p. 124; Collins, "The Water Is Our Land," pp. 24–27; Council Minutes, pp. 43–45, roll 26, Records of the Washington Superintendency of Indian Affairs, 1853–1874 (National Archives Microfilm Publication M5), Records of the Bureau of Indian Affairs, National Archives and Records Administration (NARA) [hereinafter Council Minutes, with appropriate page number].

95   **If anything, the horror made them all the more determined.** Reid, *The Sea Is My Country*, p. 136.

95   **the traditional Makah vision of ocean and whales** Dr. Barbara Lane, "Makah Economy and the Makah Treaty Circa 1855—A Cultural Analysis," pp. 44–45, *in* "Political and Economic Aspects of Indian-White Culture Contact in Western Washington in the Mid-Nineteenth Century," report prepared at request of US Justice Department (May 1973), expert testimony for *United States v. Washington*, US District Court, Seattle, No. 9213.

96   **"I ought to have the right to fish and take whales"** Council Minutes, p. 43.

96   **"I do not want to leave the salt water."** *Id.*

96   **Several chiefs spoke to the tribe's elaborate system of marine law.** Lane, "Makah Economy and the Makah Treaty Circa 1855," pp. 44–45.

96   **"I want the sea. That is my country."** Council Minutes, p. 44.

96   **The formal . . . Treaty Council . . . took place on January 31.** Lane, "Makah Economy and the Makah Treaty Circa 1855," p 37.

96   **"He knows what whalers you are"** Joanne Barker, ed., *Sovereignty Matters*, p. 132 (Lincoln: University of Nebraska Press, 2006).

96   **"This right of taking fish and of whaling or sealing"** Council Minutes, p. 43.

96   **James Swan . . . became convinced . . . that . . . the treaty did not reflect the tribe's understanding.** C. H. Hale to William P. Dole, October 19, 1862, in "Annual Report of the Commissioner of Indian Affairs for the Year 1862," p. 534 (Washington, DC, 1862).

97   **Interior Department order amending the borders** James G. Swan, "Makah Census Report, Oct. 25, 1861," copy in Jacilee Wray Collection, Olympic National Park Regional Archives, Port Angeles, Washington. The original report

is in the Swan Papers, Special Collections, University of Washington Libraries, Seattle.

97   **The reservation was expanded to a point very close to what the tribe expected.** *Id.*

97   **Chehalis Council** See generally Wray, ed., *Native Peoples of the Olympic Peninsula*, p. 129; Robert Lane and Barbara Lane, "Current Issues Arising out of the Chehalis River Treaty Council" (n.d.), Institute for the Defense of Indian Law, https://www.washingtonhistory.org/wp-content/uploads/2020/04/chehalisCouncil-1.pdf. James G. Swan attended this event in person and wrote an engaging account in *Northwest Coast*, pp. 327–360.

97   **Each of the tribes objected.** *See* Gibbs, "Record of the Proceedings," pp. 15–25; *see, e.g.,* Lane and Lane, "Chehalis River Treaty Council": "He understands it very well. He does not want to sign till he knows where he is going to. He wants to stay in his own country and not be moved elsewhere," Yowannus (Upper Chehalis), p. 19; "He wanted to put his house on the Nasal River (Shoalwater Bay). Where his dead were buried," Nah-Kot-Ti and Moos-Moos (Chinook), p. 17; "We want a piece of land in our own country. A small piece. We won't go to the Quinault. We will die on our own ground," Annan-Nata (subchief of Upper Chehalis), p. 21; "This river was all mine. While looking for food on it and fishing I do not want to be driven off. I want the river for a fishery and down below (Chehalis) for a reserve," Tu-Leh-Uk (head chief of the Lower Chehalis), p. 15.

97   **"a tract of land on the Coast of the Pacific"** *Id.* at p. 34.

98   **The tribes offered many alternative proposals.** *See, e.g., id.* at pp. 26–28.

98   **"We have now been here a week."** *Id.* at p. 32.

98   **"It having been found impracticable"** *Id.* at p. 33.

98   **Simmons's Treaty Council . . . at the mouth of the Quinault River.** *See, e.g.,* Wright, "History of Treaties and Reservations"; Robert H. Ruby and John A. Brown, *A Guide to the Indian Tribes of the Pacific Northwest*, pp. 81 (Hoh), 170–171 (Queets), 171–172 (Quileute), 174–176 (Quinault) (Norman: University of Oklahoma Press, 1992).

98   **"There shall . . . be reserved . . . for the tribes and bands"** Treaty with the Qui-Nai-elt, art. 2, 12 Stat. 971 (July 1, 1855) Article 2 (ratified March 8, 1859; proclaimed April 11, 1859).

99   **The tribes had conveyed . . . 200,000 acres of Indian title.** R. H. Milroy, "Report of the Commissioner of Indian Affairs, 1872," p. 339 (Washington, DC: Government Printing Office, 1872).

99   **Washington Superintendent of Indian Affairs R. H. Milroy recommended.** *Id.* at p. 341; Exec. Order, November 4, 1873, *reprinted in* Kappler, *Indian Affairs*, pp. 923–924.

99   **Executive orders created reservations.** Executive orders created 837 acres for

the Quileute, 1 Kappler 923 (February 19, 1889), and 443 acres for the Hoh, 1 Kappler 916–917 (September 11, 1893).

99   **Most Queets people, always closely related to the Quinault, resided on that reservation and today are considered Quinault tribal citizens.** Quinault Indian Nation, "People of the Quinault" (2003), *Quinault Indian Nation*, https://perma.cc/GQ7T-CR2Z.

99   **He probably fancied himself, and understandably so, as part of "the Vanishing Indian" phenomenon.** *See* Brian W. Dippie, *The Vanishing American: White Attitudes and U.S. Indian Policy* (Lawrence: University Press of Kansas, 1991).

6   The Long Suppression

101   **By the late 1860s, settlers . . . were complaining.** *See, e.g.,* Alexandra Harmon, *Indians in the Making: Ethnic Relations and Indian Identities around Puget Sound*, pp. 106–108 (Berkeley: University of California Press, 1999).

102   **"No panacea for the Indian problem was more persistently proposed than allotment of land"** Francis Paul Prucha, *The Great Father: The United States Government and the American Indians*, abridged ed., p. 224 (Lincoln: University of Nebraska Press, 1986).

102   **General Allotment Act of 1887** See generally Frederick E. Hoxie, *A Final Promise: The Campaign to Assimilate the Indians* (Lincoln: University of Nebraska Press, 2001); Katherine Ellinghaus, *Blood Will Tell: Native Americans and Assimilation Policy* (Lincoln: University of Nebraska Press); Jason Black, *American Indians and the Rhetoric of Removal and Allotment* (Jackson: University Press of Mississippi, 2015); Kristin Ruppel, *Unearthing Indian Land: Living with the Legacies of Allotment* (Tucson: University of Arizona Press, 2008).

103   **Flows of Indian allotments to non-Indian opportunists** Angie Debo, *A History of the Indians of the United States* (Norman: University of Oklahoma Press, 1984). On the loss of 90 million acres, *see, e.g.,* Frank Pommersheim, *Braid of Feathers*, p. 20 (Berkeley: University of California Press, 1997).

105   **"a mighty pulverizing engine"** Brian W. Dippie, *The Vanishing American: White Attitudes and U.S. Indian Policy*, p. 244 (Middletown, CT: Wesleyan University Press, 1982).

105   **"Both sides joined in seeing the massacre as the end"** David Treuer, *The Heartbeat of Wounded Knee: Native America from 1890 to the Present*, p. 8 (New York: Riverhead Books, 2019).

105   **The Bureau of Indian Affairs [and] the churches hammered home . . . the message.** See generally Kenneth R. Philp, *Termination Revisited: American Indians on the Trail to Self-Determination, 1933–1953* (Lincoln: University of Nebraska Press, 1999); Alvin M. Josephy Jr., *Now That the Buffalo's Gone: A*

Study of Today's American Indians, pp. 217–258 (New York: Alfred A. Knopf, 1982); Edgar S. Cahn, ed., *Our Brother's Keeper: The Indian in White America*, pp. 141–173 (Washington, DC: New Community Press, 1969).

105 **"Agents of the Bureau of Indian Affairs"** Josephy, *Now That the Buffalo's Gone*, p. 87.

106 **Education was a main vehicle for assimilation.** See generally Jon Reyhner and Jeanne Eder, *American Indian Education: A History*, 2nd ed. (Norman: University of Oklahoma Press, 2017); Margaret Connell Szasz, *Education and the American Indian: The Road to Self-Determination Since 1928*, pp. 8–15 (Albuquerque: University of New Mexico Press, 1999).

106 **"The Indian must have a Christian language"** Prucha, *Great Father*, p. 687.

106 **"the Indian youth should be instructed"** *Id.* at p. 703.

106 **"All the Indian there is in the race should be dead."** Richard Henry Pratt, "The Advantages of Mingling Indians with Whites," *in* ed. Francis P. Prucha, *Americanizing the American Indians*, pp. 200–261 (Cambridge, MA: Harvard University Press, 1973).

106 **"The boarding schools were highly regimented."** *See* Allen P. Slickpoo Sr., *Noon Nee-Me-Poo (We, The Nez Perces): Culture and History of the Nez Perces*, vol. 1, pp. 227–237 (Lapwai: Nez Perce Tribe of Idaho, 1973).

107 **Congress granted citizenship to all Indians.** Some Indians had already gained citizenship, upon receiving an allotment selectively by means of provisions in treaties or upon receiving allotments under the General Allotment Act of 1887. The general citizenship provision in 1924 naturalized all "Indians born within the territorial limits of the United States." 8 U.S.C. § 1401 (a)(2).

107 **1928 Meriam Report** *See* Lewis Meriam et al., "The Problem of Indian Administration," Institute for Government Research (Baltimore, MD: Johns Hopkins Press, 1928).

108 **When Franklin Roosevelt became president . . . he named . . . John Collier.** On Indian policy in the Franklin Roosevelt administration, *see* Elmer R. Rusco, *A Fateful Time: The Background and Legislative History of the Indian Reorganization Act* (Reno: University of Nevada Press, 2000); Kenneth R. Philp, *John Collier's Crusade for Indian Reform* (Tucson: University of Arizona Press, 1977); Lawrence Kelly, *The Assault on Assimilation: John Collier and the Origins of Indian Policy Reform*, pp. xvii–xviii (Albuquerque: University of New Mexico Press, 1983); John Collier, *The Indians of the Americas*, p. 15 (New York: W. W. Norton, 1947).

108 **"no interference with Indian religious life"** *See* Prucha, *Great Father*, p. 951.

108 **Felix Cohen's Handbook of Federal Indian Law** Felix S. Cohen's seminal treatise is *Handbook of Federal Indian Law* (Washington, DC: Government Printing Office, 1942). The 1982 revision of the Cohen treatise contains a discussion

of the preparation of the original edition, its importance in American law, and a complete listing of Cohen's many scholarly publications: *see* Cohen, *Handbook of Federal Indian Law*, pp. vii–xi (Charlottesville, VA: Michie Bobbs-Merrill, 1982). For the most recent revision of Cohen's *Handbook*, see Felix Cohen et al., *Cohen's Handbook of Federal Indian Law*, 2012 ed., § 15.03, pp. 997–999 (New Providence, NJ: LexisNexis, 2012).

109 **Congress announced the new Indian policy: termination.** On the termination policy, see generally Donald L. Fixico, *Termination and Relocation: Federal Indian Policy, 1945–1960* (Albuquerque: University of New Mexico Press, 1990); Philp, *Termination Revisited*.

109 **BIA officials brought termination proposals to . . . Puget Sound . . . and other . . . Washington tribes.** Harmon, *Indians in the Making*, p. 207.

109 **Senator Henry Jackson pressed for termination.** *See, e.g.,* Charles Wilkinson, *Blood Struggle: The Rise of Modern Indian Nations*, pp. 178–182 (New York: W. W. Norton, 2005).

109 **Approximately 109 tribes and bands nationally were terminated.** *See* Charles F. Wilkinson and Eric R. Biggs, "The Evolution of the Termination Policy," vol. 5 *American Indian Law Review*, p. 139 (1977).

110 **Twenty-three thousand tribal veterans returned from service.** On the returning of Indian veterans, *see, e.g.,* Alison Bernstein, *American Indians and World War II*, pp. 131–158 (Norman: University Oklahoma Press, 1991).

110 **"World War II revived the Indian's capacity"** *Id.* at p. 158.

110 **"Hang on to your lands."** Quoted in John Fahey, *Saving the Reservation: Joe Garry and the Battle to Be Indian*, p. 53 (Seattle: University of Washington Press, 2001).

111 **For two decades after the treaties, the tribes and the settlers had few disputes.** Gabriel Chrisman, "The Fish-in Protests at Frank's Landing" (2008), *Seattle Civil Rights and Labor History Project*, University of Washington, https://perma.cc/583L-6NUB.

111 **The arrival of canneries** On the early history of canning, *see* Arthur F. McEvoy, *The Fisherman's Problem: Ecology and Law in the California Fisheries, 1850–1980*, pp. 70–71 (Cambridge, MA: Cambridge University Press, 1986); Courtland L. Smith, *Salmon Fishers of the Columbia*, p. 6 (Corvallis: Oregon State University Press, 1979).

111 **Hume brothers . . . moved up to the Columbia.** *See* McEvoy, *Fisherman's Problem*, p. 132; Smith, *Salmon Fishers*, p. 6.

112 **The non-Indian commercial fishery quickly developed into a major industry.** *See, e.g.,* Russel Barsh, *The Washington Fishing Rights Controversy: An Economic Critique*, pp. 12–13 (Seattle: University of Washington, Graduate School of Business Administration, 1977).

112 **Some forty-five Puget Sound canneries were producing nearly 1,400,000**

cases of salmon annually. *See* Robert Higgs, "Legally Induced Technical Regress in the Washington Salmon Fishery: Independent Institute," *The Independent*, p. 10 (June 30, 1982).

112 **The commercial fishermen . . . built impressive harvesting operations.** *See,* e.g., Higgs, "Legally Induced Technical Regress," pp. 10–11; Barsh, *Washington Fishing Rights Controversy*, pp. 12–13.

113 **Fish wheels** See generally Francis Seufert, *Wheels of Fortune*, p. 9 (Portland: Oregon Historical Society, 1980).

113 **"Here was the fisherman's problem"** McEvoy, *Fisherman's Problem*, p. 72.

113 **"The salmon fisheries of the Columbia River"** President Theodore Roosevelt, "Special Message to Congress" (December 8, 1908), *in* James D. Richardson, *Messages and Papers of the Presidents*, vol. 10, p. 7610 (New York: Bureau of National Literature and Art, 1913).

114 **Tons of . . . salmon bound for grounds where tribes had traditionally fished were intercepted.** *See* Fay Cohen, *Treaties on Trial*, p. 40 (Seattle: University of Washington Press, 1986).

114 **"After the canneries started going good"** *See* Ann Nugent, ed., *Lummi Elders Speak*, p. 26 (Lynden, WA: Lynden Tribune, 1982).

114 **The economics and politics of Northwest salmon fishing began to change.** *See, e.g.,* Higgs, "Legally Induced Technical Regress," pp. 14–15.

114 **State officials paid little attention to tribal complaints.** *See* Thomas P. Schlosser, "Washington's Resistance to Treaty Indian Commercial Fishing: The Need for Judicial Apportionment," pp. 11–13 (October 1978), https://perma.cc/KBW6-UTND, from the website of attorneys Morisset, Schlosser, Jozwiak, & Somerville under the section American Indian Law Papers and Publications, https://www.msaj.com/indian-law-papers-1; Cohen, *Treaties on Trial*, pp. 43–44.

114 **The state made much of its purported police power** *See* Hugh D. Spitzer, "Municipal Police Power in Washington State," vol. 75 *Washington Law Review*, p. 495 (2000).

114 **Washington State Supreme Court handed down** *See State v. Alexis*, 154 P. 810 (1916); *State v. Meninock*, 197 P. 641 (1921); *State v. Towessnute*, 154 P. 805, 807 (1916).

114 **"The Indian was a child"** *State v. Towessnute*, 154 P. 805, 807 (1916). In 2020 the Washington Supreme Court overruled the Towessnute opinion. *See State v. Towessnute*, 486 P. 3d 111 (2020); Donald W. Meyers, "State Supreme Court Vacates Racist 1916 Ruling in Yakama Fishing Rights Case," *Yakima Herald* (July 10, 2020), https://perma.cc/2LTF-2MUG.

115 **Initiative in 1932, establishing the Department of Game** Washington Secretary of State, "November 1932 General [Election]" (updated March 2011), *Election Search Results*, https://perma.cc/SKW5-9Q8Z.

115 **Voters approved Initiative 77.** The initiative sought to conserve salmon runs by outlawing fish traps, which at the time were mainly used by commercial canneries. For more detail, *see* Higgs, "Legally Induced Technical Regress," pp. 13–19.

115 **Commercial fishers found ways around [Initiative 77].** *See, e.g.,* Schlosser, "Washington's Resistance to Treaty Indian Commercial Fishing," pp. 15–16.

115 **"The provisions of the Act do not apply to fishing by Indians"** *Id.* at p. 16.

115 **Sports clubs went to the Game Department and . . . demanded action.** Barsh, *Washington Fishing Rights Controversy,* p 19.

115 **"young bucks" and . . . "The state is not infringing"** *See* Joshua L. Reid, *The Sea Is My Country: The Maritime World of the Makahs,* p. 256 (New Haven, CT: Yale University Press, 2015).

116 **"After the 1950s one provision"** Harmon, *Indians in the Making,* p. 218.

7   The Tribes Come Forward

117 **In the 1942 Tulee case** *Tulee v. Washington,* 315 U.S. 681 (1942) addressed the validity of tribal rights and state authority to regulate tribal rights if necessary for "conservation."

117 **A split decision in State v. Satiacum** *State v. Satiacum,* 314 P. 2d 400 (Wash. 1957) concerned broad state authority to regulate for conservation and found tribal rights "unimpaired" unless curtailed by Congress.

118 **"I was fishing with my son"** Statement of Ted Plaster, Lummi. *See, e.g.,* Ann Nugent, ed., *Lummi Elders Speak,* p. 23 (Lynden, WA: Lynden Tribune, 1982). On private citizens interfering with tribal fishers, *see* Alvin J. Ziontz, "Tribal Report to the Presidential Task Force on Treaty Fishing Rights in the Northwest: History of Treaty Fishing Rights in the Pacific Northwest," p. 26 (October 21, 1977), which includes "Non-Indian sports fishermen vented their anger by acts of violence; cutting the Indians' nets, pushing their boats into the river . . . and threatening physical harm to Indian fishermen."

118 **Tribal fishers were taking only 6 percent of the . . . harvest** *See, e.g.,* Ziontz, "Tribal Report to the Presidential Task Force on Treaty Fishing Rights in the Northwest," p. 38; American Friends Service Committee and Mary B. Isley, *Uncommon Controversy: Fishing Rights of the Muckleshoot, Puyallup, and Nisqually Indians,* pp. 126–127 (Seattle: University of Washington Press, 1970). These figures come from the Departments of Game and Fisheries (now the Department of Fish and Wildlife).

118 **The total of all Indian fishers was approximately 800.** *See* Alvin M. Josephy Jr., *Now That the Buffalo's Gone: A Study of Today's American Indians,* p. 180 (New York: Alfred A. Knopf, 1982).

118 **Significant damage was due to wide-scale impacts on salmon habitat.** *See, e.g.,*

Anthony Netboy, *The Columbia River Salmon and Steelhead Trout, Their Fight for Survival*, chs. 5 and 6 (Seattle: University of Washington Press, 1981); J. Lichatowich, L. Mobrand, and L. Lestelle, "Depletion and Extinction of Pacific Salmon (*Oncorhynchus* spp.): A Different Perspective," vol. 56 *ICES Journal of Marine Science*, pp. 467–472 (1999). See also Russel Barsh, *Washington Fishing Rights Controversy: An Economic Critique*, p. 17 (Seattle: University of Washington, Graduate School of Business Administration, 1977); Robert T. Lackey, "Salmon Decline in Western North America: Historical Context," Department of Fisheries and Wildlife, p. 4, Oregon State University (2009); University of Washington Libraries Special Collections Division, *Salmon in the Pacific Northwest and Alaska Collection, 1890–1961* (2001), UW Libraries Digital Collections, https://perma.cc/7H38-XB2G.

119   **"it is probable that the ultimate solution will have to lie with Congress."** *See* "Indian Fishing Is Problem for Congress," *Seattle Times*, p. 12 (March 5, 1962).

119   **"Simplistic arguments . . . continued to be used"** Josephy, *Now That the Buffalo's Gone*, p. 189.

120   **[Washington] became the first state to resolve to eliminate Indian treaty rights.** See Bruce Brown, *Mountain in the Clouds: A Search for the Wild Salmon*, p. 155 (Seattle: University of Washington Press, 1995); Bradley G. Shreve, "From Time Immemorial: The Fish-in Movement and the Rise of Intertribal Activism," vol. 78, no. 3 *Pacific Historical Review*, p. 412 (August 2009).

120   **[Raid] on January 6, 1962** *See* Mark Trahant, "The Center of Everything—Native Leader Janet McCloud Finds Peace in Her Place, Her Victories, Her Family. It Has Taken Many Years to Get There," *Seattle Times* (July 4, 1999); Shreve, "From Time Immemorial," p. 412.

120   **"It was nearly a daily event"** *See* Charles Wilkinson, *Messages from Frank's Landing: A Story of Salmon, Treaties, and the Indian Way*, pp. 33–34 (Seattle: University of Washington Press, 2000).

121   **The Quinault Indian Nation protested state policies.** *See* "Lake Quinault to Be Closed to White Fishers," *Seattle Times*, p. 1 (March 26, 1961).

121   **In 1963, the Makah held their initial meeting with Al Ziontz.** Alvin J. Ziontz, *A Lawyer in Indian Country: A Memoir*, p.6 (Seattle: University of Washington Press, 2009). *See also* Alexandra Harmon, *Reclaiming the Reservation: Histories of Indian Sovereignty Suppressed and Renewed*, pp. 151–153 (Seattle: University of Washington Press, 2019).

122   **Hank Adams was born** Josephy, *Now That the Buffalo's Gone*, p. 193. *See also* Mark Trahant, "American Indian Activist Hank Adams Dies at 77," *Times Magazine* (December 25, 2020); David E. Wilkins, *The Hank Adams Reader: An Exemplary Native Activist and the Unleashing of Indigenous Sovereignty*, pp. 5–7 (Golden, CO: Fulcrum Publishing, 2011); Wilkinson, *Messages*, p. 44.

122   **Adams joined the National Indian Youth Council.** *See* Trova Heffernan, *Where the Salmon Run: The Life and Legacy of Billy Frank Jr.,* p. 72 (Seattle: University of Washington Press, 2012), which also reported Adams's interest in the NIYC.

122   **NIYC grew out of a groundbreaking anthropological experiment . . . [by] Professor Sol Tax.** On Sol Tax's influential workshops for Indian college students, *see* Nancy Oestreich Lurie, "Sol Tax and Tribal Sovereignty," vol. 58 *Human Organization,* p. 108 (Spring 1999); Paul McKenzie-Jones, "Evolving Voices of Dissent: The Workshops on American Indian Affairs," vol. 38, no. 2 *American Indian Quarterly,* p. 207 (Spring 2014).

122   **D'Arcy McNickle** On McNickle, *see, e.g.,* Dorothy R. Parker, *Singing an Indian Song: Biography of D'Arcy McNickle* (Lincoln: University of Nebraska Press, 1992); John Lloyd Purdy, ed., *The Legacy of D'Arcy McNickle: Writer, Historian, Activist* (Norman: University of Oklahoma Press, 1996); Charles Wilkinson, *Blood Struggle: The Rise of Modern Indian Nations,* pp. 902 (New York: W. W. Norton, 2005).

123   **The Washington Supreme Court, which . . . had long ruled against tribal fishing rights, handed down State v. McCoy.** On the court's rulings against tribal fishing rights, *see State v. Towessnute,* 154 P. 805, 807 (Wash. 1916); *State v. Meninock,* 197 P. 641 (1921); *State v. Alexis,* 154 P. 810 (Wash. 1916). *See also State v. McCoy,* 387 P. 2d 942 (Wash. 1963).

123   **1896 US Supreme Court opinion** *See State v. McCoy ,* 387 P. 2d at 949–951, 953. *See also Escanaba Company v. Chicago,* 107 U.S. 678, 689 (1882): "Equality of constitutional right and power is the condition of all the States of the Union, old and new."

124   **Washington had "acquired all of the sovereign powers."** *See State v. McCoy,* 387 P. 2d at 952–953.

124   **Supreme Court formally overruled [Ward v. Race Horse]** *Herrera v. Wyoming,* 139 S. Ct. 1686, 1697 (2019): "To avoid any future confusion, we make it clear today that Race Horse is repudiated to the extent that it held that treaty rights can be implicitly extinguished at statehood."

124   **Maison v. Confederated Tribes of Umatilla Indian Reservation** *Maison v. Confederated Tribes of Umatilla Indian Reservation,* 314 F. 2d 169 (1963).

124   **They decided to start by going to the governor first.** *See, e.g.,* Josephy, *Now That the Buffalo's Gone,* p. 192; Shreve, "From Time Immemorial," p. 414: "The McCoy decision reverberated throughout tribal communities in western Washington."

124   **"Nice to hear your problems"** Josephy, *Now That the Buffalo's Gone,* p. 192.

125   **January 2, 1964 . . . injunction . . . arrests** *Id.* at pp. 192–193, which describes these incidents as "the start of a war." *See, e.g.,* Don Tewkesbury, "Court Orders Indians to Stop Fishing," (Tacoma) *News Tribune,* p. 1 (January 23, 1964); Mike

Conant, "Indians Net New Troubles," *Daily Olympian*, p. 1 (March 4, 1964); "White Flag Lowered; Indian Group Ends Truce With State," *Yakima Morning Herald*, pp. 1–2 (January 22, 1964).

126 **The treaties provided for a means of support.** Ramona Bennett, Puyallup tribal member, interview with Cecelia La Pointe-Gorman (May 2009), *Oral History and Memory Project*, Northwest Indian College, Bellingham, Washington, https://perma.cc/FF8N-BEDJ.

126 **"The Nisqually River was targeted"** Trahant, "The Center of Everything."

127 **SAIA saw itself as a "fighting" organization.** Gabriel Chrisman, "The Fish-in Protests at Frank's Landing" (2008), *Seattle Civil Rights and Labor History Project*, University of Washington, https://perma.cc/XEC4-F7A3.

127 **Finding an old mimeograph machine at Goodwill** Trahant, "The Center of Everything."

127 **McCloud asked the wardens if they had a search warrant.** Forterra, "Janet McCloud—Yet-Si-Blue, 'woman who speaks her mind'" (April 10, 2022), *Honoring Women of the Past, Present and Future*, https://perma.cc/RPF7-9Q4D.

128 **"We rode the wave"** *See* Cecelia La Pointe-Gorman, "Ramona Bennett: Puyallup Tribal Indian Activities," p. 9, research essay (2009), *Tacoma Community History Project*, University of Washington Tacoma, https://perma.cc/NUA2-AYU6.

128 **Tribal people . . . were uncertain about following the Black civil rights approach.** Vine Deloria Jr., *Custer Died for Your Sins: An Indian Manifesto*, pp. 169–196 (Norman: University of Oklahoma Press, 1988); Wilkinson, *Blood Struggle*, pp. 129–130.

129 **Many older Indians and Native organizations were uncomfortable with demonstrations.** *See, e.g.,* Deloria, *Custer Died for Your Sins. See also* Shreve, "From Time Immemorial," p. 417; "State Indians Reject Marches, Sit-in Tactics," *Seattle Post-Intelligencer*, p. 10 (February 16, 1964).

129 **The fish-ins worked as planned.** On the fish-ins of March 1964, *see* Shreve, "From Time Immemorial," pp. 419–420; Chrisman, "Fish-in Protests," pp. 8–9.

130 **March on Olympia . . . to protest state actions against Indian treaty fishers.** *See, e.g.,* Shreve, "From Time Immemorial," pp. 420–423; Chrisman, "Fish-in Protests," pp. 8–9.

130 **"an indignity to the human spirit"** Shreve, "From Time Immemorial," p. 42.

130 **The meeting, which lasted four hours, ended with the governor agreeing.** *See, e.g., Id.* at p. 422.

130 **The only tribe with a tribal lawyer was the Makah, with Al Ziontz.** Ziontz, *A Lawyer in Indian Country*, pp. 5–7.

131 **SAIA and fishers brought in [attorney] Jack Tanner.** *See, e.g.,* Josephy, *Now That the Buffalo's Gone*, p. 193; Chrisman, "Fish-in Protests," pp. 8–9.

131   **Local attorneys were volunteering pro bono help. . . . the ACLU was also providing attorneys.** Chrisman, "Fish-in Protests," pp. 8–9.

131   **George Dysart had been in the Interior Department Solicitor's Office in Oregon for several years.** *See, e.g.,* Ziontz, *A Lawyer in Indian Country,* pp. 93–94; Michael C. Blumm and Cari Baermann, "The Belloni Decision and Its Legacy: United States v. Oregon and Its Far-Reaching Effects After a Half-Century," vol. 50, no. 4 *Environmental Law,* pp. 364–366 (2020). George Dysart (1923–2002) was a scholarly, vigilant man, graduating from Harvard Law with honors in 1949. It was in his capacity as general solicitor for the Department of the Interior that Dysart "dived into the business of protecting Indian treaties," paving the way for the historic Boldt Decision: Wilkinson, *Blood Struggle,* pp. 164–165. Sid Lezak, the US Attorney in Oregon from 1961 to 1982, noted that George Dysart's integrity gave him great credibility with judges: "George was the kind of guy, if he told you something, believe it. There were no mistakes. He was the consummate legal craftsman": "George Dysart, Legal Champion of Tribal Fishing Rights, Dies at 79," *The Oregonian,* p. D5 (November 27, 2002).

131   **Dysart knew Sid Lezak.** Blumm and Baermann, "The Belloni Decision and Its Legacy."

132   **The Department of Justice did authorize assistant US attorneys to defend tribal fishers in state courts.** *See, e.g.,* Fay G. Cohen, *Treaties on Trial: The Continuing Controversy over Northwest Indian Fishing Rights,* p. 76 (Seattle: University of Washington Press, 1986).

132   **The Interior Department . . . can submit a litigation request to the DOJ.** The best account of this drafting and presentation project is Ziontz, *A Lawyer in Indian Country,* pp. 93–94. These events led up to the so-called Belloni Decision, which is taken up in the next several pages of this chapter. On October 18, 2019, I delivered the keynote address at a conference at Lewis and Clark Law School commemorating the Belloni Decision and that address became an article: Charles Wilkinson, "The Belloni Decision: A Foundation for the Northwest Fisheries Cases, the National Tribal Sovereignty Movement, and an Understanding of the Rule of Law," vol. 50 *Environmental Law,* p. 331 (Spring 2020). I have drawn liberally on that article in my treatment of the Belloni Decision and related events.

133   **David Sohappy** *See, e.g.,* Yakama Nation Fisheries, "David Sohappy, Sr. 'Tucknashut' (átwai)" (2022), *Honored Elders,* https://perma.cc/729Z-9LP2.

133   **Individual Yakama tribal members filed a lawsuit, Sohappy v. Smith.** *Sohappy v. Smith,* 302 F. Supp. 899 (D. Or. 1969).

133   **"You're in state court and treaty fishing is a federal question"** George Dysart quoted in Laura Berg, "Let Them Do as They Have Promised," vol. 3 *Hastings Environmental Law Journal,* p. 10 (Fall 1995).

134 **"opposition from several Justice and Interior Departments attorneys"** *Id.* at p. 11.

135 **Issues in both cases were so similar.** Blumm and Baermann, "Belloni Decision and Its Legacy," p. 347.

135 **Now had the prestige and resources of the United States of America behind them** On the trail-blazing work of Lezak and Dysart in conceiving of, and bringing to court, *United States v. Oregon*, see Blumm and Baermann, "Belloni Decision and Its Legacy," pp. 364–369.

135 **Judge Robert Belloni . . . was raised in small towns in Coos County.** Judge Robert C. Belloni, US District Court judge for the District of Oregon, interview with Laura Berg, Portland, Oregon, December 1, 1989.

136 **The main exception was the 1905 . . . Winans case** *United States v. Winans*, 198 U.S. 371, 380 (1905).

137 **How tribes possessed fishing and water rights before the treaties** *Id.* at p. 381.

137 **"not much less necessary to the existence of the Indians than the atmosphere they breathed."** *Id.* Three years later Justice McKenna wrote the equally seminal Winters opinion, establishing reserved tribal water rights, in *Winters v. United States*, 207 U.S. 564 (1908).

137 **Tribal governmental authority** *Worcester v. Georgia*, 31 U.S. 515 (1832).

137 **The word sovereignty hadn't been used with respect to tribes by the Supreme Court in the twentieth century.** *See McClanahan v. Arizona State Tax Commission*, 411 U.S. 164 (1973).

137 **On state regulation, the courts had addressed the issue only rarely and unhelpfully.** Even *Winans* came up short, offering a two-sentence suggestion, which did not survive, of a broad state authority: *United States v. Winans*, 198 U.S. 371, 384 (1905). State regulation of tribal fishing did come up in the 1968 Supreme Court ruling in Puyallup I, *Puyallup Tribe v. Department of Game of Washington*, 391 U.S. 392 (1968), just as Judge Belloni was entering the judiciary. The brief and unconvincing opinion by Justice William O. Douglas was formidable only because it was recent. But it contained new language—suggesting that states might include authority to regulate tribes when "necessary for conservation"—that was far broader than previously believed. *See* Puyallup I, *Puyallup Tribe v. Department of Game of Washington*, 391 U.S. at 399. Judge Belloni narrowly construed the reference in Puyallup II, and in the 1973 Puyallup II decision Justice Douglas did not apply the "reasonable and necessary" standard, which effectively removed the inappropriate language in Puyallup I from Supreme Court jurisprudence. *See* Puyallup II, *Department of Game of Washington v. Puyallup Tribe*, 414 U.S. 44 (1973). On the Puyallup cases, *see also* chapter 9, The Trial, pp. 153–181, in this book.

137 **Justice Belloni responded** The most comprehensive treatment of the Belloni

Decision is found in the collected articles presented at the Fiftieth Anniversary Celebration of the Belloni Decision held at Lewis and Clark Law School on October 18, 2019. *See* Symposium, *US v. Oregon: 50th Anniversary,* vol. 50, no. 2 *Environmental Law,* pp. 327–556 (Spring 2020).

137 **Treaties must be read to reflect the intent of the tribes.** *Sohappy v. Smith,* 302 F. Supp. at 905–906.

138 **Tribes must have a specific share of the salmon resource.** *Id.* at pp. 907–908, 910–911.

138 **The court would keep continuing jurisdiction to resolve continuing conflicts.** *Id.* at p. 911.

138 **Judge Belloni also clarified and defined** *Id.* at pp. 906–909.

138 **This regulatory authority is narrow.** *Id.* at p. 908 [emphasis added].

138 **Judge Belloni . . . debunked the state's assertion** *Id.* at pp. 909–910.

138 **A key state objective was to allocate the resource to satisfy two powerful user groups.** *Id.* at pp. 910–911.

138 **The regulations of these agencies** *Id.* at p. 909.

139 **Amounted to discrimination against tribal treaty rights** *Id.* at p. 910.

139 **"[T]he case took a toll on Belloni."** Judge Owen M. Panner, US District Court judge for the District of Oregon, interview with author, May 8, 2002, quoted in Wilkinson, *Blood Struggle,* p. 166.

8   The Buildup to the Boldt Decision

141 **The case had been closely watched up in Washington.** Mike Layton, "Long Battle Over Fishing Rights May End," *Daily Olympian,* p. 2 (June 4, 1969); "Indian Fishing Rights Are Upheld," *Longview Daily News,* p. 3 (April 25, 1969).

141 **Indian country was elated** James Magner, "Judge Rules in Favor of 1855 Indian Fishing Treaty," *The Oregonian,* p. 19 (April 25, 1969).

141 **Washington tribes . . . expected . . . equal or perhaps greater legal protection.** "Indians Demand Fishing Areas," (Spokane) *Spokesman Review,* p. 3 (June 3, 1969); "Indians Fish in River," (Chehalis-Centralia) *Daily Chronicle,* p. 7 (August 5, 1969).

142 **Stan Pitkin, the United States Attorney for Western Washington** Carlyle Reed, "One Man Against City Hall," *Lodi* (California) *News-Sentinel,* p. 4 (September 3, 1981).

142 **A litigation request should be made to the Justice Department office in Washington, DC** Al Ziontz describes this process well; *see* Alvin J. Ziontz, *A Lawyer in Indian Country: A Memoir,* pp. 93–95 (Seattle: University of Washington Press, 2009).

142 **"in dire need of a case to end all cases"** Trova Heffernan, *Where the Salmon*

Run: The Life and Legacy of Billy Frank Jr., p. 129 (Seattle: University of Washington Press, 2012).

142 **Nixon's White House staff included "loyal opposition"** *See, e.g.,* Charles Wilkinson, *Blood Struggle: The Rise of Modern Indian Nations,* pp. 214–215 (New York: W. W. Norton, 2005).

142 **On July 8, 1970, Nixon issued his . . . "Special Message on Indian Affairs"** President Nixon, "Special Message on Indian Affairs, July 8, 1970," *Public Papers of the Presidents of the United States: Richard Nixon* (1970), pp. 564–567, 576, https://perma.cc/RQ4A-767M.

143 **The New York Times carried a front-page photograph of the occasion.** James M. Naughton, "President Urges Wider Indian Role in Aid for Tribes," *New York Times,* p. 1 (July 9, 1970).

143 **On September 9, 1970, . . . military-style force of seventy-five state and Tacoma officers** *See e.g.,* Alvin M. Josephy Jr., *Now That the Buffalo's Gone: A Study of Today's American Indians,* pp. 204–205 (New York: Alfred A. Knopf, 1982).

145 **Stan Pitkin . . . hit with tear gas.** Billy Frank Jr., "Treaty Rights Are Civil Rights: Being Frank," *Kitsap Daily News* (June 15, 2012), https://perma.cc /2AUT-YQKN.

145 **Stuart Pierson** "Biographical Sketch: Stuart F. Pierson, Esq.," *Historical Society of the District of Columbia Circuit* (July 16, 2014), https://perma.cc/JF6A-XJU3; *see also* Ziontz, *A Lawyer in Indian Country,* pp. 95–96.

145 **Dr. Barbara Lane** *See, e.g.,* Matthew L. M. Fletcher, "Barbara Lane Walks On" (January 21, 2014), *Turtle Talk* (blog), https://perma.cc/YKR2-9635.

146 **"Seattle Seven"** *See, e.g.,* Kit Bakke, "The Chaos, and Surprising Conclusion, of the 1970 Trial of the Seattle 7," *Seattle Times Pacific Northwest Magazine* (May 3, 2018), https://perma.cc/LAY9-HH2U.

146 **Judge Boldt . . . charged them with contempt of court.** *Id.*

146 **"will he be fair with us?"** *See, e.g.,* Rob Carson, "Boldt Decision Has Rippling Effects 40 Years Later," (Tacoma) *News Tribune* (February 15, 2014), https:// perma.cc/TN4U-PPJB.

146 **"I don't want to hear about any more of these damned Indian fishing cases."** Josephy, *Now That the Buffalo's Gone,* p. 206.

146 **Judge Boldt . . . called an early meeting with attorneys.** Alvin Ziontz, interview with author, Bellevue, Washington, March 22, 2014.

146 **[Judge Boldt] had . . . been a coauthor for a manual on complex federal litigation.** Thomas J. Clary, George H. Boldt, and Joe Ewing Estes, eds., *Manual for Complex and Multidistrict Litigation* (Washington, DC: Federal Judicial Center, 1969).

147 **George Dysart . . . agreed . . . that the tribal fishers . . . should have the right to sell fish.** Ziontz, *A Lawyer in Indian Country,* p. 98.

147 **Federal Pay Board** Philip Shabecoff, "White House Appoints 22 to Pay and Price Boards," *New York Times*, pp. 1, 15 (October 23, 1971).

148 **Judge Boldt called for a meeting of all attorneys.** Heffernan, *Where the Salmon Run*, p. 131.

148 **There was an omen** Stuart Pierson, "Stu Pierson at Boldt 40," 19:36 video (February 5, 2014), *in* Northwest Indian Fisheries Commission and Salmon Defense, "Boldt 40: A Day of Perspectives on the Boldt Decision, February 5, 2014," *Tribal Voices Archive Project*, https://perma.cc/DN6T-CWEP; Heffernan, *Where the Salmon Run*, p. 131.

148 **Two anthropologists bluntly declined to take on the task.** See comments of Dr. Frank Taylor and Dr. Angelo Anastasio *in* Angelo Anastasio letter to Joseph Coniff, May 6, 1970, Box 2032, Accession No. 04A246, Washington Department of Fish and Wildlife, Attorney General, Working Files, *United States v. Washington* Testimony and Anthropology Reports, Washington State Archives, Olympia; Joseph Coniff letter to Al Lasater, May 6, 1970, Box 2032, Accession No. 04A246, Washington Department of Fish and Wildlife, Attorney General, Working Files, *United States v. Washington* Testimony and Anthropology Reports, Washington State Archives, Olympia.

148 **"[M]ost anthropologists are reluctant to work without tribal approval"** *See* Coniff letter to Lasater, *id.*

149 **Supreme Court decisions by Chief Justice John Marshall** *See Cherokee Nation v. Georgia*, 30 U.S. 1 (1831); *Worcester v. Georgia*, 31 U.S. 515 (1832).

149 **Other older cases . . . that stood for strong tribal sovereignty.** *United States v. Winans*, 198 U.S. 371 (1905). *See, e.g.,* Charles F. Wilkinson, *American Indians, Time, and the Law: Native Societies in a Modern Constitutional Democracy* (New Haven, CT: Yale University Press, 1987).

149 **Launched by Brown v. Board of Education in 1954** *See Brown v. Board of Education*, 347 U.S. 483 (1954).

150 **Nixon sent a transformative joint message on Indian Affairs to Congress.** Nixon, "Special Message on Indian Affairs."

150 **McClanahan v. Arizona** *McClanahan v. Arizona State Tax Commission*, 411 U.S. 164 (1973).

150 **"the policy of leaving Indians free from state jurisdiction"** *Id.* at p. 169.

150 **"tradition of Indian independence."** *Id.* at p. 174.

150 **Mattz v. Arnett** *See Mattz v. Arnett*, 412 U.S. 481 (1973).

151 **The earliest . . . arrivals . . . wanted the Yurok tribal homeland.** *See, e.g.,* Chag Lowry et al., *Northwest Indigenous Gold Rush History* (Arcata, CA: Humboldt State University, 1999); The Yurok Tribe, "Gold Rush in Yurok Country" (accessed February 14, 2022), https://perma.cc/RP9Y-V46K. In response, the United States established a Yurok Reservation but pressure to open Yurok land

for non-Indian settlement and development continued. *See Mattz v. Arnett*, 412 U.S. at 485–495.

152 **"clear indication of Congressional purpose to terminate"** *Id.* at p. 498.

9 The Trial

154 **Court House Square Building** In 1992, long after the Boldt Decision, facilities of the Tacoma Division of the Western District of Washington Federal District Court were moved to another historic building, Tacoma Union Station at 1713 Pacific Avenue. The Court House Square Building continues to house federal Post Office and Customs operations and has been renovated to allow a number of high-end (and high-ceilinged) facilities. I was fortunate to visit the Court House Square Building just before the Boldt Decision's courtroom space was renovated. The room remained almost exactly as it was during the 1973 trial. I was allowed to go into the room on May 9, 2014, for a couple of hours and just take in the architecture and imagine the atmosphere. I thank Alan Stay, an attorney for the Muckleshoot Tribe, who did not participate in the 1973 trial but did represent the tribe in several hearings in post-judgment issues involving the Boldt Decision. Alan arranged for my visit to the courtroom and made many valuable observations about the courtroom and the way Judge Boldt presided.

155 **"Every witness has a right to explain"** During the month-long trial, Judge Boldt's court received 350 exhibits, and counsel from all parties appeared and presented fifty witnesses, whose testimony was reported in 4,600 pages of trial transcript. Transcript of Proceedings, *United States v. Washington*, 384 F. Supp. 310, 312 (W.D. Wash. 1974). [hereinafter Transcript of Proceedings].

155 **"reasonable and necessary"** *Department of Game of Washington v. Puyallup Tribe*, 414 U.S. 44, 45 (1973).

156 **Pierson recommended . . . Belloni's "fair share" allocation** *See Sohappy v. Smith*, 302 F. Supp. 899 (D. Or. 1969). Regarding state regulation to reevaluate tribal fishing only when it "threatens the preservation of the runs," *see* Transcript of Proceedings, p. 8.

156 **The tribes held a "deeply-felt duty . . . to preserve the resources for future generations"** Transcript of Proceedings, pp. 8–9.

156 **Getches . . . like Pierson, asserted that tribal rights included commercial, as well as subsistence, uses.** *See id.* at pp. 4–18 (Pierson) and 18–30 (Getches).

156 **"Not far from where this courthouse now stands"** *See id.* at pp. 18–19, 22, 29.

156 **"The rule of law we submit"** *Id.* at pp. 32–42.

157 **"if there is such evidence of such an exclusive right"** *Id.* at p. 64.

157 **McGimpsey agreed . . . that tribal rights covered only fish harvested for subsistence, not commercial uses.** *Id.* at pp. 73–87.

157   McGimpsey . . . did agree to a tribal "fair share," . . . that would mostly be determined by the state. *Id.* at pp. 82–87.

157   Attorneys and Judge Boldt all saw the case as resting upon two time frames. *See, e.g., id.* at pp. 73, 76.

158   "At the first pretrial conference with counsel in this litigation back in 1970, I expressed the hope." *Id.* at pp. 98–100.

158   **Dr. Barbara Lane** Barbara Savadkin Lane (1927–) and Robert B. Lane Papers, accession 1976-12 d4336, Evergreen State College Archives, p. 4 (accessed February 11, 2014), https://archives.evergreen.edu/1976/1976-12/dedanaan_l/d4336home.htm; Barbara Savadkin Lane, "A Comparative and Analytic Study of Some Aspects of Northwest Coast Religions," PhD diss., University of Washington (1953), https://digital.lib.washington.edu/researchworks/handle/1773/23903; Matthew L. M. Fletcher, "Barbara Lane Walks On" (January 21, 2014), *Turtle Talk* (blog), https://perma.cc/YKR2-9635.

159   **"The piece to understand"** Melia Lane-Kamahele, adopted Native Hawaiian daughter of Dr. Barbara Lane and Dr. Robert Lane, phone interview with Cynthia Carter, faculty assistant, October 16, 2019.

160   **"I had a very close relationship with the Lanes"** Neil Vallance, phone interview with Cynthia Carter, faculty assistant, August 14, 2019.

160   **"The Lanes' home had an incredible library."** *Id.*

160   **For evidence at trial, Dr. Lane produced original research.** The summary report is Barbara Lane, "Practical and Economic Aspects of Indian-White Culture Contact in Western Washington in the Mid-19th Century," *United States v. Washington,* Plaintiffs Exhibit USA-20, US District Court Tacoma, No. 9213 [hereinafter Lane, summary report]. The individual tribal reports are Plaintiffs Exhibits USA-20 to -30, including "The Identity, Treaty Status, and Fisheries of the Quinault Tribe of Indians" (1973). Dr. Lane's written direct testimony is Plaintiffs Exhibit USA-52.

161   **This body of work by Dr. Lane . . . is considered today to be a leading source.** Opinion in *United States v. Washington,* 384 F. Supp. 312, 350 (W.D. Washington, 1974).

161   **The treaties . . . would be the supreme law of the land.** U.S. Const. art. VI, cl. 2.

161   **Treaties are bilateral agreements** UN High Commissioner for Refugees, "Bilateral Treaties/Agreements," *Refworld* (accessed April 13, 2022), https://perma.cc/6XSA-253E.

161   **Ambiguous treaty language must be liberally construed in favor of the tribes.** *Choctaw Nation of Indians v. United States,* 318 U.S. 423, 431–32 (1943).

162   **Salmon was "the main food source, both in bulk and importance."** Transcript of Proceedings, p. 167.

162   "The first-salmon ceremony" Transcript of Proceedings, summary report, pp. 7–8.

162   Commercial trade . . . "very important, extensive" Transcript of Proceedings, p. 1778.

162   "in order to acquire food stuffs" Transcript of Proceedings, summary report, pp. 2–3.

162   "from the interior tribes across the mountains" Transcript of Proceedings, p. 1779.

163   "Chinook jargon" Transcript of Proceedings, summary report, pp. 28–29.

163   "in common with" was meant United States v. Washington, Exhibit Nos. USA-20 to -30 and -53, Civ. No. 9213.

163   "The defendants contend" Transcript of Proceedings, pp. 1678–1680.

163   "Yes, there were certainly other social controls." Id.

164   "rapid cultural decline" Transcript of Proceedings, pp. 1833–1834.

164   "I don't believe that the culture was rapidly declining." Transcript of Proceedings, p. 1833.

165   "For many Indians, fish continue to provide a vital component in their diet." Lane, summary report, p. 40.

165   "You don't feel that you yourself have any problem . . . ?" Transcript of Proceedings, pp. 1795–1796.

165   On cross-examination, the state attorneys made little or no headway. See, e.g., Alvin J. Ziontz, A Lawyer in Indian Country: A Memoir, pp. 106–107 (Seattle: University of Washington Press, 2009).

166   Dr. Carroll Riley Obituary, "Carroll Riley," Albuquerque Journal (April 11, 2017), https://perma.cc/2BCH-GTQ9.

166   "Since I have not worked with the Indian population since the 1950s" Transcript of Proceedings, pp. 2454–2455.

166   Dr. Riley . . . was notably resistant and defensive during much of the cross-examination. Id. at pp. 2273–2287.

166   "I don't know why you hesitate to answer simple questions" Id. at pp. 2277–2278.

166   Judge Boldt was moved, and often rapt See, e.g., John Hughes, chief historian, Office of Secretary of State, Legacy Washington, email to author (January 10, 2023).

167   "[T]he first agents was really mean to our Indian people." Testimony of Lena Hillaire, Transcript of Proceedings, pp. 2867–2868.

168   "I don't think that this is the prime interest." Transcript of Proceedings, pp. 3041–3042.

169   "Now, what differences do you see in the younger generation?" Id. at pp. 2599.

170 "Well, once when my grandfather was picked up for fishing and put in jail"
     Id. at p. 2696.

170 "for the simple reason your treaty says that we can fish" *Id.* at pp. 2519–2522,
     2559.

170 "And is it my understanding . . . ?" *Id.* at p. 2647.

171 Tribes had always been acknowledged as sovereign governments . . . exer-
     cising jurisdiction . . . over non-Indians. *See, e.g., Williams v. Lee*, 358 U.S.
     217 (1959); *Santa Clara Pueblo v. Martinez*, 436 U.S. 49, 65 (1978): "Tribal
     courts have repeatedly been recognized as appropriate forums for the exclusive
     adjudication of disputes affecting important personal and property interests
     of both Indians and non-Indians." *See also* Felix Cohen et. al., *Cohen's Handbook
     of Federal Indian Law*, 2012 ed., § 4.02 (New Providence, NJ: LexisNexis,
     2012).

172 Family members "had their supply of fish, then traps were lifted" Transcript
     of Proceedings, p. 3440.

172 In 1925, the Quinault Business Committee had adopted written regulations.
     Id. at pp. 3439–3442.

172 On two occasions, the committee had to close Lake Quinault to fishing. *Id.*
     at pp. 3441–3442.

172 The Business Committee also banned two harvesting methods—drift nets
     and monofilament nets. *Id.* at pp. 3445–3446 (monofilament nets) and 3451–
     3452 (drift nets).

173 Violations of the regulations *Id.* at pp. 3442.

173 Regulate their own members *Id.* at pp. 3442, 3471.

173 Joe DeLaCruz *See, e.g.,* Ross Anderson, "Indian Quinault Leader Joe DeLa-
     Cruz Dies," *Seattle Times* (April 18, 2000), https://perma.cc/AH93-VPZ3.

173 Guy McMinds *See, e.g.,* Javier Panzar, "Obituary: Quinault Leader Guy Mc-
     Minds Revered Lands, Waters," *Seattle Times* (July 14, 2012), https://perma
     .cc/3W75-HQFJ.

174 In the late 1960s, . . . Jackson, . . . DeLaCruz, and . . . McMinds . . . began
     work on . . . comprehensive management system *See* McMinds direct testi-
     mony, *United States v. Washington*, Plaintiffs Exhibit QN-2, U.S. District Court,
     Tacoma, No. 9213, pp. 2–3 .

174 Tribal fisheries staff *See* McMinds direct testimony, pp. 8–9; Transcript of Pro-
     ceedings, p. 3527.

174 Annual fisheries budget McMinds direct testimony, p. 2.

174 Full-time patrolmen and . . . judges Transcript of Proceedings, pp. 3488–3489.

174 The 1887 General Allotment Act opened the Quinault reservation to . . . tim-
     ber . . . allotments. *See, e.g.,* Pauline K. Capoeman, ed., *Land of the Quinault*, 2d
     ed. (Taholah, WA: Quinault Indian Nation, 1991); Gary Morishima and Larry

Workman, *Portrait of Our Land: A Quinault Tribal Forestry Perspective* (Tahola, WA: Quinault Indian Nation, Department of Natural Resources, 1978); Hal Neumann et al., *The Forests of the Quinault: Forest Management on the Quinault Indian Reservation, 1855–1996* (Missoula, MT: Heritage Research Center, 1997); Frank C. Fickeisen, *The Quinaults, Their Land, Their Waters* (Portland, OR: American Friends Service Committee, 1971). On the General Allotment Act, see Charles Wilkinson, *Blood Struggle: The Rise of Modern Indian Nations*, pp. 15–16, 43, 45, 50 (New York: W. W. Norton, 2005).

176 **"When I came back after forestry school"** David Martin, interview with author, Quinault Indian Reservation, Taholah, Washington, December 18, 2001.

176 **The tribes went to the BIA and to court . . . sought relief from Congress.** DeLaCruz, Transcript of Proceedings, pp. 3519–3521.

176 **Brian Allee** See, e.g., direct testimony of Allee, *United States v. Washington*, Plaintiffs Exhibit QN-3, U.S. District Court, Tacoma, No. 9213, pp. 1–6; Transcript of Proceedings, pp. 3528–3534.

177 **"the Quinault River . . . was confined to one channel"** Transcript of Proceedings, p. 3535.

177 **"This sort of picture illustrates the instability of the Upper Quinault"** *Id.* at pp. 3535–3536.

177 **"Well, I think it's very possible for the Quinaults to manage their resource"** *Id.* at pp. 3554–3555.

177 **"Thank you very much, Mr. Allee."** *Id.* at p. 3555.

178 **A decision from the US Supreme Court** *Department of Game of Washington v. Puyallup Tribe (Puyallup II)*, 414 U.S. 44 (1973).

178 **Justice William O. Douglas wrote a short, shallow, and confusing opinion** *Puyallup Tribe v. Department of Game of Washington (Puyallup I)*, 391 U.S. 392 (1968).

179 **Professor Ralph Johnson . . . wrote a scathing law review article.** Ralph W. Johnson, "The States Versus Indian Off-Reservation Fishing: A United States Supreme Court Error?" vol. 47 *Washington Law Review*, p. 28 (1972).

179 **"No valid basis for existence of such state power can be found."** *Id.* Professor Johnson styled his article as a "Supreme Court error," not because the Court in *Puyallup I* in 1968 had actually approved the "reasonable and necessary" test. Rather, he criticized Justice William O. Douglas in *Puyallup I* for not striking down the test, originally put forth by the Game Department. Of course, Douglas's later *Puyallup II* opinion, probably informed by Professor Johnson's article, made it clear that the "reasonable and necessary" test was not the law.

179 **The US Supreme Court vacated** *Department of Game of Washington v. Puyallup Tribe (Puyallup II)*, 414 U.S. 44, 48 (1973): "discrimination because all Indian net fishing is barred."

179 **The state's right to regulate treaty fishing for "conservation" is very narrow.**
Id. at p. 49. *See, e.g.,* "We do not imply that these fishing rights persist down
to the very last steelhead in the river. Rights can be controlled by the need to
conserve a species; and the time may come when the life of a steelhead is so
precarious in a particular stream that all fishing should be banned until the species regains assurance of survival. The police power of the State is adequate to
prevent the steelhead from following the fate of the passenger pigeon; and the
Treaty does not give the Indians a federal right to pursue the last living steelhead until it enters their nets."

181 **"I hope that out of all this effort"** Transcript of Proceedings, pp. 4240–4241.

10   The Boldt Decision

183 **"the most stringent protection of free speech"** *See Schenck v. United States,*
249 U.S. 47, 52 (1919).

183 **"I know it when I see it."** *See Jacobellis v. Ohio,* 378 U.S. 184, 197 (1964).

183 **"Great nations, like great men"** *See Federal Power Commission v. Tuscarora Indian Nation,* 362 U.S. 99, 142 (1960), dissenting opinion.

184 **Salmon "were not much less necessary to ... Indians than the atmosphere
they breathed."** *United States v. Winans,* 198 U.S. 371, 381 (1905).

184 **"For more than three years"** *United States v. Washington,* 384 F. Supp. 312,
328–330 (W.D. Wash. 1974).

186 **"The anthropological reports and testimony of both Dr. Barbara Lane and
Dr. Carroll Riley"** *Id.* at p. 350.

187 **Dr. Lane's report on traditional life among the treaty tribes** Plaintiff
Exhibit USA-20–30, 53, *United States v. Washington,* 384 F. Supp. 312 (W.D.
Wash. 1974).

187 **"[One] common cultural characteristic"** *United States v. Washington,* 384 F.
Supp. at 350–351.

187 **"At the time of the treaties, trade was carried on"** *Id.* at p. 351.

188 **"Those involved in negotiating the treaties"** *Id.* at pp. 351–352.

188 **He offered ... informational histories and present status of each plaintiff
tribe.** *Id.* at pp. 348–382.

188 **He looked primarily to Dr. Lane's thick package** Plaintiff Exhibits USA-21–
26, 27A, 27B, 28–30, *United States v. Washington,* 384 F. Supp. 312 (W.D. Wash.
1974).

190 **"Doesn't a father give his children a home"** Gibbs, "Record of the Proceedings," pp. 1–2.

190 **Dr. Lane concluded that the "in common with" language meant** Plaintiff Exhibit USA-20, *United States v. Washington,* 384 F. Supp. 312 (W.D. Wash. 1974).

190 "There is no indication that the Indians" *United States v. Washington*, 384 F. Supp. at 343.

191 **Tribal treaty rights included commercial harvesting.** *Id.*

191 **The tribes were entitled to 100 percent of the fish taken on the reservations.** *Id.*

191 **State legal control over wildlife ... is one of the police powers.** *See, e.g.,* chapter 8, The Buildup to the Boldt Decision, pp. 141–181 in this book: Worcester held that "Indian tribes are independent sovereign governments protected from most state laws"; Wex Definitions Team, "Police Powers" (December 2020), *Legal Information Institute*, Cornell Law School, https://perma.cc/X43C-Q58N; David Favre, "American Wildlife Law—An Introduction" (2003), *Animal Law Web Center*, Animal Legal and Historical Center, Michigan State University, https://perma.cc/T743-WP6B.

192 **The states ... argued ... state police power allows substantial actions against tribes.** *See, e.g., Puyallup Tribe v. Department of Game of Washington*, 391 U.S. 392 (1968), also known as *Puyallup I; Department of Game of Washington v. Puyallup Tribe*, 414 U.S. 44 (1973), also known as *Puyallup II.*

192 **A federal treaty right would run directly contrary to congressional power.** *See* Wex Definitions Team, "Police Powers"; Favre, "American Wildlife Law."

193 **Tribal attorneys "have submitted well researched briefs"** *United States v. Washington*, 384 F. Supp. at 334.

193 **"Conservation" [of the resource] ... defined specifically as "perpetuation of the fisheries species."** *Id.* at p. 333.

193 **All state officers "must understand"** *Id.* at p. 342.

193 **"This [state police] power does not include"** *Id.* at p. 402.

195 **"Ever since the first Indian treaties"** *Id.* at p. 339.

195 **During the century after the treaties, Congress did limit tribal authority.** *Id.* On Congressional policy during this period, see chapter 6, The Long Suppression, pp. 101–116 in this book.

195 **In [recent years] ... legislation "definitely has been in the contrary direction."** *United States v. Washington*, 384 F. Supp. at 340.

195 **"These measures and others make plain"** *Id.*

196 **The required qualifications and conditions included** *Id.* at pp. 340–342.

196 **Quinault and Yakama Tribes met the standards** *Id.* at pp. 341–342.

196 **"the evidence indicates several other plaintiff tribes have capacity"** *Id.* at p. 342.

198 **"Joint Biological Statement"** *Id.* at pp. 328–329.

198 **"General Fisheries Conservation and Management"** *Id.* at pp. 382–389. He also included sections of Department of Game fisheries policies, *id.* at pp. 389–393, and Department of Game policies, *id.* at pp. 393–399.

198 **"fisheries management is a social science"** *See* Richard Whitney, transcription of "Lecture on Work with Judge Boldt" (May 23, 2013), p. 1, University of Washington, https://archive.org/details/DickWhitneyAtTheUW.

199 **"for the life of this decree."** *United States v. Washington*, 384 F. Supp. at 408.

199 **Continuing jurisdiction is ordered only rarely** On continuing jurisdiction, *see, e.g.,* Ron J. Whitener, "The Personal Impact of the Boldt Case: A Tribute to Professor William H. Rodgers Jr.," vol. 82 *Washington Law Review*, p. 497 (2007): "The intervening tribes and the State of Washington use the continuing jurisdiction of the case as a forum to settle disputes. . . ."

200 **Judge Boldt . . . naming Professor Richard Whitney . . . technical advisor on the same day he issued his opinion.** *United States v. Washington*, 384 F. Supp. at 413.

200 **They could file . . . a "request for determination."** *Id.* at p. 419.

200 **"The biologists of defendants and . . . the tribes"** *Id.* at p. 420.

200 **Judge Boldt . . . directed the state . . . to locate seized gear and return it to the tribal fishers.** *Id.* at pp. 418–419.

201 **"In the 1960s there was a general belief"** John Echohawk, Pawnee tribal member and executive director of the Native American Rights Fund, telephone interview with the author, October 14, 2022.

201 **including the *New York Times*** *See* "Indians on Coast," *New York Times*, p. 14 (February 13, 1974).

11   Rebellion

202 **Ninth Circuit Court of Appeals** *See United States v. Washington*, 520 F.2d 676 (9th Cir. 1975).

202 **"I deplore situations that make it necessary"** *Id.* at p. 693.

202 **"The record in this case, and the history set forth"** *Id.*

203 **The Supreme Court denied the writ of certiorari.** See generally U.S. Const., art. VI, cl. 2; Caleb Nelson and Kermit Roosevelt, "Common Interpretation: The Supremacy Clause," *Interactive Constitution*, National Constitution Center (accessed May 23, 2022), https://perma.cc/C36M-86MW: "The core message of the Supremacy Clause is simple: the Constitution and federal laws [of the types listed in the first part of the Clause] take priority over any conflicting rules of state law."

203 **"I had no idea an objective adult"** Brad O'Connor, "Rights, Yes, but What "Fair Share?" *Seattle Times*, p. F6 (February 14, 1974), quoting Chuck Voss, western regional director, Northwestern Steelheaders Council of Trout Unlimited.

204 **"I was stunned."** *Id.,* quoting Gary Ellis, state president of Northwest Steelheaders Council of Trout Unlimited.

204 **"I was flabbergasted."** *Id.*, quoting Phil Tucker, chairman of the Steelhead Committee of the State Sportsmen's Council.

204 **"there should be a blanket ban on off-reservation Indian net fishing for steelhead"** "Indians Win Fishing Decision," (Chehalis-Centralia) *Daily Chronicle*, p. 3 (February 12, 1974), quoting J. Lawrence Coniff Jr., assistant attorney general for the Washington Department of Game.

205 **"If the Boldt Decision is allowed to stand"** Brad O'Connor, "Smelt Running Thick in Cowlitz, Lewis," *Seattle Times*, p. B3 (February 19, 1974), quoting Carl Crouse, director, Washington Department of Game.

206 **Objectors [to the Boldt Decision] adopted the language of the civil rights movement.** A leading source on this development with respect to the Boldt Decision is Jeffrey R. Dudas, "In the Name of Equal Rights: 'Special' Rights and the Politics of Resentment in Post-Civil Rights America," vol. 39, no. 4 *Law and Society Review*, pp. 736–748 (December 2005).

206 **These [tribal treaty] rights are governmental, not racial or individual rights.** *See, e.g., Morton v. Mancari*, 417 U.S. 535, 553 n.24 (1974), a case affirming the constitutionality, under the Fifth Amendment, of preferences given to Indians in which the Supreme Court held the Indian preference is reasonably and rationally designed to further Indian self-government: "The preference is not directed towards a 'racial' group consisting of 'Indians'; instead, it applies only to members of 'federally recognized' tribes. This operates to exclude many individuals who are racially to be classified as 'Indians.' In this sense, the preference is political rather than racial in nature." See generally Sarah Krakoff, "They Were Here First: American Indian Tribes, Race, and the Constitutional Minimum," vol. 69 *Stanford Law Review*, p. 491 (February 2017); Felix Cohen et al., *Handbook of Federal Indian Law*, 2012 ed. (New Providence, NJ: LexisNexis, 2012).

206 **[Governor Daniel Evans] strongly disapproved of the "many mass protests that got out of hand."** *See* Daniel J. Evans and John Charles Hughes, *Daniel J. Evans: An Autobiography*, John Charles Hughes, ed., p. 245 (Olympia: Washington State Legacy Project, Office of Secretary of State, 2021).

207 **Governor Evans** Daniel J. Evans, an Eagle Scout with a pioneering spirit for public service, first earned engineering degrees from the University of Washington and was then elected to the legislature in 1956. He is best known for his service as governor, serving an unprecedented three terms (1965–1977), and recognized as "One of the Ten Outstanding Governors in the Twentieth Century" (according to a University of Michigan study, 1981). *See, e.g.,* Washington Secretary of State, "Daniel J: Evans An Autobiography," *Legacy Washington*, Stories (accessed May 23, 2022), https://perma.cc/G3Z7-ZUBS; Richard G. Weingardt, "Daniel Jackson Evans," vol. 7, no. 4 *Leadership and Management in Engineering* (October 2007), https://perma.cc/B5TK-LC8X.

207   Governor Evans announced that Washington also was bound by [the Bel-
       loni Decision]. *See, e.g.,* Alvin J. Ziontz, *A Lawyer in Indian Country: A Memoir,*
       p. 94 (Seattle: University of Washington Press, 2009).

207   Evans was "one of the greatest leaders" Bill Wilkerson, former director of
       Washington Department of Fisheries, interview with author, Bremerton,
       Washington, June 23, 2015.

207   Evans . . . stated, "I discovered how intensely all fishermen" *See* Evans and
       Hughes, *Daniel J. Evans,* p. 246.

208   "Washington state legal officials refused to enforce Boldt's order." *See* Lou
       Cannon, "Salmon Is the Loser in Long Fisher War," *Washington Post* (Septem-
       ber 5, 1979), https://perma.cc/TQJ9-735P.

208   [Jim] Johnson called the Boldt Decision "morally reprehensible" and pre-
       dicted that . . . [the Boldt Decision] "shall be overturned." Fay G. Cohen,
       *Treaties on Trial: The Continuing Controversy over Northwest Indian Fishing
       Rights,* p. 91 (Seattle: University of Washington Press, 1986); *see also,* e.g.,Trova
       Heffernan, *Where the Salmon Run: The Life and Legacy of Bill Frank Jr.,* pp.
       152–153 (Seattle: University of Washington Press, 2017).

208   "Buoyed by this attitude, it is little wonder" Cohen, *Treaties on Trial,* p. 91.

208   "Despite 'an extensive commitment of both man-hours and equipment'"
       Bob Lane, "Tanner Criticizes Fish Enforcement; Boldt Warns of Resource
       Damage," (Tacoma) *News Tribune,* p. A1 (November 9, 1978).

208   "There has been so much illegal fishing" Robert H. Mottram, "Illegal Gillnet
       Fishing Rife on Sound," (Tacoma) *News Tribune,* p. A1 (October 6, 1976).

209   "It was like a city out there." Mike Grayum, former executive director of
       Northwest Indian Fisheries Commission, Zoom interview with author, Febru-
       ary 2, 2022.

209   "David C. Pratt, [Fisheries Department] biologist, produced a document"
       Robert H. Mottram, "Court Told non-Indians Topped Fish Limit," (Tacoma)
       News Tribune, p. A1 (April 7, 1978).

209   As for 1976, state biologists "estimate that more than $1 million worth of
       fish" Robert H. Mottram, "Moos: Illegal Netting May Ravage Steelhead," (Ta-
       coma) *News Tribune,* p. A4 (December 3, 1976).

209   Boldt opponents took out their anger on individual Indians. *See, e.g.,* "Indian
       Rights Mess," *The Oregonian* (November 7, 1976); Bureau of Indian Affairs,
       Department of the Interior, "Indians Treated Disgracefully," vol. 6, no. 46 *In-
       dian News Clips* (November 13, 1976); "The Fishing War: FBI Steps In," *Seattle
       Post-Intelligencer,* p. A1 (October 22, 1976); Daniel L. Boxberger, *To Fish in Com-
       mon: The Ethnohistory of Lummi Indian Salmon Fishing,* p. 155 (Seattle: Univer-
       sity of Washington Press, 2000): "The blame, of course, was laid on the Indians,
       and shortly several violent altercations ensued, with Lummi fishers shot at by

snipers on at least three occasions. In one case the target was a fourteen-year-old-boy."

209 "Initiated by a few hotheaded gillnetters, multiple assaults against officers occurred" Heffernan, *Where the Salmon Run*, p. 151.

210 "Later when we started fighting about the Boldt Decision" E. O. Connell, "Georgiana and Nugie Kautz, Nisqually Indian Tribe, on the History of the Treaty Rights Struggle," 21:58 video (December 4, 2010), *Tribal Voices Archive Project*, Northwest Indian Fisheries Commission and Salmon Defense, https://perma.cc/D9Y6-NXNG.

210 "I remember some of those fishermen yelling at us on the docks." Cathy Ballew, member of the Lummi Nation, interviewed by Althea Wilson for "Revitalizing Cultural Knowledge and Honoring Sacred Waters: An Oral History of Life on the Nooksack River," 50:44 video (June 22, 2018, a capstone project for Northwest Indian College), *Tribal Voices Archive Project*, Northwest Indian Fisheries Commission and Salmon Defense, https://archive.org/details/CathyBallewTVAP.

212 **Professor Richard Whitney was well known to both sides.** Richard Whitney, interview with author, Leavenworth, Washington, March 24, 2014; Richard Whitney, letter to Guy McMinds (February 11, 2011), copy on file with author; transcription of Richard Whitney's "Lecture on Work with Judge Boldt" (May 23, 2013), University of Washington, https://archive.org/details/DickWhitneyAtTheUW; Richard Whitney, letter to author (February 19, 2015); Northwest Treaty Tribes, "Dick Whitney at Boldt 40," 7.55 video (February 5, 2014), *Tribal Voices Archive Project*, Northwest Indian Fisheries Commission and Salmon Defense, https://vimeo.com/87499474.

212 "I already had the perfect job." *See, e.g.,* Whitney, transcription of "Lecture," p. 4.

212 **Whitney asked [Judge Boldt] when they should meet. "How can you say 'no' to a federal judge?"** Whitney, interview, March 24, 2014.

213 **In November 1974, he issued an order.** *See United States v. Washington*, 459 F. Supp. 1020, 1038 (W.D. Wash. 1978; compilation of major Boldt Decision post-trial Substantive Orders).

213 **In October 1975, Judge Boldt . . . [established] the Fisheries Advisory Board.** *Id.* at p. 1061.

214 **Emergencies that would "threaten serious harm to the resource."** *Id.*

214 **"I could make a recommendation to the court."** Whitney, transcription of "Lecture," p. 12.

214 **72 percent of [FAB] disputes were settled.** Cohen, *Treaties on Trial*, p. 95 (estimates by George Dysart, Department of Interior Solicitor during the FAB process).

215   **For decades, Washington state courts had been handing down decisions
... that belittled tribal rights.** *See* chapter 7, The Tribes Come Forward, pp.
117–139.

215   **In June 1977, the Washington Supreme Court ruled** *See Puget Sound Gillnetters Association v. Moos*, 565 P.2d 1151 (Wash. 1977).

215   **Justice Hugh Rosellini, whose unwavering contempt for Indian rights** *See,
e.g., Puget Sound Gillnetters Association v. Moos*, 565 P.2d at 1159: "that every
fisherman in a class must be treated equally, and that each should be given an
equal opportunity to fish within lawful statutes and regulations"; *Washington
State Commercial Passenger Fishing Vessel Association v. Tollefson*, 571 P.2d 1373,
1378 (Wash. 1977): "that the granting of more than 50 percent of the harvestable
fish to 0.28 percent of the population (treaty Indians) and less than 50 percent
to 2,243,069 non-Indian population, violates the equal protection clause of the
fourteenth amendment to the United States Constitution."

215   **Senator Warren Magnuson and President Jimmy Carter both expressed discomfort.** Bill Wilkerson, interview with author, June 23, 2015.

215   **Judge Boldt ... took charge with an order ... [o]n August 31, 1977, [that]
took over direct control of the fisheries.** *United States v. Washington*, 459 F.
Supp. 1020, 1104 (W.D. Wash. 1978).

215   **Federal departments ... established a pool of interagency federal enforcement officers.** *See* Cohen, *Treaties on Trial*, p. 100.

216   **The earliest announcement of this national phenomenon** See generally
C. Herb Williams and Walt Neubrech, *Indian Treaties, American Nightmare: The
First Comprehensive Account of the Most Controversial Legal Battle of the Seventies*
(Seattle: Outdoor Empire Publishing, 1977).

216   **"This is dangerously close to a dictatorship"** *Id.* at p. 75. The quote is taken
from a chapter written by Joseph Coniff, who represented the Washington Department of Game for twenty-two years, including during the Boldt Decision.

216   **"It can't happen here"** *Id.* at p. 12.

216   **The authors listed seventeen states where tribal advances were being contested.** *Id.* at p. 13.

217   **ICERR had granted membership to fourteen organizations with similar interests in the state of Washington alone.** *See* C. Montgomery Johnson Associates, *First Our Land and Now Our Treaties*, p. 3 (Hadlock, WA: C. Montgomery
Johnson Associates, 1977).

217   **"When he was chairman of the Indian affairs subcommittee ... Rep. Lloyd
Meeds"** *See* Bill Richards, "Hill Cools in Attitude on Indian Affairs," *Washington Post* (October 9, 1977), https://perma.cc/P7FW-E4EV. *See also, e.g.*, Bill
Curry, "Indians Seek to Guard Special Rights Against White Backlash," *Washington Post* (April 16, 1978), https://perma.cc/E54J-GDKZ.

217 **The most extreme proposal . . . came from Washington Congressman Jack Cunningham.** House Report No. 9054, "Native Americans Equal Opportunity Act," 95th Congress (Washington, DC: Library of Congress, 1977) [hereinafter "House Report No. 9054]; *see also, e.g.,* Robert N. Clinton, "Isolated in Their Own Country: A Defense of Federal Protection of Indian Autonomy and Self-Government," vol. 33, no. 6 *Stanford Law Review,* pp. 979, 980–982 (July 1981).

218 **Numerous other bills would have extinguished or weakened water . . . and land rights.** *See, e.g.,* Clinton, "Isolated in Their Own Country," p. 981.

218 **Pressure from the Washington congressional delegation** *See, e.g.,* Laurie Johnstonbaugh, "Indian Civil Rights Hearings: US Commission on Civil Rights Comes to Seattle, 1977," (2006), *Seattle Civil Rights and Labor History Project,* University of Washington, https://perma.cc/P2AS-3SSY; Cohen, *Treaties on Trial,* p. 101.

218 **President Carter announced the creation of the Federal Task Force on Washington State Fisheries.** United States Commission on Civil Rights, "Indian Tribes: A Continuing Quest for Survival. A Report of the United States Commission on Civil Rights," Bonnie Mathews, ed., pp. 75–91, 103–107 (Washington, DC: Government Printing Office, 1981), https://perma.cc/27VS-CM2U; see generally Cohen, *Treaties on Trial,* pp. 101–106.

219 **The . . . 490-page final plan . . . was a mishmash.** House Report No. 9054, p. 27.

219 **"Nobody liked the plan."** Cohen, *Treaties on Trial,* p. 104.

219 **Each tribe was "entitled to exercise . . . the treaty right fishing of its members without any state regulation"** *United States v. Washington,* 384 F. Supp. at 340.

220 **The conditions were demanding.** *Id.* at pp. 340–342.

220 **Federal money went out to the tribes to help support . . . fisheries programs.** *See, e.g.,* Cohen, *Treaties on Trial,* p. 86.

220 **The [Northwest Indian Fisheries Commission] was effective from the beginning.** *See, e.g.,* Jennifer Ott, "Northwest Indian Fisheries Commission" (March 28, 2011), *HistoryLink.org,* https://perma.cc/G628-NCN7; Northwest Indian Fisheries Commission, "About Us" (2016), https://perma.cc/JN9Q-A8PB: "The role of the NWIFC is to assist member tribes in their role as natural resources co-managers. The commission provides direct services to tribes in areas such as biometrics, fish health and salmon management to achieve an economy of scale that makes more efficient use of limited federal funding. The NWIFC also provides a forum for tribes to address shared natural resources management issues and enables the tribes to speak with a unified voice in Washington, D.C."

221   **Within just a few years, all Boldt Case area tribes were managing their own fisheries and members.** *See* chapter 13, Comanagement—Eliminating Overfishing and Preserving Salmon Habitat, of this book, pp. 234–247, discussing, among other things, the 1981 *Hoh Indian Tribe v. Baldridge* decision and the 1985 Port Ludlow Agreement.

221   **The Washington Supreme Court struck twice.** *Puget Sound Gillnetters Association v. Moos*, 565 P. 2d 1151 (Wash. 1977), discussed above at this chapter's notes 38 and 39; *Washington State Commercial Passenger Fishing Vessel Association v. Tollefson*, 571 P.2d 1373 (Wash. 1977).

221   **Both [Justice Hugh Rosellini's] opinions . . . were clumsily written and offered slender legal precedent.** For example, the Washington Supreme Court in the *Washington State Commercial Passenger Fishing Vessel Association* case found that awarding 50 percent of the salmon to a small minority amounted to racial discrimination and violated the Equal Protection Clause in the Fourteenth Amendment to the US Constitution. See the brief explanation, citing just two minor cases, at *Washington State Commercial Passenger Fishing Vessel Association v. Tollefson*, 571 P.2d at 1378. In the *Washington State Commercial Passenger Fishing Vessel Association* opinion, Associate Justice Utter wrote a substantial dissenting opinion concluding that the Rosellini opinion is "embarrassing to this Court" and "completely ignores the most basic principles of Indian law developed over the past 70 years by the United States Supreme Court." *Id.* at p. 1379.

221   **The state argued that the Supreme Court should . . . resolve the uncertainty.** United States Commission on Civil Rights, "Indian Tribes: A Continuing Quest for Survival," pp. 103–107.

222   **The United States threw its weight behind granting certiorari.** *Id.* at p. 105.

12   The Supreme Court Acts

223   **The pledge given in the treaties** *Washington v. Washington State Commercial Passenger Vessel Association*, Brief for the United States, pp. 45–46 (January 30, 1979).

224   **United States v. Baker** *See United States v. Baker*, 641 F.2d 1311 (9th Cir. 1981).

225   **According to Claiborne, a "mere" right of access . . . would be "meaningless."** *Washington v. Washington State Commercial Passenger Vessel Association*, Oral Argument (February 27, 1979), https://perma.cc/2FHT-RNNZ.

226   **Supreme Court papers . . . from six of the nine justices . . . present valuable insights** Ronald Collins, "Accessing the Papers of Supreme Court Justices: Online and Other Resources" (August 22, 2013), *Scotus Blog*, https://perma.cc/P7XQ-N66U.

226 **Neither side had made any breakthrough.** Lewis F. Powell, Conference Notes, March 2, 1979, Lewis Powell Papers, Supreme Court Case Files Collection, Box 494, Washington and Lee University School of Law, Virginia.

226 **Powell and Stevens had circulated "memos"** Memorandum to Lewis F. Powell from John Paul Stevens, June 14, 1979, Potter Stewart Papers, Box 349, Yale University Library, New Haven; Memorandum to John Paul Stevens from Lewis F. Powell Jr., June 18, 1979, Potter Stewart Papers, Box 349, Yale University Library, New Haven.

226 **Justice Stevens clarified that the . . . 50 percent share was a ceiling.** Memorandum to Lewis F. Powell from John Paul Stevens, June 18, 1979, Potter Stewart Papers, Box 349, Yale University Library, New Haven.

226 **Chief Justice Warren Burger . . . proposed that the case be moved into the next October term.** Memorandum to the Conference, Warren E. Burger, June 18, 1979, Potter Stewart Papers, Box 349, Yale University Library, New Haven.

226 **Justice Byron White had made the same proposal a few days earlier.** Memorandum to John Paul Stevens from Byron R. White, June 15, 1979, Byron R. White Papers, Box 435, Library of Congress, Washington, DC.

226 **"John Stevens has done a 'noble' job"** Memorandum to the Conference, Warren E. Burger, June 18, 1979, Potter Stewart Papers, Box 349, Yale University Library, New Haven.

227 **"I would like to weigh in with my comment about these cases."** Memorandum to the Conference, Harry A. Blackmun, June 22, 1979, Potter Stewart Papers, Box 349, Yale University Library, New Haven.

228 **On June 22, Chief Justice Burger reversed course . . . "I have decided to vote against reargument."** Memorandum to the Conference, Warren E. Burger, June 22, 1979, Byron R. White Papers, Box 435, Library of Congress, Washington, DC.

228 **Justice White did the same.** Memorandum to John Paul Stevens from Byron R. White, June 25, 1979, Byron R. White Papers, Box 435, Library of Congress, Washington, DC.

228 **The Supreme Court released its opinion.** *Washington v. Washington State Commercial Passenger Vessel Association*, 443 U.S. 658 (1979).

228 **The Supreme Court . . . quoted from [Judge Boldt's] opinion many times.** *See id.* at pp. 663 n. 3, 664 n. 4 and n. 5, 665 n. 6 and n. 7, 667 n. 10, 668 n. 12 and n. 13, 670 n. 15.

228 **The tribes all "shared a vital and unifying dependence on anadromous fish"** *Id.* at pp. 664–665.

228 **The right to take salmon was "not much less necessary to the existence of the Indians than the atmosphere they breathed."** *Id.* at p. 680, quoting from *United States v. Winans*, 198 U.S. 371 (1905).

229 "Are you not my children . . . ?" *Id.* at p. 667 n. 11.

230 Tribal negotiators did not comprehend the meaning of English treaty words. *Id.* at p. 667 n. 10.

230 The tribes "would forever be able to continue the same off-reservation food gathering and fishing practices" *Id.* at pp. 667–668. The quote came from the Boldt Decision, which in turn adopted words from the Yakama treaty negotiations. *See United States v. Washington*, 384 F. Supp. at 381.

230 The Supreme Court also pointed to a number of other federal cases . . . showing that an equal share would be a fair representation *See Washington v. Washington State Commercial Passenger Vessel Association*, 443 U.S. at 686–687.

230 The 50 percent share is a ceiling, not a floor. *Id.* at p. 686.

230 If a tribe were to "dwindle to just a few members" *Id.* at p. 687.

230 Neither the "moderate standard of living" nor the "dwindling to just a few members" has ever been acted upon by any court. Basically, Washington administrative agencies and non-Indian fishing groups explored trying to use these provisions, but it became clear that tribal fishing rights have not accounted for more than a moderate standard of living. As for "dwindling" tribes, most tribes see their membership numbers rising, not diminishing.

230 The Supreme Court reduced the number of tribal fish in two ways. *Washington v. Washington State Commercial Passenger Vessel Association*, 443 U.S. at 686–690.

231 "When Fisheries was ordered by the state courts" *Id.* at pp. 673–674.

232 State Attorney General Slade Gorton, who "continues to argue that the District Court exceeded its authority" *Id.* at pp. 694–695.

232 "State-law prohibition . . . cannot survive the command of the Supremacy Clause" *Id.*

232 The federal court unquestionably has the power *Id.* at pp. 695–696.

232 "In short, we trust that the spirit of cooperation" *Id.* at p. 696.

233 "The state's extraordinary machinations" *Id.* at p. 696 n. 36. The Supreme Court was quoting from a Ninth Circuit Court of Appeals opinion, which is found at *Puget Sound Gillnetters Association v. US District Court for Western District of Washington*, 573 F.2d 1123, 1126 (9th Cir. 1978).

233 On the day of the Supreme Court opinion . . . [Judge Boldt] was "quite elated" Laura Raun, "Court's Ruling on Fishing Elates Judge Boldt," (Tacoma) *News Tribune*, p. C-15 (July 2, 1979); "Ruling Pleases Boldt," *The World: Coos Bay*, p. 5 (July 3, 1979); Fay Cohen, *Treaties on Trial: The Continuing Controversy over Northwest Indian Fishing Rights*, p. 117 (Seattle: University of Washington Press, 1986).

233 Successor judges who followed [Judge Boldt] . . . have followed and enforced [his] opinion and orders. The first major case after Judge Boldt's res-

ignation was *Hoh Indian Tribe v. Baldridge*, 522 F. Supp. 683 (W.D. Wash. 1981), affirmed by 676 F.2d 710 (9th Cir. 1982), which broadly followed the Boldt Decision. The judge was Walter Early Craig, a distinguished federal district court judge from the District of Arizona, who was assigned to many *United States v. Washington* cases until 1986.

13 Comanagement

234 **Justice and Interior Departments put together major annual grants so that the tribes could establish full-scale tribal fisheries management capability.** Bill Wilkerson, former Washington director of fisheries, interview with author, Bremerton, Washington, June 23, 2015; Richard Whitney, University of Washington fisheries professor, interview with author, Leavenworth, Washington, March 24, 2014.

234 **By the late 1970s and early 1980s, most of the tribes were operating substantial and effective fishery programs.** *See, e.g.,* Alexandra Harmon, *Indians in the Making: Ethnic Relations and Indian Identities Around Puget Sound*, p.42 (Berkeley: University of California Press, 1999); Wilkerson, interview, June 23, 2015; Whitney, interview, March 24, 2014.

234 **Tribes had developed fisheries staffs . . . equal . . . to the state department staffs.** *Id.*

235 **"We were still fighting the Boldt Decision."** Wilkerson is quoted in Northwest Treaty Tribes, "Bill Wilkerson at Boldt 40," 2:09 video (February 5, 2014), *Tribal Voices Archive Project*, Northwest Indian Fisheries Commission and Salmon Defense, https://perma.cc/94ZZ-3WV7.

235 **"I was trained to believe"** *Id.* at 3:24.

235 **"It was like a debating society in court."** Wilkerson, interview, June 23, 2015.

235 **Wilkerson and Spellman came to agree that "what was needed was to end the fish war."** Northwest Treaty Tribes, "Bill Wilkerson at Boldt 40," at 7:21.

235 **"Here's what I tell Indian people"** Charles Wilkinson, *Messages from Frank's Landing: A Story of Salmon, Treaties, and the Indian Way*, pp. 103–104 (Seattle: University of Washington Press, 2000).

236 **"We were making speeches all over the state at the time."** Northwest Treaty Tribes, "Bill Wilkerson at Boldt 40," at 4:45.

237 **In Hoh Indian Tribe v. Baldridge** *Hoh Indian Tribe v. Baldridge*, 522 F. Supp. 683 (W.D. Wash. 1981).

237 **State ballot initiative declaring that only the state, not tribes, could engage in resource management.** Initiative 456 (SPAWN) is explained in Fay Cohen's *Treaties on Trial: The Continuing Controversy over Northwest Indian Fishing Rights*, pp. 184–185 (Seattle: University of Washington Press, 1986). The initia-

tive, aimed at reducing tribal rights, passed by a margin of 53–47. It was never put into action. The initiative requested the legislature to "petition" Congress to take action but that was never done.

237 **Port Ludlow [conference] . . . the Puget Sound Management Plan of 1985.** The Port Ludlow conference has been covered in many sources. *See, e.g.,* Syma A. Ebbin, "Dividing the Waters: Cooperative Management and the Allocation of Pacific Salmon," *in* eds. Brad A. Bays and Erin H. Fouberg, *The Tribes and the States: Geographies of Intergovernmental Interaction,* pp. 168–170 (Lanham, MD: Rowman & Littlefield, 2002); Trova Heffernan, *Where the Salmon Run: The Life and Legacy of Billy Frank Jr.,* pp. 187–189 (Seattle: University of Washington Press, 2017).

237 **That trail-blazing plan . . . is still in force.** Puget Sound Indian Tribes and Washington Department of Fish and Wildlife, "Comprehensive Management Plan for Puget Sound Chinook: Harvest Management Component" (February 17, 2022), Washington Department of Fish and Wildlife, https://perma.cc/ GA84-E4RJ.

238 **The spotted owl . . . conflict.** *See, e.g.,* Charles F. Wilkinson, *Crossing the Next Meridian: Land, Water, and the Future of the West,* pp. 156–167 (Washington, DC: Island Press, 1992); Forest History Society, "The Northern Spotted Owl and the Endangered Species Act" (October 29, 2017), *US Forest Service Headquarters Collection,* Policy and Law, Wildlife Management, https://perma.cc/ ZDN8-FEMM.

238 **Timber, Fish, and Wildlife (TWF) Agreement of 1987** *See, e.g.,* Jovana J. Brown, "Treaty Rights: Twenty Years after the Boldt Decision," vol. 10, no. 2 *Wicazo Sa Review,* pp. 5–8 (Autumn 1994).

238 **"In a bold move, NWIFC Chairman Billy Frank Jr. and [timber industry leaders] committed to find a way forward"** Lorraine Loomis, "Pacts Offer Path to Streamside Habitat Protection" (August 4, 2020), *Northwest Treaty Tribes,* https://perma.cc/TM37-S576.

239 **It was a "ground-breaking Agreement."** Steve Barnowe-Meyer letter to Washington State Forest Practice Board, *in* Department of Natural Resources, *Forest Practices Board Written Public Comments,* p. 21 (February 10, 2021), https:// perma.cc/8ZYZ-Z3YY.

239 **TFW "is just another way that we can try to help influence the state of Washington"** *Id.* at p. 11.

239 **Chelan Agreement of 1992** *See, e.g.,* Brown, "Treaty Rights," pp. 8–11.

239 **It was the first in the nation of its kind.** *See* Barbara Leigh Smith, "The Centennial Accord: What Has Been Its Impact on Government-to-Government Relations between Tribes and the State in Washington?" pp. 1–18, *Enduring Leg-*

acies: Native Case Studies (2018), Evergreen State College, Olympia, https://perma.cc/7B8U-PLH8.

240 **Tribes and the states agreed to respect each other's sovereignty.** *See* Washington Governor's Office of Indian Affairs, "Centennial Accord," *State-Tribal Relations* (accessed June 15, 2022), https://perma.cc/PB4M-Q92C.

240 **Millennium Agreement in 1999 and the Out of State Accord in 2004** Smith, "Centennial Accord," p. 8.

241 **Centennial Accord Agreement and subsequent agreements do not solve all disputes.** *See, e.g.,* Fawn Sharp, vice president of Quinault Indian Nation, telephone interview with author, May 31, 2022. Sharp stated that the Centennial Accord is "ceremonial" and the tribes "don't have an ability to effectively mitigate or address conflicts with the state." Additionally, Sharp stated that she has been "unsuccessful on engaging the state at the Centennial Accord on climate policy."

241 **"we are proud of the Centennial Accord"** Lorraine Loomis, "Centennial Accord from 1989 Fosters Cooperation," *Nisqually Valley News* (December 7, 2017), https://perma.cc/D4F2-BLX6.

241 **The lawsuit brought by the Hoh, Quileute, and Quinault Tribes over salmon harvesting in Alaska** *See Hoh Indian Tribe v. Baldridge,* 522 F. Supp. 683 (W.D. Wash. 1981).

242 **"the helpless salmon's life"** Livingston Stone, "A National Salmon Park," vol. 21 *Transactions of the Twenty-first Annual Meeting of the American Fisheries Society,* pp. 149–162 (address given at the meeting, New York, May 25, 1892); for the full text of Dr. Stone's address, *see* Anthony Netboy, *Salmon: The World's Most Harassed Fish,* p. 213 (Winchester, UK: Winchester University Press, 1980).

242 **"the fishermen of [Oregon and Washington] have naturally tried to take all they could get"** Theodore Roosevelt, "Annual Message to Congress (1908)," presidential message (December 8, 1908), *Teaching American History,* https://perma.cc/B6XP-37GB.

242 **1976 . . . Fishery Conservation and Management Act** *See, e.g.,* Syma A. Ebbin, "Fish and Chips: Cross-cutting Issues and Actors in a Co-managed Fishery Regime in the Pacific Northwest," vol. 45, no. 2 *Policy Sciences,* pp. 177–178 (June 2012); Charles F. Wilkinson and Daniel K. Connor, "The Law of the Pacific Salmon Fishery: Conservation and Allocation of a Transboundary Common Property Resource," vol. 32 *Kansas Law Review* pp. 48–53 (1983); Lee G. Anderson, "Marine Fisheries," *in* ed. Paul Portney, *Current Issues in Natural Resources Policy,* pp. 149–178 (New York: Routledge, 2016).

243 **Tribal seat on the [Pacific fisheries] council . . . and . . . virtually all [committees]** *See, e.g.,* Ebbin, "Fish and Chips," pp. 177–178.

243   **United States–Canada Pacific Salmon Treaty of 1985** *See, e.g.,* Joy A. Yanagida, "The Pacific Salmon Treaty," vol. 81, no. 3 *American Journal of International Law,* p. 577 (1987); Pacific Salmon Commission, "The Pacific Salmon Treaty," *Publications* (accessed June 2, 2022), https://perma.cc/XUE8-NAGK.

243   **Tribes have been deeply involved in both the negotiation and the implementation of the United States–Canada Treaty.** *See, e.g.,* Ebbin, "Fish and Chips," p. 178.

244   **North of Falcon process** *See, e.g.,* Washington Department of Fish and Wildlife, "A Guide to the Salmon Season Setting Process: North of Falcon," *Medium* (December 22, 2020), https://perma.cc/HH5D-69M7 [hereinafter Fish and Wildlife, "Guide to Salmon Season"]; Washington Department of Fish and Wildlife, "North of Falcon," *Fishing and Shellfishing* (accessed June 2, 2022), https://perma.cc/VZX9-DR4N; Kelly Susewind and Loraine Loomis, "The Struggle to Share a Shrinking Resource—Northwest Salmon," *Seattle Times* (March 29, 2021), https://perma.cc/RLD5-KCYE.

245   **Washington Department of Fish and Wildlife** In 1932 the Department of Fisheries changed its focus to just food fish, and the Department of Game was established to focus on game animals and game fish; in 1987 the Department of Game was changed to the Department of Wildlife; in 1994 the Departments of Fisheries and of Game were merged to create the Department of Fish and Wildlife.

246   **"almost everything we do at this department is with our fellow co-managers, the tribes."** Ron Warren, *in* Washington Department of Fish and Wildlife, "North of Falcon Plenary: Joint State-Tribal Public Discussion on Salmon Fisheries," 11:20 video (March 31, 2021), https://perma.cc/7BNS-289W [hereinafter Warren *in* Fish and Wildlife, "North of Falcon Plenary"].

247   **"At the core of the North of Falcon process is a fierce commitment to cooperation"** Fish and Wildlife, "Guide to Salmon Season."

247   **"Nothing in my career has been as rewarding as being a co-manager with the tribes."** Warren *in* Fish and Wildlife, "North of Falcon Plenary," at 17:07.

247   **"The institutional restructuring that came about"** Ebbin, "Fish and Chips," p. 179.

14   The Boldt Decision at Fifty

249   **"There is a saying"** Ron Allen, chairman, Jamestown S'Klallam Tribe, telephone interview with author, February 17, 2023.

251   **"Judge Boldt had a way of seeing the treaty"** Fawn Sharp, president, Quinault Indian Nation, telephone interview with author, May 31, 2022.

251   **Hundreds of cases ... were decided by Judge Boldt and successor judges**

under the continuing jurisdiction. For a list of the continuing jurisdiction cases, *see, e.g.,* Gallagher Law Library, "*United States v. Washington* (Boldt Decision)," *Indian and Tribal Law* (updated June 28, 2022), University of Washington, https://perma.cc/4UB8-CSNH; *United States v. Suquamish Indian Tribe*, 901 F.2d 772 (9th Cir. 1990), in which Judge Wright stated, "We cannot think of a more comprehensive and complex case than this. Since 1974, there have been numerous supplemental proceedings with voluminous filings. In the proceedings below, this was one of 14 sub-proceedings and over 11,000 papers had been filed with the district court."

251 **The "shellfish provision" in the Stevens treaties** The provision was included in virtually the same language in all five Stevens treaties in Western Washington. *See, e.g.,* Treaty with the Dwamish and other Tribes, January 22, 1855, 12 Stat. 927, art. V: "The right of taking fish at usual and accustomed grounds and stations is further secured to said Indians in common with all citizens of the Territory, and of erecting temporary houses for the purpose of curing, together with the privilege of hunting and gathering roots and berries on open and unclaimed lands. Provided, however, that they shall not take shell-fish from any beds staked or cultivated by citizens."

252 **The . . . Rafeedie opinion came down in 1994.** *See United States v. Washington*, 873 F. Supp. 1422 (W.D. Wash. 1994); *United States v. Washington*, 898 F. Supp. 1453 (W.D. Wash. 1995), affirmed and modified; *United States v. Washington*, 157 F.3d 630 (9th Cir. 1998); Cert. denied 526 U.S. 1060 (1999).

252 **Judge Rafeedie looked to . . . the special rule of interpretation for Indian treaties.** *United States v. Washington*, 873 F. Supp. at 1428.

252 **Judge Rafeedie seemed to have no trouble finding that shellfish were . . . "fish" under the treaties.** *Id.* at p. 1429.

252 **The treaty provided for some landowner rights in . . . "artificial, or planted, shellfish beds." . . . 50 percent of the "natural beds . . . on privately owned tidelands, are part of the tribal fishery."** *Id.* at p. 1441.

253 **Tribes had rights to fish in deep-water areas and that the right extended to all types of shellfish.** *United States v. Washington*, 157 F.3d at 643–644.

253 **Detailed orders . . . establishing procedures for shellfish gathering.** *United States v. Washington*, 898 F. Supp. at 1463–1476.

253 **Dungeness crab and other commercial shellfish revenues now exceed those for salmon.** *See, e.g.,* Dominic P. Parker, Randall R. Rucker, and Peter H. Nickerson, "The Legacy of *United States v. Washington*: Economic Effects of the Boldt and Rafeedie Decisions," *in* ed. Terry Anderson, *Unlocking the Wealth of Indian Nations*, pp. 195–223 (Lanham, MD: Lexington Books, 2016): "In 2009, nominal salmon revenues were $20.67 million and nominal shellfish revenues were $153.84 million . . ."; Mariel J. Combs, "*United States v. Washington*: The

Boldt Decision Reincarnated," vol. 29, no. 3 *Environmental Law*, p. 683 (1999); TWC Economics, "Economic Analysis of the Non-Treaty Commercial and Recreational Fisheries in Washington State," Washington Department of Fish and Wildlife (December 2008), https://perma.cc/7N7H-MNFW. In 2006, the harvest value for shellfish was $41.1 million and for salmon was $9.5 million.

253   **Nine years later, the Ninth Circuit Court of Appeals ruled that the issue . . . needed to be decided in a "particular dispute."** *United States v. Washington*, 759 F.2d 1353, 1357 (9th Cir. 1985).

254   **Evidence at trial showed that state culverts in northwestern Washington were causing significant damage to salmon passage.** *United States v. Washington*, 827 F.3d 836, 856–857 (9th Cir. 2016).

254   **In 2013, Judge Ricardo S. Martinez issued a sweeping injunction.** *United States v. Washington*, No. CV 70-9213, 2013 WL 1334391 (W.D. Wash. March 29, 2013), affirmed; *United States v. Washington*, 827 F.3d 836 (9th Cir. 2016), opinion amended and superseded; *United States v. Washington*, 853 F.2d 946 (9th Cir. 2017), and affirmed, *United States v. Washington*, 853 F.3d 946 (9th Cir. 2017).

254   **The Ninth Circuit Court of Appeals affirmed the district court opinion.** *United States v. Washington*, 827 F.3d 836 (9th Cir. 2016).

254   **"Washington has violated, and is continuing to violate"** *Id.* at pp. 851–853.

254   **Professor William Rodgers called it "a stunning ruling"** William Rodgers, University of Washington professor emeritus of law, interview with author, Seattle, Washington, 2015.

255   **[The Supreme Court] split four to four. . . . [which] meant that the Ninth Circuit Court opinion would remain in force, but only in the Ninth Circuit.** *See Washington v. United States*, 138 S. Ct. 1832 (2018), affirmed by an equally divided court.

255   **Elwha River Ecosystem and Fisheries Restoration Act** Northwest Fisheries Science Center, "Dam Removals on the Elwha River," *National Oceanic and Atmospheric Administration Fisheries* (updated April 1, 2021), https://perma.cc/4VAC-57XC.

256   **"We are salmon people."** Charles Wilkinson, "The Olympic Peninsula's Elwha River: Prisoner of History, Harbinger of Hope," *in* Mary Peck, *Away Out Over Everything: The Olympic Peninsula and the Elwha River*, p.72 (Stanford, CA: Stanford University Press, 2004).

256   **"Our elders–nobody would listen to them"** *Id.* at p. 76.

256   **"The Boldt Decision has furnished a basic template for similar decisions in other states"** *See* Reid Peyton Chambers, "Reflections on the Changes in Indian Law, Federal Indian Policies and Conditions on Indian Reservations Since the Late 1960s," vol. 46 *Arizona State Law Journal*, pp. 776–777 (Fall 2014). For examples of other states following the Boldt Decision, *see, e.g., Sohappy v. Smith,*

529 F.2d 570, 573 (9th Circ. 1976), in which, under continuing jurisdiction from *United States v. Oregon*, Judge Belloni amended his 1969 order to apply Boldt's 50 percent allocation to the Columbia River; *United States v. Oregon*, 913 F.2d 576 (9th Cir. 1985); *United States v. Michigan*, 505 F. Supp. 467 (W.D. Mich. 1980); *Mille Lacs Band of Chippewa Indians v. Minnesota*, 952 F. Supp. 1362 (D. Minn. 1997); *Lac Courte Oreilles Band of Lake Superior Chippewa Indians v. Wisconsin*, 740 F. Supp. 1400 (W.D. Wis. 1990); *City of Pocatello v. State* (In re SRBA), 180 P.3d 1048 (Idaho 2008).

256   **The decision is a foundational case.** *See* Pauline R. Hillaire, *Rights Remembered: A Salish Grandmother Speaks on American Indian History and the Future*, ed. Gregory P. Fields, pp. 21–22 (Lincoln: University of Nebraska Press, 2016): "This century of fishing rights events is very informative, from both sociological and legal standpoints, as regards the principles and dynamics of Native rights, not only in the Northwest, but for indigenous people everywhere."

257   **"The fishing rights battle helped kickstart the formal study of Federal Indian law"** *See* Bethany Berger, "Natural Resources and the Making of Modern Indian Law," vol. 51, no. 4 *Connecticut Law Review*, p. 942 (2019).

257   **"'The Boldt Decision . . . was one of the biggest court decisions . . . involving Native rights."** *See* Phil Dougherty, "Boldt Decision: *United States v. Washington*" (August 24, 2020), *HistoryLink.org*, https://perma.cc/4CWL-XSH7.

257   **In Canada, . . . the "cornerstone case" on First Nations' fishing rights, "mirrored the Boldt Decision."** On "mirrored the Boldt Decision" and other comments on the Boldt Decision in Canada, *see* Douglas C. Harris, "The Boldt Decision in Canada: Aboriginal Treaty Rights to Fish on the Pacific," *in* ed. Alexander Harmon, *The Power of Promises: Rethinking Indian Treaties in the Pacific Northwest*, p. 134 (Seattle: University of Washington Press, 2008); *see also Regina v. Sparrow* (1980) 1 SCR 1075 (1990) CNLR 160.

257   **Other Canadian court decisions . . . were informed by Judge Boldt's work.** Harris, "The Boldt Decision in Canada," pp. 133–139. *See also* Anthony Moffa, "The Oil Sands of Time," vol. 22 *Ocean and Coastal Law Journal*, p. 111 (May 2017).

257   **"Australia has struggled to redefine its relationship with indigenous peoples."** *See* Andrew Lokan, "From Recognition to Reconciliation: The Functions of Aboriginal Rights Law," vol. 22 *Melbourne University Law Review*, p. 66 (April 1999).

258   **"Spurring the process . . . were diverse efforts to draw attention to human rights"** *See* Jason Robison et al., "Indigenous Water Justice," vol. 22 *Lewis and Clark Law Review*, p. 848 (2018). *See also* the leading authority, S. James Anaya, *Indigenous Peoples in International Law*, 2nd ed. (Oxford, UK: Oxford University Press, 2004; first published 1996). For more on international fishing rights, see generally Morihiro Ichikawa, "Understanding the Fishing Rights of

the Ainu of Japan: Lessons Learned From American Indian Law, the Japanese Constitution, and International Law," vol. 12 *Colorado Journal of International Environmental Law and Policy*, p. 245 (2001); Kristi Stanton, Comment, "A Call for Co-Management: Treaty Fishing Allocation in New Zealand and Western Washington," vol. 11 *Pacific Rim Law and Policy Journal*, p. 745 (2002).

260 **American Fisheries Society . . . made an early finding that more than a hundred salmon runs had a "high risk of extinction."** *See* Willa Nehlsen, Jack E. Williams, and James A. Lichatowich, "Pacific Salmon at the Crossroads: Stocks at Risk from California, Oregon, Idaho, and Washington," vol. 16, no. 2 *American Fisheries Society Fisheries Magazine*, pp. 4–21 (March 1991).

260 **In 1991 . . . granted a petition by the Shoshone-Bannock Tribe of Idaho and listed the imperiled Snake River sockeye run under the Endangered Species Act** *See, e.g.,* Andre E. Kohler, Robert G. Griswold, and Doug Taki, "Snake River Sockeye Salmon Habitat and Limnological Research," Annual Report 2002, Project No. 199107100, Bonneville Power Administration, US Department of Energy, BPA Report DOE/BP-00004343-5 (August 2004), https://perma.cc/8E63-UUX6.

260 **"[Too] many salmon remain on the brink of extinction."** *See* Governor's Salmon Recovery Office, "2020 State of Salmon in Watersheds: Executive Summary" (December 2020), p. 3, *Salmon and Orca Recovery*, Washington State Recreation and Conservation Office, https://perma.cc/EKG6-JKFB.

261 **Washington as a place has built a truly imposing system . . . to carry out . . . salmon protection and preservation.** On Washington's system of salmon protection, *see* Washington Forest Protection Association, "Salmon Recovery Is a Shared Responsibility in the Northwest," *Seattle Times* (December 16, 2021), https://perma.cc/A4JP-XSPQ: "For more than two decades, private forest landowners have joined state and tribal governments, regulators, and other interested parties in sharing the responsibility by improving their roads, removing fish blockages, and replacing culverts and bridges"; Washington Forest Protection Association, "Forest and Fish Law: 20 Years of Collaboration in Washington State," *Seattle Times* (June 7, 2019), https://perma.cc/Q2A8-DRNA: "Today, salmon recovery remains a top legislative priority as policymakers, interest groups and lawmakers strive to achieve sustainable salmon"; Thomas G. Safford and Karma C. Norman, "Water Water Everywhere, but Not Enough for Salmon? Organizing Integrated Water and Fisheries Management in Puget Sound," vol. 92 *Journal of Environmental Management*, p. 838 (2011): "The disappearance of salmon populations has not gone unnoticed, and both governmental and non-governmental actors have mobilized to protect and restore salmon habitat."

261 **A notable hallmark . . . the ways that individual citizens can help salmon
protection** Washington State University Extension and Stewardship Partners
are leading a campaign that encourages Washingtonians to install rain gardens.
See, e.g., 12,000 Rain Gardens in Puget Sound (accessed July 8, 2022), https://
perma.cc/SJJ6-NEJ5; *see also* Lisa Stiffler, "Rain Gardens Could Make Runoff
Safe for Salmon: Filtering Polluted Stormwater through Soil Makes It Non-le-
thal for Fish," *Sightline Institute* (January 22, 2015), https://perma.cc
/N9P8-9LLY: "Across the Northwest there is a movement to install more rain
gardens and green stormwater technologies, which also include green roofs and
permeable pavements, as well as protecting native vegetation and shrinking the
amount of water-repelling impervious surfaces being built." Skagit Fisheries
Enhancement Group and other organizations plan planting parties where volunteers can plant trees to help restore stream banks. *See, e.g.,* Skagit Fisheries
Enhancement Group, "Volunteer" (accessed July 8, 2022), https://perma.cc
/2N2B-X9ET. Northwest Artists Against Extinction encourage individuals
to pick a salmon template, color it, and send it to government officials with a
message about salmon conservation. *See* Northwest Artists Against Extinction,
"Speak for the Salmon" (accessed July 8, 2022), https://perma.cc/C7US-RCV5.

262 **"If we are to leave future generations a legacy of wild salmon"** Jim Lichatowich et al., *Wild Pacific Salmon: A Threatened Legacy*, pp. 29–30 (St. Helens,
OR: Bemis Printing, 2017).

262 **"But salmon matter to people beyond those who harvest them."** Michael
Blumm, *Pacific Salmon Law and the Environment: Treaties, Endangered Species,
Dam Removal, Climate Change, and Beyond*, p. 207 (Washington, DC: Environ-
mental Law Institute, 2022).

263 **The outrage in Washington** *Sohappy v. Smith*, 529 F.2d 570, 573 (9th Circ.
1976).

263 **In Washington, Senator Slade Gorton and Congressman Jack Cunningham
did exactly that.** *See, e.g.,* Hearing Before the Select Committee on Indian Affairs United States Senate, "To Provide for Additional Protection of Steelhead
Trout as a Game Fish, and for Other Purposes," 99th Congress, 1st Session
(July 11, 1985; text in ProQuest Congressional Hearings Digital Collection, accessed July 7, 2022), which proposed legislation to abrogate tribal treaty rights
to harvest steelhead.

265 **The Washington State Legislature produced a statute** *See* Final Bill Report
SHB 2080, "Vacating Convictions for Certain Tribal Fishing Activities," Wash-
ington State Legislature, House Committee on Development, Housing and
Tribal Affairs, Senate Committee on Law and Justice (February 14, 2014).

265 **"it is incumbent on us as a society to admit that we were wrong"** *See* Wash-

ington State House Democrats, "Senate Sends Governor Rep. Sawyer's Bill to Erase 'Fish War' Convictions," *Washington State House Democrats* (March 6, 2014), https://perma.cc/9ALY-S4TP.

265 **Johnson Meninick . . . was finally able to vacate his great-uncle's 1917 conviction.** Kate Prengaman, "Court Overturns Nearly Century-old Conviction for Fishing at Traditional Yakama Location," *Yakima Herald* (November 13, 2015), https://perma.cc/639P-VZ8T.

265 **President Barack Obama signed the act changing the title . . . now named the Billy Frank Jr. Nisqually National Wildlife Refuge.** *See* "Nisqually Wildlife Refuge to Be Renamed for Activist Billy Frank Jr.," *Seattle Times* (December 14, 2015), https://perma.cc/3ZXR-BSAQ; Joel Connelly, "Billy Frank Lives . . . in Words, Stories and a Namesake National Wildlife Refuge," *Seattle Post-Intelligencer* (July 19, 2016), https://perma.cc/M3KP-KMXN; US Fish and Wildlife Service, "About Us," *Billy Frank Jr. Nisqually National Wildlife Refuge* (accessed July 7, 2022), https://perma.cc/4F2D-SAWF.

265 **Billy Frank Jr. passed on in 2014.** For publications on Billy's passing, *see* Craig Welch and Aaron Spencer, "Billy Frank Jr., Nisqually Elder Who Fought for Treaty Rights, Dies," *Seattle Times* (May 5, 2014), https://perma.cc/F4PE -EEEW; William Yardley, "Billy Frank Jr., 83, Defiant Fighter for Native Fishing Rights," *New York Times* (May 9, 2014), https://perma.cc/2PPH-RNJV.

265 [**Billy Frank's**] **memorial service** *See* Paige Cornwell, "Billy Frank Jr. Remembered as Humanitarian, 'Spokesman for the Salmon,'" *Seattle Times* (May 11, 2014), https://perma.cc/8DSP-BENW; "Large Crowd at Memorial for Billy Frank Jr.," *Nisqually Valley News* (May 19, 2014), https://perma.cc/QGA7-4KUL.

266 **President Obama . . . in a press release stated** The White House, President Barack Obama, "Statement by the President on the Passing of Billy Frank, Jr." (May 5, 2014), *Statements and Releases*, https://perma.cc/BZD7-REGA.

266 **Bill Wilkerson . . . reflected, "I don't think there is probably any single leader"** Bill Wilkerson, former director of Washington Department of Fisheries, telephone interview with author, June 2, 2022.

266 **National Statuary Hall Collection** *See, e.g.,* Architect of the Capitol, "National Statuary Hall Collection by Location," *Explore the Capitol Campus* (accessed July 7, 2022), https://perma.cc/D7P4-PTJV.

266 **In 2021, Governor Jay Inslee signed into law a bill [to replace the statue] . . . with a statue of Billy Frank Jr.** *See* Final Bill Report ESHB 1372, "Replacing the Marcus Whitman Statue in the National Statuary Hall Collection with a Statue of Billy Frank Jr.," Washington State Legislature, House Committee on State Government and Tribal Relations, House Committee on Appropriations, Senate Committee on State Government and Elections (February 20, 2021).

267 **The bill passed the state House of Representatives by a vote of 92–5 and the state Senate approved it by a 44–5 vote.** *Id.*

267 **"We expect to send our best."** Tom Banse, "It's Official: Statue Honoring Billy Frank Jr. to Replace Marcus Whitman at U.S. Capitol," *Northwest Public Broadcasting* (April 14, 2021), https://perma.cc/TR8H-8HFS.

Index

An italicized page number followed by an *f* refers to a figure or a caption.

About the Author

CHARLES WILKINSON (1941–2023) was the Moses Lasky Professor of Law at the University of Colorado and an internationally recognized expert on federal Indian law. *Treaty Justice* is his fifteenth book. In 2021 he received the Colorado Book Award for Lifetime Achievement for his fourteen previous books on the American West. His publications include *Blood Struggle: The Rise of Modern Indian Nations*; *Messages from Frank's Landing: A Story of Salmon, Treaties, and the Indian Way*; *The People Are Dancing Again: The History of the Siletz Tribe of Western Oregon*; and *American Indians, Time, and the Law*. Wilkinson's books often taught as much about history, geography, and the revitalization of Indian nations as they did about the law.

Over the years, Wilkinson served as a key advisor to many Indian tribes and the US Departments of Interior, Agriculture, and Justice on Native American legal issues. He was counsel to the Menominee Tribe of Wisconsin for the Menominee Restoration Act of 1973 and to the Siletz Tribe of Oregon for the Siletz Restoration Act of 1977. He served as special counsel to the Interior Department for the drafting of President Clinton's 1996 Presidential Proclamation establishing the Grand Staircase-Escalante National Monument in Utah. He acted as facilitator in negotiations between the National Park Service and the Timbisha Shoshone Tribe concerning a tribal land base in Death Valley National Park;

in 2000, Congress enacted legislation ratifying the resulting agreement. He served as mediator in successful negotiations, involving salmon runs in the Cedar River, between the City of Seattle and the Muckleshoot Indian Tribe. He was Special Advisor to the Bears Ears Inter-Tribal Coalition in regard to the creation of the Bears Ears National Monument, proclaimed by President Obama in 2016.

Wilkinson has received other awards, including many teaching awards as well as the National Wildlife Federation's National Conservation Award; the Warm Springs Tribal Museum's Twanat Award for tireless work for Indian people; the High Desert Museum in Bend Oregon's Earle A. Chiles Award for exceptional commitment to the high desert's land and Indian tribes; the Grand Canyon Trust's Lifetime Achievement Award for extraordinary vision, passion, and commitment to the Colorado Plateau; and the Federal Bar Association's Lawrence R. Baca Award for Lifetime Achievement in Indian Law. Throughout his life, Wilkinson has been recognized for his advocacy and tireless pursuit of justice for Indigenous peoples.